THE CHANGING
NATURE OF WORK

FRONTIER ISSUES IN ECONOMIC THOUGHT
VOLUME 4
NEVA R. GOODWIN, SERIES EDITOR

Titles published by Island Press
in the Frontier Issues in Economic Thought series include:

R. Krishnan, J. M Harris, and N. R. Goodwin (eds.),
A Survey of Ecological Economics, 1995

N. R. Goodwin, F. Ackerman, and D. Kiron (eds.),
The Consumer Society, 1997

F. Ackerman, D. Kiron, N. R. Goodwin, J. M. Harris, and K. Gallagher (eds.),
Human Well-Being and Economic Goals, 1997

Upcoming volumes
in the Frontier Issues in Economic Thought series address:

The Political Economy of Inequality
Fully Sustainable Development

THE CHANGING NATURE OF WORK

Edited by
Frank Ackerman,
Neva R. Goodwin,
Laurie Dougherty,
and Kevin Gallagher

The Global Development
And Environment Institute
Tufts University

ISLAND PRESS

Washington, D.C. ■ Covelo, California

ISLAND PRESS is a trademark of The Center for Resource Economics.

Library of Congress Cataloging-in-Publication Data
The changing nature of work / edited by Frank Ackerman . . . [et al.].
    p.   cm. — (Frontier issues in economic thought ; v. 4)
   "The Global Development and Environment Institute, Tufts University."
   Includes bibliographical references (p.) and index.
   ISBN 1–55963–665–3 (alk. paper). — ISBN 1–55963–666–1 (pbk. : alk. paper)
   1. Work. 2. Labor economics. 3. Foreign trade and employment.
4. Employees—Effect of technological innovations on. 5. Industrial relations. 6. Diversity in the workplace. 7. Women—Employment.
I. Ackerman, Frank. II. Series.
HD4901.C427 1998   98–35988
331—dc21   CIP

Printed on recycled, acid-free paper ♲
Manufactured in the United States of America
10 9 8 7 6 5 4 3 2 1

Note to the Reader

In general, the summaries presented here do not repeat material from the original articles verbatim. In a few instances it has seemed appropriate to include in the summaries direct quotations from the original text ranging from a phrase to a few sentences. Where this has been done, the page reference to the original article is given in square brackets. The complete citation for the article always appears at the beginning of the summary. References to other books or articles appear in endnotes following each summary.

Contents

Authors of Original Articles   xvii

Foreword by Robert B. Reich   xxiii

Acknowledgments   xxvii

Volume Introduction by Neva R. Goodwin   xxix

PART I

The History of Work   1

Frank Ackerman

PART II

New Directions in Labor Economics

Overview Essay   15
Frank Ackerman

An Introduction to the Wage Curve   25
David G. Blanchflower and Andrew J. Oswald

The Production Process in a Competitive Economy:
Walrasian, Neo-Hobbesian, and Marxian Models   29
Samuel S. Bowles

Industrial Relations and Productivity Growth:
A Comparative Perspective   32
Robert A. Buchele and Jens Christiansen

Radical Political Economy and the Economics of Labor Markets   35
James Rebitzer

Labor Market Segmentation Theory: Reconsidering the Evidence   40
William T. Dickens and Kevin Lang

Supervision and High Wages as Competing Incentives:
A Basis for Labor Segmentation Theory   43
Robert W. Drago and Richard Perlman

The Fair Wage–Effort Hypothesis and Unemployment   47
George A. Akerlof and Janet Yellen

The Exit-Voice Tradeoff in the Labor Market:
Unionism, Job Tenure, Quits, and Separations   50
Richard B. Freeman

An Alternative Approach to Labor Markets   53
David Marsden

An Analytical Frame   56
Chris Tilly and Charles Tilly

PART III
Globalization and Labor

Overview Essay   61
Frank Ackerman

How Trade Hurt Unskilled Workers   69
Adrian Wood

International Trade and American Wages in the 1980s:
Giant Sucking Sound or Small Hiccup?   73
Robert Z. Lawrence and Matthew Slaughter

International Trade and the Performance of U.S. Labor Markets 76
Dale Belman and Thea M. Lee

Skills Mismatch or Globalization?   80
David Gordon

The Causes and Consequences of Changing Earnings Inequality:
W(h)ither the Debate?   84
David G. Blanchflower and Matthew Slaughter

Consequences of Trade for Labor Markets and the
Employment Relationship   88
Dani Rodrik

The Transformation of the Japanese Employment System:
Nature, Depth, and Origins   91
James R. Lincoln and Yoshifumi Nakata

Labor Squeeze and Ethnic/Racial Recomposition in the
U.S. Apparel Industry   94
Evelyn Blumenberg and Paul Ong

Gender and the Global Economy   98
Lourdes Benería

The Politics and Economics of Global Employment:
A Perspective from Latin America   101
Hernando Gómez-Buendía

Globalization and Labor Standards: A Review of Issues   105
Eddy Lee

Policy Options for the North   109
Adrian Wood

PART IV
New Technologies and Work Organization

Overview Essay   113
Laurie Dougherty

Sociotechnical Organizational Change:
Technological and Organizational Coevolution   121
John A. Mathews

Alternative Models of Production   125
Eileen Appelbaum and Rosemary Batt

Integrating Technology and Human Resources for High-Performance
Manufacturing: Evidence from the International Auto Industry   129
John Paul MacDuffie and John F. Krafcik

Toward Post-Lean Production   133
Christian Berggren

Japanese Work Organization in Mexico   136
Harley Shaiken and Harry Browne

The Effect of Human Resource Management Practices on Productivity:
A Study of Steel Finishing Lines   140
Casey Ichniowski, Kathryn Shaw, and Giovanna Prennushi

The Limits of Hierarchy in an Informated Organization
and
The Information Panopticon   143
Shoshana Zuboff

The End of Skill?   146
Stanley Aronowitz and William DeFazio

The Transformation of Work Revisited:
The Limits of Flexibility in American Manufacturing   149
Steven Vallas and John Beck

Computer Rationalization and the Transformation of Work:
Lessons from the Insurance Industry   153
Eileen Appelbaum and Peter Albin

Effects of Technological Change: The Quality of Employment   157
Heidi Hartmann, Robert E. Kraut, and Louise A. Tilly

Computing Inequality: Have Computers Changed the Labor Market?   161
David Autor, Lawrence Katz, and Alan Krueger

The Returns to Computer Use Revisited:
Have Pencils Changed the Wage Structure Too?   164
John E. DiNardo and John-Steffen Pischke

Technology, Power, and the Social Organization of Work:
Toward a Pragmatic Theory of Skilling and Deskilling   167
Stephen R. Barley

PART V
Restructuring Employment: Flexibility versus Security

Overview Essay   171
Laurie Dougherty

Employment and Productivity in Industrialized Economies   177
Eileen Appelbaum and Ronald Schettkat

Nonstandard Work, Substandard Jobs:
Flexible Work Arrangements in the United States   181
Arne L. Kalleberg et al.

Restructuring the Employment Relationship:
The Growth of Market-Mediated Work Arrangements   185
Katharine G. Abraham

Rethinking Employment   189
Peter Cappelli

Internal Labor Markets: Theory and Change   192
Paul S. Osterman

Toward a New Labor Market Segmentation   195
Thierry J. Noyelle

World Underneath: The Origins, Dynamics,
and Effects of the Informal Economy   199
Manuel Castells and Alejandro Portes

Informalization at the Core: Hispanic Women,
Home-Based Work, and the Advanced Capitalist State   202
M. Patricia Fernández-Kelly and Anna M. Garcia

Reevaluating Union Policy Toward White-Collar Home-Based Work   205
Kathleen E. Christensen

Sustainable Flexibility: A Prospective Study on Work, Family,
and Society in the Information Age   208
Martin Carnoy and Manuel Castells

PART VI
Emerging Patterns of Industrial Relations

Overview Essay   215
Kevin Gallagher

International Difference in Male Wage Inequality:
Institutions versus Market Forces   224
Francine Blau

Participation, Productivity, and the Firm's Environment   227
David I. Levine and Laura D'Andrea Tyson

Conclusion: The Transformation of Industrial Relations?
A Cross-National Review of the Evidence   231
Richard M. Locke and Thomas Kochan

Microchips and Macroharvests:
Labor-Management Relations in Agriculture   234
Robert J. Thomas

Alternative Forms of Work Organization
Under Programmable Automation   238
Maryellen R. Kelley

A Strategy for Labor   241
Joel E. Rogers

An Economic Analysis of Works Councils   245
Richard B. Freeman and Edward Lazear

Theoretical and Empirical Studies of Producer Cooperatives:
Will Ever the Twain Meet?   248
John P. Bonin, Derek C. Jones, and Louis Putterman

Labor-Managed Cooperatives and Private Firms in North Central Italy:
An Empirical Comparison   252
Will Bartlett, John Cable, Saul Estrin, Derek C. Jones, and Stephen C. Smith

Financial Markets and the Political Structure of the Enterprise   255
Herbert Gintis

PART VII
Difference and Diversity in the Workplace

Overview Essay   259
Laurie Dougherty

Queuing and Changing Occupational Composition   269
Barbara F. Reskin and Patricia A. Roos

Between the Toe and the Heel—Jobs and Emotional Labor
and Gender, Status, and Feeling   273
Arlie Russell Hochschild

Race, Class, and Occupational Mobility: Black and White Women
in Service Work in the United States   276
Marilyn Power and Sam Rosenberg

Black Mobility in White Corporations:
Up the Corporate Ladder But Out on a Limb   280
Sharon M. Collins

What Went Wrong? The Erosion of Relative Earnings and Employment
Among Young Black Men in the 1980s   283
John Bound and Richard B. Freeman

"Soft" Skills and Race: An Investigation
of Black Men's Employment Problems   286
Philip Moss and Chris Tilly

Feminization of the Labor Force: The Effects of Long-Term
Development and Structural Adjustment   290
Nilüfer Çagatay and Sule Özler

Engendering the Worlds of Labor: Women Workers, Labor Markets,
and Production Politics in the South China Economic Miracle   292
Ching Kwan Lee

Notes on the Incorporation of Third World Women into Wage-Labor
through Immigration and Offshore Production   295
Saskia Sassen-Koob

PART VIII
The Household Economy and Caring Labor

Overview Essay 299
Neva Goodwin

Introduction to *Gender and Family Issues in the Workplace* 312
Francine Blau and Ronald Ehrenberg

Historical Changes in the Household Division of Labor 316
Jonathan I. Gershuny and John P. Robinson

Accounting for Women's Work: The Progress of Two Decades 319
Lourdes Benería

Women's Employment or Return to "Family Values"
in Central-Eastern Europe 323
Barbara Lobodzinskc

Changing the Conditions of Work: Responding to Increasing
Work Force Diversity and New Family Patterns 326
Lotte Bailyn

The Third Shift 329
Arlie Russell Hochschild

Overwork in the Household 333
Juliet B. Schor

The Triangle of the Human Economy—Household,
Cultivation, Industrial Production: An Attempt
at Making Visible the Human Economy in Toto 336
Hilkka Pietila

Global Development and Personal Dependency:
The High Cost of Doing Well 339
Allan R. Meyers

Holding Hands at Midnight: The Paradox of Caring Labor 341
Nancy Folbre

Children as Public Goods 345
Nancy Folbre

PART IX
Human Values in Work

Overview Essay   349
Neva Goodwin

Learning at Work: Beyond Human Capital   361
Robert Lane

On Work and Alienation   365
Kai Erikson

Ghetto-Related Behavior and the Structure of Opportunity   368
William Julius Wilson

Unhappiness and Unemployment   371
Andrew Clark and Andrew J. Oswald

Social Psychology, Unemployment, and Macroeconomics   373
William A. Darity, Jr., and Arthur Goldsmith

The Need for Work as Such: Self-Expression and Belonging   376
Edward J. O'Boyle

Shifting Perspectives: The Decoupling of Work and Money   379
Robert J. Wuthnow

Position in the Class Structure and Psychological Functioning
in the United States, Japan, and Poland   382
Melvin L. Kohn et al.

Dignity in the Workplace Under Participative Management:
Alienation and Freedom Revisited   385
Randy D. Hodson

Work, Labor, and Action: Work Experience in
a System of Flexible Production   388
Michael J. Piore

Subject Index   393
Name Index   415

Authors of Original Articles

Katharine G. Abraham Bureau of Labor Statistics, United States Department of Labor, Washington, D.C.

George A. Akerlof Dept. of Economics, University of California, Berkeley, California

Eileen Appelbaum Economic Policy Institute, Washington, D.C.

Stanley Aronowitz Dept. of Sociology, The Graduate School and University Center, CUNY, New York, New York

David Autor John F. Kennedy School of Government, Harvard University, Cambridge, Massachusetts

Lotte Bailyn Sloan School of Management, Massachusetts Institute of Technology, Cambridge, Massachusetts

Stephen R. Barley Dept. of Industrial Engineering, Stanford University, Stanford, California

Will Bartlett Deputy Director of the Centre for Mediterranean Studies, University of Bristol, Bristol, United Kingdom

Dale Belman Dept. of Industrial and Labor Relations, University of Wisconsin, Milwaukee, Wisconsin

Lourdes Benería Dept. of City and Regional Planning, Cornell University, Ithaca, New York

Christian Berggren EKI industriell organisation, Linkopings Universitet, Linkoping, Sweden

David G. Blanchflower Dept. of Economics, Dartmouth College, Hanover, New Hampshire

Francine Blau Dept. of Labor Economics, School of Industrial and Labor Relations, Cornell University, Ithaca, New York

Evelyn Blumenberg Dept. of Political Studies, University of California, Los Angeles, California

John P. Bonin Dept. of Economics, Wesleyan University, Middletown, Connecticut

John Bound Population Studies Center, University of Michigan, Ann Arbor, Michigan

Samuel S. Bowles Dept. of Economics, University of Massachusetts, Amherst, Massachusetts

Robert A. Buchele Dept. of Economics, Smith College, Northampton, Massachusetts

Nilüfer Çagatay Dept. of Economics, University of Utah, Salt Lake City, Utah

Peter Cappelli Dept. of Management and Co-Director of the Center for Human Resources, The Wharton School of Business, University of Pennsylvania, Philadelphia, Pennsylvania

Martin Carnoy School of Education, Stanford University, Stanford, California

Manuel Castells Professor and Center for Western European Studies Chair, Dept. of City and Regional Planning, University of California, Berkeley, California

Kathleen E. Christensen Graduate School and University Center, CUNY, New York, New York

Andrew Clark Directorate of Education, Employment, Labor and Social Affairs (DEELSA), Organisation for Economic Co-operation and Development (OECD), Paris, France

Sharon M. Collins Dept. of Sociology, University of Illinois, Chicago, Illinois

William A. Darity, Jr. Boshamer Professor, Dept. of Economics, University of North Carolina, Chapel Hill, North Carolina

William T. Dickens Brookings Institution, Washington, D.C.

John E. DiNardo Dept. of Social Science, University of California, Irvine, California

Robert W. Drago Dept. of Economics and Department of Industrial and Labor Relations, University of Wisconsin, Milwaukee, Wisconsin

Kai Erikson Dept. of Sociology, Yale University, New Haven, Connecticut

M. Patricia Fernández-Kelly Dept. of Sociology and the Office of Population Research, Princeton University, Princeton, New Jersey

Nancy Folbre Dept. of Economics, University of Massachusetts, Amherst, Massachusetts

Richard B. Freeman Ascherman Chair of Economics, Harvard University, Cambridge, Massachusetts

Jonathon I. Gershuny Dept. of Social Sciences, School of Social and Policy Sciences, University of Bath, Claverton Down, Bath, Avon, England

Herbert Gintis Dept. of Economics, University of Massachusetts, Amherst, Massachusetts

Hernando Gómez-Buendía Bogotá, Colombia

David Gordon Deceased

Heidi Hartmann Institute for Women's Policy Research, Washington, D. C.

Arlie Russell Hochschild Dept. of Sociology, University of California, Berkeley, California

Randy D. Hodson Dept. of Sociology, College of Social and Behavioral Science, Ohio State University, Columbus, Ohio

Casey Ichniowski Graduate School of Business, Columbia University, New York, New York

Arne L. Kalleberg Economic Policy Institute, Washington, D.C.

Maryellen R. Kelley H. John Heinz III School of Public Policy and Management, Carnegie Mellon University, Pittsburgh, Pennsylvania

Melvin L. Kohn Dept. of Sociology, The Johns Hopkins University, Baltimore, Maryland

Robert Lane Eugene Meyer Professor Emeritus, Dept. of Political Science, Yale University, New Haven, Connecticut

Robert Z. Lawrence John F. Kennedy School of Government, Harvard University, Cambridge, Massachusetts

Ching Kwan Lee Dept. of Sociology, The Chinese University of Hong Kong, Shatin, New Territories, Hong Kong

Eddy Lee International Labour Organization, Geneva, Switzerland

David I. Levine Dept. of Economics, Haas School of Business, University of California, Berkeley, California

James R. Lincoln Haas School of Business, University of California, Berkeley, California

Barbara Lobodzinska New Brighton, Minnesota

Richard M. Locke Dept. of Political Science, Sloan School of Management, Massachusetts Institute of Technology, Cambridge, Massachusetts

John Paul MacDuffie Wharton School of Business, University of Pennsylvania, Philadelphia, Pennsylvania

David Marsden Dept. of Industrial Relations, London School of Economics, London, England

John A. Mathews School of Industrial Relations and Organizational Behavior, University of New South Wales, Sydney, Australia

Allan R. Meyers Dept. of Health Services, School of Public Health, Boston University, Boston, Massachusetts

Philip Moss Dept. of Policy and Planning, University of Massachusetts, Lowell, Massachusetts

Thierry J. Noyelle New York, New York

Edward J. O'Boyle Dept. of Economics and Finance, College of Administration and Business, Louisiana Tech University, Ruston, Louisiana

Paul S. Osterman Sloan School of Management, Massachusetts Institute of Technology, Cambridge, Massachusetts

Hilkka Pietila Institute of Development Studies, University of Helsinki, Helsinki, Finland

Michael J. Piore Dept. of Economics, Massachusetts Institute of Technology, Cambridge, Massachusetts

Marilyn Power Dept. of Economics, Sarah Lawrence College, Bronxville, New York

James Rebitzer Sloan School of Management, Massachusetts Institute of Technology, Cambridge, Massachusetts

Barbara F. Reskin Department of Sociology, Harvard University, Cambridge, Massachusetts

Dani Rodrik Rafiq Hariri Professor of International Political Economy, John F. Kennedy School of Government, Harvard University, Cambridge, Massachusetts

Joel E. Rogers Industrial Relations Research Institute, University of Wisconsin, Madison, Wisconsin

Saskia Sassen-Koob School of Architecture, Planning, and Preservation, Columbia University, New York, New York

Juliet B. Schor Dept. of Women's Studies, Harvard University, Cambridge, Massachusetts

Harley Shaiken University of California, Berkeley, California

Robert J. Thomas School of Business, Georgetown University, Washington, D.C.

Chris Tilly Dept. of Policy and Planning, University of Massachusetts, Lowell, Massachusetts

Steven Vallas Dept. of History, Georgia Institute of Technology, Atlanta, Georgia

William Julius Wilson Dept. of African American Policy, Harvard University, Cambridge, Massachusetts

Adrian Wood Institute of Development Studies, University of Sussex, Brighton, United Kingdom

Robert J. Wuthnow Dept. of Sociology, Princeton University, Princeton, New Jersey

Shoshana Zuboff Harvard University Business School, Boston, Massachusetts

Foreword

Robert B. Reich

"What do you do?" is typically the second question asked when meeting some-one for the first time. Occupation establishes one's identity. It demarcates a par-ticular place in society and implies a set of values and ideals. There is nothing new in this. The slave, the serf, the skilled craftsman, the warrior, the nobleman were all defined by their roles in society. But it is a peculiarity of modern life that the question must be asked at all. Until quite recently, in historical time, the answer was obvious. One's "job" was conferred by birth, part of a given set of social obligations and standings.

In modern society there are assumed to be choices, and the choices are as-sumed to reflect the unique attributes of the answerer. For some—profession-als, artists, caregivers, evangelists, and others with personal missions—what they "do" gives meaning to their lives. That they are paid to do their job is almost beside the point. For many others, a job is a means of gaining enough money to do what they want outside of paid employment. The job may give their lives structure, but not meaning. But what they value most comes from things they are not paid to do, such as caring for their children, or writing, or working in a soup kitchen, or visiting with their friends.

It is only very recently, and only in the middle and upper reaches of the world's richest societies, like America's, that significant numbers of people can make conscious choices about what they "do" for a living, and how they allo-cate their lives between paid and unpaid work. That is partly a consequence of prosperity. But it is also a result of the changing nature of work, as many of the essays summarized in this volume make clear.

The age of mass production is ending. Relatively fewer middle-class jobs are to be found any longer in factories or in what had been routinized services, such as banking, insurance, sales, or office clerical work. Many routinized or stan-dardized jobs are on their way to being done by a computer (i.e., stored in dig-ital memory) or else are being farmed out to people around the globe who are eager to do repetitive tasks for a fraction of American wages. This trend is leav-ing just two broad types of paid work in all advanced nations: technical jobs, which entail solving problems, and interpersonal jobs, which require a human touch.

Mass production demanded full-time employees who would report to a cer-tain place and remain there, usually five days a week and at least eight hours a day. But the emerging economy allows a greater range of possibility and less predictability. The most sought-after technicians are the successful inventors, surgeons, lawyers, investment bankers, and software engineers who are compensated for the quality of what they produce, not the quantity. I have elsewhere described their work as being symbolic and analytic.[1] The same is true for gifted and skilled providers of interpersonal services—the "rainmakers" who bring in clients, "dealmakers" who consummate transactions, and top sellers, marketers, and management consultants who effectively advise and persuade their corporate customers.

Lower-paid technicians (e.g., installers, repairers, and troubleshooters of all types) are also in demand in the emerging economy, as are lower-paid providers of interpersonal services (e.g., teachers, caretakers of children, the sick, and the elderly, executive secretaries, and personal trainers). They are working particularly hard when demand is high, in order to make up for fallow periods when demand slackens. There is less and less steady work in the new economy. So even for them, "jobs" are taking on more varied meanings, and the borders between paid work and unpaid work is blurring.

But the bottom third of the nation is coming to have less choice than before. What they "do" requires exceedingly long hours and, increasingly, multiple jobs. Mass production work had been a gateway into the American middle class during the last half of the twentieth century. But the decline of mass production work has reduced the bargaining power of workers without the education, skills, or the connections needed to become technicians or interpersonal workers. Wage-setting institutions of all types are disappearing: "oligopolies" that once coordinated wages have given way to highly competitive industries without clear borders; regulated industries, whose prices and wages were established by commission, have been deregulated; and labor unions, whose organization had been premised on large numbers of people working together at a single place with similar tasks and predictable routines, continue to shrink as a percentage of the workforce. As a consequence, real average hourly earnings of production workers, most of whom have only high school degrees, dropped from $13.75 in 1979 to $11.80 in 1997 (in 1997 dollars). Those who left high school before completion have experienced an ever more precipitous drop in hourly wages, from $9.50 an hour to $6.80.

The United States is rapidly becoming a two-tiered society, composed of the "have-mores," who enjoy ever-greater choice over the nature of the work they do, and the "have-lesses," whose choices are becoming more constrained. The wealthiest 1 percent of the population now owns almost 39 percent of the total household wealth of the nation. Excluding the value of homes, they own 47 percent. The top fifth owns 93 percent. While hardly a representative sample, Bill Gates, the chief executive of Microsoft, has a net worth larger than the combined net worth of the bottom 40 percent of American households. This accumulation of wealth at the top has few parallels in American history. Perhaps the closest analogy is the Gilded Age of a century ago.

A major challenge for this nation in the next century is to reverse this troubling trend. To do so will require several steps. Again, the essays summarized herein establish some of the context for understanding why these steps are important. First and foremost, we must bring all of our young people to a high minimum level of competence. This means establishing national education standards, putting extra resources into schools in poor areas, paying teachers enough so that top-quality people are attracted to the teaching profession, and giving parents a choice of which public school to send their children to.

Second, the nation will have to subsidize the wages of people who are working, but who do not earn enough to lift themselves and their families out of the range of poverty. A "reverse" income tax is already in place, providing about $3,000 per year to full-time workers who earn the minimum wage of $5.15 an hour. But this refundable tax credit will need to be expanded. In addition, the current unemployment-insurance system—designed for people who are temporarily laid off from their jobs—must be changed into a "re-employment" system, reflecting the fact that most people who now lose their jobs lose them permanently. Those who lose their jobs and get new ones at lower pay should have a portion of the difference subsidized, for a certain length of time, so as to make the transition easier.

Third, the nation must provide health insurance to all its citizens. At this writing, almost 18 percent of the population lacks access to health care, including more than 20 percent of the nation's children.

All three of these initiatives will be expensive. But the cost of failing to act could be much greater. A two-tiered society is ultimately an unstable society. It will require ever-greater expenditure on police, prisons, and private security. Already, an estimated 3 million American households live within 20,000 "gated" communities, featuring private security guards and electronic surveillance. In 1970, there were fewer than 2,000 such entities.

A two-tiered society also is susceptible to political backlashes against trade, immigration, and vulnerable groups. One recent example occured at the close of 1997, when the U.S. Congress refused to give President Clinton the authority he sought to move trade treaties quickly through Congress without amendment. Trade is good for a nation, but it also can impose special burdens on workers who are displaced by it, and they (and others who see their displacement) are the ones who are most in fear of declining wages and lost jobs. Their insecurities were reflected in Congress's decision to withhold "fast track" authority from the president. The tension between economic nationalism and globalism is already emerging as the most significant fissure in American politics today. Economic nationalism is replacing cold-war nationalism as a rallying cry for blue-collar voters who have been frustrated by their inability to get ahead. When the economy slows, the debate can only intensify.

The choice for America in the twenty-first century is clear. Other advanced nations face a similar choice. If adequate steps are taken to bring more people into the circle of prosperity, a strong economy can become even stronger, and nationalist and protectionist backlashes can be avoided. But if the nation fails to act and allows the economic divide to remain wide, or to widen further, it may gradually become two societies. Its most prosperous citizens will become citizens of the globe, engaged in global production, technology, and finance. But its poor and working-class citizens may seek to secede from the rest of the world behind a veil of nationalism.

The central political question is whether those who have gained the most from the current prosperity will be willing to sacrifice some of their fortunes in order to create new opportunities for those who have lost ground. The essays summarized in this volume do not answer that question, but they do provide a context for understanding why it has become so vitally important.

Note

1. *The Work of Nations*, Robert B. Reich (Alfred A. Knopf, 1991).

Acknowledgments

In the process of working on the successive volumes in this series we find ourselves agreeably indebted to many people. The first group are in-house: that is, within Tufts University, and sometimes closer to home, in the Global Development And Environment Institute (G-DAE), which is the sponsor for the series.

Our G-DAE colleague, Jonathan Harris, was a coeditor on two previous Frontiers volumes and has maintained a close association with this one, attending frequent group meetings, giving excellent feedback on essays written by the editors, and aiding us in a variety of ways throughout the process.

A number of Tufts students have assisted in this project, becoming, along the way, valued members of the Frontiers team. Graduate students Rhae Parkes and Mike Strauss did heroic work in researching and assembling articles to consider for summarization. Undergraduates Stacie Bowman and Gabriel Safar were excellent and hard-working library assistants. Copy editing was most ably performed by graduate students Carol Chouchani and John Nordgren. Others who briefly became members of the team, drafting some of the summaries, were Tufts alumnus Martin Hughes and an outside writer, Marc Breslow. Essential backup and support for all of our activities is supplied by the G-DAE office administrator, Dave Plancon.

Early in 1997 we met with a group of scholars in the field whose exceptional insight and experience aided our development of the outlines and the organizational scheme for the book. These included Barry Bluestone, Francois Carre, Peter Doeringer, Robert Forrant, Robert Kuttner, Paula Raymon, and Chris Tilly.

Another group of experts gave very helpful responses to a draft of the bibliography. We appreciate their contributions of time and thought, were relieved to receive their general approval, and believe that the final bibliography has benefited from their suggested changes. These reviewers included Eileen Applebaum, Sam Bowles, Robert Buchele, John Dunlop, Nancy Folbre, Clark Kerr, Mehrene Larude, Lisa Lynch, Molly Mead, Susan Ostrander, Michael Piore, and Robert Solow.

We have also been fortunate in receiving institutional support of several kinds. Among the values of being at Tufts University, we wish to single out for especially warm thanks the interlibrary loan office at Tisch Library, which has assisted in retrieving an astonishing volume of material for this project. The age of electronic information is a marvelous thing, but without real people in a real library it would be impossible to turn the electrons into the tangible books or journals we often require. We have also benefited from the solid support of our editor, Todd Baldwin, and our publisher, Island Press.

The funders of the Frontiers project, along with those who support the core activities of the Global Development And Environment Institute, provide another, essential type of institutional support. G-DAE's ability to take on and successfully complete a variety of projects in recent years has been undergirded by a series of generous grants from the Ford Foundation and the Fund For the Future. Work on The Changing Nature of Work, in particular, started up under two grants from the Bauman Foundation. We are grateful to Patricia Bauman for her involvement, which both encouraged the writing of graduate theses on related topics (the winners of the Bauman Thesis Awards at Tufts were Sutherland Miller, Rhae Parkes, and Saskia Wilhelms), and also gave us a solid financial base at an early stage of the project. The other major funder for this book was the John D. and Catherine T. MacArthur Foundation. We appreciate greatly the recognition of these foundations (evidenced in their other grant activities, as well) of the timeliness and the practical and theoretical importance of the topic of work, and of the forces affecting the experience and impact of work in people's lives.

Volume Introduction

by Neva R. Goodwin

The eighty-six articles that have been summarized for this volume present an interweaving of observation and theory that will be of use to the many people who are concerned about the topic of work and about its future in a time of rapid globalization and technical change. It is relevant to workers in general, including those who care about the evolution of unions; to people who are involved in a wide variety of work-related policy issues; and to journalists who write on allied subjects. It also has an important function for scholars. We expect this volume to be read and used in classes by labor economists, as well as by scholars in related fields who want an efficient means of surveying the writings that are most likely to lead toward new understandings of work in the twenty-first century.

While the editors have come to this material primarily via the discipline of economics, we believe that students and scholars in such related fields as political theory, sociology, history, anthropology, and philosophy will find this a good introduction to what contemporary economics can contribute to an understanding of the changing nature and conditions of work. We also believe that economists have much to gain by exploring, in this format, the frontiers of their own field, along with some of the most relevant work from neighboring disciplines.

The series, Frontier Issues in Economic Thought, has developed a unique format for providing access to the topics it covers. In this volume, for example, summaries of eighty-six articles, along with nine Overview Essays, tell an intriguing story about the forces affecting our working lives and the interrelations between production, labor organization, and technology.

The editors of *The Changing Nature of Work* have taken pains to present this material in nontechnical language. We hope that this will make this volume widely accessible. At the same time, we believe that, in order to understand what is happening in the world, it is necessary to do more than look at the facts. Indeed, it is rarely possible to "look only at the facts"; we understand what we see by supplying, from our mental models of the world, some kind of interpretation. The function of theory is to provide a framework for such interpretation. Hence many of the articles summarized here are theoretical, in the sense that they attempt to see the underlying patterns in accumulated experiences, or to suggest generalizations that embrace a range of specifics.

Three Points of View on Work

The topic of work may be viewed from three quite different perspectives: that of (1) the workers; (2) the stockholders, owners, and managers whose interest is in the profits accruing to a production process; and (3) the whole of society. From the workers' point of view the topics of interest include what the worker is paid. Wage influences, and indeed largely determines, what the worker and his or her family can purchase and consume. This is, of course, a major issue. However, the quality of life is not only a function of the consumption of marketed goods and services that occurs outside of work; to an important extent it is also determined by the quality of the work experience. Occupying a large part of most people's lives, work affects not only the feelings of anxiety, trust, boredom, challenge, empowerment, ignominy, and self-respect that may be engendered during the work process, but also carries over into the rest of life, shaping character, aspirations, and the sense of self.

From the point of view of owners and managers, the relationship between work and profits hinges on labor productivity—that is, the value of output that can be contributed by each hour of work. From this point of view, the complex issues of work are often boiled down to a single one: motivation. If productivity is what you want from your workers, motivation is what you have to foster.

According to some management theories, the principal motivators are the carrot of monetary reward and the threat of dismissal. Other theories focus on that intangible issue, morale, which is more clearly tied to other aspects of workers' experience. For example, it has long been recognized that owners and managers can create or enhance an atmosphere of trust by setting standards and practices of fair dealing. Managers know, too, that they can ratchet up or down the level of anxiety in a workplace through myriad ways of applying pressure. They are also aware of the importance to worker morale of the many intangible aspects of the work experience. Yet it seems inevitable that a tension must remain between the owners' interest in morale and motivation as means to the end of productivity versus the workers' experience of morale as resulting from a quality of experience that is an end in itself.

The interest of society at large embraces all of the issues of the first two views, with some refinements. Since the well-being of its members is a major societal goal, the experience of people in their roles as workers must be—or should be—an important focus. To the extent that societal goals are defined in a longer time frame than individual goals, there should be an added interest in the education that occurs through work—in the economist's terms, the development of on-the-job human capital. The importance of this extends beyond "labor productivity" as such; demoralized, cynical workers are diminished in their capacity to be good citizens or good parents. Conversely, those who have opportunities at work to stretch their capacities, think creatively, and take responsibility also have more to offer to others and to themselves in the rest of their lives.

Thus, there are substantial overlaps between the meanings to workers, and to society at large, of the issues concerning quality of worklife and its concomitant, morale. The larger society also has a keen interest in the closely related issues of motivation and productivity that concern owners, shareholders, and managers. Again, however, there is a slightly different twist to society's interest.

Labor productivity is valuable to owners and managers because it reduces cost per unit of output. It can be equally valuable to the rest of society if several conditions are met. To wit:

- If the income produced by the sale of society's total product is shared sufficiently widely among the members of the society, then there is a broad base of people with enough income to be able to purchase that product. At its most fundamental this has to do with how the income from production is divided between labor and capital.

- Another way for the results of labor productivity to be shared widely in the society is for cost reductions to be passed on to consumers. This objective explains economists' emphasis on competition: wherever there is an uncompetitive concentration of economic power (e.g., in monopolies), productivity will do less to benefit the consumer (through lower prices) and more to benefit the owners (through higher profits).

The two issues just cited have to do with how a society's total income (i.e., its gross national product) is shared, between owners and workers and between owners and consumers. It is a curious fact, requiring a sociological explanation that will not be attempted here, that the second division, between owners and consumers, is a respectable economic subject, with considerable agreement that more competition is virtually always better than less. In contrast, the first division, between owners and workers, is far less often discussed these days, and then usually by people regarded as radicals within the economics profession.

There is also a third issue that determines how valuable labor productivity is to society at large. This one receives, if anything, even less attention from economists than the division between labor and capital:

- Labor productivity is socially valuable not simply to the extent that it produces "more," but with some regard to the question, "more of what?"

For example, there is general agreement that we do not benefit from increases in the productivity of those who produce and distribute illegal, addictive drugs. Given the growing awareness that nicotine is also a harmful and addictive drug, it is an interesting question whether or not productivity increases in the production and sale of tobacco products are actually desirable. Probably most members of the public would say, "of course they are not." It is not so clear what answers to expect from economists.

As another example, similar questions could be raised about the effectiveness of the advertising industry in general (which may be thought of in terms of the

labor productivity of the workers in this industry). One of the academic de-
fenses of advertising is that it makes no difference in consumers' preferences—
it simply ensures that they have all the relevant information. Obviously this industry would have much less business if this defense were based in fact. Instead
it is evident that advertising is creating a culture of consumption in which wants
are actively created—wants for particular things and for consumption in general. As discussed by various authors in the two previous volumes in this series,
there is considerable reason, both empirical and theoretical, to believe that
human well-being is decreased by the effectiveness of this industry. Again the
question can be raised: Is it always better to be more productive, no matter
what the product?

How are questions such as these related to the specific investigation of work
and workplace issues? To answer that requires a little more explanation of the
special character of this book, as part of the Frontier series.

How Topics Were Defined, and Articles Selected, for This Book

The projected volumes in the Frontier Issues in Economic Thought Series are
as follows:

Vol. 1: A Survey of Ecological Economics (published 1995)

Vol. 2: The Consumer Society (published 1997)

Vol. 3: Human Well-Being and Economic Goals (published 1997)

Vol. 4: The Changing Nature of Work (this volume)

Vol. 5: The Political Economy of Inequality

Vol. 6: Fully Sustainable Development

This volume may be seen as part of an ongoing exploration of a closely inter-
linked set of topics, with one fundamental issue threading through them all;
that is, the question of what is the ultimate purpose of economic development—of economic progress. A summary of our answer to that question may
be inferred from the title of Volume 3: we have accepted the assumption that
human well-being, most broadly understood, is the central goal that defines
economic progress. By contrast, the maximization of physical output, which is
often accepted as the goal of economic development, should, in fact, be regarded as intermediate—a means to the ultimate end of increased human well-
being. When this means/end distinction is forgotten, the result is often an exclusive focus on maximizing physical output that makes it easy to ignore such
critical issues as:

- who gets that output (e.g., the division among rich and poor, workers and
  owners, or among different nations and groups)

- how access to a society's product is related to the work of individuals, and what this relationship means for individuals and for society

- how the processes of production and consumption feed back into the health of the natural world

- how these processes affect the aspects of human well-being that are often swept aside as "just" moral, spiritual, or cultural issues.

Volume 2 (The Consumer Society) gave an important focus to these issues with the question: If consumption is not the final goal, what is? As we continued to pursue these issues into our fourth volume, it became clear that, given the scope of this topic, not all aspects of "the changing nature of work" could be covered. The following is a brief description of how we proceeded to accommodate this reality.

Our selection criteria started from a broad interest in the ways that work is important to human well-being (from the three points of view described earlier). Then, of necessity, we also applied several other screens. One (relating to the title of the volume) was the question: Which are the work-related issues where significant change is now occurring? Another asked: Where is there a body of constructive new thinking? By overlaying these questions on the issue of how work affects human well-being we defined the area of the intellectual frontier to be explored in this volume. The critical topics that emerged from this process include:

- *Work opportunities, wage differences, and varieties of labor markets:* influences on labor supply and demand, work opportunities, and the price of labor (including discrimination, education, and socialization) that appear significantly different from influences in other markets.

- *The experience of work:* the forces that increase or decrease involvement, autonomy, shared authority, and other generally positive aspects of the work experience, as well as negative aspects (often summarized as alienation).

- *Management and industrial relations:* the evolution of production systems (e.g., away from Taylorist/Fordist approaches), the institutions through which workers and owners relate, and the goals sought through these institutions.

- *Globalization:* how international competition, in particular, affects the changing nature of work.

- *Technology:* its role in determining the distribution of different types of jobs, and its interactions with management practices and other aspects of the work experience.

Two points should be noted regarding this list. One is that, while a number of the parts of this volume have headings that are close to one or another of the topics just listed, every one of these topics is to be found in more than one part, and most are themes that run throughout the book. The other point is that the list suggests many places where issues of economic power and inequality arise. However, these issues have been dealt with relatively lightly, because they will be the focus of the next volume in the Frontier series.

Another constraint on our selection of material for summary has been the necessity to limit our literature search, for practical reasons, to English language publications. Beyond these specific constraints is the most general one, emerging from our commitment to presenting frontier writings in the area of each book in this series. The frustrating implication of this commitment is that, where the literature—even that on the frontier of economics or the other areas surveyed—has not reached a topic that we regard as important, we cannot represent that topic in the summaries that make up a major portion of the book. In this case we use our Overview Essays or (as in this case) the Volume Introduction to define the research agenda that still lies ahead. Some notes toward such an agenda will be offered later. Before getting there, we will take a detour to lay out the theoretical backdrop against which it is necessary to understand contemporary economic contributions to the subject of work.

The Two Legacies of Adam Smith

Neoclassical and Marxian economics—both offsprings of Adam Smith's political economy—have each to some extent avoided positions and topics most strongly associated with the other. At some point in the development of neoclassical economics, this paradigm—now prevailing in the West and rapidly spreading into formerly communist countries—was impoverished by some of what it ceded to the Marxian stream. The areas surrendered by neoclassical economics included the Marxian recognition of the importance of power and inequality, both as explanatory and as normative categories. In particular, issues of power and inequality in the workplace gained special attention in a theory whose proponents saw labor as the source of all value.

The economics of power and inequality will be the focus of Volume 5 in the Frontier series, while the current volume aims to bring back to a central place in economics a general focus on work. However, this statement is not meant to suggest that neoclassical economics has altogether neglected the topic of work. On the contrary, this is an area where there has been much excellent analysis and description, so that The Changing Nature of Work will summarize more writings from mainstream economics publications than any of the previous volumes in the series. At the same time we find that, in relation to the topic of this book, an unusual amount of institutionalist, Marxist, and neo-Marxist thinking has been given a hearing in the mainstream, since these other approaches were filling such obvious lacunae.

How can we best describe the way in which neoclassical economics biased its own approach to the topic of work? The answer is, in fact, implicit in the two previous Frontier volumes: The Consumer Society and Human Well-Being and Economic Goals. The goals of neoclassical economics—the goals, for example, that are to be achieved through the means of economic efficiency—do not relate to the whole of human experience, but only to one part. Economic efficiency is intended to maximize output. That, in turn, is intended to maximize consumer choice. Neoclassical economics pays lip service to the idea of maximizing general human welfare, but in fact what it shows how to maximize is one aspect of consumer welfare: the opportunity (for those who have the purchasing power) to consume goods and services produced through the market.

Economic theory has traditionally conceptualized people in the labor force as though they were divided into two parts—the worker and the consumer. This convenient fiction is, indeed, so common, that much of the time its fictional quality is not remembered. Given this division, neoclassical economics has structured its goals with respect to a particular conception of the well-being of the consumer, while Marxian economics focused on the well-being of the worker. However, it is not possible in reality, and perhaps not desirable in conception, to divide people into the two roles of worker and consumer. When either the consumer's or the worker's needs are neglected the whole person will suffer; and many of us also identify with other significant roles (such as parent, citizen).

With the collapse of eastern European communism, neoclassical economics has become the dominant paradigm for virtually all of the world. This dominance may finally permit economists to forget the sibling rivalry that had constricted the field. An effort to make economics whole requires both giving equal weight to our working selves as to our consuming selves, and also reintegrating, within economic theory, and within our broader culture, these two halves of our selves.

Insofar as there are Marxian or neo-Marxian (or institutionalist or other unorthodox) writings that accomplish some of these ambitions, they have been summarized in this volume. However, some of the topics we would have liked to represent here simply could not be found in sufficiently thoughtful and informed treatments in any school of economics. Those topics are proposed in the next section.

An Agenda for Research on Work

In considering the gaps we have found in contemporary research, let us start with the question that was raised earlier, but not answered: Is it always better to be more productive, no matter what the product? Economic theory assesses the worker's achievement, or product, according to how it is priced through the forces of demand and supply that create economic value. A very different assessment relates to the contribution to human well-being of each piece of work. The problematical relation between these two evaluations is revealed in the fact that, roughly speaking, the more an act is essential to the survival of the human species, the lower its monetary reward is likely to be. Economics has long prided itself on being able to explain this hierarchy[1] (e.g., Adam Smith's paradox of the relative value of diamonds and water), but what it means for human life is only barely beginning to be recognized as a core problem for market economies. A few authors, summarized or discussed in Part VIII, represent a small movement, which has not yet penetrated far into academic discourse, that explicitly addresses the problem of the wage divergence between human values and economic values.

Insofar as domestic activities, along with some of the other work that supplies our basic needs, receive little compensation in either pay or recognition, we face the reality that the quality of civilization and the very possibility of human life may increasingly depend on the willingness of a sizable part of the human population—most often women—to continue to perform these tasks with ever-less economic incentive. Our very definitions of a nation's economic success may be read, in this respect, as sign-posts for trouble. Broad equality of opportunity is a widely accepted and benign social goal. At the same time, a vision of "the good life" defined in terms of high income and high consumption creates a more questionable, but also widely accepted, goal. Where there is real success in achieving both of these together, what will motivate people to do the jobs that are necessary for the social weal?

The dilemma is that, on the one hand, we have not found ways to reward, with the means for a decent livelihood, much of our societies' most important work. On the other hand, our system contains strong rewards and incentives that motivate people to do and to produce many things that have a negative impact on human and ecological health and well-being. Incentives that diverge sharply from human values can lead to counterproductive growth: that is, increases in economic output whose benefits are outweighed by their costs (e.g., to the environment, as with polluting effects of production and consumption; to culture, as with media or chemical products that have a mind-numbing effect; or to health, as with excessive consumption of fatty foods). Counterproductive growth becomes increasingly likely as a society gets richer, both because the absorptive capacity of the natural environment becomes increasingly saturated, and because the marginal value of more stuff declines as people fill their most urgent needs, then their dearest desires, and so on, through less and less urgent or meaningful wants.

In capitalist societies (and conventional economic theories) today, there is no place for a discussion of ways of evaluating work other than in terms of the market value of its output and the wage it can command. A lack of jobs, or insecurity about future access to jobs, causes such distress and hardship that there is little effort to focus on the distinction between work that produces genuine human well-being and work that detracts from it. Instead, efforts on behalf of workers tend to rate the creation of jobs only according to the characteristics of the job (especially wages), regardless of the output. Yet valueless jobs may, in the long run, turn out to be as harmful for society as jobless growth. (The worst of all, of course, is valueless, jobless growth.)

There is a difficult transition ahead, to progressively reduce incentives for the jobs that drain society's resources without enhancing well-being; to shift our focus to creating and valuing (in economic and other terms) more of the jobs that are needed by society; and to find ways of sharing fairly among all members of society the income, respect, and product that result from useful work. Until this transition is managed, we will be stuck with a severe misallocation of human, financial, and other resources: doing work that does not produce well-being, and remaining unable to afford much of the work that is sorely needed.

These are issues that should be of central interest in economic theory. Why should the profitability of counterproductive activities not be viewed by economic researchers in the same way that cancer is viewed by researchers in biology?—not as an immutable fact, but as an unfortunate by-product of the system, something we should try to understand in order to find the levers for change. When it suits economists to do so, they claim to be "pure" researchers, doing "positive science." However most of the best economists do some normative work, developing theories and policies aimed at increasing consumption in one part of the world or another. If it is legitimate to espouse the normative goal of increasing consumption, it is equally legitimate to ask the question, "consumption of what?," and to follow that with proposals for finding ways to encourage the consumption (hence the production) of some things (e.g., food grains, social services), while discouraging the consumption of other things (e.g., unsustainably harvested meat and fish products, weapons).[2]

To conclude, several additional topics for a research agenda arise from the earlier sections of this introduction. One is the need for a more constructive and realistic understanding of the relation between what continue to be posed as two separate sets of interests: those of the consumer and those of the worker. Why does this conflict appear so strongly in modern economic theory? Such a division is not nearly so marked in other studies of human behavior. Are the rest of the social sciences overlooking something critical that is only apparent through the lens of economics? Or has the discipline of economics in this respect made an error in how it organizes its subject matter?

A related topic, also mentioned earlier, is the need for more attention to the value of work to the worker. At the same time as it ignores the possibility of viewing the work experience as an end in itself, mainstream theory privileges two presumed goals—to maximize consumption and to maximize profits. What are the consequences of embedding economic goals within models where workers are only the means to these other ends? As will be noted in several later essays in this book, this bias downplays or makes invisible a number of important realities about the human values that may be achieved through work, as well as practical facts about the human nature of workers.

The failure to develop theory that can adequately recognize the far more complex reality, in which not all consumption is good and not all work is in itself bad, is connected to the poverty of the goal structure of neoclassical economics. That poverty (as was suggested in Frontier Volume 3, Human Well-Being and Economic Goals) is, in turn, related to a reluctance within the discipline to admit that it does operate in relation to internally articulated goals.

If economic theory were to expand its goal to the enhancement of the welfare of humans as whole beings—including their working as well as their consuming selves—there might be significant increases in the efficiency with which we approach this overarching goal. The current, neoclassical logic shows work leading to income, leading to consumption, leading to well-being. For some aspects of each working person's life this logic could be abbreviated, with meaningful work leading directly to well-being.

An economics that defined the goal of the economy as human well-being would recognize ways in which work can be an important means of achieving human values; it would also seek ways of recognizing the social, as well as the economic, value of the output. We hope that this volume, while not yet providing the full basis for such an economics, will at least indicate the areas to which research effort should be devoted in order to achieve a better understanding of the many ways in which work affects human well-being.

Notes

1. The counterintuitive finding that wages tend to decline as the human value of their output rises may be briefly explained as follows.

There is, of course, a large demand for the things that most people value highly in their lives, such as food, health care, and education. However, the majority of the people in the world are poor, and while they spend a large proportion of their money on basic needs, the price they can pay remains low, hence their demand is "ineffective." When it is not backed up by purchasing power, it is invisible to a market economy.

On the supply side, the skills required to supply basic needs, while often extensive (consider the knowledge requirements for tending a baby or growing a crop), tend to be very common; if they were not, the human race would not have survived. Thus the most essential skills are available at low cost, while richer people can pay higher prices for luxuries and novelties that often require new skills that are hard to acquire, rare, and, hence, expensive.

2. In this note I will be more specific about my opinions on the existing misallocation of resources, as viewed from the perspective of well-being. (Though I could cite supporting evidence, such conclusions are more appropriately termed opinion than fact.)

An unprioritized, incomplete, but suggestive list of areas where the appropriate application of more resources would increase human well-being includes: nursing; day care; repair services (for many items whose useful life is curtailed for lack of repair possibilities); social protection (e.g., police); teaching (especially precollegiate); genuinely educational, ad-free TV for kids; foster parenting and other care for children whose parents can't care for them; social casework to assist with foster children and to give support to nursing, daycare, and other areas; and maintenance of public spaces, parks, and natural resources.

In contrast, the following are areas where too much is being produced and too many resources are being used: weapons; addictive drugs, including tobacco and alcohol; violent, degrading, overly sexualized films, TV programs, video games; advertisement; and status goods (i.e., things that are sold, and bought, primarily to enhance the purchaser's status. This is a zero sum game that can never add to overall well-being.).

The second list does not constitute a proposal for banning or otherwise restricting any specific activities. The point, instead, is to apply creative practical and theoretical thought to the question of how resources can be diverted from producing goods and services of the second type, toward the first. Of course, recognizing that others would generate somewhat different lists, such a goal remains well in the future. It must be preceded by public and academic discussion of how to distinguish between the productive activities that enhance, and those that detract from, human well-being.

PART I

The History of Work

Essay

by Frank Ackerman

Work is unseen and almost unchanging. It is best thought of as a well-defined unpleasantness or disutility, which people engage in solely in order to obtain the income needed for private consumption—the real goal of economic activity. Over time, thanks to productivity increases, the same amount of disutility at work leads to more consumption, which is the definition of progress.

Or so one could easily conclude from the simplest and most widely circulated versions of conventional economics. The simplistic analysis of work is often what is learned by those students whose exposure to economics is limited to an introductory course, or those citizens who listen to the increasingly passionate public discussion of the efficiency of the market—in short, by almost everyone who encounters economic theory.

Labor economists, of course, have always known better. In contrast to some other areas of economics, there is a lively ongoing debate about alternative theories in labor economics, integrated with impressively detailed empirical research on many questions about employment and wages. To a far greater extent than in any of our previous volumes, our review of the frontiers of economic thought on the nature of work draws on articles from the established academic journals in the field.

Yet there is still a need to explore and expand the frontiers of economics in this area. The conventional constraints of neoclassical theory sometimes threaten to stifle, or at least obscure, the innovative approaches appearing in labor economics. Moreover, even the new research by labor economists often reduces the work process to a matter of individual maximizing behavior over a narrow set of quantifiable choices, leaving little scope for the analysis of social interaction, institutional contexts, or historical change.

Three concerns, three often-overlooked issues, motivate our investigation and our selection of topics and articles in this book. First, work as an essential human activity and economic process encompasses much more than paid employment. Second, work is a social process that shapes and is shaped by work-

1

ers' actions and beliefs, not just a question of individual employment decisions and wages. Finally, as our title suggests, institutional, technological, and political forces are changing the nature of work in ways that may require corresponding changes in our theories. This essay offers a brief look at the latter subject, the history of work, and then introduces the subjects of the more detailed discussions that occupy the rest of this book.

In the Beginning

Until the last 200 years or so, work, for the vast majority of people in every society, meant agricultural and related household labor. Agriculture remains an essential activity and still accounts for a large part of the work done in much of the world. However, it accounts for only a very small fraction of work in developed countries today and is shrinking in other countries as they develop. For brevity and clarity of focus, the discussion in this essay, and in the volume as a whole, largely omits the special problems of work on the farm.

Even farther back in time is the intriguing possibility of a preagricultural life that has been described as "Stone Age affluence."[1] Throughout the long prehistory of human existence, prior to the appearance of agriculture roughly 10,000 years ago, people lived by hunting and gathering. Hunter–gatherer communities, with low population densities and minimal material possessions, seem to have allowed easier work lives and a more sociable existence than any society that has followed them. But such a relaxed way of life is entirely disconnected from the modern world of work.

For a feasible, short version of the history of work, we will focus largely on the postagricultural, Anglo-American experience—both because this was the first and best-researched case, and because it has had such a powerful effect (sometimes through voluntary emulation, sometimes through forcible imposition) in shaping the later experience of other countries. We begin with a look at preindustrial patterns of work, then turn to a three-stage classification of modes of work since industrialization, and finally consider in greater detail the puzzling nature of the latest developments.

Preindustrial Work

In the century before the Industrial Revolution there were many different kinds of work and workers. Even in England, agriculture still employed a majority of the population, increasingly including wage laborers as well as those who owned their own land. Perhaps the next most common was rural household industry, particularly spinning and weaving. Some were self-employed, while many worked for merchants via the "putting-out" system. In the towns, artisans worked in many skilled trades, either individually or in very small enterprises.

The only important city, metropolitan London (which had a population of more than half a million by 1700), employed many men in work crews on the docks and in the building trades. Many women and some men were shopkeepers, street vendors, and domestic servants. Large enterprises were the exception rather than the rule, but could be found in mining and in scattered other industries. Thousands of sailors worked on England's merchant ships and in the navy.

Some of these workers were insecure and destitute. Many lived relatively comfortable lives—in comparison both to their contemporaries in continental Europe and to their descendants in the first half of the nineteenth century. It might appear that the different types of preindustrial workers had little in common, except that the industrial proletariat was later recruited from among their ranks. Yet E.P. Thompson[2] argued that many of the forms of preindustrial work shared a task-oriented rhythm, quite unlike the regular, disciplined time orientation of industry or bureaucracy. The rhythms of nature dictated the schedule for many types of work: Farmers had to plant and harvest according to the seasons, while fishermen had to "attend to the tides" and sailed, night or day, when the seas permitted. Work on the docks and in construction was governed by the tides and the weather, even more than it is today. (Those who cared for children, Thompson noted, had to attend to the tides of infancy, as they largely still do today.) The rhythm of work governed by nature leads to an uneven alternation between exhaustingly long, hard days and more relaxed interludes.

Other types of preindustrial work also followed varying rhythms of task-oriented exertion followed by periods of near idleness. Artisans frequently worked day and night as the end of the week approached, then observed the "feast of Saint Monday" (the widely used metaphor for absenteeism) as the next week began. This ritual, on occasion extended to honor Saint Tuesday as well, existed in a context of traditional fairs and holidays that made work time quite variable throughout the year. Employers naturally sought to stamp out such interruptions in work, as did temperance groups—Saint Monday's celebrations were far from dry. But despite growing labor discipline, traces of the old artisan rhythms could be found in rural and small-town England into the twentieth century, with a few coopers reportedly still honoring Saint Monday in the traditional manner as late as the 1960s.

Such a task-oriented rhythm, with bouts of very hard work interspersed with frequent relaxation and celebration, is incompatible with the efficiency of the market, in theory and in practice. The market is efficient because increased demand for anything leads to higher prices, resulting in increased supply. Yet for the preindustrial artisans described by Thompson, higher hourly wages might result in less work and more frequent celebration of Saint Tuesday. This is the backward-bending supply curve of labor, often exhibited as a classroom curiosity but excluded by assumption from the main body of economic theory.

To make markets work, and indeed to make capitalism profitable and expandable, the labor supply curve had to be bent forward. To make people work more rather than less when wages went up, a combination of strict workplace discipline and acquisitive consumerism was required—and was created over the course of the first century of industrialization. This process occurred earlier in England than elsewhere. According to Thompson,

> By the 1830s and 1840s it was commonly observed that the English industrial worker was marked off from his fellow Irish worker, not by a greater capacity for hard work, but by his regularity, his methodical paying-out of energy, and perhaps also by a repression, not of enjoyments, but of the capacity to relax in the old, uninhibited ways.[3]

Work Discipline and Technology

A useful framework for understanding the history of work since the Industrial Revolution is suggested by David Gordon, Richard Edwards, and Michael Reich.[4] They identify three logical stages, which are chronologically somewhat overlapping. The first stage, *proletarianization,* moved increasing numbers of people into wage labor in large enterprises, but often continued to rely on old crafts and technical skills. This stage lasted from the beginnings of industrialization—the 1780s in England, the 1820s in the United States—through the 1890s.

In the second stage, *homogenization,* employers challenged and often eliminated the power of the skilled craft workers. This allowed the introduction of assembly lines, continuous process technologies, and other innovations. It also allowed employers to compel the increasingly homogeneous workforce to work harder than ever. The second stage occurred at different times in different industries, stretching from the 1870s through the beginning of World War II.

The third stage, *segmentation,* saw the rise of industrial unionism and the adoption of more moderate, enlightened industrial management, followed by the decline in industrial employment (first in relative terms, later in absolute terms as well) and increasing segmentation of the labor force. This stage began in the 1920s and, according to Gordon, Edwards, and Reich, extended at least into the 1980s, the time when they wrote about it.

What happened in the beginning? Industrialization occurred first in textiles, not only in Britain but also in the United States. Before about 1840, according to economic historian Alfred Chandler, textile mills were virtually the only large industrial enterprises in America.[5] They were unique in labor discipline as well as in size:

> The work was far more routine than even that of plantation slaves. Indeed, the

[textile] mill workers were the first sizable group of Americans to be totally isolated from seasonal variations in the tempo of their work.[6]

This familiar portrait of labor at the dawn of industrialization involves women and children working at massive new machines. Not only were women and children cheaper to hire than adult men; employers believed that they would form a more docile, manageable workforce, avoiding the self-confident independence of male artisans and other workers. Yet the story of the textile industry, important as it is in its own right, may be atypical of other nineteenth-century developments in two respects.

First, early factories did not always involve new production technologies. Large enterprises emerged in many U.S. industries in the late nineteenth century, made possible by advances in transportation and communications (particularly the spread of the railroads), the availability of cheap energy (coal), the growth of management expertise, and other factors. In some industries such as papermaking, revolutionary new production processes appeared at about the same time. The technique for making paper from wood, rather than from cloth rags, was introduced in America in the 1860s, transforming and expanding the industry. But in other important industries, such as iron and steel, the new factories initially brought existing crafts and processes together under one roof. In nineteenth-century steel mills, each skilled craft carefully guarded its technical secrets. Some craft workers functioned virtually as subcontractors, hiring their own helpers and contracting to deliver a certain amount of production. In such cases, early industrialization changed the place and pace of work, but left the techniques of production unchanged.

Second, the industrial labor force did not remain predominantly women and children; skilled and unskilled adult men were drawn in as well.[7] The 1890 census, the first one to provide detailed information on workers' occupations, found that 79 percent of industrial workers were adult men. At the end of the nineteenth century, about one-fourth of all women who worked for wages were in manufacturing; a larger number were domestic servants, and almost as many were farm laborers. (In this era, paid work was extremely rare for married women—most of whom performed domestic and/or farm labor without pay.)[8]

Changes in production processes were the focus of struggles in the workplace. The results were far from being predetermined or deducible from macroeconomic contexts. Chris Tilly and Charles Tilly, examining the history of nineteenth-century English and American industries, find that both textiles and coal mining offered a choice between more capital-intensive processes that required less skilled labor, and less capital-intensive processes that depended more heavily on skilled workers.[9] However, neither country had a consistent comparative advantage in capital or skilled labor. The more capital-intensive approach was adopted in England in coal mining, but in the United States, in textiles. Modernization did not proceed uniformly throughout the economy; the newest industries often remained dependent on, and intertwined with, the oldest modes of production. The crucial raw material of early industrialization, cotton, was produced by slave labor until the 1860s, and often by semi-feudal sharecroppers for the rest of the century.

Factories and Families

In the next broad stage of industrialization ("homogenization," as identified by Gordon et al.), employers challenged the power of skilled workers, defeating the small craft-based unions that had emerged in steel and other industries. The expanded scope of capitalist control over the production process allowed the reorganization of work and the introduction of assembly lines, continuous process technologies, and other innovations. The power and the wages of skilled workers could thereby be reduced. Workers were increasingly pushed to the limits of their endurance, in what contemporary observers called the "drive system." In the early twentieth century new waves of immigration to the United States, and internal migration of African-Americans from Southern farms to industrial cities, provided a rapidly growing labor force.

Meanwhile, the growth of commerce and of corporate hierarchies spawned a growing middle class, and the spreading patterns of conspicuous consumption that Thorstein Veblen so effectively satirized. The Victorian ideal of domesticity spread to all those who could afford it. The images of the home as refuge from work, and the wife as homemaker and consumer, became important parts of the cultural landscape.

Indeed, the modern concept of the "housewife" was essentially created in this era. In earlier times, although there were clearly differentiated gender roles, there was little doubt that men and women were both involved in production. No one would have described the wife in a household of European peasants, or American pioneers, as primarily a consumer. In mid-nineteenth century America, households still carried out a vast range of productive activities: growing and preparing food; sewing and mending clothes, and reusing fabric scraps in quilts, rugs, and homemade upholstery; making and repairing furniture, tools, and other household goods; even making candles and soap from household wastes.[10]

The expansion of consumer goods industries toward the end of the nineteenth century began to change all this, providing affordable mass-produced substitutes for many things that had formerly been made at home. This industrial change allowed, and perhaps required, the rise of a consumer society.[11] In the new regime, the work of the housewife shifted away from material production toward consumption of marketed goods combined with caring for, or "nurturing," other family members. The change was a contradictory one, at once liberating women from exhausting toil and commercializing daily life to an ever-expanding extent.

The industrial development of the same era also had contradictory results: It delivered some material rewards—by 1929, a majority of American households owned cars—but it required oppressive, exhausting labor, and increasingly eliminated the security and privileges of skilled workers. The combination of the 1930s Depression and World War II ushered in the next phase, based on widespread unionization, more cooperative labor relations (at least in the more profitable major corporations), and the social and labor legislation of the New Deal. Gordon et al. identify these features as the basis of the third stage of industry, "segmentation" of the labor force.

Three Theories: Stuck in the Past?

All of the traditional theories of labor economics—neoclassical, Marxist, and institutionalist—seem designed to describe the nature of work in the early or mid-twentieth century. The destruction of traditional skilled crafts and homogenization of industrial labor could be seen as consistent with the neoclassical image of an abstract market: Nothing matters, as a first approximation, except the quantity of labor to be bought and sold, and the wage rate that is offered or demanded. The same reality, seen in broader social and political terms, could be taken as confirmation of Marxist predictions about the evolution of capitalism and the role of labor within that system. And the subsequent rise of unions and less antagonistic labor relations led to the heyday of institutionalist economics, which described in detail the bargaining processes and other institutional regularities of the era.

All three theories have fared badly in the second half of the twentieth century—which is why it is important to explore the new frontiers of labor economics. As labor markets have become segmented, differentiated, and increasingly unequal in outcomes, the neoclassical market paradigm has looked less and less appropriate. Extensions of the basic model, such as search theory and human capital theory, have led to selected insights, but are far from sufficient as a comprehensive analysis of labor. Newer approaches, such as efficiency wage and market segmentation theories, allow economists to model some of the more complex behavior patterns that are observed in real-world labor markets, as we will see in Part II. Yet the latest theories lead ever farther from the original market paradigm, still leave important questions unanswered, and to date have not produced a unified new account of the economics of labor. Other voices, also heard in Part II, doubt that even the newest formal models are adequate for a theoretical understanding of work and labor markets.

Many aspects of work, through the "homogenization" phase of industrial labor, were described remarkably well by Marxist theory. Proletarianization, deskilling of workers, intensification of the pace of work, a decade-long depression in the 1930s, an upsurge in union activity—all seemed consistent with the predictions made by Karl Marx in the nineteenth century. Few social scientists have looked so far and so successfully into the future. Yet after the 1930s, events in the United States bore a decreasing resemblance to the classical tenets of Marxism. Such trends as widespread apolitical unionization, the comparative affluence of large parts of the working class, the new segmentation and stratification of labor, and then the decline of industrial employment after the 1970s, all challenged the established theories of the left.

As with neoclassical economists, a number of creative neo-Marxists have sought to adapt and rescue their theory. Harry Braverman, for example, argued that proletarianization and deskilling will continue to expand in the future into higher and higher strata of the working population. Reality is more complex than that, however, with new skills rising at the same time that old ones decline; the contradictory changes in the levels of workplace skills are discussed in Part IV. There is not yet a successful, comprehensive neo-Marxist account of the economics of labor in the second half of the twentieth century.

Institutionalist economics has long excelled in describing the context and structures of unions, bargaining, and labor relations. At mid-century the labor movement looked like an established fact of economic life, and institutionalists looked similarly established in the world of labor economics. Through unionization, Galbraith suggested, workers achieved "countervailing power" vis-à-vis corporate America. Wage contours and other patterns of bargaining were better understood in institutional terms than with more abstract models. Neither the reality nor the theory was destined to endure. Both the labor movement and the institutionalist approach to labor economics soon suffered precipitous declines. Neoinstitutionalist analyses, attuned to the more difficult circumstances of labor at the end of the century, are only beginning to appear.[12]

In short, none of the existing theories offers an adequate description of recent developments in the world of work. This book is an attempt to answer the resulting questions: What has happened to work in the late twentieth century, and how can economics be expanded and enriched to understand the nature of work today?

The Rise and Fall of the Late Twentieth Century

Work in America, in the middle of the century, existed within the institutional structure that emerged from the New Deal and the wartime economy of World War II: strong unions in many industries; labor legislation that tolerated and bureaucratized existing unions, while limiting their activism and growth; new styles of industrial relations in many major corporations; and social welfare systems that alleviated some of the worst forms of poverty. While there were important international similarities, the corresponding institutional framework for postwar reconstruction was somewhat different in other developed countries, notably being more favorable to unions and welfare state initiatives in most of Europe, while drawing on unique social and cultural norms in Japan.

For employers, this was a regime that imposed uncomfortably high labor costs. From the beginning of the postwar era, there were attempts to segment the labor market, limiting the proportion of work done under high-cost conditions. Skilled workers, and the production workers in the largest, most profitable firms, enjoyed the relatively high wages and job security of the "primary labor market"; but at the same time, they represented a declining fraction of the working population. Routine, low-skilled production and service work was increasingly done under the much less attractive conditions of the "secondary labor market." Technological and organizational change led to an increasing proportion of white-collar work, often done by female clerical workers, and almost always nonunionized.

The first quarter-century after World War II has been called the "golden age" of capitalism.[13] (The term, it should be emphasized, refers solely to the macroeconomic performance of the era, not to the concurrent social, cultural, or political context.) Growth was rapid throughout the developed world. Although the "good jobs" in the primary labor market were declining as a percentage of the labor force, they were still growing in absolute numbers. Wages and productivity were rising steadily from year to year. Among other social consequences for the United States, this appeared to be a golden age for African-American workers, as increasing numbers moved from the rural South to urban, industrial areas. The public acceptance of civil rights and affirmative action suggested that a new era was beginning in race relations. Black-white income differentials were narrowing, many professions were taking first steps toward integration, and a classic pattern of upward mobility—work hard all your life at a unionized factory job, and send your children to college—seemed to be spreading across the color line.

And then, in the 1970s, it ended. Observers at the time might have picked the oil crisis or the social turbulence surrounding the Vietnam war as the decisive turning points of the decade. In retrospect, it appears that a quieter economic reversal was taking place. Productivity and real wages stagnated, manufacturing employment began to decline in absolute (not just relative) terms, income inequalities based on race, education, and other factors began to widen, and unions were visibly in retreat. The decline in employment and real wages has been most severe for men without college degrees, including, in the United States, a disproportionate number of African-American men. This loss of employment has been plausibly blamed for many interwoven social problems of minority communities.[14] The decline is significant for less educated whites, as well. Those of any race who lose formerly secure "good jobs" often fail to find new work with comparable wages or working conditions.

The underlying economic problem was not uniquely an American one. A similar stagnation spread throughout Europe by the 1980s, and to Japan a decade later. There is, however, a difference in the consequences of stagnation. In most of Europe, stronger unions, labor legislation, and social welfare programs mean that workers who lose good jobs are more likely to remain unemployed, while in America, and increasingly in Britain, the unemployed are more often forced to take worse jobs. The merits of the two approaches can be debated. On the one hand, the European response appears to prolong stagnation; on the other hand, the Anglo-American response appears to stimulate increasingly unequal growth, with many people relegated to an inferior status. It is not clear which route leads more quickly to equitable growth, as neither has yet reached that goal.

A Preview of Coming Attractions

Now that the macroeconomic golden age has passed into history, what are the forces shaping the nature of work in its more tarnished, contemporary condition? The subsequent parts of this volume address different aspects of this and related questions. New theories of labor economics, as described above, are the subject of Part II. The articles presented there should prompt discussion on two different levels, concerning both the merits of specific new models and theories, and the adequacy of the conventional style of formal economic modeling.

Several parts of the book present different views that bear on the great debate about recent history: What caused the transformation of work in developed countries, including the decline of traditional industrial employment, starting in the 1970s? At least three culprits have been proposed: trade, technology, and changes in the political and institutional context. There is no need to view this as an either/or choice; the evidence suggests that all three have played important, interconnected roles. Yet the inevitably polarized debate may illuminate the underlying causal mechanisms. The different poles of the debate can be found throughout Parts III through VI, along with many related issues.

Trade suggests itself as a cause of recent changes in work because the era of decline in developed-country manufacturing has also been an era of cheap imports of clothing, electronics, and other goods. It is easy to see stagnation and industrial decline in the First World as a direct result of the beginnings of industrialization in the Third World. However, many economists have concluded that trade has only a minor influence on employment and wages. Counterarguments include the suggestions that trade with low-wage countries is too small to have massive effects on work. Similar declines in low-skill employment and wages have been observed in industries that are sheltered from trade. And signs of the impending decline can be seen in the slowdown in productivity growth beginning in the late 1960s, well before effective competition from low-wage manufacturing countries began.[15] In response, a few economists have argued that the impact of trade is much greater than conventional analyses would suggest, reshaping the industries that remain in developed countries as well as causing some to leave. The articles in Part III include several views from each side of this debate, along with discussion of some of the varied effects of globalization on labor and proposals for policy responses to the problems of trade.

A second possible cause of the transformation of work, changes in technology and work organization, is the subject of Part IV. Some analysts see technological change as deskilling and disempowering workers, if not replacing them altogether; others find the process to be more ambiguous or contestable in its implications for labor. Access to new technologies such as computers is strongly correlated with employment and wage gains within the workforce, but such empirical findings are subject to a variety of interpretations. Intensified competition has brought not only new technologies, but also new systems of organization to the workplace. Despite scattered experiments with very democratic, participatory work systems, major corporate employers have tended to adopt systems of tightly managed employee participation, inspired by Japanese management practices. As with new technologies, there are differences of opinion about the meaning of new work systems for the workers involved.

Along with the adoption of new technologies and management systems, corporations have sought to preserve flexibility in a rapidly changing marketplace by reducing the number of workers to whom they have long-term commitments. The result is that fewer people spend their work lives in the internal labor markets within large establishments, while more find themselves in some form of contingent or nonstandard work. This is the topic of Part V. In the United States, about a third of female and a quarter of male workers are in job arrangements other than regular full-time work, such as temp agency jobs, self-employment, or part-time work. A minority of these nonstandard workers, such as successful contractors and consultants, are doing better than full-time employees. Most are doing worse. That is, the majority of nonstandard workers are stuck in an inferior segment of the labor market, with low pay, minimal benefits, and little security. Most ominous is the tendency toward "informalization," recreating patterns typical of much poorer countries or earlier periods of history: Those who lack formal employment are pushed into activities such as scavenging, drug trafficking, or the new wave of sweatshops and industrial home-based work. These extremes, as well as the inequality between standard and nonstandard jobs in general, highlight the need for creative policy responses.

The problems of inequity and insecurity in work today contain echoes of the historical motivation for the organization of unions. However, the labor movement has been declining for some time. This suggests the third major hypothesis about the transformation of work since the 1970s: Could institutional and political changes, such as the weakening of unions, explain the problem? Part VI examines the emerging patterns of industrial relations, both in unionized settings and in alternative institutional frameworks. Despite their weakened state, unions still make an important difference in labor market outcomes. International comparison shows that countries with stronger unions have less inequality. The lower half of the income distribution, in particular, gains from widespread unionization. An intriguing and unexpected finding is that new employee participation schemes appear to be much more productive in unionized workplaces. None of this changes the fact that current economic trends are unfavorable to traditional unionism. Revival of the labor movement may require bold new strategies emphasizing democratization and the public interest as well as the members' own well-being.

Other important approaches to worker representation include works councils, widely used in Germany and elsewhere in Europe to allow employee participation on issues not covered by union contracts. Works councils are attractive in theory but almost unknown in the United States—a fate they share with another innovative idea, producer cooperatives. When workers own and manage the firms they work for, promising solutions are available for many problems of equity, participation, and motivation. The comparative handful of existing cooperatives, largely in Italy, France, and Spain, have been extensively studied. Their impressive combination of efficiency and participation should attract much more attention. Some of the articles included here attempt to identify the barriers to the formation of cooperatives.

The stratification of employment, and the inequality of labor market opportunities and outcomes, has always occurred in part along gender and racial lines. Part VII explores the problems of difference and diversity in the workplace today. Job niches are often stereotyped as appropriate for a particular race or gender. For example, jobs involving emotional empathy or nurturing are often thought to be women's work. As women move out of the home and into paid employment in industries around the world, their choices at work are often limited to those that reflect aspects of traditional female roles.

Racial minorities, long kept in inferior or subordinate occupations, benefited from the combination of economic expansion and affirmative action in the 1960s and early 1970s. Their availability as a supply of industrial workers was important to post–World War II economic growth. More recently, economic stagnation and the retreat from liberal activism have led to a worsening position for minorities. The perception that African-American men, in particular, lack the increasingly important relational and motivational "soft skills" is cited by employers as a reason for preferring other workers. Such a judgment, if it is not just another disguise for prejudice, suggests avenues for improving the skills and prospects of those at the bottom of the job market.

The decline of traditional industry was only part of the transformation of work in the post–World War II era. While employment of production workers in manufacturing was declining in relative terms throughout the period, other forms of employment were rising. Services such as education, health, and retail distribution were expanding, as was clerical and other nonproduction employment in industry itself. Many of these jobs were filled by women, whose participation in paid employment has risen steadily. The nuclear family held together by a stay-at-home mom lasted long enough to become a dominant cultural myth and television sitcom classic, but quickly declined as women increasingly worked for wages.

A crucial but less visible implication of these trends can be seen in Part VIII. Traditionally, women's unpaid work played an essential social role in childrearing, nurturing family members, and providing "caring labor" in general. Yet that role rarely earned social standing or power within the family comparable to that of the male "breadwinner." As paid job opportunities attract ever-growing numbers of women, the caring labor formerly done by housewives is in danger of being left undone. A socially sustainable society must find a way to provide caring labor for the young, the old, and the sick, while ensuring equal access to paid employment.

Finally, the discussion of economic trends should not be allowed to obscure the importance of the human meaning of work. This is the subject of Part IX. Work is not just a disutility endured in order to earn the means of consumption. Rather, it is an essential human activity that shapes our personalities, creates social connections, and contributes to self-esteem. Sociological research amply confirms the importance of work in these regards, as well as the corresponding personal damage that is often done by involuntary unemployment. Several theoretical traditions highlight the human implications of work, ranging from Marxists writing about alienated labor to the pioneers of modern management theory writing about worker motivation. Concern for the quality of work experience has become, at least in principle, an important part of new approaches to industrial relations; but there remains a tension in the discussion between the promise of utopian restructuring and the danger of manipulative personnel management. The nature of the work process, the varied motivations for work, and the potential for fundamental reorganization—all these issues are raised by the changing nature of work at the end of the twentieth century.

Notes

1. Marshall Sahlins, *Stone Age Economics* (Chicago: Aldine and Atherton, 1972); a chapter is summarized in *The Consumer Society*, eds. Neva R. Goodwin, Frank Ackerman, and David Kiron (Washington, D.C.: Island Press, 1997), Volume 2 of this series.
2. E.P. Thompson, "Time, Work-Discipline, and Industrial Capitalism," in *Past and Present* 38 (December 1967), 56-97.

3. Ibid., 91.

4. David Gordon, Richard Edwards, and Michael Reich, *Segmented Work, Divided Workers: The Historical Transformation of Labor in the United States* (New York: Cambridge University Press, 1982).

5. A survey of the ten leading industrial states in 1832 found that textile mills accounted for 88 of the 106 industrial enterprises with over $100,000 in assets, and 31 of the 36 enterprises with more than 250 workers. Alfred D. Chandler, Jr., *The Visible Hand: The Managerial Revolution in American Business* (Cambridge, MA: Harvard University Press, 1977), 60.

6. Ibid., 68.

7. The same may be happening today in the rapidly industrializing East Asian countries: The labor force is heavily female in the earliest stages of industry, but comes to include more male workers as skills and technologies become more complex.

8. Claudia Goldin, *Understanding the Gender Gap: An Economic History of American Women* (New York: Oxford University Press, 1990), Chapter 3.

9. Chris Tilly and Charles Tilly, *Work Under Capitalism* (Boulder, CO: Westview Press, 1998); a chapter of this book is summarized in Part II.

10. See Susan Strasser's forthcoming *Waste and Want: Disposal, Recycling, and American Consumer Culture* (New York: Metropolitan Books, 1998), and Frank Ackerman, *Why Do We Recycle? Markets, Values, and Public Policy* (Washington, D.C.: Island Press, 1997), Chapter 10.

11. See our earlier volume, *The Consumer Society,* eds. Goodwin, Ackerman, and Kiron.

12. See, for example, Tilly and Tilly, *Work Under Capitalism* (Note 9 above).

13. Stephen A. Marglin and Juliet B. Schor, eds. *The Golden Age: Reinterpreting the Postwar Experience* (New York: Oxford University Press, 1990).

14. William Julius Wilson, *When Work Disappears* (New York: Alfred A. Knopf, 1997); a chapter of this book is summarized in Part IX.

15. The latter point is documented in detail in Andrew Glyn, Alan Hughes, Alain Lipietz, and Ajit Singh, "The Rise and Fall of the Golden Age," in eds. Marglin and Schor, *The Golden Age* (see Note 13 above). See also the work by David Gordon, "Skills Mismatch or Globalization?" in *Fat and Mean: The Corporate Squeeze of Working Americans and the Myth of Managerial "Downsizing"* (New York: Martin Kessler Books, The Free Press, 1996), summarized in Part III.

PART II

New Directions in Labor Economics

Overview Essay

by Frank Ackerman

How, if at all, is labor different? Is it a unique entity that calls for a unique economic analysis, or just a case in which the well-established theory of market behavior explains yet another mass of data? Odd as it may seem to outsiders, the latter view has its supporters. As Robert Solow has said,

> Among economists, it is not obvious at all that labor as a commodity is sufficiently different from artichokes and rental apartments to require a different mode of analysis.[1]

Fortunately, there are also many economists (including Solow) who do believe that labor is different enough to require its own analysis. Indeed, the theory of labor economics is one of the most active and creative fields of economics. This essay and the summaries that follow it will identify some of the leading new themes that have emerged in recent years.

Labor economics is also an area with an unusually close connection between theory and empirical evidence. Systematic, quantitative evidence is available in the form of massive computer databases describing individual workers and jobs. More than in many other areas of economics, it is common for innovative theoretical articles—including several that are summarized here—to include empirical tests of their theories.

The need for new theories flows directly from the obvious facts about labor. Two related types of evidence make it clear that labor is not just another commodity, and cannot usefully be understood as if it were simply a particularly prickly form of artichoke. First, the process of wage determination and its relationship to employment is unique; labor markets are indeed different from other markets. The most striking fact is the persistence of unemployment. Even a substantial level of involuntary unemployment leads to only gradual and modest changes in the wages of employed workers and the total supply of labor. (Artichokes do not experience unemployment; if there are too many on the market, the price and/or quantity supplied will fall relatively quickly to the market-clearing level.) Among workers who are employed, there is persistent inequality in wages and salaries, which is only partially related to visible differences in skill requirements or the inherent difficulty of the work being done.

A second type of evidence for the uniqueness of labor concerns the nature of work itself. Unlike other inputs into production processes, workers are conscious of what they are doing. Thus the subjective experience and involvement of the workers cannot be ignored. Systems of labor relations reflect the unique character of work. Many employers as well as workers accept union contracts, seniority-based pay scales, and other long-term employment commitments that bear no clear or direct relationship to the marginal product of individual workers. (Needless to say, artichokes, machinery, and other inanimate resources do not demand or get similar treatment.)

These categories of facts, which are discussed throughout this volume, make it hard to accept the simple market paradigm, and thus provide much of the motivation for the creation of new approaches in labor economics.

The History of Labor Economics

Before turning to contemporary developments, it will be helpful to take a look at the history of labor economics.[2] In the earliest stages of economic theory, it was taken for granted that labor was both unique and central to economic life. Classical economists from Adam Smith through Karl Marx relied on the labor theory of value, and examined at great length such questions as the division of labor, the level of employment, and the determination of wages.

The view of labor as just another commodity first became possible with the "marginalist revolution" of the 1870s. The labor theory of value was replaced by the idea that values and prices both depended on marginal utility. The formalization of general equilibrium reflected a fascination with the symmetrical treatment of all markets. The leading figure of late nineteenth-century economics, Alfred Marshall, played a contradictory role in this, as in other areas. On the one hand, Marshall developed the analysis of the marginal productivity of labor, which made it possible to extend the theoretical formalism of supply and demand to the labor market. On the other hand, he wrote in more practical, applied terms about the social, institutional, and political aspects of the labor questions of the day.

Later theorists generally chose one or the other of Marshall's contradictory leanings. In the 1930s the macroeconomics of John Maynard Keynes acknowledged the significance of unemployment and examined the factors affecting wages, emphasizing labor's uniqueness and institutional specificity. At the same time, the elaboration of microeconomic theory by John Hicks and Paul Samuelson completed the formal symmetry of the market model, later epitomized by Samuelson's famous remark that, in theory, it makes no difference whether capital hires labor, or the other way around.

Such microeconomic theories were not shared by the first few generations of American labor economists. In the early twentieth century the institutionalist school, including John Commons, Richard Ely, and their successors, produced many important studies of labor problems. They typically focused on questions of equity for labor, and were supportive of unions and of government intervention in the market on behalf of workers. Their work had little connection to the simultaneous development of neoclassical theory. In the 1940s and 1950s a later generation of economists, including John Dunlop and Clark Kerr, used neoclassical tools to analyze institutional issues concerning labor, addressing the problems of imperfect competition, bargaining structures, wage contours, and internal labor markets.

In short, at midcentury there was a diverse, pluralist understanding of the economics of labor. While the complex mathematics of the simple market model was of growing importance in microeconomics, a Keynesian view of unemployment and wage determination held sway in macroeconomics, and a variety of institutional insights into bargaining and wage structures remained central in labor economics itself. The labor movement was at its peak of membership, representing one-third of the paid workforce in the United States in the 1950s; thus a theoretical focus on the bargaining process seemed only natural.

The Market Model and the New Dissent

As in other areas of economics, the neoclassical microeconomic model eventually came to dominate over alternative theoretical approaches to labor. Yet only in the 1960s, with the addition of two innovations, human capital and search theory, did neoclassical theory begin to offer a plausible account of employment, unemployment, and wage determination.

Discussion of the role of skills in explaining income differentials dates back at least to Adam Smith. In the 1960s Gary Becker formalized this idea in the notion of human capital. Education and training could be seen as investments in workers' skills, which, like capital goods, are then available for use in production. At about the same time, George Stigler suggested that time and effort spent in searching for a new job could also be viewed as a productive investment; a longer search leads to a greater probability of a higher return.[3] As a result, it appeared that many types of inequality, and many types of unemployment, could be explained in conventional market terms without reference to institutional or historical factors. If not quite artichokes, perhaps workers are like machine tools, whose varying degrees of sophistication, age, and obsolescence account for their differential rewards.

These theories have led to valuable insights—but they also threaten to exaggerate the explanatory power of the simple market model. It is one thing to say that observable investment in education and training explains *some* observable patterns of employment and wages; it is another thing to assume that there must be unobservable differences in human capital that explain *all* differential labor market outcomes. Likewise, productive investment of time and effort in searching for a new job explains selected aspects of unemployment, but it defies common sense to interpret all unemployment in this manner. However, defying common sense often seems fashionable in economic theory. This was never more true than in the heyday of "rational expectations" and "microfoundations" models in the 1980s, when the principle of well-informed individual maximization was axiomatically assumed to explain virtually all behavior, and involuntary unemployment was defined out of existence.

Fortunately, a new wave of dissent, and a variety of theoretical innovations, have appeared in labor economics in recent years. Some of the new approaches preserve most of the neoclassical mathematical apparatus of individual maximization, showing that even modest changes in the assumptions can lead to different, more realistic outcomes. Others question the adequacy of the assumptions of individualism and maximization, raising more fundamental, if messier, questions about the direction of economic theory. A sampling of these new approaches are represented in the summaries following this essay, to which we now turn.

Work Incentives, Efficiency, and Unemployment

The strength of the new approaches to labor economics rests on their ability to explain a range of facts that fit awkwardly, if at all, into the standard market model. Thus it is appropriate to begin our look at the theories with a massive empirical study, the "wage curve" of David Blanchflower and Andrew Oswald. The wage curve addresses a deceptively simple question: Is higher unemployment associated with higher or lower wages? The standard model of supply and demand suggests that if wages are raised by unions or minimum wage laws, employers' demand for labor should drop (since the demand curve is downward-sloping), and unemployment should rise; in other words, higher wages should be associated with higher unemployment.

Blanchflower and Oswald show, however, that the opposite is true, in a study encompassing data on literally millions of workers in a dozen countries. They find that, when controlling for a vast range of individual and industry characteristics, workers in regions of a country with higher unemployment have lower wages than comparable workers in regions with lower unemployment. This finding, consistent with the results of other investigators, shows that something "non-neoclassical" is going on in labor markets. As Blanchflower and Oswald explain, their results are compatible with models of bargaining strength for countries with high rates of unionization, or with "efficiency wage" models for less unionized countries such as the United States.

The efficiency wage model is the best-known recent innovation in labor economics, and has been widely studied and debated. The essential idea is that if payment of higher wages has a positive effect on a worker's productivity, then employers face contradictory incentives. Their usual desire to cut costs will be tempered by the recognition that lower wages mean lower productivity. This idea can be traced back to Harvey Leibenstein's 1963 suggestion that in the poorest of developing countries, higher wages lead to better nutrition and hence to increased productivity. As a model of labor markets in developed countries, the efficiency wage theory first gained prominence in the 1980s.[4]

The most common version of the theory assumes that it is costly or difficult for employers to observe employee effort on the job, and that employees in general want to shirk, or avoid, effort at work. A worker weighing the costs and benefits of working hard will compare the joys of laziness with the probability of being caught shirking and the costs of being fired (the assumed result of being caught). A higher wage increases the cost of losing the current job, and hence makes it more attractive to work hard. An alternate, but compatible, explanation assumes that payment of above-market wages will induce worker loyalty to the firm, leading to greater effort. In either case, firms find it profitable to pay some workers more than their full-effort marginal product, that is, more than they add to production, even when working as hard as possible. This means that the demand for labor is below the market-clearing level, implying that there is involuntary unemployment.[5]

In the next article summarized here, Sam Bowles presents a model formalizing aspects of Marxian theory, using the mathematical techniques of neoclassical economics. The efficiency wage mechanism is central to Bowles' model of the firm, since profit-maximizing employers face a trade-off between increased surveillance of workers and increased wage payments, as alternate means of extracting additional work effort. Bowles extends the theory to its implications for the choice of technology and explains the functional role of unemployment, from the employers' point of view, in terms consistent with Blanchflower and Oswald's findings. Discrimination, too, is functional for employers, since it reduces labor unity and bargaining strength. Although relentlessly pursuing the mathematics of individual maximization in developing his model, Bowles also stresses the unique and social character of the work process. He is perhaps least persuasive in differentiating his version of efficiency wage theory from the very similar approaches that have appeared in recent non-Marxian theories of the firm.

Does the individualism of the efficiency wage model misrepresent the essential nature of the labor process? This question is raised in the article by Robert Buchele and Jens Christiansen. They observe that many workers, especially the best paid, are protected by union agreements, seniority systems, or other mechanisms that limit the threat of individual firing based on individual performance. Moreover, individual effort is not always the decisive factor in determining productivity. The effective organization of individual effort into a productive, collective process is at least as important.

For Buchele and Christiansen, a cooperative system of industrial relations can elicit worker participation, a source of productivity that is not available in an antagonistic system. They present a comparative analysis of data on the leading industrial countries, suggesting both that cooperation boosts productivity, and that, in a cooperative regime, lower unemployment is good for productivity, while the opposite is true in an antagonistic setting. In more recent empirical work Buchele and Christiansen have used this framework to study the trade-off between employment growth in the United States and productivity growth in leading European economies, suggesting that deregulating and "Americanizing" European labor markets could lead to greater insecurity and inequality, rather than to economic growth.[6]

Like Bowles, Buchele and Christiansen (and a number of other authors represented in this volume) are members of the school of "radical political economy" that emerged as part of the general political and cultural radicalism of the late 1960s and 1970s. In the next summary, James Rebitzer reviews the contributions of this school of thought to labor economics. Several of his themes echo the Bowles article, including the theory of the firm, the efficiency wage model, and the potential for adoption of technologies that enhance control over workers, even at the expense of efficiency. The important question of employee ownership, raised by Rebitzer and many of the authors he reviews, is discussed in much greater detail in Part VI of this volume. While Rebitzer is generally sympathetic to the radical political economy school, he also makes a number of important criticisms of its work, including a tendency to oversimplify the role of management, the actual process of bargaining, and the nature of work incentives.[7]

Labor Market Segmentation

The second major area addressed by Rebitzer, theories of labor market segmentation, is also the subject of the next three summaries. Segmentation theories typically assume that the labor market is divided into two sectors: a primary sector with relatively high wages, long average job tenure, rewards for skills and experience, and chances for advancement on the job; and a secondary sector with none of these characteristics. As with efficiency wage theory, the boundary between radical and mainstream segmentation theories has blurred in recent years (to the benefit of both, as Rebitzer notes).

"Dual labor market" theories attracted attention in the 1970s, as a possible explanation of inequality. The theories typically suggested that most members of racial minorities, and many women, were stuck in the secondary labor market and denied access to good jobs. An influential early account of dual labor markets from an institutionalist perspective, by Peter Doeringer and Michael Piore,[8] was extended by a number of radical economists exploring issues of discrimination. Yet the explanation of the basis for segmentation has been problematical. As Rebitzer explains, the most popular explanation, efficiency wage theory, does not fit some of the crucial facts.

A critique of labor market segmentation has suggested that the early theories could not explain the number of segments or the assignment of workers to those segments. Indeed, many economists have concluded that human capital theory provides a better explanation of inequality of labor market outcomes. The next article, by William Dickens and Kevin Lang, responds to this critique and insists that a model of market segmentation is superior to human capital theory in accounting for inequality. The defining characteristic of the theory, for Dickens and Lang, is not the inequality between better and worse segments of the market, but the nonmarket rationing of access to good jobs. This need not imply lifelong assignment of individuals to one or the other market segment; indeed, some patterns of racial inequality are consistent with the assumption that minorities spend more time queuing for access to primary-sector openings.

Using detailed individual data on male workers, Dickens and Lang estimate earnings functions for the primary and secondary sectors, based on education, race, age, location, and other factors. The distinctive feature of their model is that, while estimating earnings functions, it simultaneously assigns each worker to the segment in which that worker fits best. As predicted, the two-sector model fits the data much better than any one-sector model. Returns to education and experience are substantial in the primary sector, while minimal in the secondary sector; and the definition of the sectors, while subtler than in most theories, follows the expected demographic patterns.

Dickens and Lang argue effectively against explanations of inequality based solely on human capital. But they, like Rebitzer, suggest a diverse range of possible explanations for segmentation. The next two articles explore two of those explanations in greater detail. Robert Drago and Richard Perlman present a "competing incentives" theory, in which employers must choose between two incompatible routes to worker motivation. One alternative is based on a high level of trust, requiring high wages and minimal supervision; the other involves little trust, low wages, and intense supervision. Drago and Perlman propose that the heterogeneity of technology determines which regime is more profitable for which firms. The choice facing employers is a discontinuous one. Small moves toward the opposite system of motivation will simply reduce the efficiency of production. Thus there are two labor market segments because there are two incompatible systems of motivation. One or the other is more effective for each production technology. Even if workers are identical, many will queue for opportunities to enter the better jobs.

George Akerlof and Janet Yellen, two economists who have played an important part in the development of efficiency wage theories, examine the role of norms of fairness in the next article. In psychology, sociology, and elsewhere outside of economic theory, it is taken for granted that people have strong feelings about fairness, and that norms of fairness are influenced by the observed treatment of others. Akerlof and Yellen assume that workers have a notion of fair wages, and reduce their work effort when wages fall below that level. If the standard of fairness depends in part on what one's coworkers receive, then, in an enterprise with varied skill levels, the low-skilled workers will set their standard of fairness above the market-clearing wage for their labor. As Akerlof and Yellen explain, this leads to higher than market wages, and lower demand, for low-skilled labor in major enterprises,[9] the result is either involuntary unemployment of lower-skilled groups, and/or the creation of low-wage firms that employ only low-skilled workers.

The Persistence of Institutions

Many of the recent innovations in labor economics preserve the methodology, though not all the underlying assumptions, of neoclassical theory. That is, an austere, minimalist set of assumptions are made about individual options and objectives, allowing a rigorous mathematical exploration of the implications of individual maximization subject to constraints. It is impressive that, with slight modifications of the assumptions about information flows and the nature of the firm and the labor market, this methodology produces much more realistic outcomes.

Yet at the same time there is something frustrating about this approach to theory. When the conclusions are more obvious than the proofs, how much value has been added by the theory? Several pages of calculus can "prove," for example, that rational employers do not always cut their employees' wages when sales decline, for fear of damaging morale and productivity—or that more generous unemployment benefits allow laid-off workers to take longer looking for new jobs. Many noneconomists would readily accept these and other theoretical results, while dismissing the proofs as hopelessly opaque.

Moreover, it is worth noting that the realism of the new models is less than complete. In some cases, the new models look like a success; in other cases, the narrowness of the assumptions still seems to lead to artificially narrow conclusions, suggesting the need for a broader theoretical framework.

The last three articles summarized in this section address a range of institutional questions, which remain crucial for an understanding of the economics of labor. In the best-known article included here, Richard Freeman asks a question that older, descriptive institutionalist theories had no trouble answering: What do unions do? Newer, quantitative theories often reduce the role of unions to their effects on wages, and hence indirectly on output and employment levels. Freeman insists that there is more to the impact of unions than the wages they win.

In terms of Albert Hirschman's dichotomy between exit and voice as means of expressing discontent, employees always have the option of exit from a job. Unions can also give workers a voice for their concerns. This should reduce quit rates and lengthen average job tenure for unionized workers—and Freeman demonstrates that this is exactly what happens. Much of the article is devoted to empirical analysis, disentangling the effect of union voice from the effect of other confounding influences, such as the effect of union wages (which would also be expected to reduce quit rates and lengthen tenure). Freeman also observes that grievance and arbitration procedures, seniority systems, and what he calls "industrial jurisprudence" may have a public-goods character within the workplace. The only plausible means to pursue these objectives is through collective action.

Though they are clearly in a minority today, self-described institutionalist economists have not vanished. The article by David Marsden, an institutionalist labor economist, examines one of the ways in which conventional economic theory fails to describe the reality of labor markets. The common picture of markets matching jobs with workers who have transferable skills, says Marsden, ignores the problem of the origins of skills and the financing of the training process. The more transferable the skills, the more they resemble public goods; therefore, private firms will not provide the efficient level of training in such skills. Public education partially fills the gap, but many skills, even transferable ones, must be learned on the job.

In such circumstances, labor markets are fragile. Firms that provide training have a clear incentive to discourage interfirm mobility. This is a reason for steep seniority-based pay increases. To the extent that firms succeed in discouraging mobility, there may be inefficient allocation of skilled labor between firms, and significantly different rates of pay for the same skills in the same region. Market outcomes will not be optimal by the usual criteria, and questions will arise of fairness and comparability among workers at different firms.

The final entry in this section takes the broadest view of the nature of work. It is taken from a new book by Chris Tilly and Charles Tilly (an economist and a historian, who are also son and father), which offers a comparative analysis of social change in the work process, focusing on case studies of the English and American textile, coal mining, and health care industries. Their most theoretical chapter, summarized here, draws on institutionalist, Marxist, and even some neoclassical insights into the labor process. They begin, not with individuals or firms, but with transactions and the contracts that embody them; these are grouped into social roles, particularly jobs, which are embedded in networks (such as markets and hierarchies) and organizations. Incentives that can be used to motivate the completion of transactions and contracts include compensation, commitment, and coercion. Each of these three incentives can be separately present or absent, giving rise to eight different patterns of work (all three are present in a military command hierarchy, for example, while all are absent in scavenging). For Tilly and Tilly, the social context within which work transactions are embedded give rise to a range of possible outcomes and meanings, challenging us to think more expansively about the theory of labor economics.

Conclusion

How well have the new theories done in analyzing the unique characteristics of work processes and labor markets? The most widely discussed recent innovation, efficiency wage theory, offers a plausible mechanism that is compatible with the important "wage curve" findings, and can help explain the simultaneous existence of relatively well-paid "good jobs" and involuntary unemployment. Yet there are other realities, such as the social nature of production and the employment security of many good jobs, that call for a different conceptual framework. Not all the statistical evidence is compatible with an efficiency wage framework.

The hypothesis of labor market segmentation provides a straightforward explanation of many inequalities; relatively subtle empirical analysis appears to support the hypothesis, but more work is needed here. Like efficiency wage theory, labor market segmentation could arise from any of several institutional and behavioral foundations. That is, market segmentation may be the mechanism leading to unequal outcomes, but that conclusion alone does not identify the underlying causes of segmentation, or of inequality.

Along with these relatively successful formal models, there is a lively debate over institutional questions that have, thus far, resisted useful formalization. The mathematics of individual maximization explains more than the simplest neoclassical theories would suggest, but less than we need to know in order to understand the economics of labor. The broader realities of work, as described throughout this volume, still present an ample unfinished agenda for the formulation of new theories of labor economics.

Notes

1. Robert M. Solow, *The Labor Market as a Social Institution* (Cambridge, MA: Basil Blackwell, 1990), 4.
2. This account draws heavily on Bruce E. Kaufman, "The Evolution of Thought on the Competitive Nature of Labor Markets," in *Labor Economics and Industrial Relations: Markets and Institutions,* eds. Clark Kerr and Paul D. Staudohar (Cambridge, MA: Harvard University Press, 1994). See also the essays in that volume by George H. Hildebrand, Jack Barbash, and Clark Kerr.

3. For an introduction to these topics, see Jacob Mincer, "Human Capital: A Review," in Kerr and Staudohar (Note 2, above) and David Sapsford, "The Labour Market: Un employment and Search Theory," in David Greenaway, Michael Bleaney, and Ian Stewart, eds., *Companion to Contemporary Economic Thought* (New York: Routledge, 1991).

4. The articles by Leibenstein and other early contributors to the efficiency wage discussion are reprinted in George A. Akerlof and Janet L. Yellen, eds. *Efficiency Wage Models of the Labor Market* (New York: Cambridge University Press, 1986).

5. There appears to be a conflict between efficiency wage theory and the wage curve, but in fact the two ideas are compatible. The efficiency wage theory examines the overall effects of wages on employment: The need to pay wages above the marginal product of labor implies a low demand for labor, "explaining" the existence of unemployment in general. However, it is also true that when unemployment is higher (for reasons unrelated to wage levels), then wages are lower. If unemployment is higher, the cost of job loss is greater, so workers are motivated to work hard even for relatively modest wages— and profit-maximizing employers can therefore pay less. This argument provides an efficiency wage explanation of the wage curve.

6. Robert Buchele and Jens Christiansen, "Employment and Productivity Growth in Europe and North America: The Impact of Labor Market Institutions," forthcoming in *International Review of Applied Economics*.

7. For another sympathetic but critical view of the treatment of individual incentives and behavior in radical theories, see Nancy Folbre, "Hearts and Spades: Paradigms of Household Economics," *World Development* 14 (1986), 245–255.

8. Peter B. Doeringer and Michael J. Piore, *Internal Labor Markets and Manpower Analysis* (Lexington, MA: Heath, 1971).

9. That is, the wage structure will be compressed upward in enterprises that have to hire high-wage workers; there is a premium on being an "insider" in a high-wage firm, even for those in low-wage occupations. Other "insider-outsider" models identify other mechanisms that lead to the same result: The firm's need for cooperation from incumbent workers, and its desire to avoid strikes when its operations are profitable, can lead to persistent payment of above-market wages for insiders. See, for example, Assar Lindbeck and Dennis J. Snower, "Cooperation, Harassment, and Involuntary Unemployment: An Insider-Outsider Approach," *American Economic Review* 78 (March 1988), 167–188.

Summary of

An Introduction to the Wage Curve

by David G. Blanchflower and Andrew J. Oswald

[Published in *Journal of Economic Perspectives* 9 (Summer 1995), 153–167.]

What is the relationship between unemployment and wages? A simple model of supply and demand in a competitive labor market—and some not so simple models built on the same foundation—suggest a positive relationship: Higher wages reduce the demand for labor and lead to higher unemployment. However, there is massive empirical evidence for a negative relationship: all else being equal, higher unemployment is associated with lower wages, not higher. This pathbreaking study discusses the components of the negatively sloped "wage curve,"[1] other empirical research, and the implications of these findings for theories about the labor market.

Uncovering the Wage Curve

Empirical support for the wage curve—the negative relationship between the level of unemployment and the level of wages—comes from analysis of random samples of data on individual workers in many countries. In some cases the samples were extremely large, including more than a million workers in both the United States and South Korea and more than 80,000 in both Britain and Canada. For each worker, the data set includes annual earnings, occupation, the unemployment rate in the worker's state or region, and personal characteristics such as age, gender, race, years of schooling, and so on. An estimate of the wage curve is obtained from the regression of wages on regional unemployment, personal characteristics, and other effects (such as controls for regions or industries).

The estimated equation typically follows the pattern

$$\ln w = -0.1 \ln U + \text{ other terms}$$

where ln means logarithm, w is the wage, and U is the unemployment rate in the worker's area. Since the equation is logarithmic, the coefficient measures proportional change, or elasticity, and represents the unemployment-elasticity of wages. The estimated elasticity is surprisingly close to -0.1 in almost all of the countries studied. It falls between -0.08 and -0.13 in eight of the twelve countries studied and is often found in the same range in similar work by other researchers. No explanation has been offered for this international near-constancy of the effect of unemployment on wages. An elasticity of -0.1 means that, all else being equal, a doubling of the regional unemployment rate should cause a 10 percent drop in regional wages. The wage curve is negatively sloped, but fairly flat.

Corrections have been made for several technical statistical problems that might arise. None of these corrections have altered the substantive findings of the research. It might be objected that real wages in different regions should be measured with regional consumer price index. It was found, however, that controlling for regional prices in Britain, where the data are available, leaves the wage curve intact.

Explanations and Interpretations

Could a conventional supply-and-demand analysis explain the wage curve? At first glance, perhaps not. In the neoclassical model, unemployment results when the wage exceeds the market-clearing level. The higher the wage, the greater the resulting unemployment should be—contrary to the empirically estimated wage curve.

A different story could be told about supply and demand, by reinterpreting higher unemployment as meaning lower employment. The wage curve then would say that lower employment is associated with lower wages, and higher employment with higher wages. In other words, it would look like a familiar labor supply curve. However, on this interpretation, unemployment is entirely voluntary, which runs counter to official definitions of unemployment and to common sense. Moreover, it suggests that measures of employment should do even better as a predictor of wages than does the unemployment rate. Empirically, this is not the case.

Standard models in regional economics, based on the assumption of competitive labor markets, also make predictions that are disproved by the wage curve. That is, they predict that high-unemployment regions should be high-wage regions, whereas in fact high unemployment is associated with lower wages. Some of the ideas and techniques developed in these models may still be useful, but they should be used in a different framework.

Noncompetitive Labor Market Explanations

If the competitive model has failed, there are several possible noncompetitive accounts of the labor market to consider. In a bargaining model, high rates of local unemployment might frighten workers, perhaps because it is harder to change jobs if it becomes necessary, leading them to demand or obtain a smaller share of available surplus. Likewise, assume that a union responds to both its employed members' desire for higher remuneration and its unemployed members' desire for employment. When more people are out of work, the union will tilt toward the concerns of the unemployed. Lower wages are more likely to expand the number of jobs.

In nonunion regions, including most of the U.S. economy, such interpretations may not apply. Instead, efficiency wage theory provides an explanation of the wage curve for nonunionized workers. In the efficiency wage theory, workers choose how hard to work, weighing the disutility of labor against the costs of job loss if they are found to be shirking. When unemployment is high, employees are frightened of losing their jobs, and so work hard even if pay is comparatively low. This means that profit-maximizing firms can reduce pay slightly while still maintaining a motivated workforce. Unemployment thus serves to discipline workers.

Other variants on these theories are possible. The wage curve can be explained in a "labor contract" model, in which efficient contracts are reached that maximize the joint welfare of employers and employees. The higher the wage rate, the more desirable it is, from this joint welfare perspective, to have more people working and fewer drawing unemployment benefits. Thus, some labor contract models predict a positive correlation between wages and employment, or a negative correlation between wages and unemployment.

Alternatively, if there are enough random demand shocks so that labor demand fluctuates widely, a risk-averse firm will want wages to rise in good times, attracting more workers, and to fall in bad times, leading to lower employment. Again, there is a basis for finding that pay and unemployment are negatively related. However, this explanation, like the labor contract model, is really about employment rather than unemployment. Such explanations have the problems noted above in connection with the competitive supply and demand model.

A new generation of macroeconomic models has begun to appear in which an aggregate wage curve is assumed, much like the one discussed here. The new models make conventional assumptions about labor demand, but address labor supply via a wage-fixing function based on a fairly flat but negatively sloped relationship between the level of pay and the level of unemployment; this is consistent with the empirical wage curve.

The wage curve is not the same as the Phillips curve, although the two are easily confused. The Phillips curve links aggregate unemployment to the rate of change of pay, while the wage curve links regional unemployment to the level of pay. The Phillips curve is a disequilibrium dynamic model estimated on time series macroeconomic data, while the wage curve is an equilibrium model estimated on cross-section microeconomic data. Nevertheless, the wage curve is part of the tradition that Phillips began of trying to understand the macroeconomic influence of joblessness on wage setting.

In conclusion, there is strong empirical support for the existence of the wage curve. Those who work in areas of high unemployment earn less, other things constant, than those in areas of low unemployment. The curve is almost identical in numerous countries where it has been studied, with estimated unemployment elasticity of wages approximately equal to -0.1. It is difficult to see how the wage curve can be compatible with the textbook competitive model of the labor market or with theories of regional economics based on that model. In contrast, bargaining and efficiency wage theories make predictions that are consistent with the observed wage curve pattern.

Note

1. Blanchflower and Oswald, The Wage Curve (Cambridge: MIT Press, 1994).

Summary of

The Production Process in a Competitive Economy: Walrasian, Neo-Hobbesian, and Marxian Models

by Samuel S. Bowles

[Published in *American Economic Review* 75 (March 1985), 16–36.]

Economists have proposed a range of theories of the firm and the production process, with differing implications for the analysis of labor markets and employment. This article presents a mathematical model formalizing a Marxian theory of the firm, based on the hypothesis of a fundamental conflict of interests between employers and workers. The model can be contrasted to both a Walrasian theory, which views production in technological rather than institutional terms, and a neo-Hobbesian view, which sees the firm as a mechanism to reduce transaction costs and prevent workers from shirking or "free riding" on the job.

Three propositions that are surprising or counterintuitive from a conventional perspective arise as natural deductions from the Marxian model. First, capitalists will generally favor mechanisms that maintain control over workers, even at the cost of some inefficiency. Second, it is in the interest of capitalists to foster division among workers, even if this means discriminating among equally productive workers. Third, significant involuntary unemployment—Marx's "reserve army of the unemployed"—is a permanent, necessary feature of a capitalist economy. These are not based on collusion, market imperfections, or a failure to maximize profits. Rather, they are normal outcomes of market competition among profit-maximizing firms.

The Extraction of Labor from Labor Power

The analysis of production depends crucially on the social relations within the firm, which are not entirely reducible to technological or market relationships. Labor is a unique factor of production, which is inherently social in three respects. First, labor cannot be separated from the people in whom it is embodied. Second, work is generally less costly when done by many people together in one location. Finally, the work process shapes the attitudes, skills, and preferences of workers, as well as being shaped by them.

The fact that employers own and control the means of production creates a fundamental conflict of interest between them and their employees. This does not mean that workers always want to avoid work. It just means that it is more profitable for employers to control the pace and direction of the work process, rather than leaving such decisions to the employees' discretion. Because employers control the terms of employment, they can impose costs on employees who fail to carry out their wishes. In particular, employers can modify the pay or other conditions of employment, or even fire workers for nonperformance on the job.

Although it is profitable for employers to control their employees on the job, it is also costly to do so. Analysis of these costs creates the distinctive features of the model presented here. Employers hire hours of labor, but the input needed for production is labor *effort*. Labor effort per hour depends on both the employer's level of surveillance of the workforce and the cost to the employees of losing their jobs. Either more surveillance or greater costs of job loss will make workers work harder and more steadily, to increase their chances of keeping their jobs.

For the employer, the problem is to find the least-cost strategy for obtaining the maximum effort from the employees. In Marx's terms, the employer is extracting labor from labor power. In more modern language, he is extracting work from the workers. Increased surveillance is presumably available, at a known cost. The employer can also increase the cost of job loss, by paying employees more than they can earn elsewhere. The "carrot" and "stick" strategies are close but not perfect substitutes for each other, so there is an "iso-effort curve" showing the combinations of surveillance and wage increases that result in the same effort level (comparable to the production isoquants of standard microeconomics). The price of surveillance determines the least-cost point on the iso-effort curve. That point represents the unique mix of surveillance and wage increases that is the employer's optimal strategy.

The Reserve Army of the Unemployed

Paul Samuelson's famous remark, "in the competitive model, it makes no difference whether capital hires labor or the other way around," is consistent with the non-Marxian models of the firm, but not with reality. In fact, there is a basic asymmetry between the positions of capital and labor. The effect of involuntary unemployment is to render labor time a nonscarce input, weakening the bargaining power of workers. In a full employment economy there would be little cost to job loss, since workers could find new jobs with little trouble or delay. This would remove the employers' most powerful threat, allowing workers to demand escalating wages and/or reduce their effort to levels of their own choosing.

The existence of unemployment makes the threat of job loss a serious one, and hence motivates workers to exert increased effort. However, unemployment will persist only if labor costs exceed the competitively determined, market-clearing level of wages. Why would employers pay more than the market-clearing cost for labor, particularly since it is not scarce? There are two answers.

First, the cost of labor to the employer includes surveillance costs as well as wages and benefits. Second, employers may choose to pay workers more in order to increase the cost of job loss, motivating workers to provide greater, more consistent effort.

Capitalist Technology

Similar reasoning shows that a profit-maximizing employer will not always choose the most efficient technology. Efficiency means that a given output is produced with the smallest possible quantity of inputs. In a conventional model, efficient production is always the profit-maximizing strategy. However, the Marxian model shows that it is sometimes more profitable for an employer to choose an inefficient technology because it allows greater control over employees.

Some kinds of machinery, computers, and other information technologies play a joint role in production, both contributing to the marketed output of the firm and producing information on the work performance of employees. Such capital goods will be "overused." The rational capitalist will not just use such inputs up to the point at which their marginal contribution to output equals the input price (the conventional standard for efficiency), but will use more of them, up to the point at which their combined contributions to output and to the extraction of labor effort equal the input price. That is, control-enhancing capital goods will be used beyond the efficient level.

An alternative argument makes the same point. Any given level of labor effort can be extracted with many different combinations of surveillance and wage increases. Surveillance consumes real resources, while wage increases do not. Hence, if the employer's optimal strategy involves any surveillance—as it virtually always does—then there are other ways of obtaining the same effort and the same quantity of final output, while using fewer surveillance inputs and the same amount of all other inputs.

Divide and Rule

It is sometimes rational for employers to pay different amounts to identically productive workers. The rationality of discrimination rests on the effects of worker unity on the work process and the level of labor effort. Increased unity— for simplicity, assumed to be measured by the degree of wage equality within the workforce—may lower both the probability that a worker will be detected pursuing nonwork activities during working hours, and the probability of being terminated if detected. Thus, all else being equal, increased unity among workers reduces the amount of labor effort that is provided. Discrimination that fosters inequality would therefore increase labor effort by reducing solidarity.

Neo-Hobbesian and Marxian Models

Could the undesirable outcomes of involuntary unemployment, technological inefficiency, and discrimination be deduced from a different model? The neo-Hobbesian model, focusing on the need for the firm to control worker malfeasance, or shirking, is superficially similar to the Marxian model presented here. Ronald Coase proposed an influential conception of the firm as a mini-command economy that exists to minimize transaction costs. This suggests that workplace hierarchy is an efficient response to the universal tendency to shirk responsibilities on the job.

Yet derivation of the results presented above within the Coasian or neo-Hobbesian framework requires restrictive and implausible assumptions about human nature and exogenously given technologies. Perhaps more fundamentally, the claim that the hierarchical firm is an efficient response to shirking can be refuted. A different workplace organization, if perceived to be more fair or respectful to the workers, might lead to more labor effort with less surveillance inputs. The inability of the hierarchical firm to reach this outcome constitutes a market failure. Only in the Marxian model is this outcome understandable as a result of the endogenous creation of worker (and capitalist) attitudes, and of the labor extraction function.

Summary of

Industrial Relations and Productivity Growth: A Comparative Perspective

by Robert A. Buchele and Jens Christiansen

[Published in *International Contributions to Labor Studies* 2 (1992), 77–97.]

This article presents a theoretical model of the relationship between industrial relations systems and productivity, and applies that model in an empirical investigation of productivity growth rates in the leading industrial countries. The model challenges the assumption, common in other recent theories, that productivity depends largely on the effort exerted by individual workers; it focuses instead on the social determinants of productivity. The empirical work explores the relationship between productivity growth, unemployment, the extent of cooperation in labor-management relations, and the strength of workers rights, in the "Group of Seven" nations.

Theoretical Framework

Labor productivity depends on both the efforts of the workforce and the effective organization of work. Management can elicit work effort either through coercion, in what can be called the "conflict model," or through inducement, in the "cooperative model."

Many recent theories of the labor process are based on the conflict model. In such theories, the threat of job loss secures the power of capital over labor. A worker's effort depends on the cost of job loss, which increases as unemployment rises; therefore increases in unemployment should raise labor productivity. The same effect would result from other factors that increase the cost of job loss, such as a reduction in the "social wage" (cutbacks in public-sector health and welfare benefits) or an increased differential between current earnings and the wages at other available jobs.

In the long run, productivity growth depends on technical change and innovation. The conflict model suggests that workers resist technical change whenever they can. An increase in unemployment undermines workers' ability to resist changes, and hence should be positively related to productivity gains in the long run.

Critique of the Conflict Model

The conflict model is too narrow, both in its emphasis on the effort of individual workers and in its exclusive focus on shop floor activity rather than the production process as a whole. The threat of dismissal is not a day-to-day concern for most primary sector workers, who are often protected by seniority rules or other due process procedures. Therefore, calculations based on the cost of individual job loss are inappropriate for this group. The fear of massive layoffs has become important in recent years, but this concerns *collective* job loss due to larger economic forces, not individual job loss related to individual performance.

Furthermore, individual effort is not the decisive determinant of productivity in most modern production processes. In highly mechanized, integrated, or continuous flow processes, it is the effective interaction of many different people that leads to increases in the quantity and quality of output. Conversely, ineffective or uncoordinated interaction can waste labor hours and effort in any part of a large enterprise, not just among production workers.

Two stages can be distinguished in the transformation of labor hours into final output. The first is the transformation of hours into effort. This is the subject addressed in "efficiency wage" and "cost of job loss" models. The second, and perhaps more important, stage is the transformation of effort into final output. This involves the effective organization of work. Inefficiency in the first stage leads to waste of labor hours; inefficiency in the second stage leads to waste of labor effort.

The Cooperative Model

In a cooperative system of industrial relations, increased worker participation can significantly raise the rate of productivity growth. With their unique experience and knowledge of the production process, workers can make important contributions to innovation. This allows gains in the effective organization of work, of a sort not readily available in the conflict model. But the cooperative model requires that workers have a stake in the long-run success of the enterprise that employs them. Job security and profit-sharing measures are needed to motivate workers to innovate and improve the organization of production.

In such a context, the relationship of unemployment to productivity is quite different from that found in the conflict model. Long-term employment guarantees and other workers' rights on the job help create the basis for productivity-enhancing participation. High or fluctuating unemployment threatens the stability of employment, and thus tends to lower productivity growth in the cooperative model.

Productivity growth, in general, depends on the degree of cooperation achieved in labor-management relations. The effect of unemployment, or changes in workers' rights on the job, is ambiguous. If labor relations are antagonistic, unemployment (because it gives employers the upper hand) is good for productivity growth, and workers' rights are bad; if labor relations are cooperative, the reverse is true.

Empirical Analysis

The theoretical arguments developed here can be tested through international comparisons, using the wealth of data available for the seven largest industrial economies for the 1960s through the 1980s. An index of the cooperativeness of labor relations can be constructed, combining the prevalence of long-term employment, the ratio of supervisors to production workers (a lower ratio indicates greater cooperativeness), and the portion of total compensation paid as bonuses (because bonuses increase the workers' stake in the company's success). The ranking of the countries, from least to most cooperative, is the United States, the United Kingdom, Canada, France, Germany, Italy, Japan.

Similarly, an index of workers' rights can be created, combining measures of the adequacy of unemployment insurance, legal restrictions on layoffs, the percentage of health care expenditures funded by the government, public expenditures on labor market programs, level of unionization, and interindustry wage dispersion (lower dispersion indicates greater workers' rights). In this case the ranking, from weakest to strongest rights, is the United States, Japan, Canada, Italy, France, the United Kingdom, Germany.

Both of these indices can be used in an analysis of international differences in productivity growth rates. There is a wide divergence among the seven countries in average annual growth rates of real GDP per hour of work, an aggregate measure of labor productivity. In each of the three periods examined here, 1960–73, 1973–79, and 1979–88, the United States had the slowest, and Canada the second-slowest, growth in productivity. The numbers, and the rankings of the other five countries, varied from one period to the next. (Japan's productivity growth was fastest in two of the three periods.)

The theory discussed above suggests several hypotheses: Cooperation should have a positive effect on productivity; the interaction of average unemployment with cooperation should have a negative effect (since low unemployment and high cooperation, or vice versa, are good for productivity); and the interaction of workers' rights with cooperation should have a positive effect. All of these hypotheses are confirmed by regression analysis, a result that provides additional support for the theoretical model. Interpretation of the quantitative results is difficult because two of the key explanatory variables are arbitrarily scaled indices, not expressed in any natural units. Nonetheless, the qualitative results are entirely consistent with the theory, highlighting the role of cooperative systems of industrial relations in promoting productivity growth.

Summary of

Radical Political Economy and the Economics of Labor Markets

by James Rebitzer

[Published in *Journal of Economic Literature* 31 (September 1993), 1393–1434.]

Radical political economy (RPE) is a school of thought that has emerged from, and draws on, both Marxian and neoclassical economics. Three fundamental ideas define RPE. First, economics is intrinsically political: Key economic processes depend on society's institutional power relationships. Second, institutional change is desirable. Existing institutions are less efficient, and/or less just, than some feasible alternatives. Third, existing economic structures are the contingent results of particular historical events and therefore need not be optimal or efficient.

The RPE perspective has produced an important body of theory and empirical research in labor economics. This article reviews and critiques the RPE contributions in two broad areas: the nature of the firm, technology, and work; and the segmentation of labor markets. An exhaustive bibliography appears in the original article.

The Structure of the Firm

The RPE theory of the firm assumes a hierarchical structure, dominated by the owners of capital. The firm uses the threat of dismissal to elicit work effort from employees, in order to maximize profits. This is no different from the independently developed "efficiency wage" models, in which firms monitor work effort and threaten to dismiss those whose work is substandard. Both the intensity of supervision and the cost of job loss (the value of the current job relative to alternatives) are positively associated with intensity of work effort.

Empirical estimates confirm that the cost of job loss is positively correlated with productivity. Either increases in wages, or increases in unemployment, can boost the cost of job loss—and both of these factors are correlated with productivity. Intensity of supervision is more difficult to measure. It appears to be both higher and more rapidly increasing in the United States than in other industrial countries.

Work and Technology

The hypothesis of "de-skilling" technical change can be traced back at least to Marx, and was forcefully restated by Harry Braverman, in *Labor and Monopoly Capital*, in 1974. Technical change designed to replace skilled labor with machines and unskilled labor, combined with Taylorism in work relations, were said by Braverman to be widespread and successful in breaking the power of early craft unions and allowing a profitable speedup of work. More recent historical studies, while influenced by Braverman, have often failed to support his conclusions. Some have suggested that Taylorism was not always very successful, creating semiskilled industrial labor that was difficult to motivate or control. Others have found that average skill levels are not declining. In fact, increasing education has facilitated the creation of a labor force with new attitudes and behavior patterns.

Is the choice of technology made by the capitalist firm necessarily efficient? One form of inefficiency emerges from the theory of the firm discussed above. Since the same output could be produced with less supervisory inputs, the profit-maximizing production plan is not efficient (see Bowles' summary in Part II). A broader question concerns the choice of technologies and work organization in general.

The RPE literature claims that capitalist firms are less efficient than democratically run, employee-owned firms, both because incentive problems are minimized by worker ownership and because ownership motivates workers to share their unique knowledge of the production process, allowing valuable innovations.

If employee ownership is more efficient, why is it so rare in the marketplace? There are a variety of answers. The economic environment may make it difficult for isolated worker-owned businesses to survive, perhaps because lending institutions demand traditional forms of collateral, which capitalist firms are more likely to have. The history of technological development has undoubtedly favored hierarchical, control-oriented technologies over participatory, democratic alternatives. Skilled craftwork may lend itself to worker-managed firms, in contrast to industrial mass production. Finally, even if worker ownership has an advantage in short-run, static efficiency, private ownership may be more dynamically efficient. A hierarchical corporation is both less risk-averse and more able to appropriate the full long-run return on its investment than a workers cooperative. Hence the traditional firm is less prone to underinvestment.

The RPE theories discussed here offer important insights, but at the cost of several theoretical oversimplifications. Specifically, they ignore management functions other than labor supervision; they leave no room for the intricacy of actual bargaining processes between labor and management; and they rely on a poorly developed psychological treatment of work incentives.

Labor Market Segmentation

Institutionalist and radical economists have pioneered the study of labor market segmentation. There is no clear boundary between radical and mainstream writing on labor market segmentation; however, the RPE literature encompasses historical and institutional topics that are rarely examined by most of the economics profession.

The theory of labor market segmentation argues that even in long-run equilibrium, workers of identical wages will be paid different amounts—or equivalently, there will be nonmarket rationing of high-wage, desirable ("primary sector") jobs. Segmentation is often said to arise from differences in work incentives. For example, Richard Edwards proposed that there are three fundamental mechanisms of labor control: (1) simple control by supervisors, (2) technical control based on the use of machinery such as assembly lines, and (3) bureaucratic control designed to induce workers to internalize the goals of the enterprise. These correspond, respectively, to the secondary, subordinate primary, and primary sectors of the labor market.

Primary sector jobs exist, in such theories, either because they are difficult to monitor (making it more effective to "discipline" them with high wages, raising the cost of job loss and encouraging enterprise loyalty) or because they are intrinsically unsuited to negative sanctions and require workers to internalize their employers' goals. Less attractive and less stable secondary jobs exist either because they are easier and cheaper to monitor or because fluctuations in product demand make it costly to provide long-term employment for all.

Firms may have a choice between "high trust" and "close supervision" incentive schemes, with different wages and average job tenure depending on which they choose. The psychological attributes that employees bring to the job must be compatible with the employer's incentive scheme. In a broad view of political economy, worker attitudes can be seen as endogenously shaped by schools, family life, and by work itself.

An important theme in labor market segmentation literature is that women and minorities have limited access to primary jobs. Discrimination by employers would be "rational" (profitable) if ascriptive characteristics were correlated with unobservable characteristics that are relevant to work performance. Possible unobservable characteristics playing this role include workers' expected job tenure and preferred hours of work. The longer an employee expects to remain in the same job, and the longer the hours that he or she prefers to work, the cheaper it is (the lower the wage premium required) to induce loyalty and identification with the firm. If men, on average, expect longer job tenure and prefer longer weekly hours than women—due to both childbearing requirements and traditional gender roles in the household—then there is an "explanation" for primary sector employers' preference for male workers.

The same argument does not directly apply to racial differences. Here the RPE literature offers an alternative hypothesis, the "divide and rule" theory of discrimination. Consistently treating one group of workers better than another reduces worker solidarity and bargaining power, thus lowering the cost of supervising workers and extracting effort from them. However, such models are not consistent with the emphasis on reciprocity and mutual obligation between employers and primary sector workers, nor do they apply to entirely segregated workplaces.

Wages and Productivity

As predicted by labor market segmentation theory (but not by conventional microeconomics), there are large, persistent wage differentials correlated with plant size, firm size, and industry. These differentials remain even when one controls for education, other worker characteristics, and job characteristics such as unionization. The relationship of wages to plant size is consistent with one of the explanations of segmentation, namely the difficulty of monitoring primary sector workers. The harder it is to monitor workers, the more employers will rely on higher wages rather than closer supervision. It seems plausible to assume that it is harder to monitor workers in larger establishments; hence their wages will be higher, all else being equal.

Wage differentials associated with firm size or industry may reflect differences in profitability. Firm size may be a rough indicator of profitability, and industries have persistent differences in profit rates. In a more profitable enterprise, rent-sharing—dividing the excess profits between employers and employees—becomes possible. Norms of fairness may develop, suggesting in general that high-profit firms should pay high wages, or specifying expected "fair" wages for particular occupations in particular industries or firms. Refusal to share a visible surplus with employees might undermine the sense of loyalty and obligation that primary sector employers strive to create.

Differential wage payments mean that the cost of job loss is substantial for workers in the primary sector, but insignificant in the secondary sector (because other poorly paid secondary jobs are readily available). When unemployment increases, the cost of job loss also rises—which should increase productivity, as discussed above. However, the effect of unemployment on productivity is much greater for workers in the secondary sector than in the primary sector. This somewhat paradoxical finding suggests a limit to the applicability of efficiency wage and monitoring models of the labor process. If primary sector workers have extensive firm-specific human capital, it may be very expensive to replace them, reducing the threat of dismissal. Theories of rent-sharing in profitable firms, and sociological models involving norms of fairness, may therefore be more relevant to wage and employment practices in the primary sector.

Many questions remain to be answered in the RPE framework. For example, broad issues of institutional change and stability have been addressed by some authors in terms of long-lasting, but gradually changing, "social structures of accumulation." This intriguing notion has inspired some interesting research into business cycles, "long waves" of growth, and institutional change. In theoretical terms, however, it remains ambiguous and problematical.

> Looking solely at its ability to stimulate provocative and influential research, the intellectual project constituting RPE must be judged a success. Moreover . . . the RPE conception of economic relationships as political, remedial, and historically contingent has increasingly been incorporated into the mainstream of economic research. Over time, this process is likely to erode much of the distinction between RPE and the rest of the economics profession—to the benefit of both. [1429–1430]

Summary of

Labor Market Segmentation Theory: Reconsidering the Evidence

by William T. Dickens and Kevin Lang

[Published in *Labor Economics: Problems in Analyzing Labor Markets,* ed. William Darity, Jr. (Boston: Kluwer Academic Publishers, 1993), 141–180.]

The theory of labor market segmentation was widely discussed in labor economics in the early 1970s, as an explanation of inequality in job opportunities and earnings. Since then, the theory has faded in popularity. Most economists prefer human capital theory as an explanation of labor market inequalities. This essay examines the theoretical basis for segmentation, offers an improved specification and empirical test of the theory, and concludes that it provides both a good fit to the data and a more promising research agenda than human capital theory.

What Is Labor Market Segmentation?

There are two crucial assumptions in a theory of labor market segmentation. First, the labor market is made up of distinct segments with different rules for determining wages and employment. Second, access to jobs in some segments is limited by nonmarket mechanisms (at the prevailing wage, the supply of qualified applicants for primary sector "good jobs" exceeds the demand). Segmentation alone, without the second assumption, would not imply market failure or require a new theory; it might simply reflect a bimodal distribution of skills.

Early writing on labor market segmentation emphasized lack of mobility between sectors; however, this is not essential to the theory. Empirical evidence shows that in an economic expansion, black workers are more likely than whites to move into better jobs. In general, wages rise more rapidly with age and experience for blacks, but more slowly within any single job. "This is precisely what would be expected if blacks were more likely to be employed in low-wage jobs with little return to seniority while queuing for good jobs." [145] The existence of excess labor supply and queuing for high-wage jobs, and wage differences unrelated to ability or job quality, provide evidence of labor market segmentation, regardless of mobility.

The most common form of segmentation theory distinguishes between primary and secondary segments, sometimes with further subdivisions within these categories. The primary sector has good wages and working conditions, opportunity for advancement, returns to education and training, and formalized labor relations that circumscribe supervisors' authority.

As a result, employees tend to stay on the job for a long time. The secondary sector of the labor market offers the opposite in most or all of these respects.

Several economic theories can explain why high wages persist for primary sector workers, even in the face of excess labor supply. Efficiency wage theories suggest that labor productivity depends in part on the wage level. Employers may pay more than the market-clearing wage in order to increase the cost of job loss, or to meet workers' expectations about what constitutes a fair wage. Employers may also want to reduce turnover and protect their investment in training of skilled workers, or to ensure that they attract high-quality workers, in the presence of adverse selection problems (employers may not be able to fully observe worker quality either before or after hiring). Unions can raise wages; so, too, can management efforts to forestall unionization. In a firm that is earning monopoly profits, rent-sharing—giving workers part of the excess profits—becomes possible. Thus there is no logical inconsistency in the hypothesis that primary sector workers routinely earn more than the market-clearing wage for their labor.

Empirical Evidence of Segmentation

Numerous studies have found large and persistent interindustry differences in wages. These differences remain significant even when controlling for location and for a wide range of worker characteristics. There is a high degree of collinearity among worker and industry characteristics that might affect wages, including capital/labor ratio, labor productivity, average education, average job tenure, unionization, firm size, profit rates, and many others. As a result, the attempt to establish which of these factors are most important has been largely fruitless. This is, however, exactly the pattern one would expect if there is an underlying segmentation of the labor market, with industries differing sharply in the proportion of primary sector workers. Similar patterns have been found for differences among specific employers within an industry.

Human capital theory explains such interindustry and interemployer differences by assuming the existence of unobserved or unobservable skill differences. This assumption is hard to maintain in the face of the evidence. Some industries and firms pay higher than average wages across the board; why would the same pattern of unobserved industry or employer-specific characteristics be shared by secretaries and truck drivers? Most studies find that when workers change industries, their wages change by nearly the full difference between the old and new industry averages. Thus the unobserved skills do not appear to be transferable from one industry to another. Increasingly difficult and contorted versions of human capital theory are required to explain such findings, while market segmentation theory provides a natural explanation.

Testing the Theory

Early empirical tests of segmentation theory provided useful information, but were criticized for failing to provide an endogenous explanation of which segment a worker ends up in. A new approach, developed by the authors, addresses this problem directly.

The authors' model makes no a priori assumptions about which individuals, occupations, or industries are associated with the primary or secondary sectors. Using data on individual workers, it estimates three equations simultaneously. Two are wage determination equations, specifying primary and secondary sector wage-setting mechanisms; the model assigns individuals to sectors so as to produce the best possible fit with these two equations. The third is the "switching" equation, describing the probability that an individual with given characteristics will be found in the primary or secondary sector.

Hypotheses about the model include: The two wage determination equations will fit the data much better than any single equation; the higher-wage market segment will have substantial returns to education and work experience, while the lower-wage segment will have almost none; and a majority of adult male workers are in the higher-wage segment. A test of the model using 1983 data on some 48,000 employed male heads of household, ages 20 to 65, strongly confirms these hypotheses. A man is more likely to be in the primary sector if he has ever been married, is white, lives in a metropolitan area, and has more years of work experience and education.

An interesting anomaly, which requires further study, appears in the results for race. While being white has a large, expected effect on primary/secondary status, and a significant positive effect on primary sector wages, it has a negative effect on secondary sector wages.

The distribution of primary and secondary sector workers in specific industries and occupations follows the expected pattern. Industries with virtually all workers in the primary sector include paper, primary metals, and advertising, research, and computers, while eating and drinking places and liquor stores have only about half their (adult male) workers in the primary sector. Managers and supervisors are almost always in the primary sector, while retail clerks and unskilled labor have a smaller proportion of primary sector workers. However, no major industries or occupations have a clear majority of their adult male workers in the secondary sector. The classification schemes used in previous studies, typically identifying whole occupations or industries as secondary, have only a modest level of agreement with this scheme.

Can the findings described here be made consistent with standard theories? If technologies were sharply discontinuous, there could be two distinct market segments with no market failure. It is harder to explain the observed income differences. It is implausible, and inconsistent with other evidence, to suggest that low-income workers prefer the conditions of employment in the secondary sector, and that they are willing to give up substantial income to obtain those conditions. It is also hard to explain why blacks and more educated workers are as likely to be found in the secondary sector as they are, given the advantages to them of primary sector employment. Other objections have been dealt with by the authors in earlier publications. For instance, the model does not prove that there are two, rather than more, labor market segments. It does, however, demonstrate that the hypothesis of two segments fits the data much better than the hypothesis of an unsegmented market.

Summary of

Supervision and High Wages as Competing Incentives: A Basis for Labor Segmentation Theory

by Robert W. Drago and Richard Perlman

[Published in *Microeconomic Issues in Labour Economics: New Approaches,* eds. Robert Drago and Richard Perlman (Hertfordshire: Harvester Wheatsheaf, 1989), 43–61.]

Efficiency wage theories link wages to work effort by hypothesizing that higher pay elicits increased effort. The most prevalent variant of efficiency wage theory—the work-discipline version—predicts that imperfect information concerning work effort will lead to both a positive level of supervision and to wages above the market-clearing level. This article presents a "competing incentives" model in which high wages play a role in enhancing trust; however, this effect is often incompatible with an emphasis on supervision.

Efficiency Wages

The competing incentives approach and the work-discipline model both recognize the heterogeneity of technology, along with its implication that monitoring costs (the costs of obtaining information about work effort) may be expected to vary from one production setting to another. A difference between these two variants of efficiency wage theory is that, while the work discipline model predicts a continuum of jobs, in the competing incentives model it is proposed that "workers do not always choose effort levels by smoothly trading-off the pains and pleasures associated with work and leisure." [44] Indeed, this model predicts a bifurcation among jobs depending on the kinds of incentives used to promote work effort. One package of incentives comprises low wages and close supervision; the other combines high wages with little or no supervision.

The second possibility could not exist if workers were always opportunistic, for such workers would shirk when unsupervised, and the too-trusting firm would become bankrupt. A critical assumption of the competing incentives approach is that "low levels of supervision will promote trust so that employees will choose effort in an equitable fashion while, under higher levels of supervision, employees will act opportunistically, consistent with work-discipline arguments, and the threat of job loss will be required to counter potential opportunism." [42] In fact, the literature on participatory management has made a strong case that high productivity may result from the job satisfaction and good morale, which are strongly correlated with worker autonomy (lack of monitoring). The trust that links autonomy, morale, and productivity is difficult to achieve. A management structure emphasizing supervision can make shirking harder to achieve, but it undermines trust.

High wages on the one hand, and intensive supervision on the other, may thus be seen as competing incentives to work effort that will be self-defeating if applied simultaneously. This bifurcation can explain a picture of labor market segmentation in which primary sector jobs have high wages, low supervision, and technology that makes it difficult for management to monitor effort, while secondary sector jobs have low pay, high supervision, and technology that makes it simple to monitor effort.

The competing incentives model will be analyzed with the aid of the following simplifying assumptions: (1) Workers are homogeneous with respect to productivity and preferences, and are employed by profit-maximizing firms that generally fit the competitive model, except that obtaining information about work effort is costly; (2) technology is given; and (3) the only costs are those required to motivate workers.

The Firm Under Heterogeneous Technology and Competing Incentives

Given competing incentives, there are two different decision rules under which workers may operate. With low supervision the worker will act according to an equity rule (Rule I), seeking to equate work effort and compensation fairly. Here higher pay induces greater effort. Alternatively, with high supervision the worker will act according to an opportunistic rule (Rule II), seeking to minimize effort to the extent possible without jeopardizing the job. One simple way to express this choice is

$$e = (1 - s) \, (\text{Rule I}) + s \, (\text{Rule II})$$

where e is effort and s is supervision. As supervision approaches zero, the worker behaves according to Rule I; as supervision approaches one, the worker behaves according to Rule II.

The firm faces a choice between two strategies, one dependent on trust and the other on supervision. The strategies face different kinds of costs: The trust strategy implies higher than average wages; the other has lower wages but higher supervision costs. Under a given set of conditions (including the technologies that affect ease or difficulty of supervision) there are likely to be two points that are local optima. A profit-maximizing firm that is not initially swayed by history, or by preconceptions about what constitutes good management, could, theoretically, survey the relative costs and effort levels associated with the two strategies and adopt the more profitable one.

Once a strategy has been selected, however, marginal changes away from the local profit optimum will lead to reduced profits. When a trust regime is in place, a marginal change to more supervision will decrease effort "because the worker begins to shirk as soon as it is perceived that the firm does not trust him or her." [47] Similarly, under a supervision regime, where workers are already looking for ways to shirk, a small move in the direction of trust will not accomplish a regime-switch—it will only lead to more shirking. Only a complete regime switch can replace the benefits of high supervision/low wages with the benefits of high trust/low supervision, or vice versa.

Given the heterogeneity of technology, at any given time it will be found that the trust regime is the profit-maximizing choice for some firms, while for others the high-supervision regime is rational. Given change in technology, and consequent changes (in either direction) in the cost of supervision, it may be expected that the profit motive would cause firms to switch from one regime to the other when a technology change makes such a switch profitable. However, it is hard for firms to know when they are at such a switch point, since marginal experiments (increasing or decreasing supervision by small amounts) are unlikely to yield useful information. For reasons just cited, such experiments will probably reduce effort whether or not the firm is at a potential switch point. "Firms may respond to this uncertainty by maintaining work motivation practices over time, and hence segmented jobs, even if technological change dictates managerial change." [51]

Explaining Segmentation and Discrimination

This model can help to explain some important facts about the segmentation of workers and jobs. All workers will queue for primary sector jobs, which are rationed by virtue of their higher-than-market-clearing wages. With more qualified workers than jobs in this sector, and given diverse monitoring costs, there may be a shortage of good jobs even for workers with the same productivity potentials. In this case, the cost of discrimination is zero, primary sector jobs are rationed, and secondary jobs go to groups facing discrimination.

In primary jobs, where job security is important to employee trust, employers will try to minimize layoffs, even when there is a shortage of such jobs. Preferred jobs are rationed by noneconomic criteria such as race or gender, rather than by the productivity differences emphasized by human capital theory.

Unemployment also plays a role in the structure of incentives. "Because primary sector jobs are more desirable, they will be rationed, while unemployment is required with regard to secondary sector jobs in order to maintain work discipline." [51] It is evident that the worker's welfare is greater in low supervision jobs, not only because working conditions are less pleasant when supervision is higher, but because firms using the high supervision strategy will offset the extra supervision cost either by requiring greater effort for the same wage or by lowering the wage.

However, there is research indicating another explanation for discrimination related to the trust hypothesis. Where piece-work type incentive plans are prevalent, researchers have noted less racial discrimination, suggesting that where such plans are absent and trust is a key issue, mistrust between minority employees and white managers may be a factor in employment outcomes. Where this is true, "Rule I" effort, induced by equity considerations, may be difficult to achieve.

In further applications of the competing incentives model it will be important to make a sharper distinction between supervision and monitoring. Some supervision occurs for coordinating purposes, while in other cases monitoring might be done via output measurement or market responses rather than through direct supervision. Nonsupervisory monitoring may be perceived as fairer, and may therefore be more compatible with a trust model.

Conclusion

Management theory recognizes that people are "motivated by carrots and sticks, but that the two do not work well in tandem and are not generally provided to the same employees." [54] However, economic theory usually subsumes both under the concept of opportunity costs, blurring the incompatibility of incentives noted here, and ignoring considerations based on trust.

Summary of

The Fair Wage–Effort Hypothesis and Unemployment

by George A. Akerlof and Janet Yellen

[Published in *Quarterly Journal of Economics* 105 (May 1990), 255–283.]

In conventional economic theory, the supply of labor is determined by the balance between the attractiveness of wages and the unpleasantness of work. Each worker responds only to his or her own wages and work situation and is indifferent to the circumstances of others. This article proposes a hypothesis, widely accepted by psychologists and sociologists, that people are motivated by perceptions of fairness. "When people do not get what they deserve, they try to get even." [256] In the labor market, if wages are reduced below the level that workers consider fair, they will reduce their effort on the job proportionally. The "fair wage–effort hypothesis" may explain the negative correlation between skill and unemployment; in addition, it can explain wage differentials and labor market segmentation.

Motivation for the Hypothesis

Several types of evidence support the fair wage–effort hypothesis. Equity theory in psychology and social exchange theory in sociology both suggest that in a voluntary social exchange, each party perceives the value of "inputs" and "outcomes" to be equal. If there is an accepted fair wage for a standard level of work effort, then payment above the fair wage should elicit greater effort, and payment below the fair wage should lead to correspondingly less effort. Psychological experiments have more often examined the results of overpayment—this does not always lead to increased effort, since it is easier to revise upward one's opinion of a fair wage than to work harder. The few experiments that have studied underpayment have confirmed that it leads to a higher proportion of substandard work and to higher rates of quitting the job (or experiment).

Relative deprivation theory suggests that perceptions of fairness are based on comparisons with others. Psychological theory, however, does not tell us which others are most relevant. Those most similar to ourselves are surely important, but visible others—dissimilar workers in the same firm, for example—are also significant.

Sociologists have documented the conscious restriction of effort in the workplace, in retaliation for unfair wages or working conditions. Workers can often cause machinery to fail, or to need excessive levels of maintenance, by minor modification of work procedures. Two-tier wage structures are sometimes inefficient, since the resentment of the lower-wage workers can lead to withdrawal of effort or refusal to cooperate with higher-wage workers.

Personnel management texts regard the need for equitable pay schedules as obvious. The common policy of secrecy about wages and salaries is evidence of the interest that workers feel in the payment received by others. Workers generally believe that pay should reflect performance—but virtually everyone believes that their own performance is well above average. Thus a pay schedule that is perceived as fair will be more compressed than one based strictly on management's evaluation of performance.

Considerations of fairness can also help explain the persistent pattern of wage differentials between industries, which cannot be entirely accounted for by differences in productivity or compensation for the differential nature of work. If high wages must be paid to one group of workers in an industry, perhaps to attract a scarce skill, then other workers in the industry will have a higher standard of fair payment. That is, the other workers will expect, and will often get, more than they would for the same work in another industry.

A Rudimentary Model

Suppose that a normal effort is supplied by workers if actual wages are at or above the (fixed, exogenous) fair wage, but if wages are reduced below the fair level, then effort is reduced in the same proportion. For half the fair wage, an employer gets half the normal level of effort. Suppose also that there is a perfectly competitive economy, with many identical firms whose output is proportional to their labor input and to the level of effort. How much labor will firms choose to employ?

The marginal cost of a unit of labor effort is simply equal to the wage, so long as the wage is above the fair wage level. At lower wages, however, the cost of a unit of labor effort is always the fair wage (since, for example, half the fair wage gets half a unit of effort). Thus if the marginal product of labor is below the fair wage, it is not profitable to hire anyone or produce anything. If the marginal product of labor is above the fair wage, competition among employers will bid wages up to the marginal product of labor (as in the standard textbook model), and there will be full employment. Although this model is simplistic, it demonstrates one reason why wages do not fall below the fair wage level: Under the model's assumptions, no profits can be made by pushing down to the point where workers withhold effort.

A Relative Deprivation Model

A more sophisticated model allows the fair wage level itself to be endogenous and examines the interactions between two groups of workers who supply distinct types of labor. Each group sets its effort level as in the simple model, based on its own idea of a fair wage. In this case, however, the fair wage for each group is variable, dependent partly on the relative demand for its own labor and partly on the wages received by the other group. (More formally, each group's fair wage is a weighted average of the market-clearing wage for its own labor and the current wage received by the other group.)

With the addition of some technical assumptions about firms and production, this model leads to three types of equilibria. In an integrated equilibrium, all firms hire both types of workers, and some low-paid workers are unemployed. In a partially segregated equilibrium, some firms hire both types of workers, and some hire only low-paid workers. And in a fully segregated equilibrium, each firm hires only one or the other type of workers. There is no unemployment in the partially and fully segregated equilibria, but there can be persistent wage differences and labor market segmentation.

Consider, first, the integrated equilibrium. It is impossible, or unstable, for both groups of workers to be fully employed and providing normal effort. Low-paid workers would consider their wages unfair, since they would receive less than the others, and would reduce their effort accordingly. This would make it less attractive to employ the low-paid group, causing a decline in the demand for their labor. On the other hand, there cannot be unemployment of the higher-paid group in equilibrium. If there were, it would be doubly profitable for employers to reduce their wages, since this would also reduce the lower-paid group's idea of fair wages.

From these arguments it can be deduced that the low-paid group will receive its fair wage. Since they experience unemployment in equilibrium, firms can set the cost-minimizing wage for low-paid labor; but, as in the simple model, there are no profits to be gained by cutting wages below the fair wage level. The high-paid group, on the other hand, receives its market-clearing wage and is fully employed. (The market-clearing wage is above the fair level for the high-paid group, so fairness is not a binding constraint for this group.)

Segregated Equilibria and Segmentation

The integrated equilibrium creates an opportunity for "deviant" firms to profit by hiring only low-paid workers. Fairness is not an issue within the deviant, or segregated, firms, since there are no higher-paid workers for the employees to compare themselves to. These firms are free to pay the market-clearing wage. The presence of segregated firms increases the demand, and hence the market-clearing wage, for low-paid workers. This increases the fair wage for low-paid workers at integrated firms (since the fair wage depends on the market-clearing wage), and hence increases the wage these workers receive at integrated firms. If enough segregated firms enter the market, there will be full employment for low-paid workers. However, they will earn less at segregated firms (the market-clearing wage) than at integrated firms (the fair wage). This corresponds to standard descriptions of dual labor markets, with jobs for low-skilled workers in both the primary and the secondary sectors.

As segregated firms begin hiring low-paid workers, their fair wage rises, leading integrated firms to reduce their employment of this group. In the extreme, the formerly integrated firms might become unwilling to hire any low-paid workers. All firms would then hire only one or the other group of workers. With segregated workforces, fairness issues would not arise within firms. Both groups of workers would be fully employed at their market-clearing wages. However, this is not necessarily an efficient outcome. In the fully segregated equilibrium, considerations of fairness prevent any firm from employing both types of labor (since low-paid workers would then demand higher, fair wages)—even though it is almost always efficient to combine workers of different skill levels in complex production processes.

Summary of

The Exit-Voice Trade-Off in the Labor Market: Unionism, Job Tenure, Quits, and Separations

by Richard B. Freeman

[Published in *Quarterly Journal of Economics* 94 (June 1980), 643–673.]

What do unions do? Much of the economics literature on unions has focused on their effects on wages and benefits. It is clear that unions, on average, increase worker compensation. This classic article demonstrates that unions have an additional, independent effect on labor relations: They reduce the rate at which workers leave their jobs, and hence increase average job tenure. It seems likely that this occurs because union members have an institutionalized opportunity to voice their discontents and to attempt to change their conditions of work. The article first elaborates this argument in theory, and then tests it empirically on four large sets of data on individual U.S. workers in the late 1960s and the 1970s.

Exit, Voice, and Labor

Albert Hirschman's "exit-voice" model proposes that individuals can react to discontent either by exiting from undesirable situations or by voicing their discomfort to decision-makers in the hopes of affecting change. In the case of the labor market, workers can exit from undesirable jobs by quitting; and, in unionized workplaces, they can give voice to their concerns through the collective bargaining system and grievance procedures. If, as usually assumed, there is a trade-off between the use of exit and voice, then union members should have lower quit rates and longer average job tenure than comparable nonunion workers.

This is a testable hypothesis, and the principal finding reported in this article is that the hypothesis is quite strongly supported by the available data. The empirical analysis involves much more than the observation that union members have longer average job tenure. The familiar effect of unions on wages also increases tenure. Workers are naturally more interested in keeping better-paid jobs. The major empirical challenge is to distinguish between the effect of union wages and the separate effect of union "voice" on quit rates and tenure.

There are several ways in which unions operate as an institutional form of worker "voice" within the firm. Perhaps the most important is the grievance and arbitration system, which is found in virtually all firms covered by major U.S. collective bargaining contracts, but in only a small minority of nonunion firms. The regular process of negotiation of labor contracts also allows institutional expression of workers' desires for change. If desired working conditions and rules have a public-good character within the workplace, it may be inefficient or even impossible for workers to seek these objectives individually rather than collectively. Union contracts create a set of negotiated rules that can be viewed as an industrial jurisprudence system, requiring that certain decisions be made on the basis of principles such as seniority, rather than supervisory authority. If workers desire such a system and it is provided largely by unions, then even with the same pay and other benefits, quit rates will be lower in unionized firms.

If institutions such as grievance and arbitration systems and "industrial jurisprudence" are so desirable that they lower employee turnover, why do nonunion enterprises so rarely offer these options? ". . . [T]he essence of voice is to reduce managerial power and create a dual authority channel within the firm. Such a change in power relations would be difficult to attain in the absence of a genuine independent union or union-like organization." [647] Among the minority of nonunion firms that do have grievance systems, managers frequently report that the systems were instituted in part to reduce worker desires for unions.

Empirical Analysis

Exit is measured by three variables: job tenure, quits, and total separations. Tenure reflects longer-run behavior than current rates of quits or separations; however, tenure depends on past as well as present job characteristics. Quits appear to measure current worker decisions, while separations include layoffs initiated by the employer; however, the line between the two is not always clear (an employer may harass a worker into quitting; a disaffected worker may perform so poorly that firing becomes inevitable). Fortunately, the results for all three variables are qualitatively similar.

The empirical analysis uses large data sets describing individual worker characteristics and behavior. The strategy is to estimate equations expressing tenure, or probability of quits or separations, as functions of numerous explanatory variables, including wage levels and union membership as well as education, experience, industry, occupation, local labor market conditions, and others. While it is impossible to identify all factors that affect tenure or quit rates, one can hope that the unobserved factors are highly correlated with some of the variables that are included. If so, the estimated effects of the included variables include the actual effects of the unobserved factors.

If union membership continues to have a positive effect on tenure and a negative effect on probability of quits or separations, even when controlling for all the other factors, one would conclude that the evidence is consistent with the union voice hypothesis. This is exactly what happens in the empirical analysis (which occupies most of the original article).

Of the four data sets, one includes only men aged 50 to 64, another includes only men aged 17 to 27 (all data sets exclude anyone who was in school or retired during the survey period), and two include men and women of all ages. All estimated effects of union membership on tenure, quits, and separations are significant and substantial. The effects are relatively largest for older men and smallest for younger men. This suggests that union status is most valuable for older men and least valuable for younger employees with less commitment to and seniority in a particular job, consistent with common images of the role of unions.

Several other analyses largely strengthen the basic conclusion. Does the relationship between union membership and job tenure simply show that more stable employees are likely to be in unions? One of the data sets allows a test of the empirical relationships restricted only to those who quit a job at least once during the survey period. Union membership decreases the estimated probability of quitting among "quitters," just as it does in the entire sample.

The voice interpretation of the empirical results implies that union membership should have the greatest effect on those who are most dissatisfied with their jobs. They are the workers most at risk of quitting, for whom the union voice should be most important. Two of the data sets include questions on job satisfaction, allowing an examination of this question. Separate tests for workers at different levels of satisfaction largely confirm that the effect of unions is greatest for the most dissatisfied, although there is some ambiguity in the results in this case.

The union effect on employee turnover should be larger in firms with stronger or more inclusive grievance systems. This, too, is empirically confirmed, to the limited extent that it can be tested with the available data.

The analysis presented here, stressing the institutional role of unions, is consistent with the way that unions are typically viewed in the industrial relations literature. It is also consistent with other economic findings. The greater average tenure and lower quit rates in unionized firms suggests that they would rely on temporary layoffs and recalls over the course of the business cycle, to a greater extent than nonunionized firms. This is confirmed by other research. Longer tenure may also allow greater investment in firm-specific human capital, boosting productivity in unionized firms. In general, there are many aspects of unions, beyond their effects on wages, that should be of central concern to theory and research in labor economics.

Summary of

An Alternative Approach to Labor Markets

by David Marsden

[Published in *The End of Economic Man? Custom and Competition in Labor Markets* (New York: St. Martin's Press, 1986), 230–263.]

This article distinguishes between three main types of labor markets: markets for unskilled or casual labor; internal markets, in which firms allocate jobs among workers with nontransferable skills; and occupational labor markets, which match up jobs with workers who possess readily transferable skills. The latter are taken as the norm of conventional economic theory, which assumes competitive conditions in the long-run. By contrast, the position of this book is that occupational labor markets possess a number of the characteristics of "public goods"; they are difficult to maintain and susceptible to breakdown in the long-run unless supported by some institutional framework. If this is true, then

> at any time the number of occupational markets will be limited, remaining skill requirements being met usually by internal labor markets, and . . . firms will usually fall back on their own internal markets if occupational markets fail or are not available. Consequently the scope for competitive pressures within the labor market is greatly reduced. [231]

Occupational Labor Markets and Transferable Skills as Public Goods

Occupational labor markets (OLMs) are institutional creations that are fairly unstable unless they have a high degree of institutional support. This becomes clear if occupational labor markets and the transferable skills they distribute are recognized as public goods.

A public good has two defining characteristics. First, once it is produced and supplied to anyone, it is not feasible to exclude others from using it. Second, use of the good by one person does not diminish its availability to others. Occupational labor markets and transferable skills have both of these characteristics.

In occupational labor markets skills are highly transferable because of skill mix standards and training levels, along with standardized job training and standardized job descriptions across firms. Once these features are established, employers draw from this pool and workers seek training to gain access to it. These traits enable employers to treat skilled labor as a variable rather than as a fixed cost. They can lay off such workers without losing essential firm capital.

Thus, OLMs function much like public goods. "In an economy in which labor has the right to change employers freely, the standardization of skills means that firms cannot easily be deprived of access to the market. Moreover, once the system of standardized skills is established, in the long run its use by other employers may even enhance it, spreading some of the fixed costs of regulation more widely." [235]

Difficulties of Establishing and Maintaining Stable OLMs

Conventional theory states that, under competitive conditions, workers learning transferable skills will bear the whole cost of training. This is exemplified when trainees accept a special trainee rate below the value of their output. However, in reality skilled employees often possess enough power to force employers to accept most or all of such training costs. The skilled workers may, for example, insist on a good deal of institutional supervision of trainees, thus raising the cost to the employer.

To obtain an adequate pool of skilled labor in an OLM, workers must invest in standardized training and employers must design jobs that match such training. When establishing OLMs, many firms develop their own in-house training programs to supplement outside training. The first firms that participate in an OLM therefore face a danger of "poaching" by other firms that lack in-house training. The same logic can be applied to technological change within firms. As workers are trained to use a new technology they become attractive to competitors adopting the same technology. These dangers create incentives for firms to reduce turnover through the design of internal labor markets. Though there are also costs associated with the latter, once firms turn their training investment in this direction the possibility of establishing standardized skills is reduced, as is the firm's motivation to return to the more open OLM form.

Other factors that could cause firms to move to internal labor markets are (1) free riders—firms who dilute training standards; (2) the fear of losing flexibility when accepting standardized skill norms (as in the face of rapid technological change); (3) cyclical skills shortages, when firms are in danger of losing their workers unless the latter are tied in to internal labor markets; and (4) the fear that workers with more transferable skills will gain bargaining power.

Public funding for training is a logical solution to this public good problem, but "often fails to provide the work experience (often itself transferable) which has to be gained in the firm, and which is nevertheless costly to provide." [238] Skilled workers, who may play a necessary part in the training, will resist assisting in this process if they see it as leading to a reduction of their own job security.

Institutional regulation can help alleviate these problems. By overseeing the quality of training and maintaining uniform standards, institutions can reduce the use of trainees as cheap labor and ease the free rider problem. In such a framework, training costs could be shared among employers or with trainees. In addition, regulation can increase trust among firms and workers and increase the acceptability of low trainee wages, reflecting their actual marginal product.

We have seen, here, two types of solutions to the inherent instability of OLMs: internal markets and institutional regulation. It should be noted that neither of these solutions supports the mainstream economic expectation of a reassertion of unregulated competitive markets.

Conclusion: Implications for Labor Market Theory

The foregoing discussion reveals that occupational labor markets operate much like public goods in that it is often difficult to exclude those who are not prepared to contribute to their funding. Implications that can be derived from this study of labor markets include the following:

1. Occupational labor markets will be limited in number.

2. Because of limited numbers of OLMs, firms will have to provide internal labor markets for other needed skills.

3. The public good analogy implies that employers will be prevented from passing training costs to workers and will therefore have additional motivation to develop internal labor markets. This further implies that the Hicks–Marshall long-run competitive equilibrium may not be achieved.

4. As institutional regulation of OLMs break down, competitive markets are not reestablished. In fact, the use of internal labor markets may increase.

5. OLMs will be confined to higher paid groups, especially if the workers have to bear some portion of the cost.

6. The market power of workers in OLMs will be greater than that of their fellow workers in internal labor markets. This "contributes to frequent higher pay of workers on occupational markets; and it suggests that there is a strong incentive for groups on such markets to use their organization to exploit their bargaining advantage." [249]

7. The reduced elasticity of demand for workers in occupational markets creates an opportunity for monopolistic bargaining. Employers may respond by adopting policies to counter job mobility, such as by giving rewards to seniority.

8. OLMs require institutional support to regulate standards and adapt them to a changing environment.

9. When institutions are given a more central role in labor markets, more weight can be given to questions of comparability and fairness of wage comparisons.

10. "As many firms will have recruited only a limited number of their workers from occupational markets, with the remainder on internal markets or recruited from unskilled markets, competitive pressures from their local labor markets will be limited." [250] In contrast to what conventional theory would argue, mobility of transferable skills is only a potential. Job tenure can be high and turnover low even where there are significant wage differences for comparable jobs among firms in the same region. Similarly, it cannot be expected that labor market pressures alone will reduce inter-country differences in internal pay and grading structures.

Framed in this manner, it is evident that the economic analysis of labor markets could benefit from collaborations with members of other disciplines as well as from cross-country comparisons.

Summary of

An Analytical Frame

by Chris Tilly and Charles Tilly

[Published in *Work Under Capitalism* (Boulder, CO: Westview Press, 1998).]

Existing theories of work and labor markets, whether neoclassical, institutionalist, or Marxist, generally err in one of two ways. Some theories opt for individualism, building their models on the analysis of the confrontation between a single employer and a single worker. This strategy is intellectually tidy but inhibits serious consideration of networks, organizations, culture, history, and collective action. Other theories that offer dense social analysis usually narrow their focus to small areas of inquiry, failing to match or challenge the broad theorizing offered by the individualist models.

The chapter summarized here, from a forthcoming historical and economic analysis of work under capitalism, seeks to establish the framework for a more adequate theory of work. Much of it is necessarily schematic, identifying the often-overlooked categories that should be central to a new understanding of the labor process and the labor market. It is a collaborative effort of an economist and a historian.[1]

What's the Problem?

A theory of work should begin by defining a set of key concepts that are needed to understand the role of social interactions. The transaction is the fundamental relationship that links the producer and recipient of use value. Transactions are organized through contracts, which may be formal or informal. Contracts, in turn, are bundled into roles, notably jobs but also including the roles involved in family membership.

Work contracts also compound into networks, such as markets and hierarchies. Organizations are bounded networks in which some agents have the power to act for the whole; industries are connected networks and organizations maintaining similar relations to upstream and downstream markets.

What happens within these categories? Producers and recipients of work-created value pursue objectives of quality, efficiency, and power. Contracts and networks embody various mechanisms to achieve these objectives. Among the most important of these mechanisms is the provision of incentives—coercion, compensation, and/or commitment—which play a central part in motivating work. These allow us to address the basic question: How does one person get useful effort from another?

Transactions, Contracts, and Networks

Every work transaction involves costs. In fact, "transaction costs constitute a major expense of doing business, challenge any suggestion that workers and employers strike Walrasian bargains based on perfect information, and largely explain why people settle so regularly for second-best solutions that happen to be ready at hand." (74) Every transaction involves some or all of the three types of incentives. The threat of harm (coercion), the offer of contingent payment (compensation), and the invocation of solidarity (commitment) are all means of ensuring that a transaction is carried out.

The question of incentives arises not only in capitalist labor markets, but also in the home, in the underground economy, and in precapitalist work settings. While capitalist labor markets superficially appear to rely solely on compensation, the real story is more complex. Whole departments of business schools are built on the premise that it takes more than a job description and a wage offer to motivate workers.

Like the transactions they incorporate, contracts have costs. Continuous surveillance of an employee is usually unaffordable, so employers rely on indirect controls and incentives, giving rise to intricate patterns of trust, implicit and explicit bargains, threats, espionage, and other responses. Contracts specify many but not all possible contingencies. Trust is an essential part of most contracts, though to greatly varying extents. Contracts often link more than two individuals, and may place a single individual in differing roles—a teacher relates to the school principal and to the pupils in the classroom in opposite ways.

Economic activity is embedded in extensive networks of many types. Most modern production processes depend on extensive networks of suppliers, distributors, and customers. Less obvious, but also of central importance, are the nonproduction networks of friendship, kinship, religion, ethnicity, class, education, and so on, which organize social interactions. These social networks often define what is possible in the realm of economic organization. For example, it is extremely common for people to learn about job openings from friends and associates. Ethnic groups and close-knit families often mobilize the capital needed to start small enterprises. More generally, nonwork networks often define or constrain people's choices about whom to contract with, and what kinds of contracts to form.

Social networks tend to be segregated by gender, race, ethnicity, age, schooling, and neighborhood. Thus recruitment of employees through such networks tends to perpetuate job segregation, especially when high-status and low-status jobs are filled through different networks. Recruitment following conventional boundaries comes to seem natural to people on both sides of the boundary, giving rise to myths about innate differences among categories of people and reproducing traditional prejudices.

Objectives, Incentives, and Mechanisms

The recipients of value in work transactions (often, but not always, employers) have three main objectives, or standards for judging the performance of producers: quality, efficiency, and power. The weight of these objectives varies according to the job being performed. A symphony musician is judged almost entirely on quality of output. A fast-food worker is evaluated almost entirely on efficiency. For a domestic servant, power—the employer's ability to elicit work in response to relatively small incentives—typically matters most. Existing theories of work often go wrong in assuming that one of these objectives has absolute priority in production. Neoclassical economics accords priority to static efficiency, while Marxist theories often make power the predominant factor.

The incentives of commitment, compensation, and coercion are, as noted above, used to achieve the objectives of work contracts. To some extent, the choice of incentives mirrors the choice of objectives. Commitment is particularly used to elicit quality, compensation to support efficiency, and coercion to buttress power. However, many jobs combine two or three objectives, and likewise many contracts rely on two or three incentives.

Even if each of the three incentives is reduced to a dichotomy of present or absent (rather than a more realistically complex, continuous variable), there are eight possible incentive systems. Examples range from military command, combining commitment, compensation, and coercion, to scavenging, which involves none of the three. Work in (civilian) bureaucratic organizations involves a combination of commitment and compensation, though not usually coercion. "Capitalism stands out from other economic systems for its stress not only on compensation relative to commitment and coercion, but also on fungible forms of compensation: money and similar rewards that easily convert into other goods." (87)

While incentives are central to the design of work contracts, other mechanisms also shape the work process. Work is embedded in cultural and institutional contexts, which may limit, for example, what can be paid and what can be asked of workers. Any particular job is characterized by a pattern of contracting, a level of autonomy, and a degree of time discipline that constrain the nature of work to be performed. Over time, the systems of matching workers to particular jobs, allowing mobility of workers between jobs, and providing training for more advanced or desirable skills will determine the "laws of motion" of the employment system.

Although the choices and dimensions of variation may seem endless, there are in fact strict limits on the sets of mechanisms that are functionally compatible with each other. Only a few of the countless imaginable arrangements actually occur. Given the conflicting objectives of the parties to work contracts, some form of bargaining over the outcomes is common. Employers generally have more power than workers, but do not wield anything like absolute power. Thus systems of work often rest on compromises established through a process of conflict and contention.

The remainder of the book spells out these themes in greater detail and specificity, in historical case studies of the evolution of the cotton textile, coal mining, and health care industries in the United States and Britain.

Note

1. In addition to many relevant works written by each of the authors individually, there is one other joint publication that presents some of the themes covered here, with far more historical detail: Chris Tilly and Charles Tilly, "Capitalist Work and Labor Markets," in eds. Neil J. Smelser and Richard Swedberg, *The Handbook of Economic Sociology* (Princeton University Press and Russell Sage Foundation, 1995), 283–312.

PART III

Globalization and Labor

Overview Essay

by Frank Ackerman

Two trends have reshaped the nature and location of work over the course of the last few decades. One trend is often called "globalization." The world economy has become increasingly integrated. Rising levels of trade, foreign investment, and migration are connecting national economies to each other. In particular, many developing countries are rapidly expanding their manufacturing production and exports. At the same time, there has been a disturbing trend in developed countries of declines in manufacturing employment, often accompanied by stagnant or falling real wages, leading to increasingly bleak job prospects for workers with limited skills.

Is there a causal relationship between these two trends, or just the coincidence of simultaneous appearance? Is globalization responsible for the plight of industrial workers in developed countries, or should we be looking for a different culprit? In the words of the title of one of the articles in Part III, if we listen to jobs leaving for lower-wage destinations abroad, do we hear a giant sucking sound or a small hiccup? The questions are not rhetorical, and the answers are not obvious. There are strongly held, carefully argued and documented positions on both sides.

This part begins with six articles drawn from the lively debate over the effects of trade on wages and employment levels in developed countries. It then turns to four articles examining the impacts of globalization on particular aspects of work and concludes with two articles on policy responses to the problems of the global economy.

Trade, Technology, and Measurement

The first problem is to explain why there is a debate at all. Casual observation suggests that the giant sucking sound of jobs heading south is unmistakably audible. There is ample anecdotal evidence that some factories do indeed move to Mexico, Southeast Asia, or elsewhere in pursuit of cheaper labor. Moreover, conventional economic theory implies that (under the usual, unrealistic textbook assumptions) free trade would lead rich countries to specialize in capital- and skill-intensive products, while poor countries would specialize in unskilled-labor-intensive products. As a result, wages would rise for skilled workers in rich countries and for unskilled workers in poor countries. In this simple model, employment and wages for unskilled labor in rich countries should fall, just as has happened in recent years.

There are economists who would agree with the casual observer, although they appear to be in the minority among economists who have examined the question. One of the most prominent members of this minority is Adrian Wood, who presents his analysis of the effects of trade, and responds to critics of his earlier work, in the first article in Part III. Wood maintains that declining barriers to trade, due to technological change and declining costs in transportation and communication, have led to increased international specialization, as predicted by simple trade models. Several types of evidence are consistent with this view. Among developed countries, there is a clear, negative correlation between changes in the share of employment in manufacturing and manufactured imports from developing countries as a percentage of GDP. Within the United States, declines in output have been most rapid in the industries that are most reliant on unskilled labor.

Wood identifies several important factors that are omitted from simple statistical comparisons, all of which suggest a greater role for trade in reducing the demand for unskilled labor in developed countries. Some of the most labor-intensive industrial processes, such as assembly of electronic consumer goods, have almost entirely moved to developing countries; thus analysis of developed-country employment tends to overlook the labor content of these processes. Competition from low-wage producers has led to "defensive innovation," introducing technology that reduces the demand for unskilled labor in high-wage countries. (This point reveals the difficulty of separating the effects of trade and technology. In practice, it will be almost impossible to distinguish between defensive innovation and technical change unrelated to trade.) Labor-intensive services such as data entry are increasingly performed in developing countries, but do not show up in studies restricted to manufacturing. Wood's admittedly rough estimate is that, as of 1990, trade with developing countries reduced the demand for unskilled labor in developed countries as a whole by about 20 percent.

Nonetheless, as suggested by Wood's detailed responses to his numerous critics, his is not the majority position among economists.[1] An influential version of the majority view is presented here in the article by Robert Lawrence and Matthew Slaughter. There is no doubt about their answer to the question posed in their title. They find that, if we listen carefully, we hear only a small hiccup. To demonstrate this, they introduce a numerical comparison that at first glance seems almost unrelated: a recalculation of the relationship between employee compensation and productivity in the United States in the 1980s. This calculation is relevant because, in an idealized competitive market, hourly wages and labor productivity should increase at the same rate. Lawrence and Slaughter view the apparently wide gap between productivity and wage growth in the 1980s as potentially strong evidence that some external factor, such as trade, was depressing wages. However, they show that with a surprising but sensible-sounding recalculation of the data on employee compensation, the gap all but disappears. The absence of a gap between compensation and productivity implies the absence of a trade effect on wages.

For these authors, other data also point in the same direction. Most U.S. manufactured imports come from other high-wage countries. The U.S. terms of trade (ratio of export to import prices) did not fall, as they should have if cheap imports were an important factor; the union/nonunion pay differential barely changed (suggesting that unionized industry was not uniquely impacted by trade). Far more important, in their analysis, is the very slow growth of productivity in the areas where most workers are employed—that is, outside of manufacturing. This slow productivity growth would be expected to cause slow real wage growth, which is of course what happened. While the problem is serious, Lawrence and Slaughter conclude that it must be understood in terms of technological change, or the lack thereof, in nonmanufacturing, largely nontraded, sectors of the economy.

The disagreement between Wood on the one hand and Lawrence and Slaughter on the other has a parallel among those economists who have been advisors and educators for the labor movement—though the majority, within this circle, may be on the side that sees a larger effect of trade. Dale Belman and Thea Lee offer a thoughtful review of the literature, arguing that the impacts of trade are among the most important problems facing labor. They cite a number of studies finding substantial industrial job losses due to trade, and intriguing preliminary evidence that the employment impact of any given amount of trade may be increasing over time. Employment effects look larger than wage effects, they suggest, in part because the loss of low-wage jobs indirectly raises the average wage of those who remain employed. Responding to Lawrence and Slaughter's recalculation of the relationship between wages and productivity, Belman and Lee accept the underlying idea but not the specific data series used in that recalculation. Other data series embodying the same concepts show that there is a large gap between wage and productivity growth rates, demonstrating that there is potentially a "trade effect" to be explained.

Belman and Lee stress the use by employers of the threat of moving overseas as a means to win concessions from workers, even when no actual movement of jobs occurs. While trade may lower average wages, the evidence as they see it is stronger for trade as a cause of growing inequality of wages within the U.S. labor force. There is no need to argue about whether trade is the leading cause of the problems of industrial labor in developed countries. For Belman and Lee it is enough that trade is one of the very important problems, with clear, measurable effects.

An opposite perspective, equally written from the point of view of labor, is provided by the late David Gordon in his last book. He maintains that simple stories about both technology and trade are inadequate to explain the discouraging trends in wages and employment. Rather, the trends reflect corporate behavior and strategy, as suggested by Gordon's book title, *Fat and Mean*. In the chapter summarized here, he argues that technology leading to a skills mismatch between jobs and workers is not an adequate explanation of recent trends. Economists frequently treat technology as a residual, accounting for all unexplained effects, an approach that is prone to ambiguity and overstatement. Direct measurements of technological change have a hard time accounting for changes in wages and employment—for example, the collapse in real hourly earnings began a decade before computerization became a significant factor in the workplace.

Regarding globalization, Gordon emphasizes, as do Lawrence and Slaughter, that the decline in wages was slower in manufacturing than in many nonmanufacturing sectors that are largely unaffected by trade. Moreover, most of the U.S. trade deficit in manufactured goods is with other developed countries, including Japan and Western Europe, where manufacturing wages are at least as high as in the United States. Imports from countries with equally high or higher wages suggest that the problem lies in other factors, such as the productivity of U.S. manufacturing.

The last article included here on the trade debate presents a somewhat different perspective. Moving beyond the debate on the aggregate impacts of trade, Dani Rodrik suggests that trade has increased the elasticity of demand for unskilled labor. Due to global competition the same change in wages now leads to a larger change in employment than before, since it has become easier to substitute foreign labor for domestic. A strength of this analysis is that it applies to trade between developed countries as well as with lower-wage competitors. If two countries with equal wages open their economies to trade with each other, there is no reduction in the demand for unskilled labor, but there is a new barrier to wage increases in one country if they are not matched in the other country. Skilled labor, often performing more differentiated tasks, is subject to the same effect to a much smaller extent. Greater elasticity of labor demand leads not only to a weakened bargaining position for unions, but also to greater volatility of employment levels. Volatility of employment has increased, particularly for the least-skilled workers, and is a major contributor to the growing inequality of incomes.

While the debate is interesting and illuminating, it is difficult to come to a decisive yes-or-no resolution. There is a strong case for trade effects as one of the important causes of the declining prospects for low-skilled labor in developed countries, but also a strong case for the view that other effects must be of equal or greater importance. Perhaps the most surprising conclusion is the difficulty of precisely defining and measuring the effects of trade, and the extent to which the evaluation of these effects rests on a series of subtle technical judgments. The difference between a giant sucking sound and a small hiccup, unfortunately, depends on exactly how you listen.

Grappling with Globalization

The effects of globalization on work can also be examined on a more detailed, specific level. Even among the developed countries there is a broad diversity of impacts and responses. Much of the discussion so far has drawn on U.S. data, or on international comparisons that inevitably exclude most country-specific experiences. As a general rule, the smaller a country is, the more it tends to be dependent on foreign trade. Small developed countries have always had to cope with "globalization," evolving varied strategies for integrating trade and employment policies.[2]

Among developed countries, Japan has a unique system of labor relations in many ways. Until the 1990s, Japan also had a consistently rapid rate of growth, leading to frequent suggestions by foreign observers that copying the Japanese model was a key to growth. Admiration for Japan's success intensified in the 1980s, as other developed countries entered a period of slow growth, rising unemployment, and stagnant or declining wages.[3] However, when the speculative "bubble" of 1988–90 burst, Japan entered an economic slump of its own. The worldwide slowdown now merely seems to have arrived a decade later in Japan than elsewhere.

The article by James Lincoln and Yoshifumi Nakata, summarized here, is one of the first academic analyses of the impact of the stagnation of the 1990s on the Japanese employment system. The legitimacy of traditional practices remains a powerful force, and corporations have gone to considerable effort to bend rather than break the precedents set in more expansive times. The famous system of permanent employment was available, even in good times, only to roughly one-third of the labor force, largely the male employees of big companies. Now it is being constrained, though not abandoned, through increased hiring of temporary workers, pressure to accept early retirement, transfer of permanent employees to less prestigious, lower-paying jobs with subsidiaries and suppliers, and a gradual shift from salary increases based almost entirely on seniority toward monetary rewards for merit, performance, and technical skills. The authors emphasize, though, that the changes have thus far been only incremental, and that Japanese employment practices remain distinctively shaped by the country's traditional institutions.

Low-skill, labor-intensive industries in developed countries are down but not out. The surviving firms in such industries have somehow found ways to cope with low-wage foreign competitors. This is where the grim image of a "race to the bottom" arises, as the poorest nations seem to force everyone else's wages down to their level. The article by Evelyn Blumenberg and Paul Ong looks at the U.S. apparel industry in three regions: New York, North Carolina, and Southern California. Nationally, the industry suffered both job losses and real wage declines after 1970, as foreign competition intensified. In each of the three regions the industry responded by shifting its employment to a lower-status, lower-wage demographic group: recent immigrants, particularly from China, in New York, black women in the South, and Hispanic and Asian immigrants in California. Even after moving down the demographic ladder, the industry appears to be thriving only in California. In all areas, its short-run survival seems to rest on the introduction of what the authors call "Third World working conditions."

A more direct analysis of Third World working conditions is the subject of the next two articles. Lourdes Benería assesses the effects of globalization on women's work roles around the world. Although the expansion of multinational capital has begun to transform women's work and depends on women workers, Benería points out that only a tiny fraction of the female labor force in developing countries actually works for international firms. More often, women remain employed in agriculture, services, or other activities in the informal sector, frequently outside the world of wage labor. Those who do work in the modern sector in expanding economies are valued not only for their lower wages, but also because they are thought to be more easily controlled and more willing to accept varying or irregular hours of employment. The view that women have "nimble little fingers" is significant in hiring for some kinds of assembly work. While work in the modern sector brings economic opportunities to some, global integration has also brought the extraordinary exploitation of sex-related tourism, a shameful growth industry that employs large numbers of poor women in several countries. There is no single meaning of global integration for women. Age-old inequalities are likely to persist in new forms unless there is a conscious effort to change them.

The effects of the global economy on work in developing countries differs from one region to another; many aspects of the problem must be examined at the regional, if not national, level.[4] Hernando Gómez-Buendía offers a unique perspective on the long-standing dualism of leading Latin American economies and its implications for employment relations. A small modern sector has emerged, with, in theory, nearly European conditions of employment, benefits, and legal protection. The basis for this modern sector is the early strength of the region's export industries, followed by a period of import substituting industrialization. Unionization of these industries, combined with populist traditions and Catholic social influence, led to outstanding labor-oriented legislation. Yet modernization did not continue to expand. In reality, Latin American nations cannot afford to extend their ambitious labor and social legislation to a majority of workers. The large informal sector continues as a labor market buffer. Workers forced out of formal employment are more likely to end up in the informal sector than in the small pool of the formally unemployed. Gómez ends with an impassioned advocacy of the development of new public policies that will lead to meaningful formal employment for all who want it.

Racing Back from the Bottom: Policy Responses

In view of the diversity of experience and impacts of globalization, the near-impossibility of national control of international trends, and the apparent pressure to engage in a race to the bottom, what can be accomplished by public policy responses? The simplest response, protective tariffs or quotas as barriers against trade, receives almost no support among economists, at least as a policy for use in developed countries (and even its use in poor countries has become controversial, as earlier import substitution strategies have generally been abandoned). What else, then, is possible? At least two answers have been suggested, which are the subjects of the last two articles in Part III.

Debate about trade policy and labor has often focused on the possibility of imposing international labor standards. Is it reasonable to demand that all countries meet certain minimum standards in terms of working conditions? If so, how high should the standards be? Should developed countries refuse to import goods from nations that fail to meet the standards? The dilemma is that, as Alice Amsden has explained,[5] too high a standard—for instance, demanding that a country like Mexico adopt U.S. minimum wage, child labor, and hours-of-work standards within ten years—is unaffordable, and amounts to little more than a new form of protectionism. Yet no standards, or too low a level, may mean that none of the world's workers, North or South, are assured of prospering from globalization.

In the article summarized here, Eddy Lee reviews the recent literature on labor standards, finding a frustratingly wide range of conflicting views. While there is essentially universal agreement with the goals of labor standards in areas such as limits on child labor, protection of worker health and safety, and other social goals, there is no such uniformity in the economic analysis of potential standards. The effects and the desirability of the unilateral imposition of standards continue to be debated. Some argue for the moral imperative of standards, while others emphasize the economic gains from free trade. One view proposes that labor standards are a form of public good, which everyone wants but no one can afford to introduce alone. Others would say that standards are a suboptimal interference with the market, and that economic growth will eventually raise standards more effectively than any public intervention.

Despite hopes for concerted international action, public policy will largely continue to be made on a national basis for the foreseeable future. What, then, can a single country do about the pressures of trade? For our final article, we return to the author whose work opened this part. Adrian Wood, who argues that trade does hurt unskilled labor in developed countries, nonetheless rejects protectionist policies and offers a range of alternative suggestions. Wood proposes a combination of education and training programs, measures to increase the demand for unskilled labor (either public works spending or taxes and subsidies to stimulate private sector employment) and redistribution of income to provide for those hardest hit by trade. He addresses the difficult problems of financing these initiatives, recognizing the danger of creating perverse incentives: Making it too attractive could stimulate an increased supply of unskilled labor. Differing labor market conditions in America and Europe call for somewhat different policy approaches.

Wood's final point focuses on the human impact of these policies, and provides a fitting note on which to end the discussion. As shown in the articles summarized earlier in Part III, there is considerable uncertainty about the magnitude of the future impacts of trade on labor. In terms of the policy responses Wood proposes, there is a danger of doing too much if the problem turns out to be small, and an opposite danger of doing too little if the problem turns out to be large. The human costs of providing too much education and training, job creation, and income support seem far less serious than the costs of providing too little.

Notes

1. In addition to the Lawrence and Slaughter article summarized here, other statements of the majority view include Richard Freeman, "Are your wages set in Beijing?" *Journal of Economic Perspectives* 9, 3 (Summer 1995), 15–32; Jagdish Bhagwati and Marvin Kosters, eds., *Trade and Wages: Leveling Wages Down?* (Washington, D.C.: AEI Press, 1995); and Paul Krugman, "Does Third World growth hurt First World prosperity?" *Harvard Business Review* July–August 1994, 113–121.

2. For a comparison of two very different trade policies, each of which allowed a small developed country to sustain full employment for several decades, see Deborah Mabbett, *Trade, Employment, and Welfare: A Comparative Study of Trade and Labour Market Policies in Sweden and New Zealand, 1880–1980* (New York: Oxford University Press, 1995).

3. One of the best analyses from this era, including an extensive analysis of the Japanese employment system and review of other literature on the subject, is William Lazonick, "Cooperative employment relations and Japanese economic growth," in *Capital, the*

State, and Labour: A Global Perspective, eds. Juliet Schor and Jong-Il You (Aldershot, U.K.; Brookfield, VT: Edward Elgar/United Nations University Press, 1993).

4. For an ambitious attempt at broad regional analyses, see Robert Boyer, "Do labor institutions matter for economic development? A "regulation" approach for the OECD and Latin America with an extension to Asia," in *Workers, Institutions, and Economic Growth in Asia,* ed. Gerry Rodgers (Geneva: International Institute for Labour Studies, 1992).

5. Alice Amsden, "Macro-sweating policies and labour standards," in Werner Sengenbrenner and Duncan Campbell, *International Labour Standards and Economic Interdependence* (Geneva: International Institute for Labor Studies, 1993).

Summary of

How Trade Hurt Unskilled Workers

by Adrian Wood

[Published in *Journal of Economic Perspectives* 9, 3 (Summer 1995), 57–80.]

Adrian Wood's 1994 book (see the summary of his conclusions and policy recommendations, later in Part III) forcefully stated the case that "the main cause of the deteriorating situation of unskilled workers in developed countries has been expansion of trade with developing countries." [57] In this article he summarizes the theory and evidence supporting his position, responds to criticisms of his work, and critiques the leading alternative explanations.

The starting point for the discussion is the recognition that the demand for unskilled labor has fallen substantially in developed countries, leading to increased wage inequality and/or unemployment. Manufacturing employment has fallen faster than previous trends would have predicted. At the same time, imports of low-skill-intensive manufactures from developing countries have increased, as has the diffusion of computers and related technology into the workplace. Thus many empirical studies have evaluated the role of trade versus technology, usually finding that trade makes only a small contribution, and so concluding by default that technology must be much more important. In contrast, this article argues that trade effects are quite large, and that the effects of technology are inseparable from the recent patterns of trade.

Theoretical Framework

Economic theory conventionally asserts that countries export goods that intensively utilize those factors of production that are relatively abundant, and import goods that utilize those factors that are relatively scarce at home. If the mix of factors is sufficiently different from one country to another, each country will specialize—for example, developed countries producing only those manufactures that have high skill requirements, and developing countries producing only manufactures with low skill requirements.

The huge growth in trade over the last few decades can be seen as leading developed countries toward such specialization. As advances in transportation and communication have lowered the cost of trade, many of the most unskilled-labor-intensive manufacturing processes, such as final assembly of consumer electronics, have moved entirely to developing countries. This is one of several ways in which trade and technology are intertwined—new transport and communications technologies have effectively lowered the barriers to trade.

A Review of the Evidence

Empirical evidence clearly suggests a link between trade and labor market changes. Among OECD (developed) countries, there is a strong negative correlation between the change from 1970 to 1990 in net manufacturing imports from developing countries, as a percentage of GDP, and the change in the percentage of the labor force in manufacturing. The change in imports is quite small. Both the OECD average and the U.S. figure are around 1 percent of GDP over the 20-year period. However, there is a disproportionately large impact on unskilled labor, because the imports depress the prices of labor-intensive goods and force firms to find ways of using less labor in order to stay competitive. Moreover, since the imports displace labor-intensive production, they directly affect more workers than their share of GDP would suggest.

A common method of estimating the effect of trade on labor is to calculate its factor content—that is, the amount of labor used to produce the country's exports, and the amount that would have been used to produce its imports in the absence of trade. A study of the factor content of U.S. trade by Jeffrey Sachs and Howard Shatz[1] found that the increase in trade from 1978 to 1990 did reduce the domestic demand for labor, but had only slightly greater effects on unskilled than on skilled labor. This study, like most published studies of factor content, errs in assuming that the labor content of imports is similar to that of goods currently produced in developed countries. Since many imports are actually more labor-intensive than goods currently produced in developed countries, the true effect is much larger. With this and other technical changes, a revised factor content analysis shows that trade from 1978 to 1990 barely changed the demand for skilled labor, but caused a large drop in the demand for unskilled labor.

Furthermore, trade leads to "defensive innovation," in which firms threatened by imports adopt new technologies that hopefully allow them to remain competitive—typically involving a reduction in the demand for unskilled labor.

This is another way in which trade and technology cannot be separated. While most empirical studies focus exclusively on manufactures, trade in services is also growing, with labor-intensive activities such as data entry increasingly moving to low-wage countries.

An admittedly rough estimate incorporating all of these factors is that as of 1990, trade lowered the overall developed-country demand for unskilled labor, relative to skilled labor, by about 20 percent.

Response to Critics

Four major criticisms of the author's position merit special attention. First, Sachs and Shatz found that, contrary to expectations, the industrial sectors that began the 1980s with low skill intensity had a slightly smaller than average increase in skill levels during the decade. This is a surprising result that requires further study, but it is a very indirect test of the theory.

Second, the calculation of large trade impacts assumes that currently imported goods would have been produced and sold domestically in the absence of trade. However, in that case the prices would have been higher, since developed-country labor is paid more. If the price elasticities are high enough (the higher prices would have deterred enough customers from buying), there is no possibility of domestic production even in the absence of trade. The author has defended his price elasticity estimates in his 1994 book. He believes that there is a general tendency for elasticities to be overestimated.

Third, even the estimated 20 percent reduction in demand for unskilled labor might not be enough to explain the observed changes in labor markets. There was apparently a preexisting downward trend in the relative demand for unskilled labor, [70] which may exist because increases in the supply of skilled labor create additional needs or opportunities to employ even more skilled labor. "But whatever the cause of the secular demand shift, it has been amplified by recent changes in trade. . . ." [71]

Finally, a series of technical objections have been raised against the use of factor content calculations, and are answered by the author. Perhaps the most serious objection is that, in Heckscher–Ohlin trade theory, trade affects wages only through product prices; therefore prices should provide a more direct test of the theory. Answering this requires a look at price data.

Evidence on Prices and Skill Intensity

If trade has reduced the wages of unskilled workers, then according to Heckscher–Ohlin theory, it must have reduced the relative prices of labor-intensive goods. Lawrence and Slaughter (see article summarized in Part III) find that this did not occur for the United States, Japan, or Germany in the 1980s.

However, they use an unusual and intricate method of calculation. Sachs and Shatz reanalyze the U.S. data and find that prices fell slightly for the least skill-intensive products relative to the most skill-intensive ones—though, in the opinion of Sachs and Shatz, the decline appeared too small to explain the change in wages. This is not a serious problem: The changes in wages would be expected to be much larger than the changes in prices. Additional puzzling results in other authors' analyses suggest that products within individual industrial sectors are becoming more heterogeneous over time, making studies of prices at the sectoral level less appropriate in testing the underlying theory.

A last category of evidence, which several economists use to support the technology explanation over the trade explanation, is the rising proportion of skilled workers within most sectors, despite the rise in their relative wages. This certainly implies that the demand for labor has shifted, possibly due to technical change biased against unskilled labor. However, this does not mean that trade is absent from the picture. Studies of U.S. manufacturing, analyzing as many as 400 detailed sectors, find a high, positive correlation between increases in import penetration and the rise in skill intensity during the 1980s. Other studies find a positive relationship between exporting and increasing skill levels. At the very least, technology is advancing most rapidly in the sectors most affected by trade. Studies of direct expenditure on new technology are ambiguous and cannot distinguish whether technology is a cause or an effect of other changes.

> Where does all this leave the 'trade versus technology' debate? It seems certain that new technology contributed to the recent deterioration in the relative economic position of unskilled workers—as a background trend, as a cause of lower trade barriers, and as a response to foreign competition. The key question, though, is whether spontaneous diffusion of computers and new management methods would have reduced unskilled workers to anything like their current plight [in the absence of imports from developing countries]. . . . The answer to this question, on the basis of the evidence now available, appears to me to be 'probably not.' [77]

For the author's concluding suggestions about policy responses, see the other summary of his work in Part III.

Note

1. Jeffrey D. Sachs and Howard J. Shatz, "Trade and Jobs in U.S. Manufacturing," *Brookings Papers on Economic Activity* 1 (1994), 1–84.

Summary of

International Trade and American Wages in the 1980s: Giant Sucking Sound or Small Hiccup?

by Robert Z. Lawrence and Matthew Slaughter

[Published in *Brookings Papers on Economic Activity* 2 (1993), 161–210.]

In the 1980s, average wages in the United States (as conventionally measured) stopped growing and actually declined, while earnings inequalities related to skills and education increased dramatically. At the same time, the volume of international trade was expanding rapidly. It is scarcely surprising that many observers blamed wage stagnation and inequality on trade. In Ross Perot's memorable phrase, under the North American Free Trade Agreement we would expect to hear "a giant sucking sound" of wages and jobs being siphoned off to Mexico. This study analyzes the data on the effects of international trade on American wages, finding that trade played only a relatively small role in the changes of the 1980s. More important, the authors find, were the slowdown of productivity growth in services and the patterns of technological change.

Average Wages

Economic theory suggests that in a competitive labor market, workers' compensation should grow at the same rate as output. However, from 1979 to 1991 output per worker grew by 10.5 percent, far faster than the reported growth in hourly earnings. Did trade pressure hold the growth of wages below productivity increases? There is little evidence for this. Rather, it turns out that labor compensation, appropriately measured, actually did keep up with productivity.

Three different statistics can be used to measure average wages or labor compensation. The most common figure, average real hourly earnings of production workers, declined by almost 11 percent between 1979 and 1991. A second measure, average real hourly compensation in the business sector, increased by 1.5 percent in the same period. These two series differ because business sector compensation includes nonproduction workers and self-employed people. It also includes fringe benefits, while the common hourly earnings series covers only the wages of production workers. From the point of view of economic theory, it is total labor cost, or compensation, not wages alone, that should affect employers' demand for labor.

The gap between output and compensation growth disappears if a third, less common measure of compensation is used. Both output and compensation are expressed in real (inflation-adjusted) terms, but different price indexes are typically used for the two adjustments. Output is deflated by an index of prices of goods produced in the U.S. business sector; compensation is deflated by the Consumer Price Index (CPI), measuring the price of goods consumed in the United States. Since about 1980, producer prices have risen more slowly than consumer prices.

Wages deflated by the CPI measure workers' real purchasing power. However, compensation deflated by producer prices is a better measure of the cost of labor to employers. The latter is the figure that should grow at the same rate as productivity—and, roughly speaking, it does. Hourly compensation deflated by producer prices grew by 9.5 percent from 1979 to 1991, very close to the growth in output per worker.

Producer and consumer prices have differed for two principal reasons, of about equal importance. First, producer prices include the prices of investment goods, which have fallen relative to consumption goods. Second, consumer prices include the cost of owner-occupied housing, which rose faster than most other prices in the 1980s. A third conceptual difference between the two price indexes, namely that consumer prices include the prices of imported goods, played almost no role in practice. The terms of trade (the ratio of export to import prices) moved slightly in favor of the United States during the 1980s—meaning that, for the same amount of resources, the United States could buy slightly more from abroad at the end of the decade than at the beginning.

Since compensation grew at about the same rate as output per worker, the slowdown in wage growth can be traced to a corresponding slowdown in productivity growth. Between 1979 and 1990, real output per hour in manufacturing grew 30.7 percent, while nonmanufacturing output per hour grew only 4.5 percent. Thus it is the near-stagnation in nonmanufacturing productivity that ultimately limited wage growth—not the more robust productivity growth in manufacturing, the sector most affected by international trade. Although there are many problems in the measurement of service sector productivity, it is noteworthy that before 1973 reported productivity growth was only slightly slower in services than in manufacturing.

Relative Wage Performance

During the 1980s, average pay in manufacturing rose faster for nonproduction workers than for production workers, reversing the trend of the previous 25 years. At the same time, almost all of the decade's employment growth in manufacturing consisted of nonproduction workers, largely managers and professionals. Thus demand for nonproduction workers must have increased substantially. Could this have resulted from international trade?

The standard theory of international trade leads to the Stolper–Samuelson theorem: an increase in the price of a product raises the return to factors used relatively intensively in its production, and lowers the return to factors used relatively sparsely. If international trade leads to the United States specializing in knowledge-intensive or high-technology industries, then the Stolper–Samuelson theorem would predict an increase in the relative wages of skilled, nonprofessional workers, a "factor" of production used heavily by those industries. However, the evidence for such specialization is not as obvious as it seems, since most U.S. manufactured imports come from developed countries with comparable levels of wages and technology.

If the Stolper–Samuelson mechanism is at work, then prices should have increased more rapidly in industries that make greater use of skilled, nonproduction labor. Such price increases would then allow the corresponding increase in wages. However, data on price changes in the 1980s by disaggregated industries (two-digit and three-digit Standard Industrial Classification (SIC) categories) show that price changes were nearly unrelated to the nonproduction-worker intensity of industry. If anything, there was a slight decline in the relative prices of nonproduction-labor-intensive goods.

On the other hand, technological progress was apparently concentrated in the skilled-labor-intensive industries. Again using disaggregated data, it can be shown that in the 1980s, productivity grew faster in these industries than in production-labor-intensive industries. This difference in productivity growth rates was much less pronounced in the 1960s and 1970s, suggesting that a new pattern of technological change emerged in the 1980s. It is possible, for example, that a new round of production-labor-saving technologies was introduced, or that the use of computers became an important source of productivity gains for the first time.

Qualifications and Conclusions

The simplest theories about the harmful effects of international trade on U.S. wages can be rejected. These theories would imply a noticeable improvement in the U.S. terms of trade (an increase in the ratio of U.S. export to import prices, due to cheap imports). In fact, the terms of trade barely rose in the 1980s, after declining in the 1970s.

More complex economic theories have examined the possibility of complete specialization of a country in one type of industry, combined with analysis of technological diffusion between countries. Such theories, while intricate, also lead to the wrong predictions for the 1980s. One such model, for example, predicts declining terms of trade, and labor compensation (deflated by producer prices) falling behind productivity growth, contrary to what actually happened.

Another hypothesis is that trade has been particularly harmful to unionized workers, by reducing either the number of unionized jobs or the wage premium earned by union members. However, the union/nonunion pay differential barely changed in the 1980s, and the decline in unionized jobs explains very little of the increase in inequality during the decade.

Much more important is the slowdown in nonmanufacturing productivity growth, and the emergence of new patterns of technological change, during the 1980s. Since rapid productivity increases continued in manufacturing, the result was that goods production absorbed a smaller share of spending, relative to services, and accounted for a smaller share of total employment. This reduced the demand for production workers (since they remain a much larger share of the labor force in manufacturing than in other sectors), and thus contributed to their declining wages.

In conclusion, "trade has not been the major contributor to the performance of U.S. average and relative wages in the 1980s." [208] The near-constancy of the U.S. terms of trade, the fact that compensation (deflated by producer prices) has kept up with productivity, and the absence of the price patterns predicted by the Stolper–Samuelson theorem all argue against theories that make trade a principal cause of wage and employment changes. The differential patterns of technological change, both within manufacturing and between manufacturing and services, are much more important than trade effects. "Finally, those who focus on real wage behavior without paying attention to productivity growth outside manufacturing are writing *Hamlet* without the Prince." [209]

Summary of

International Trade and the Performance of U.S. Labor Markets

by Dale Belman and Thea M. Lee

[Published in Robert A. Blecker, ed., *U.S. Trade Policy and Global Growth: New Directions in the International Economy* (Armonk, NY: M.E. Sharpe, 1992), 61–107.]

Since the 1970s, average real wages in the United States have stagnated or fallen, and there has been a widening gap between the earnings of college-educated workers and those with high school degrees or less. During the same time period, the U.S. economy has become progressively more open to international trade. Is there a connection between these two trends? And to what degree can increased trade be held responsible for declining wages and rising inequality? This article reviews the theoretical and empirical debates on the subject, finding that

the preponderance of evidence indicates that increased trade has had a negative effect on wages in manufacturing and has accelerated the decline in employment in this sector. The consequent movement of jobs out of manufacturing and into lower-wage service sectors has also contributed to the
declining average real wage in the U.S. economy as a whole. By eliminating
high-quality jobs for non-college-educated workers, this process has also ex-
acerbated wage inequality between the most and least educated workers. . . .
[63]

Patterns of Trade, Wages, and Inequality

By many measures, trade has been of growing importance. From 1960 to 1993
merchandise imports and exports combined rose from 6.7 percent to 16.5 percent of U.S. GDP. The merchandise trade deficit rose from $25.5 billion in
1980 to $132.5 billion in 1993. In the 1990s the United States has had a trade
deficit not only with Japan, but also with a number of newly industrializing
Asian and Latin American nations. In 1980 the U.S. had a trade surplus with
these newly industrializing countries.

Meanwhile, real hourly wages in the United States have been stagnant since
1973 and falling since 1977. Inequality rose as well: For example, there was a
decline in the percentage of the labor force earning between 125 and 300 percent of the poverty wage, while the percentages above and below those boundaries rose. In manufacturing, wages rose slightly, but employment fell from a
peak of 21 million in 1979 to 17.8 million in 1993—while service sector employment was rising rapidly. Manufacturing wages and employment are sensitive to an industry's place in trade patterns. Export industries paid an average of
$9.55 an hour in 1983, while import-competing industries paid $8.28 per
hour.

Trade Theory and Causation

The traditional Heckscher–Ohlin–Samuelson trade model predicts that both
countries involved in trade will benefit. However, it does not claim that every
individual in the countries will be better off. In fact, the related Stolper–
Samuelson theorem predicts that where there are two factors of production
(such as capital and labor), the owners of the relatively scarce factor will be
made worse off by a reduction in trade barriers, while the owners of the abundant factor will be made better off. This change takes place because the scarce
factor becomes more abundant due to expanded trade.

The United States is relatively scarce in labor and abundant in capital, so the
Stolper–Samuelson theorem would predict losses to labor and gains to capital.

If the model is expanded to encompass three sectors, with labor divided into skilled and relatively unskilled groups, the model implies that the wages of the more skilled will rise while those of the less skilled will fall.

Another aspect of conventional trade economics, "factor price equalization" theory, asserts that if trade barriers are eliminated, commodity prices will be equalized across nations, leading to equalization of "factor" prices—meaning that wages in industrialized countries and those in low-income countries will converge. However, for the theory to hold, several stringent conditions must be met: Each country must produce each commodity involved in trade, with constant returns to scale, using the same technology and quality of inputs in each country, and both labor and capital must be able to move freely between countries. In practice, it is unlikely that all these conditions will be met entirely. But as trade and investment barriers fall the world may be moving closer to fulfilling the conditions for factor price equalization.

Trade can also affect wages and employment through a variety of other channels that are difficult to capture within formal economic models. Workers may be threatened with outsourcing or runaway shops if they do not accept pay cuts. This is not an idle threat. The movement of jobs to low-wage countries may be accelerated by lower trade barriers. Movement within the United States has an effect as well, since manufacturing industries are more likely to be oligopolies with higher profits, and higher wage and benefit levels, than service industries. If manufacturing workers are displaced by trade and are forced to switch to lower-wage service industries, the economywide average wage can fall—even if wages in each industry remain unchanged. However, it is a mistake to look solely at wage effects. Standard trade models assume full employment, and therefore show all trade impacts as movements in prices and wages. In reality, prices and wages are not completely flexible, so some of the effects of trade will be felt in lower employment.

Empirical Studies of Trade and Labor Markets

A number of researchers have tried to estimate the effects of trade on manufacturing. One study found that the 1987 trade deficit was associated with the loss of 5.1 million jobs, of which 3.1 million were in manufacturing. Another study estimated that the increase in the U.S. trade deficit in manufactured goods between 1978 and 1990 reduced employment of manufacturing production workers by 6.5 percent. A third found that a 10 percent rise in imports reduces wages within an industry by 0.0 to 0.64 percent and employment by 5 to 6 percent. [Citations to these and many other studies can be found in the original article.] There is some evidence, though it is still preliminary, that the effects of trade on U.S. wages and employment are growing more severe over time; that is, the same level of imports may have had more effect on U.S. industry in the 1990s than in the 1970s.

Theory predicts that trade will have its greatest negative effects in industries that require lower levels of skill and pay relatively low wages, and where the international differences in wages of workers are greatest. Consistent with this theory, from 1978 to 1990 U.S. trade deficits with developing countries were largest in those industries with the highest proportions of low-skilled workers.

Empirical studies consistently find that employment effects are larger than wage effects. But the lack of large wage effects could reflect a statistical quirk. If imports greatly reduce employment in low-productivity, low-wage U.S. industries, while the wages of the surviving employees remain unchanged, the change in the mix of high-wage and low-wage jobs could tend to increase the overall average wage. This effect might offset the tendency of trade to lower manufacturing wages in general.

The debate about the effect of trade on wages usually begins with an agreement that average real wages have stagnated in the United States—despite sharp disagreement about the role of trade in causing that stagnation. However, Lawrence and Slaughter (see summary in Part III) argue that when changes in real wages are properly measured, they have changed at about the same rate as productivity, so that there is no "trade" effect to be explained. Standard measures suggest a gap between the growth of productivity and wages of 21 percent for the period 1979 to 1991. Lawrence and Slaughter show that, if total compensation (including benefits) is used instead of wages and the GDP deflator (reflecting the prices received by industry) is used instead of the consumer price index, then the gap between productivity growth and compensation growth is less than 1 percent for the 12-year period.

Several corrections should be made to Lawrence and Slaughter's corrections of the data. The figures they use for total compensation rise quite rapidly, perhaps because of the inclusion of self-employment income and managerial salaries. A Bureau of Labor Statistics employment cost index (which includes benefits) should be used instead. The appropriate price series to use, to reflect prices received by industry, is the price deflator for final products. With these further corrections, there is a 17 percent gap between productivity and wage growth from 1979 to 1991, almost as great as the "naive" gap before any recalculations.

In addition to aggregate effects, trade may change the wages of some portions of the labor force relative to others. One estimate is that trade explains between 8 and 15 percent of the increase in inequality between high school and college graduates during the 1980s. Trade and immigration combined may have accounted for about 40 percent of the relative decline in wages for high school dropouts in the same decade. A 1993 study found that falling relative prices of labor-intensive goods cause a small rise in the returns to capital, a large increase in the earnings of professional and technical labor, and a substantial fall in the wages of other workers.

If trade is not responsible for all of the recent changes in wages and employment, what else is involved? Technology is frequently invoked as an alternative explanation. Yet economists often estimate the effects of technology as a residual that cannot be explained by other factors. Such estimates actually reflect the effects of technology combined with anything else that economists have not measured correctly. Studies that use direct measures of the introduction of technology, or expenditures on new technology, often find little or no correlation with the wage and employment effects discussed here. A deeper problem is that trade and technological effects need not be separate, if trade accelerates the adoption of labor-saving technology.

Are trade effects small? With a big enough denominator, anything can be made to look small. Manufactured imports from developing countries are small as a percentage of U.S. GDP, but may still have noticeable effects on employment and wages in manufacturing. In this connection, it is important to remember that manufacturing has traditionally been a high-wage sector that is important in establishing expectations for wages throughout the economy. Several estimates find that trade accounts for between 10 and 20 percent of the increase in wage inequality in the 1980s, particularly lowering the wages and employment prospects of less-educated workers. Finally, it is not reasonable to simultaneously claim that trade is unimportant to wages and unemployment while arguing that barriers to trade are costing consumers tens of billions of dollars. If changes in trade are large enough to matter to consumers, they are also large enough to matter to workers.

Summary of

Skills Mismatch or Globalization?

by David Gordon

[Published in *Fat and Mean: The Corporate Squeeze of Working Americans and the Myth of Managerial "Downsizing"* (New York: Martin Kessler Books, The Free Press, 1996), 175–203.]

Most economists have emphasized one of two standard explanations of falling real wages and rising inequality—the "wage squeeze"—among U.S. workers today. Some attribute the problems to the changing skill requirements of the economy, creating a "skills mismatch" between labor supply and demand. Others see globalization as the cause of the problem, including both the growing competition from industry in low-wage developing countries, and immigration of relatively low-skilled workers from the same regions. The chapter summarized here argues that neither of these views comes close to a complete or adequate explanation of the wage squeeze. Other chapters of the book present the author's alternative explanation, in which "fat and mean" corporate management strategies are the principal cause of the problem.

The Skills Mismatch

In the most popular explanation of the wage squeeze, it is argued that low-skilled workers have suffered most acutely because they are out of step with the rising, technologically driven demand for high-skilled labor. The facts seem to support this view. Since the early 1980s, real earnings of those with the most education have increased, while real earnings of nearly everyone else have declined.

However, these figures only show that better educated workers fared better, not that a skills mismatch was responsible for the differential outcomes. The educational differential cannot be attributed to labor supply shifts, since the supply of highly educated workers is rising faster than the supply of those with less education. Changes in labor demand must therefore be responsible; yet identifying the demand-side effect has proved difficult. There have been important interindustry shifts in labor demand, but researchers have found that these are not responsible for increasing wage inequality. The changes in average wages have occurred within industries—not as a result of movement of labor from one industry to another.

At this point, many economists simply assume that technological change is the only plausible explanation for changes in earnings. Technology is often treated as a residual, accounting for everything about wages and productivity that cannot be explained more directly by other factors. In a study of the rise in earnings inequality, two economists said, referring to possible explanations of the problem, "The term 'technological change' comes to mind, but it only underscores our ignorance."[1] The claim that the unexplained residual represents the effects of technology is at best based on circumstantial evidence, at worst a tautological explanation.

There are at least four substantive problems with the skills mismatch argument. First is the problem of timing. Much of the collapse in low-skilled workers' earnings and employment had occurred by 1984, well before the widespread computerization of the workplace. "Were businesses so shrewd and prescient that they *anticipated* the coming trends in computerization and began dumping their lower-skilled workers, as it were, before the deluge?" [182–183] Wages for male college graduates, on the other hand, fared worse after the mid-1980s than before. Thus the timing makes it difficult to attribute the relative gains of the best-educated workers over the last few decades to a rise in computer use.

A second problem lies in the assumption that rising educational levels imply rising skill requirements on the job. More detailed examination of skill requirements suggests that they have grown steadily over the past thirty years or more, with no particular acceleration in recent years. Computerization in manufacturing appears to have had little effect on actual job requirements. Computerization in offices raises the skill levels needed for some jobs but lowers the skills needed for others.

A third problem is the absence of productivity gains in many sectors. Rapid technological change and an increase in the demand for skilled labor should result in rising productivity. Yet during the 1980s and early 1990s there was little productivity growth in nonmanufacturing sectors, despite the increasing educational level of the workforce.

Finally, the skills mismatch argument assumes that earnings are directly related to skills and educational levels. This has proved problematical both in general and in specific terms. In general, empirical studies find little or no correlation between skills and earnings for nonsupervisory, nonprofessional workers. More specifically, highly skilled occupations involved in the use of new technologies, such as computer operators and engineering technicians, have had only slow increases, or even decreases, in real earnings. Meanwhile, nontechnological professions such as lawyers have had rapid earnings gains.

Globalization

If technology didn't do it, perhaps globalization is the culprit. Imports have risen rapidly, while manufacturing employment has fallen, making the trade-and-wages argument seem plausible. Specific industries and communities have certainly suffered from trade competition. But as with the skills mismatch argument, the evidence here turns out to be largely circumstantial.

One concern is that trade largely affects manufacturing and other industries, such as mining, that produce tradeable goods. If import competition were the primary explanation of the wage squeeze, the problem should be more severe in manufacturing and mining than in other, nontradeable sectors. This is not the case. Between 1979 and 1994, real wages fell faster in construction, transportation and public utilities, and retail trade than in either manufacturing or mining.

Even in manufacturing it is important to distinguish between import competition caused by low foreign wages and other causes. In the early 1980s, a critical period of job losses and real wage declines, the value of the dollar was unusually (and unsustainably) high relative to other currencies. This made it unusually cheap for Americans to buy foreign goods, even those produced with labor paid as well as in the United States.

In fact, most manufactured imports do come from countries where labor is paid well. A majority of the U.S. trade deficit in manufactured goods is with Japan and Western Europe, where labor costs are slightly higher than in America, rather than with low-wage developing countries. "[I]f we want to understand the trade advantages that many other advanced countries have enjoyed, we should pay more attention to the sluggish pace of our productivity growth than to the levels of our workers' wages." [193]

Economists studying the effects of trade have estimated that between 1978 and 1990 the United States lost almost a million production worker jobs in manufacturing due to trade with developing countries. While this is a large absolute number, it is less than 1 percent of private nonfarm employment in 1990, and thus cannot account for much of the overall decline in real wages.

Other evidence of the importance of trade also appears problematical on closer inspection. Widely quoted estimates that trade accounts for 10 to 15 percent of the increased inequality of wages in the 1980s are based on a study that did not consider other possible explanations, such as the decline in unionization.

The much-discussed idea that transnational corporations are transferring their production facilities to low-wage countries has some local or anecdotal validity, but it is not a growing trend. During the 1980s, the amount of U.S. trade controlled by transnational corporations actually dropped, and their manufacturing employment in the United States and in foreign affiliates declined at the same rate. Moreover, most of their majority-owned affiliates are in developed, not developing, countries.

A final argument about globalization is that immigration of low-skilled foreign workers is driving down U.S. wages. The most influential study of the subject finds virtually no effect of immigration on the relative wages of college graduates versus high school graduates, but a sizeable effect on the wages of high school dropouts. Yet as in several of the other studies discussed here, this analysis assumes that there are direct links between education, skills, and earnings, and ignores other possible explanations such as the decline in union strength. Other discussion of the effects of immigration points out that immigrant-owned businesses and the additional purchasing power of immigrant households create about as many jobs as are taken by immigrant workers.

Veil the Corporations, Blame the Victims

Strong skepticism about both the skills mismatch and the globalization explanations could seem like nihilism. In explaining the wage squeeze, what else is there?

Both the skills mismatch and the globalization arguments rely on the assumption that markets work in a way that closely resembles the competitive models of traditional economic theory. Employers simply reflect and respond to market forces that compel, for example, payment of growing skill differentials or movement of production to low-wage countries. In this theory, corporate power is invisible, indeed even impossible to imagine. The problems of the market can then be blamed on individuals, who failed to become sufficiently educated and skilled, or who refused to compete hard enough to win the battle against foreign producers.

However, the world does not behave according to the competitive model. Our economy cannot be explained without reference to the exercise of corporate power. An older generation of institutionalist economists recognized this fact. Fortunately, the awareness of institutional factors is gradually reappearing within the mainstream of labor economics. A better explanation of the wage squeeze (the subject of the next chapter of Gordon's book *Fat and Mean*) places the spotlight directly on corporate power, rather than on the individuals who are its victims.

Note

1. Kevin Murphy and Finis Welch "Industrial Change and the Rising Importance of Skill," in *Fat and Mean*, p. 131.

Summary of

The Causes and Consequences of Changing Earnings Inequality: W(h)ither the Debate?

by David G. Blanchflower and Matthew Slaughter

[Published in *Global Trade and Wages* (New York: Council on Foreign Relations, forthcoming 1998).]

The relationship of international trade to income inequality and unemployment has been widely debated by both labor economists and trade economists. The two groups typically use incompatible analytical frameworks, making it difficult to compare their results. This summary, a collaborative effort by a labor economist and a trade economist, reviews the research to date on internationalization and labor markets, tentatively identifies areas of consensus and areas of remaining uncertainty, and observes that public policy choices may not depend on the fine points of debate among economists.

The Basic Facts

In the early 1970s, the U.S. labor market began changing in three ways. First, average real earnings stopped growing—in fact have declined slightly since 1973. Second, earnings differentials based on skills have become larger: For example, the gap between the earnings of male college graduates and high school graduates has widened substantially. The combination of these two changes has led to a sharp drop in real earnings for low-skilled workers. Finally, there has been increasing inequality among workers within the same skill level. There has been a rise in the so-called "residual inequality" that remains after controlling for education, work experience, race, and gender. This is an important part of the rise in overall inequality.

The same changes have occurred to a mixed extent in other OECD (developed) countries. In contrast to the U.S. pattern, average real earnings have continued to grow since the 1970s in most countries. Overall inequality has generally increased in recent years, but only in the United Kingdom has the magnitude of the change approached U.S. levels. There is some tendency for countries with less increase in inequality to have more increase in unemployment, but the relationship is far from perfect. The United Kingdom has done poorly on both measures, with a rise in earnings inequality and unemployment. Residual inequality appears to have increased in most countries, although again the U.S. and U.K. may have more pronounced increases than others.

Explanations of rising inequality, therefore, should include factors that distinguish the United States and the United Kingdom from other OECD nations, as well as trends that have affected all countries.

The Role of Trade

Inequality can be increased by shifts in relative demand for different types of labor, shifts in relative supply of labor, or changes in labor market institutions. It is clear that supply shifts alone cannot explain increasing inequality, since the quantity of skilled labor and the relative wages paid to skilled workers have been increasing at the same time. This strongly suggests a shift in demand toward more skilled labor.

How much of that shift in demand is due to international trade? When analyzing this question, trade economists generally use the Heckscher–Ohlin framework, assuming all countries have perfectly competitive economies, making the same diversified mix of products, with perfect factor mobility between industries. In this framework, the Stolper–Samuelson theorem predicts that international trade affects product prices, which in turn affect the demand for, and prices of, factors of production. Thus if trade has led to an increase in the demand for skilled-labor-intensive products in developed countries, the prices of those products and the earnings of skilled workers would both increase as a result of trade. However, there is on balance very little evidence that trade has increased prices of technology-intensive or skill-intensive products.

Other studies, often by labor economists, have looked at quantities of employment, or of exports and imports. These, too, have often found little or no role for trade. One model estimates that the expected effects of trade with developing countries on U.S. prices and wages would be within the margin of measurement error. Others have found less than 10 percent of U.S. earnings inequality to be due to trade. While debate continues, the majority of studies, regardless of methodology, find only a small role for trade in explaining rising inequality in the United States.

Alternative Explanations

Skill-biased technical change is a favorite alternative explanation for rising inequality. Often this is just a residual category that has resisted other explanations—"it is largely a name for our ignorance." [10] Anecdotal or industry-specific evidence has been presented regarding particular technologies, but this, too, is controversial. Correlation between wage increases and use of new technologies does not imply causation (see the articles on computer use by Autor, Katz, and Krueger, and by DiNardo and Pischke, summarized in Part IV). The same technologies have not produced even roughly similar trends in inequality in different countries.

Changes in labor supply, while inadequate to explain the entire trend toward inequality, might well explain differences between countries and time periods in the strength of this trend. The relative supply of college-educated workers grew more rapidly in Europe than in the United States in the 1980s. This would tend to cause slower growth in skill differentials in Europe. Also, the growth of the college-educated labor force was more rapid in the 1970s, leading to declining skill differentials—a pattern that was reversed in the following decade.

Another labor supply change related to globalization, namely immigration, may play a role in the U.S. earnings distribution. Immigration has increased rapidly since 1970, and the average skill and education level of immigrants has declined. While some studies find that immigration has little effect on U.S. earnings, others find it explains much of the drop in relative earnings for high school dropouts (though having little effect on relative earnings of college and high school graduates). In Europe, immigration seems to have had little effect on inequality.

The factor most closely related to the international pattern of inequality is the change in labor market institutions. The United States and the United Kingdom have both had decreases in "union density" (the unionized percentage of the labor force). In the United States, union density dropped throughout the

1970s as well as the 1980s (and later), while in the United Kingdom the decline began in the 1980s, matching the pattern of growing earnings inequality in the two countries. Moreover, the real value of the U.S. minimum wage declined sharply during the 1970s and 1980s, while in the U.K. the councils that set sectoral minimum wages were abolished in the 1980s. No other OECD country had comparable changes in both of these institutions, suggesting that institutional factors account for the distinctive Anglo-American trends in inequality.

The Nature of Globalization

Much remains to be done in assessing the effects of globalization on earnings and employment. Trade economists and labor economists approach the problem differently, the former emphasizing clear theoretical reasoning and the latter valuing careful empirical work. It is important to think about the interaction of many markets simultaneously, as trade economists assert. It is also important to recognize, as labor economists point out, that perfect competition and factor mobility, the foundations of the Heckscher–Ohlin framework, are highly unrealistic assumptions. Thus the published findings that trade has little effect on earnings inequality must be viewed as tentative, since they generally rely on these assumptions. The economics literature has only begun to look beyond the Heckscher–Ohlin framework at other effects of globalization on the U.S. labor market. Such factors as exchange-rate volatility, increases in international capital mobility, and competitive pressures resulting from international trade, are anecdotally said to be important. Some initial analyses of these factors suggest a much larger role for globalization in explaining rising inequality than most of the Heckscher–Ohlin studies.

Finally, do the causes of inequality matter for public policy purposes? In a word, no. If there is to be public intervention aimed at reducing inequality—a point that is by no means certain today—then the appropriate policy responses are independent of the underlying causes. Short-term solutions such as earned-income tax credits and long-term solutions such as subsidies to education and skill acquisition should be pursued regardless of our understanding of globalization. Even though skill differentials in earnings have increased, market failures (such as imperfect capital markets for borrowing to finance education) prevent some individuals from obtaining skills that they desire. In contrast, policies such as trade barriers, or limits on the use of new technologies that are associated with earnings inequality, would not be desirable regardless of the outcome of future research.

While research and debate on the issues raised here are ongoing, the most important message is that economists are much closer to unanimity on policy recommendations than on the causes of the problems that the policies are designed to solve.

Summary of

Consequences of Trade for Labor Markets and the Employment Relationship

by Dani Rodrik

[Published in *Has Globalization Gone Too Far?* (Washington, D.C.: Institute for International Economics, 1997), 11–27.]

Since the second half of the 1970s the United States and Western Europe have experienced a widening wage premium for skills and a significant increase in labor market instability and insecurity. This article examines the impacts of globalization on workers (especially low-skilled workers) in the North. It focuses on how trade affects the relative demands for skilled and unskilled workers, increasing the ease with which domestic producers can be substituted across national borders through outsourcing or foreign direct investment. One result is an inward shift and a flattening of the demand curves for low-skilled workers, reducing their average wages while increasing the volatility of their wages and hours worked. Another result is increased inequality in earnings within skill-groups.

Consequences of Trade with Countries Having Abundant Unskilled Labor

> A cornerstone of traditional trade theory is that trade with labor-abundant countries reduces real wages in rich countries—or increased unemployment if wages are artificially fixed. Indeed, in the standard factor-endowment model, trade creates gains for nations precisely by altering the relative domestic scarcity of factors of production such as labor . . . if one believes that trade has been a source of many of the good things that advanced industrial economies have experienced in the last few decades, one is forced to presume that trade has also had many of the negative consequences that its opponents have alleged. [12]

In spite of this logic, most trade economists are in the curious position of crediting expanded trade with the "good things" just cited, while minimizing the negative impacts of trade on developed countries' jobs and wages.

The Heckscher–Ohlin–Samuelson trade models provide solid theoretical reasoning for the belief that increased exposure to trade with low-income nations will increase the skill premium in the North. Against this background recent empirical studies have asked: How much has trade reduced the demand for unskilled labor in the developed nations? The answer is commonly "some, but not a whole lot." The reasons for this answer are, first, that North–South trade flows are small. The bulk of international trade takes place among industrial nations with similar factor endowments. Second, the theory states that more skilled workers can gain higher wages only if there is a corresponding fall in the relative price of goods produced with low skill intensity. Absent evidence for such a relative price-shift, economists infer that shifts in wages must stem from causes other than trade.

However, looking beyond Heckscher–Ohlin theory, one can see a much larger role for trade in recent wage inequalities. For example, Adrian Wood notes that import competition has driven out many low-skill-intensive activities in the developing world, while inducing labor-saving technological change in the industrialized world. "Calculations of the implied factor content of trade that look at existing factor proportions in the remaining import-competing activities therefore underestimate the reduction in the demand for unskilled workers as a consequence of trade." [14–15]

Technology is the leading alternative to trade as an explanation for the recent rise in wage inequality. In fact, these two forces are highly interdependent. Even while theoretical arguments continue, most trade economists would agree that trade can account for somewhere between 10 and 20 percent of the rise in wage inequality during the 1980s. This is by no means a small number, and it has been derived by taking a very narrow cut of the issues.

Consequences of a More Elastic Demand for Workers

Economists have largely focused on looking at how far the demand curve for low-skilled labor has shifted, with less emphasis on the implications of the fact that, as economies become more open to foreign trade and investment, the demand for labor becomes more elastic. The reason for this increased elasticity is that employers and consumers can substitute foreign workers for domestic workers by investing abroad or by importing the products made by foreign workers. "[I]ncreased substitutability of low-skilled workers across borders affects three key ingredients of the employment relationship: the incidence of nonwage costs, volatility of earnings and hours worked, and bargaining in the workplace." [17] It is important to note that North–North trade, while having little effect on the overall demand for unskilled labor, does increase opportunities for substituting workers within the now enormous, tightly integrated market of the developed world. The resulting contribution to elasticity of demand for (especially low-skilled) labor has been largely overlooked as economists have focused on the effects of North–South trade.

Incidence

Labor standards can be seen as a tax on employment resulting in a shift up the labor supply curve by an amount corresponding to the per-worker cost of introducing the standard. Elasticity determines how the cost is distributed between workers and employers. The more elastic labor demand is, the more difficult it is for workers to make other groups in society—especially employers—share such costs. Thus, in industries where the demand for labor has become more elastic and competition has made employers more cost-sensitive (because there is a smaller cushion of rents), higher labor standards cost workers in terms of jobs as well as wages. "Hence, globalization makes it difficult to sustain the post-war bargain under which workers' pay and benefits steadily improved in return for labor peace and loyalty." [19]

Volatility

As globalization causes labor demand curves to flatten, there is greater instability in the labor market. Shocks in demand can result in much greater volatility in both earnings and hours worked. Such an increase in volatility has been well documented in the United States where, according to a study by Gottschalk and Moffitt, it appears that one-third of the widening of the measured earnings distribution results from an increase in earnings instability. This increase is nearly double for the least-skilled groups. These numbers do not in themselves explain the underlying causes for the changes, but the facts are "consistent with a picture of labor markets in which greater openness to trade interacting with short-term fluctuations in labor demand (or labor productivity) has resulted in greater inequality across and within skill groups and greater instability in wages and employment." [22]

This can be shown in the following numerical exercise. Suppose that an individual firm faces a labor elasticity of one in the short- to medium-run. In addition, assume that trade has resulted in an increase in the elasticity of demand for labor from -0.5 to -0.75. One could then calculate that the standard deviation would increase by 29 percent.

Via increased churning in labor markets, globalization can contribute to inequality in other ways. Job-specific skills may constitute a larger share of earnings for less-educated workers than for college graduates. Since less-educated workers are subject to longer unemployment spells and larger wage cuts upon reemployment, this also puts downward pressure on the relative wages of less-educated workers as a whole, widening the skill premium.

Bargaining

As seen above, increased substitutability of labor affects the balance of power between workers and employers. Because the focus of academic economics has been on perfectly competitive settings where wages are determined in spot markets, solely on the basis of marginal productivity (with no room for the influence of bargaining power), this effect of trade has received relatively little attention.

To the extent that wages are, in fact, determined through bargaining, an increase in the substitutability of workers results in a lower share of the rents that go to workers. Unions also become weaker. Richard Freeman has estimated that about one-fifth of the rise in U.S. wage inequality is due to the decline in unionization. In Europe, where unions are stronger, the effect has been shifted to an increase in unemployment. In general, the rise in global competitiveness has caused a change in norms, lowering expectations, especially for the low-skilled workers whose bargaining power has been most eroded.

Summary of

The Transformation of the Japanese Employment System: Nature, Depth, and Origins

by James R. Lincoln and Yoshifumi Nakata

[Published in *Work and Occupations* 24 (February 1997), 33–55.]

In the 1980s, as in earlier years, the rapid economic growth of Japan was often attributed in part to the nation's unique employment system. However, in the 1990s the Japanese economy entered a period of stagnation, which has started to undermine past employment practices. This article describes the changes in the Japanese employment system that have resulted from the economic slowdown and intensified competitive pressures of the 1990s. The article is based on interviews with corporate and union leaders, and on a review of reporting in the Japanese business press.

Legitimacy and Change

There is a high degree of legitimacy attached to the "three pillars" of the traditional Japanese employment system: lifetime employment guarantees for most employees of big companies; steep, automatic salary increases based on seniority; and enterprise unions that work cooperatively with business and government to find consensus solutions to economic problems. The widespread acceptance and legitimacy of these institutions is an important constraint on Japanese management. Even when firms announce that they are making a dramatic break with tradition, to create a public image of forward-looking innovation, they often prove to be adopting only cautious and incremental changes in existing employment practices.

Yet there are powerful forces for change. Japanese corporations are increasingly investing and expanding abroad rather than at home. U.S. and European firms, having absorbed some Japanese manufacturing techniques (such as "lean production" methods, discussed in Part IV of this book), are increasingly effective competitors. Deregulation is opening formerly protected industries to both foreign and domestic competition. The aging of Japan's population makes the seniority system increasingly expensive to maintain. The rise of the service sector, with a largely female and more mobile workforce, has increased labor turnover and reduced long-term commitment on the part of both employers and employees.

Responding to such changes, Japanese employers have, to a remarkable extent, bent rather than broken traditional employment practices.

The End of Permanent Employment?

Japanese corporations have always found ways to achieve some flexibility in staffing levels, despite lifetime employment guarantees to permanent employees. The use of flexible staffing arrangements, often hidden from view, has increased markedly in the 1990s, but is not an entirely new phenomenon. Workers past the retirement age (formerly 55, now 60) are often rehired on a temporary or subcontract basis. They are usually willing to work at much lower pay rates since they are also receiving pensions. Part-time, seasonal, and temporary work, though used much less than in the United States, are on the increase. Most temporary workers are women, while almost all permanent employees at major firms are men.

"The line between a forced layoff or dismissal and voluntary early retirement has always been thin in Japan." [40] In the past, those who resisted the "tap on the shoulder" could rely on the lifetime employment guarantee, though at the cost of isolation in a dead-end career. Now firms are more aggressively seeking to dislodge the "sitting by the window tribe," although they are facing resistance from unions and from individual lawsuits. The Ministry of Labor sometimes intervenes to block what it views as excessive workforce reduction policies.

Within the *keiretsu* (interfirm networks), the dominant firms can transfer excess employees to affiliates, suppliers, and other partners. This practice, known as *shukko*, has become more common in recent years. Because wages and benefits depend on the size of the firm, the *shukko* worker suffers an economic loss. One manager said that the use of *shukko* left the leading firm with the best and the worst employees: the ones it wanted to keep, and the ones the affiliates would not accept. For the firms on the receiving end, *shukko* could mean increased communication and links with the leading firm. On the other hand, it often saddles the recipient with employees who have proved ineffective in another job and who have the wrong skills for their new positions. Nonetheless, the deeply entrenched legitimacy of the hierarchical *keiretsu* structure means that *shukko* is almost always accepted.

Recruitment, Seniority, and Pay

In the past, Japanese corporations hired bright, inexperienced college graduates for most managerial, professional, and technical positions, and trained them on the job as they moved up the seniority ladder. While this approach remains common, many firms are finding that it is no longer entirely adequate in an era of rapid technical change. Midcareer hiring of workers with desirable skills, and recruitment based on specific technical abilities rather than general aptitude, are both beginning to appear. The traditional hierarchy of management titles is still used in many contexts, but new career patterns are emerging. The Ministry of Labor recommends, and several leading firms have adopted, three separate promotion tracks for managers, researchers and planners, and skilled workers and technicians—with promotion and pay based on ability within each track, not simply on seniority.

This is potentially an important challenge to the seniority system. In the past, workers started at very low salaries but could look forward to a lifetime of steady raises. Young workers were paid less than their productivity warranted, while older ones were paid wages in excess of productivity. This system assumes, and encourages, lifetime employment guarantees. In the absence of such guarantees, young workers would not accept it. However, performance reviews have always played a part in this system (although this fact has rarely been discussed in the English-language literature). The qualities that are rewarded are signs of commitment to the corporation, skill acquisition, and long-term potential, rather than short-term achievement. Evaluation of merit, in these terms, blends into rewarding seniority and loyalty.

Although the seniority-based system of pay remains much in evidence, it is of gradually decreasing importance. During the 1980s, the age-earnings profile for male university graduates became significantly flatter, with the greatest change occurring in the lowest-paid categories. As economic conditions have threatened to disrupt the stability of labor relations in the 1990s, unions have opted to protect permanent employment rather than seniority-based pay and promotions. This is a noteworthy shift for Japanese unions, which formerly defended both principles. However, there are limits to the extent of change in this, as in other areas: systems of executive compensation based largely on short-term (such as previous year) performance, while much discussed in the press, are apparently used by only a small minority of firms.

Conclusion

Economic forces are propelling broad and sweeping changes in the Japanese employment system; but it would be easy to overstate the extent to which new practices have been implemented. As a Japanese reporter said about labor trends in 1995, "Most companies are phasing in change at a snail's pace." [50] Resistance from unions, government ministries, and public opinion plays some part in limiting the speed of change. So does the strength of the postwar consensus and the legitimacy attached to established Japanese employment practices and industrial relations. "[W]elfare corporatism remains a pervasive organizing principle of the Japanese employment system." [50]

Previous research by one of the authors showed that, as of the early 1980s, age, family obligations, seniority, and on-the-job training were more important determinants of wages in Japan than in the United States. While that analysis has not been formally updated, the present article suggests that only incremental changes have occurred in the past pattern of Japanese labor relations. "Assuming that real economic recovery takes hold, we envision considerable stabilization of Japanese employment practice, albeit at a higher level of market-oriented flexibility than the three pillars system has thus far allowed." [51]

Summary of

Labor Squeeze and Ethnic/Racial Recomposition in the U.S. Apparel Industry

by Evelyn Blumenberg and Paul Ong

[Published in *Global Production—The Apparel Industry in the Pacific Rim*, eds. Edna Bonachich, Lucie Cheng, Norma Chinchilla, Nora Hamilton, and Paul Ong (Philadelphia: Temple University Press, 1994): 309–327.]

The apparel industry is one of the signature industries of the global economy. Sweatshop conditions in Caribbean and Asian garment factories have been the target of well-publicized picket lines and boycotts among activists sympathetic to labor, to the point that a popular U.S. TV personality was reduced to public tears when the line of women's clothes she endorsed was exposed as the product of oppressive factories. Most clothing items are easily made with unskilled labor and a few simple machines, so manufacturers can move quickly to take advantage of lower wages or a more favorable business climate. For years producers have been moving out of the United States or contracting with off-shore suppliers to reduce costs, particularly labor costs. However, the global restructuring of the apparel industry has also reshaped what remains of the industry in the United States, intensifying or shifting the direction of changes already underway.

Import Competition

In 1960 only 2 percent of apparel goods purchased in the United States were imported. By the late 1980s, imports were 30 percent of the market. Industrialization in the Third World opened low-wage production locations, while free-trade advocacy during the Reagan administration blocked the erection of new trade barriers in the form of increased quotas or tariffs. The surge of cheaper imports put severe cost pressures on the domestic industry. Garment prices, which had been in concert with prices for other goods from 1950 to 1970, fell dramatically in relative terms from 1970 to 1985 before leveling off. Employment also dropped from a high of 1.43 million in 1973 to 1.03 million in 1991 and wages declined from a peak of $8.00/hour in the late 1960s (in 1990 dollars) to $6.50/hour in 1991. Working conditions worsened as unions weakened and workers were pressed to work harder to achieve greater productivity. Much of the industry has gone underground, further eroding working conditions and making accurate assessment difficult. Three regions of the United States—New York, North Carolina, and California—house substantial portions of garment production, but each exhibits a different pattern of growth and employment.

The Rise and Fall of the New York Apparel Industry

New York has long been a hub of fashion in the United States and became the center of the garment industry in the 1800s. Initially, immigration provided abundant, inexpensive labor. However, cost factors in the New York garment industry changed rapidly between the two world wars. Legislation restricted immigration, unions took hold and gained substantial bargaining power, and rents began to rise. Firms that could afford to move did so, while weaker firms closed. Employment dropped after World War II, although unions were able to maintain a high wage structure in the New York industry until the 1970s. After that, union membership declined and wages began to fall as employment continued to drop.

Small shops and contract production fragmented the industry making union organization even more difficult. A new wave of immigration, particularly from China, replenished the pool of cheap labor, while the trend toward smaller shops producing less formal, easier to manufacture clothing opened opportunities to immigrant entrepreneurs. Even with these changes, however, the pace of job loss in the industry increased in the 1970s and 1980s.

Growth and Stagnation in North Carolina

Unlike New York, North Carolina and other areas of the South experienced growth in apparel production after World War II. Better transportation was one among several inducements to growth. The textile industry had already moved from its birthplace in the Northeast to the South and, as apparel manufacturing moved into the area, some integration of the two industries took place. Many state governments made strenuous efforts to attract industry with financing and loan subsidies, assistance with recruitment and in some cases outright land giveaways. A key element in "the selling of the South" was suppression of unionization. Most southern states enacted right-to-work legislation that made it illegal to require union membership as a condition of employment.

With the mechanization of agriculture, more southern workers sought industrial employment. White women moved into the garment industry in large numbers, but racial discrimination kept black workers out of the factories until the 1970s. After that, the civil rights movement made employment of black women acceptable at the same time that import competition and the diminishing pool of white female labor led employers to seek other, cheaper sources of labor. In North Carolina, where the apparel industry is heavily concentrated and has experienced growth, the proportion of black workers rose from 5 percent in 1960 to 28 percent in 1990. In Mississippi, 44 percent of apparel workers were black by 1990. But in Mississippi and several other Southern states, employment in the industry has dropped since 1970. Overall, apparel employment in the South has stabilized. Many analysts and industry insiders are concerned that even the low wages paid to black women are too high to compete with imports.

California Garment Boom

California provides a contrast to the rest of the country. There the apparel industry is booming. Southern California has had a substantial proportion of garment production since the 1920s, drawn by the fashion-conscious movie industry. Expansion after World War II continued into the 1970s as a consequence of burgeoning immigration, low unionization, lucrative products, and "an industrial organization that insulates manufacturers from legal responsibility for labor." The structural aspects of the industry and the characteristics of the labor force reinforce each other.

Legal immigration increased the U.S. labor force by 19 percent in the 1970s. California was, and still is, a major destination for immigrants, particularly from Asia and Mexico. The dramatic recomposition of the labor force as a whole is reflected in the apparel industry. Non-Hispanic whites once were the vast majority of California's garment workers (86 percent during the World War II era); by 1980, only 24 percent of the state's apparel workers were non-Hispanic whites, 50 percent were Latino, and 18 percent were Asian. Black representation in the industry dropped from 8 percent in 1950 to 5 percent in 1980. Latinos and Asians were an even higher proportion of production workers in the industry.

Immigration reinforces low wage rates both by increasing the labor pool and by discouraging unionization. Many immigrant workers are undocumented and fear deportation if they exhibit militant behavior. The entrenched white male leadership of the most prominent unions has had difficulty building rapport with the largely Latina workforce. Fragmentation in the industry, which is composed of numerous small shops, is also a hindrance to union organization.

The availability of a large unskilled labor force willing to work for low wages is compatible with the shift in fashion, after World War II, to casual wear. Casual clothing is less expensive and requires less skill to produce than dressier clothing.

Industrial organization also matches the product base and the workforce, with separable functions parceled out among a large number of small shops often owned by Asian entrepreneurs employing Latino workers.

> This fragmented structure enables large manufacturers to pass the financial risks of fluctuating product demand to small contractors . . . [and] to avoid legal problems associated with subminimum wages, poor working conditions, and the infraction of labor standards. Asian and other contractors are thus left in 'middlemen positions,' where labor and union conflicts are most likely to occur. [324]

Taking a look at apparel industry trends in New York, North Carolina, and California together leads to the bleak conclusion that U.S. and Third World working conditions are converging. In the long run, U.S. manufacturers may choose to compete on the basis of quality, style, or flexibility; but for the near future the apparel industry depends for survival on deteriorating conditions of work and the availability of low-wage labor.

Summary of

Gender and the Global Economy

by Lourdes Benería

[Published in *Instability and Change in the Global Economy,* eds. Arthur MacEwan and William Tabb (New York: Monthly Review Press, 1989), 241–259.]

[A]s the globalization of economic relations proceeds, the need to understand the role of gender from a global perspective emerges with greater intensity. Where are women located in the new international division of labor? Can we assume that women's labor force participation is increasing worldwide? As international capitalism expands, how are class and gender integrated in the face of a rapidly changing economic landscape? What are the major issues emerging with respect to how gender is used in the global economy? [242]

The internationalization of the economy intersects with the economic and social position of women in complex ways. This summary offers an overview and an assessment of major global trends affecting women's experience of work.

Is There a Feminization of the International Labor Force?

This question exemplifies the difficulties that arise because trends differ by geographic area and economic sector. Some trends are contradictory, and good statistical information is not always available. Furthermore, women's work in subsistence and family labor is often undercounted. When official statistics show an increase in women's labor force participation, they may really reflect a shift of women from agricultural or household production to more formal and "visible" work. [243]

In industrialized countries, there has been a large measured increase in women's labor force participation rates, which reached beyond 50 percent in most OECD countries by 1980. In developing countries the pattern is less clear. Some countries witnessed increases, while others did not. Unlike industrialized countries where most women entered the service sector, in the newly industrializing areas of the developing world the greatest increase in women's employment has been in the industrial sector. What is therefore becoming clearer is the trend toward the feminization of wage labor.

Recent attention to the new international division of labor may have exaggerated the scale of employment of women in less developed countries by transnational corporations, especially when we are reminded that the large majority of Third World women are not working with multinational capital; for example, even in the industrializing economies of Asia, Africa, and the Middle East, 70 percent of women in the labor force still work in agriculture. (Women in Latin America, however, tend to work in service or informal sectors.)

International firms directly employ less than 1 percent of the female labor force in the developing world; however, multinational investment is nevertheless a significant factor in the growth of many newly industrializing countries, and has a wide influence on employment patterns in host countries. Many women work for suppliers in subcontracting chains linked to multinational corporations. In some countries, women's share of employment in export processing zones can reach 80 to 90 percent. Local firms may mimic the employment practices of large foreign companies, increasing the demand for female labor even more.

Women's Work and Wages

In the 1960s, the introduction of large-scale industry to developing countries often drove family-based industries out of business and deprived women of work opportunities. This pattern is documented in a well-known study by Ester Boserup, published in 1970. The pattern no longer holds true now that women, particularly young, single, relatively well-educated women, are desirable employees for low-wage, labor-intensive production. The fact that women are highly segregated by occupation all over the world makes it easier to segment the wage structure—women's wages are generally lower than men's. While occupational segregation is common, what is defined as women's work differs from one country to another. For example, 80 percent of clerical workers in the United States were women in 1986, while only 2 percent were women in Togo in 1981. These gender constructions are changeable—when a male occupation becomes feminized its relative wages generally decline.

It is not only because of low wages, however, that women workers are sought in newly expanding economies. Women are also regarded as more docile, more malleable, and easier to control. In some cases, women are considered to be more dexterous in manipulating small objects and therefore more productive for many kinds of assembly work. Women also provide a source of flexible labor, taking part-time or unstable work assignments when demand oscillates.

Prostitution and Sex-Related Tourism

A different kind of work associated with internationalization is the expansion of sex-related tourism. Several Southeast Asian countries (for example, Thailand, South Korea, and the Philippines) are well-known for state-licensed prostitution. Sexual "hospitality services" are part of the global tourist trade, but are also connected to the presence of foreign military bases and to international business travel. Prostitution in some countries has become a significant source

of foreign currency and is used by corporate and government interests to promote business ventures. In Bangkok the estimated number of prostitutes in
1981 is comparable to 10 percent of employment by multinationals.

Poverty among women in many rural areas and city slums translates into low
prices for prostitutes and is also related to the docility and servility perceived
and sought after by visiting men. "What a perfect symbol this is of the connections between the pleasures of international jet-setting and the survival pains of
everyday life in the global economy." [252]

Change and Action

What is the significance of the increasing visibility of women in the global economy? The answers must depend on both labor market and household circumstances. In the industrialized world (and probably some other areas as well),
women's participation in the global economy represents growing labor force attachment and economic autonomy. In the newly industrialized countries, however, many women face unstable labor markets as multinational corporations
shift from country to country in search of lower wages. As one commentator in
a January 1987 issue of *The Economist* put it, when young women lose jobs in
Malaysia, "will, as the cynics say, the pretty ones become bar girls and the plain
ones turn to Islam?" [254] In spite of such comments, the acceptance of
women as paid workers has generally increased and is generally followed (with
some lag) by more equality and a gradual breakdown of gender stereotypes.

With respect to household work, the double burden for women remains
widespread. However, there are hopeful signs—difficult to capture but worthy
of further research—that point to increasingly egalitarian family structures. Evidence exists that, for women in high-income countries, hours spent in domestic work are dropping and men are sharing more chores in the home. One researcher even noted a challenge to patriarchal authority in countries like Puerto
Rico and the Dominican Republic, where women's contribution to family income has taken on greater importance.

> The existence of a large pool of female labor at a world scale is being used to
> deal with the pressures of international competition, profitability crises, and
> economic restructuring that characterize the current reorganization of pro-
> duction. [250]

Forces of multinational investment draw women into the industrial labor
force, but often through informal or casualized channels. Women's work in the
home is intensified when the debt crisis in developing countries throws
economics into disarray and forces the poor to rely on their own meager resources. Increased participation in paid employment might result in greater autonomy for women and more equality between the sexes. "On the other hand,

these changes are based on inequalities that are likely to persist stubbornly precisely because they are instrumental in the current functioning of the global economy." [255]

Structural adjustment policies in many developing countries has made austerity a way of life, straining household budgets and particularly those of the poor. Women bear a large share of the burden of coping with lower incomes and deteriorating access to resources. To use what is available more efficiently, or to generate new resources, households may change their patterns of purchasing, preparation, and consumption; produce more at home; rely on extended families; send more family members (most likely to be women and children) into the labor force; or migrate. In some areas women have been key in collective coping strategies like communal kitchens.

Other possible responses at a more macro scale include the use of traditional channels of action such as trade unions or minimum wage enforcement. Governments can provide or enact policies with respect to health care, reproductive rights, maternity leave, day care, equal pay for equal work, and working conditions affecting women. Unfortunately, progressive organizations often do not incorporate women's issues into their agendas when the class dimension is not clearly identified, and traditional paths of action may not be effective. Women's organizations are important to exert pressure on trade unions, political organizations, and governments—but they should recognize the class dimensions that influence women's conditions. This lack of integration of issues is a loss to movements for social change. Some commentators have called for a new politics; however, for solidarity among different groups to be useful to women, gender issues must play a fundamental role.

Summary of

The Politics and Economics of Global Employment: A Perspective from Latin America

by Hernando Gómez-Buendía

[Published in *Global Employment: An International Investigation into the Future of Work*, ed. Mihály Simai (London and New Jersey: Zed Books, 1995), vol. 2, 65–93.]

The standard methodology for analyzing levels of employment, namely a comparison of trends affecting labor supply and demand, may lead to an understanding of the reported rate of unemployment in developed countries. The same methods fail, however, to comprehend a crucial problem in developing countries: the large volume of low-productivity underemployment, often in the informal sector of the economy. Many Latin American countries, in particular, have a very modern, but relatively small, high-productivity formal sector along-side a much larger urban informal sector. This essay, by a Colombian econo-mist, relates Latin America's dual structure of employment to the political and economic history of the region.

The Politics of Unemployment

Global reviews of employment problems often overlook the important distinc-tion between formal unemployment and informal underemployment. Academic and political interest in employment issues varies with the formal unemploy-ment rate in developed countries. In historical terms, unemployment only be-comes a political issue when a society is able to afford comprehensive, publicly funded unemployment insurance, an innovation that makes the costs of unem-ployment a matter of concern to everyone. Common strategies of public inter-vention in labor markets—better information about job openings, public works employment, changes in labor regulations, and retraining and small business loan programs—are designed to address the formal unemployment of a small minority, not the informal underemployment of a large fraction of the labor force.

Formal and Informal Labor Markets

[There is a] political dimension behind each of the four most commonly rec-ognized economic peculiarities of the Latin American labor market, that is: the large size of the informal sector; the early and uneven development of labor protection regimes; the lag in technological development which blocks further expansions in productive employment; and the large extent of state interven-tion reflected in the large share of the public sector in overall employment. [66]

The urban informal sector, a set of heterogeneous activities characterized by small-scale, labor-intensive technologies, free entry, competition, and absence of regulation, includes a large portion of the labor force in developing coun-tries. Though statistics are unreliable, estimates for Latin America are often be-tween 20 and 30 percent of the nonagricultural labor force, if not higher. Moreover, informal employment appears to have grown during both the debt-adjustment crisis of the 1980s and the more recent move toward flexible labor markets.

Informal organization of urban life is not restricted to employment; it also encompasses approaches to housing, transportation, and access to public utili-ties. Some authors view the informal sector as a reaction to excessive regulation in the formal sector. The present author has argued elsewhere that the informal economy can be understood as private appropriation of public goods. Informal work takes place in the streets, or in enterprises that do not pay taxes and utility bills. Squatter settlements do not pay for public land, sanitation, and other services, nor do they meet public health and safety standards. Informal access to utility networks is simply unpaid appropriation of these services.

Formal labor protection and social service legislation in Latin America is generous to the worker, roughly on a par with Western Europe. Compensation for workplace injuries, and retirement pensions for some categories of workers, were introduced earlier in several Latin American countries than in the United States. Labor oriented legal systems are a result of the region's history of industrial protectionism. A strategy of import substitution led to the successful development of a manufacturing sector, beginning around the 1910s. This allowed the rise of powerful unions in the protected industrial sector. Other factors promoting labor legislation included the social teachings of the Catholic Church, the earlier unionization of selected agricultural and mining export industries, and the region's populist traditions.

However, the generosity of the resulting system is more than Latin American economies can afford. "There is an abyss between law and reality" [76]. Basic social security covers less than half of the economically active population throughout the region, and less than one-fourth in many countries. Those who are covered often receive inequitable treatment, varying widely by occupation and region.

Protectionism and the State

The puzzle of Latin American development is the sharp slowdown in industrialization in the 1970s, followed by a decline in the 1980s. The standard economic explanation is that import substitution turned out to be self-defeating. More complex manufactures required more, not fewer, imported inputs, while the distortion in prices caused by protectionism made export industries uncompetitive in the world market. A complementary explanation rests on the politics of protectionism. Latin American industrialists, having prospered for decades on the basis of political connections and regulation, naturally remained focused on preserving access to government policy makers and protected domestic markets, rather than competing with more efficient foreign producers.

The state plays a crucial role in molding the labor markets of Latin America, in part through its generous but unevenly applied labor and social welfare legislation (which defines the informal sector by exclusion from these provisions). The state is also an important employer, accounting for 10 to 15 percent of total nonagricultural employment in the larger countries—more than the average for developing countries in Africa and Asia, but less than in many industrialized countries. Public workers in Latin America appear to be more active in politics than their counterparts in developed nations. As with labor legislation, there is a gap between formal and informal reality. Governments often refuse to recognize powerful unions, yet negotiate with them anyway. Collective bargaining and strikes by public sector workers are legally prohibited or restricted, yet routinely occur, in many countries. Benefits and privileges somewhat beyond the law are often available to lawmakers, the military, and employees of major public enterprises.

Labor Dualism Revisited

There is a long-standing debate on the nature of economic dualism in Latin America. Parts of the regional economy began to modernize much earlier than other developing countries. There are wide disparities both between and within Latin American countries. Argentina is not Haiti, nor is Brazil's impoverished Northeast comparable to the modern industry of São Paulo. Such trends as the demographic transition to slower population growth, and the increased participation of women in formal employment, began earlier in the more affluent Latin American countries than in other developing nations.

Yet modernization and industrialization did not continue to expand. Employment in agriculture fell from 55 percent of the region's workforce in the 1950s to 26 percent by the end of the 1980s, and 72 percent of the population now lives in cities. At the same time, employment in modern manufacturing has remained around 14 percent of the regional labor force for four decades, and overall per capita productivity has barely increased. The result has been the coexistence of formal and informal labor markets, with open unemployment and disguised, informal underemployment side by side.

The formal and informal labor markets interact with each other. Those who lose jobs in the formal sector often end up in informal occupations, while times of prosperity and expansion in the formal sector will draw workers out of informal activities. There is little evidence of a long-term trend, either up or down, in formal unemployment. The existence of the vast reserve of informal sector workers undercuts most interventions in the labor market aimed at reducing formal unemployment. Indeed, formal unemployment may be a luxury, available only to those who qualify for unemployment assistance or have other resources that allow them to search for more desirable jobs rather than immediately pursuing low-paid, informal activity.

The economy of the future, it appears, will rely even more heavily on skills and knowledge, rather than the simple, unskilled labor that is so abundant in the informal sector of Latin America. What will become of those who cannot join the technologically defined global village of the future? Even more intensive informalization of the economy is one scenario. Another, more ominous possibility is demagogic or xenophobic opposition to technology and globalization, under the guise of neopopulist alternatives. "One can only hope that some others will discover that asserting the public interest and constructing a nation where all can be gainfully employed can be a task far more rewarding." [90]

Summary of

Globalization and Labor Standards: A Review of Issues

by Eddy Lee

[Published in *International Labor Review* 136 (Summer 1997), 172–189.]

This article reviews the issues relating to the impact of globalization on labor standards. It examines political and economic aspects of this topic and concludes by assessing the current state of the debate.

Background

Questions concerning globalization and labor standards are not new. In fact, international labor conditions were the impetus behind the founding of the International Labor Organization in 1919. The ILO's constitution cites the motives of social justice and humanitarian concerns as well as a fear of labor unrest as a threat to national and international peace. Improved labor standards in one country were seen to be threatened by others that remained backward. Since its establishment, the ILO has adopted 176 conventions and now has 174 member nations.

Support for international labor standards has waned in recent years, for several reasons. First, a shift toward neoliberal economic policy in industrialized countries has questioned the value of labor regulation. This is part of a generally negative view of government action, wherein labor standards are seen as distorting the efficiency of markets, hurting growth and employment. In addition, economic globalization has changed the nature of competition. International competition creates pressure to cut labor and other costs while it increases the need for greater flexibility in production. Furthermore, many governments are eager to attract foreign direct investment, so strengthening the bargaining power of employers.

The Political and Economic Debate

The foregoing trends have been associated with other broad shifts in the emphasis of public awareness and concern. Increasing public awareness of exploitative labor practices and rising public anxieties over job loss both support a call for a "social clause" that would inject labor standards into international trade agreements. This would mean that trade sanctions could be invoked when there are violations of agreed upon international labor standards "relating to the freedom of association, the right to collective bargaining, the prohibition of forced labour, equality of treatment and nondiscrimination in employment, and minimum wage." [176] Such a clause would aim to eliminate unfair trade advantages accruing to countries that benefit from inhumane labor practices.

Opponents, mainly developing countries, perceive a linkage between trade and labor standards as a disguised form of protectionism. While the (mostly First World) proponents of a social clause in trade agreements stress the economic efficiency of trade sanctions, the opponents fear that higher labor standards would act as an economic drag. "Although the existence of child labour and other forms of labour exploitation is not denied, this is seen as the unavoidable side-effect of underdevelopment and poverty. . . . Thus the appropriate response should be expanded access to industrialized markets in order to raise growth. . . ." [177] These opposing positions have introduced yet another layer of mistrust between industrialized and developing countries.

The economic literature deals with these issues within three categories. The first concerns the question of whether harmonization of labor standards with other (such as trade) agreements is necessary to ensure fairness. Second is whether trade liberalization causes a "race to the bottom" with respect to labor standards. The third category asks whether there is a real need for a formal link between trade agreements and labor standards.

Is Harmonization Necessary?

"The broad case for harmonization rests on the argument that some domestic policies, such as rules relating to market entry for foreign investors and environmental and labour standards, have an effect on a country's international competitiveness." [179] Harmonization is viewed as a way to "level the playing field."

A standard response to this argument is that any country will gain from trade if it uses the differentials between its production costs and the costs of other countries to define its comparative advantage. It does not make any theoretical difference what causes these cost differentials. This argument, however, assumes certain ideal conditions of competition and undistorted markets. Lacking these conditions in the real world, there are "second best" arguments, as well as noneconomic considerations, that support the idea of pushing for uniform international standards of human rights and humane economic treatment.

Fairness arguments that do not depend on economic theory start from the premise that practices such as child labor and forced labor are intrinsically wrong. When some groups of producers and workers find themselves disadvantaged—as some inevitably will be—by trade liberalization, their loss is especially hard to justify and accept if exploitative labor practices are known to undergird the successfully competing imports.

A more theoretical argument notes that "the impact of trade liberalization on the distribution of income in a given country is different depending on whether or not there is policy harmonization. Without harmonization the extra cost of unilaterally maintaining, say, a higher labor standard is borne by producers in the country concerned because the world market price of the good produced does not change." [180] With harmonization, which is intended to alter production practices throughout the world (presumably in the direction of higher costs), there will be a rise in the world prices, and the cost burden is then shifted from producers to consumers.

A Race to the Bottom?

A common view is that, without international action, increasing economic competition in an era of globalization will put downward pressure on labor standards. This pressure comes from need for firms to cut costs, as well as the possibility that governments will attract foreign direct investment by lowering labor standards. From this perspective, labor standards can be seen as public goods that can only be produced at the international level. Isolated national action will not suffice because, without universal, enforced standards, defectors who choose not to comply will gain an unfair competitive advantage.

The counter argument is that producers who choose to adopt high labor standards can shield themselves from loss of competitiveness by shifting the cost to workers in the form of lower wages. (There is some evidence that this does commonly occur.) Similarly, on the national level, it is possible to adjust for the cost of higher standards by depreciating a nation's exchange rate (thus shifting the burden to consumers who have to pay more for imports) or by redistributing the burden through higher taxes. These solutions may, however, be infeasible on account of political or distributional considerations.

Arguments on this topic continue, due to a lack of empirical evidence that could support the theoretical positions. It is not convincingly evident that the incidence or intensity of labor exploitation has increased with globalization, either in low-wage, low labor standard countries or in the developed countries that complain of unfair competition.

Should There Be a Link between Trade and Labor Standards?

While there is wide acceptance of the basic principles that have been enshrined in the Constitution of the ILO and, more recently, in the Declaration of the World Summit on Social Development, there is continuing disagreement on whether such standards should be formally linked to trade agreements. One controversy concerns national and cultural sovereignty. It is argued that labor standards are culturally specific and therefore do not lend themselves to universal moral consensus. Similarly, on economic grounds it has been said that "Each country will arrive at its own optimum equilibrium point, given its level of development, resource endowments, path of institutional development, etc." [184]

A second area of controversy over a social clause concerns the relative costs and benefits of alternative instruments for achieving the objective of labor standards. Neoliberals argue that public intervention is distortionary and that higher standards can have unintended effects on their targeted beneficiaries, such as child workers and their families. From this perspective, economic growth driven by free trade will indirectly raise labor standards via rising labor demand and wages. Other alternatives include instruments such as consumer boycotts of goods produced by unacceptable labor conditions; these, however, are likely to be plagued by free-rider problems.

A number of responses have been made to these suggestions. Empirically, the evidence on growth retardation due to the spread of labor standards is mixed. The idea that better standards will follow economic growth is rebutted with the observation that "growth in undemocratic countries resolutely hostile to labour rights is unlikely to lead to any improvement. In countries with high inequality in the distribution of wealth and income the trickle-down effect from growth to improving labour standards is likely to be weak. . . ." [187]

In fact, a case can be made on the opposite side—that labor standards enhance productivity, encourage cooperative work organization and higher investment in worker training, and push economic systems onto the healthy development path that depends on high productivity rather than on cheap labor.

Widely applied labor standards are not only recognized as morally necessary—they also offer economic benefits to both rich and poor nations. The benefits to the latter were just mentioned. The gain to industrialized nations is in the removal of "international public bads." The remaining controversies are not about whether such standards should be implemented, but about how—and how closely they should be linked to other policies.

Regardless of their findings, however, economic considerations cannot override the strong moral case in favor of observing the core standards that are basic human rights.

Summary of

Policy Options for the North

by Adrian Wood

[Published in *North–South Trade, Employment and Inequality: Changing Fortunes in a Skill-Driven World* (Oxford: Clarendon Press, 1994), 346–94.]

Most economists have concluded that trade with developing countries has at most a minor impact on employment and wages in industrialized nations. Adrian Wood, however, argues that trade with the South has played a major role in depressing the demand for less-skilled labor in the North, as seen in the earlier chapters of his book, and in the related article summarized in Part III (see "How Trade Hurt Unskilled Workers"). In the concluding chapter of his book, summarized here, Wood examines the available responses to the effects of trade for developed countries.

Motives for Intervention

Trade has increased the aggregate welfare of Northern nations by providing consumers with inexpensive imported goods. However, it has harmed workers (and owners of immobile capital) in the specific industries most affected by foreign competition. It has also lowered the demand for less-skilled workers throughout the economy, perhaps by as much as 20 percent by 1990.

Is it appropriate for governments to take action in response to the decline in the demand for unskilled labor? There are three possible motives for intervention. First, policy intervention could promote efficiency; this is most relevant where wage rigidities limit the market demand for unskilled labor, as in Europe. Second, because unskilled workers and their families are among the poorer members of society, it seems inequitable that they should be made even poorer by trade that benefits the nation as a whole. The third motive is related to equity, but conceptually distinct: Falling wages and rising unemployment lead to social corrosion, including increased crime, drug abuse, racial tension, homelessness, and other forms of degradation and decay. Such problems predate recent labor market trends—but they are clearly made worse by those trends.

Protectionism and Education

There are four possible policy responses: trade barriers, education and training, increases in the demand for unskilled labor, and redistribution of income. Of the four, trade barriers are the least desirable. The best arguments for protectionism—sheltering infant industries, achieving economies of scale, and stimulating innovation—do not generally apply to richer countries facing competition from poorer ones. However, there will be recurring political pressure for protectionism for workers affected by trade, unless better means of promoting equity are adopted.

Education and training are in many ways the most attractive solution to the problems caused by trade. While trade causes a decrease in the demand for unskilled labor, education and training cause a decrease in the supply of unskilled labor (and a corresponding increase in the supply of skilled labor). Those who remain unskilled also benefit, since their type of labor becomes scarcer, improving their prospects for employment and wage increases.

However, there are limitations and difficulties facing a labor strategy of education and training. Since educational initiatives are usually expensive, it is necessary to consider the sources of financing. New taxes to fund such programs will inevitably be paid (directly or indirectly) largely by workers. If taxes fall differentially on unskilled workers, the problems of equity and social corrosion will be worsened. If, as seems more feasible, the taxes are largely borne by skilled workers, then there will be a decline in the after-tax rewards to skills, and hence a decline in the market incentives to acquire and use skills. This disincentive partially offsets the benefits of educational efforts that are intended to increase the supply of skills. In a poorly designed program, the financing disincentive could even outweigh the educational benefits, resulting in a net decrease in skilled labor. Policies must be carefully designed to avoid such perverse outcomes.

Employment Programs and Redistribution

A third option is the use of taxes and public expenditure to boost the relative demand for unskilled labor. In theory this could be done via a payroll tax/subsidy scheme, giving employers a subsidy for hiring unskilled workers and taxing them when they hire skilled workers. More realistic options include a progressive payroll tax, taking a larger percentage of higher-wage employees' pay—or public works programs, such as the United States adopted in the 1930s.

When relative wages of skilled and unskilled workers are flexible, as is nearly true in the United States, then there is no efficiency justification for boosting the demand for unskilled labor. In this case the market reflects the relative need for different grades of labor. It may still be desirable to increase demand for unskilled labor, to improve equity or reduce social corrosion. On the other hand, when relative wages are rigid, as in much of Europe, then job-creating initiatives can be supported on efficiency grounds as well. Labor market rigidities mean that the wages of unskilled workers are above the opportunity cost of their labor. This reduces the demand for unskilled labor below the most efficient level. Government programs that raise the demand for such labor may move the economy toward the optimal level of unskilled employment.

A final option is redistribution of income from skilled to unskilled workers through income taxes and transfer payments. Redistribution is already practiced on a large, though varying, scale in most Northern countries. It is typically designed to benefit low-income people in general, or families with children, and addresses many other social goals in addition to the welfare of unskilled workers. Any new initiative must be carefully integrated into a country's existing systems of redistribution.

If wages are flexible, the analysis of redistribution to unskilled workers is very similar to that of subsidies designed to create jobs, as discussed above. Economists are familiar with the idea that the ultimate incidence of a subsidy to unskilled workers, or to their employers, depends on the elasticities of supply and demand functions—not on who actually receives the subsidy. However, voters and politicians may have a preference for subsidies to workers rather than their employers—making direct redistribution more feasible than job-creation efforts.

If wages are rigid, job creation and income redistribution are no longer analytically similar. In this case there is less need for supplements to low wages and more need for transfers to the unemployed. Despite some reductions and restrictions in recent years, Northern countries generally accept government income transfers to the unemployed.

Alternative Policy Packages

No one policy alone is likely to be effective. Trade protection should not in general be part of the policy package for a Northern country. The other options may all play an important role. The first step should be to assess the maximum scope for cost-effective education and training programs, that is, programs for which the positive effect on the supply of skilled labor outweighs the disincentive effect of increased taxes. The remaining gap should be filled by demand-side and/or redistributive programs.

In America, where wages are flexible and there is less social concern about inequality than in other countries, one might question whether to implement *any* demand-side or redistributive programs. However, reduction in social corrosion is important for any society, and there is some ethical concern about poverty in all countries. Since job-creation subsidies and income redistribution are analytically equivalent in a flexible wage economy, the choice of policy will be dictated by political practicality. A combination of education and training with income supplements for low-income workers appears the most appropriate.

In Europe there is greater concern about inequality, and wage rigidity means that there are additional efficiency arguments for public policy intervention. Job-creation subsidies and redistribution are not equivalent in a rigid wage economy, and Europe already has extensive income redistribution programs.

Here the most appropriate package is a combination of education and training with a progressive payroll tax that creates an incentive for employers to hire low-skilled workers. The simplest way to implement such a tax would be to modify the existing structure of employers' social security contributions.

Finally, what are the costs of being wrong—that is, the costs of doing too much, or too little, because the underlying analysis was mistaken? If the recommended policy initiatives are adopted, but trade turns out to be a smaller problem than assumed here, the cost is that unneeded education and training, job creation, and income redistribution initiatives were undertaken. On the other hand, if nothing is done, but trade does turn out to cause large labor market problems, the resulting cost would be measured in increased, unalleviated poverty, unemployment, inequality, crime, urban decay, and other forms of social corrosion. The costs of doing too much appear far more bearable than the costs of doing too little.

PART IV

New Technologies and Work Organization

Overview Essay

by Laurie Dougherty

Industrialization on the March

> The world is entering a new age—the age of total industrialization. Some countries are far along the road; many more are just beginning the journey. But everywhere, at a faster or slower pace, the peoples of the world are on the march toward industrialization. They are launched on a long course that is certain to change their communities into new and vastly different societies whose forms cannot yet be clearly foreseen. The twentieth century is an age of enormous and profound and worldwide transformation.[1]

Although these words, from the introduction to *Industrialization and Industrial Man* by Clark Kerr, John Dunlop, Frederick Harbison, and Charles Myers, were written in the early 1960s, they parallel the sense of onrushing change on a global scale found in the prologue to Manuel Castells' three-volume discussion of the information age, published in 1996.

> Toward the end of the second millennium of the Christian Era several events of historical significance have transformed the social landscape of human life. A technological revolution, centered around information technologies, is reshaping, at accelerating pace, the material basis of society. Economies throughout the world have become globally interdependent, introducing a new form of relationship between economy, state, and society, in a system of variable geometry.[2]

Besides a vision of sweeping transformation, each of these paragraphs takes the method of production of goods and services as a system, an organizing principle for human life and society. The method of production situates the society in time and space. What is different is the vision of the outcome. Although the earlier paragraph, written by several of the most renowned analysts of industrial

113

relations, does not claim to predict precisely what the final form of an industrialized world will look like, the reader is left with the impression of a coming homogenized, industrialized world—something that is all of a piece, only awaiting the completion of a process undertaken "at a faster or slower pace" by people around the world. For Castells, however, the outcome is not a homogenized world, but one of "variable geometry" in which differences are not dissolved, but rather are linked up, played off against each other, and incorporated into a complex global network.

In preparing this book on the changing nature of work, we have been faced with a need to come to grips with the fact that not only is work changing, but the direction of change is shifting and the discussion of work is changing. For two centuries work changed in the direction that Kerr and his coauthors perceived: spreading industrialization and the growth of large-scale organizations—cities, enterprises, governments—that operated according to a "web of rules" to integrate and manage a complex system of social and economic relationships. Although the word "web" might seem to prefigure the free-wheeling information web we know today, for Kerr and his coauthors, this web of rules is a constraining one that holds together a hierarchical structure. In the workplace this structure contains a "few managers . . . and many to be managed."[3]

The industrial economy was essentially a manufacturing economy with clerical and service occupations integrated into a vast system for the assembly and distribution of mass produced goods. Work was organized around an ever-increasing division of labor within large enterprises regulated by large-scale government. As these enterprises absorbed more and more of the work once done in homes and farms and workshops, work relocated to mass production factories, vast complexes for processing chemicals and ores, and towering office buildings that centralized the bureaucratic administration of both firms and governments. The family shrank into a small mobile unit for consumption and cultural activity, able to move up with an advancing career or to absorb the shock of technological change. While new technologies might render a product or process (and therefore a particular job) obsolete, technology also opened up new opportunities that were easily grasped by a well-educated workforce. New technology meant progress in the form of both products and production techniques, resulting in a better quality of life for all. With the spread of industrialization throughout the world, it could be imagined that all people would eventually come to share in the well-being produced by the industrial age.

For Kerr and his coauthors the march toward the industrial age was a campaign of the new against the old, waged by elites (of various persuasions—capitalist, communist, nationalist, dynastic, and so on). Science-based technology was the basis for material progress and the source of its universality, because science-based technology could be shared and understood across political boundaries and despite cultural differences. Management, by members of the industrializing elites or their delegates, was the pivotal process for coordination of complex organizations and subordination of the labor force to the "web of rules" by which the industrial enterprise operates.

The Labor Process Under Industrialization

The workplace came under intense scrutiny during the restless period of protest and rebellion that marked the late 1960s and early 1970s. Strikes broke out in many mass production industries and young black workers in Detroit began to display the same resistance to the white-dominated establishment exhibited on a community level by militant civil rights organizations. The discourse around work turned toward a revival of interest in Marx's critique of capitalism. Harry Braverman's *Labor and Monopoly Capital*[4] stripped the Industrial Age of its grandeur and revealed a labor process marked by loss: loss of skill, of autonomy, and of technical understanding of the production system as a whole. Workers in the factories and offices were not participants in the march of progress, but cogs in the machinery of profit-seeking capitalism.[5]

What Braverman shares with earlier analysts of industrial relations is not their vision of progress, but rather the understanding that in industrialized society labor is situated within a hierarchical system that is emblematic of the organization of society as a whole. While Kerr et al. accepted the "inevitable and eternal separation of industrial men into managers and the managed"[6] as part of the structure of the industrial system, for Braverman the managers and the managed exist in an antagonistic relationship—one that is neither inevitable nor eternal, but rather is the result of a particular historical process.

In the course of industrialization, technology became, in addition to a source of greater productivity, a tool that extended and intensified the reach of managerial control. Scientific knowledge was appropriated by industrialists and transformed into usable technology that an educational establishment harnessed to the needs of industry.[7] This idea has been developed in detail in David Noble's discussion of the rise of the engineering profession in the late nineteenth and early twentieth centuries and its integration with emerging structures of corporate management.[8] As engineering and management became entwined, innovation and productivity became more and more a matter of wresting control from workers and situating it in intricately engineered machines and the planning departments of large industrial firms.

Marxist analysts reinterpreted the construction of "industrial man" as a process of deskilling and disempowerment of workers. Their understanding was based both on empirical data from research on contemporary work sites and on review of books, articles, and published presentations by late nineteenth and early twentieth century practitioners of scientific management—particularly its outspoken founder, Frederick Taylor. Taylor and his colleagues were quite open about their search for the "one best way" to accomplish any given task. They aimed to improve efficiency. Taylor felt that management should be willing to pay for productivity. One element of scientific management, as he conceived it, was an incentive-based system of compensation. However, he also thought that the skill of the craftsman, gained through years of experience and indoctrination into the customary knowledge and practices of the craft, was an impediment to a rational understanding of technique; and that the craftsman's control over the pace and sequence of tasks was an impediment to efficiency. Taylorism brought the stopwatch and the trained observer to the workplace, translating experience and skill into time and motion studies and specialized equipment.[9]

Henry Ford took this process even further when he arrayed rigidly specified and carefully sequenced jobs beside a moving conveyer to produce vast quantities of automobiles quickly and cheaply for a burgeoning mass market. Mass production spread to other industries and became one of the core institutions of the Industrial Age. But where some analysts saw an organization grand enough to lead the march of progress, others saw a bloated bureaucracy set up to coordinate a carefully engineered work environment and discipline a reluctant workforce that had been robbed of initiative and skill.

It is fair to say that work has been changing at a rapid pace since the earliest days of the industrial era, but the changes we are most concerned with in the summaries in Part IV are those sparked by computerized technologies and the transition in the last quarter of the twentieth century, from the industrial to the information age. The mood at the end of the millennium is uncertain rather than triumphant, marked by both opportunity and risk—a loss of the sense that progress is inevitable.

New Directions and New Technologies

If the impact of industrialization proved not to be universally progressive, the drive toward industrialization proved not to be as straightforward as Kerr and his colleagues imagined. After World War II, the United States was the only industrial economy unscathed by the war. For twenty-five years, the United States played a hegemonic role in world economic and political affairs. U.S. military presence around the world enforced a Pax Americana in the face of a perceived threat from the Soviet bloc. An international monetary agreement signed at Bretton Woods, NH, in 1944 established the U.S. dollar as the world's leading currency. U.S. corporations invested in overseas factories, mergers, and joint ventures.

Eventually, the recovering economies of Europe and Japan began to compete with the United States for world markets. The Bretton Woods agreement broke down. Other political and economic factors, including falling profit rates (beginning in the late 1960s) and the oil price shocks of the 1970s contributed to spreading economic stagnation.[10] Competition led firms to seek greater efficiencies, lower costs, and improved quality. Cheaper labor in developing countries induced many corporations to outsource production to low-wage areas. The process of industrialization in developing countries shifted away from attempts to become self-sufficient in manufactured goods toward production for export. In the developed countries the confident, expansive discourse of the Industrial Age gave way to images of decay and uncertainty. Aging factories closed or cut back production. Recession swept one country after another.

At the same time, computers and factory automation had increasing effects on the workplace. They enhanced the mobility of capital through improved communication and transportation capabilities. Bluestone and Harrison called them permissive technologies because they permitted or enabled "managers to shift capital (and products) across long distances, and to operate far-reaching networks of production facilities."[11] New technologies used in this way fostered the emergence of regionally or even globally integrated networks of production and distribution.

Computer-based technologies also changed the conduct of work within the workplace. In his book *Work Transformed*, Harley Shaiken (who also has an article summarized in Part IV) investigated the impact of several forms of electronic technology, including numerical control and computer numerical control of machine tools, flexible manufacturing systems, robotics, and computer-aided design/computer-aided manufacturing (CAD/CAM) systems. He saw a disjuncture between the potential for these programmable technologies to reintegrate the mental and manual aspects of production and to relieve the worker of the more tedious or strenuous or dangerous jobs, and the actual uses of these technologies in the same controlling, deskilling manner promoted by the tenets of scientific management a century ago.[12] Shaiken's own experience working as a machinist under very different forms of work organization led him to understand that technology could be adopted in ways that either enhanced or degraded the work experience.

Like earlier researchers, the authors of summaries in Part IV are concerned with the relationships between technology, work organization, and skill and autonomy in the workforce. But those relationships are no longer sheltered within a well-structured web of rules. Intense competition is pervasive, leading to drastic measures to cut costs and improve efficiency. When information technology combines with communications technology, not only is the individual workplace restructured, but the work is redistributed with little concern for time or distance. The dynamic is not one that tends to homogenize societies under the steady march of industrialization, but one that exploits differences and sets workers in competition with each other as investors seek out lower costs and higher short-term returns.

At the same time the competitive environment demands that firms command consistently high performance from their workers. As Peter Cappelli points out in an article summarized in Part V, these goals may conflict: One view sees workers as a liability, the other as an asset. Part V will take up the discussion of the tendency to detach workers from long association with employers. Part IV takes up the discussion of technology, skills, and work organization in the context of computerization and global competition.

John Mathews, an industrial relations analyst from Australia, leads off with an introduction to sociotechnical organizational change. The sociotechnical perspective is an historical one that holds that the effective use of technology and organizational form are mutually dependent. Eileen Appelbaum and Rosemary Batt analyze several work systems that exist as alternatives to mass production. It is worth noting that each one is associated with a different country, having evolved within a particular set of institutions and product and labor market conditions.

Two of those work systems are examined in more detail: lean production in the article by John MacDuffie and John Krafcik, and Swedish sociotechnical design by Christian Berggren. Here the term sociotechnical is used in a more limited sense to mean a form of work organization designed with concern for the needs of the human worker. In the Swedish case, young workers at Volvo were so alienated by the tedium of mass production that the company dismantled the assembly line in its newer plants in favor of team-based work units. (One interesting point made in a different part of Berggren's book is that Volvo's Belgian factory had no problems with turnover because unemployment was high and workers had few other opportunities. No efforts were made there to make working conditions more congenial.)

Lean production, a system that originated in Japan and can now be found in many parts of the world, has been applauded for its ability to raise efficiency and reduce defects. Critics of lean production claim that it creates a very stressful work environment, while supporters claim that it eliminates wasteful procedures and involves the workforce in continuous improvement of tools and techniques. Its methods call to mind the X-efficiency theory of Harvey Leibenstein.[13] According to this theory, although economics is based on the assumption that efficiencies are maximized, in reality there are gaps between what is actually achieved and what could be achieved. The goal of lean production appears to be the closing of that gap by inducing the highest level of human effort and by incremental redesign of equipment and procedures.

Besides claims for high performance, supporters of lean production claim that it is the wave of the future and will come to dominate manufacturing on a worldwide basis in the way the Fordist factory dominated the mid-twentieth century. Harley Shaiken and Harry Browne investigated this claim at several Japanese-owned factories in Mexico. They found little evidence of lean production techniques in these plants even though lean production had been effectively implemented at a Ford plant in Mexico and many factories in the United States.

Sociologists Shoshana Zuboff and Steven Vallas and John Beck undertook qualitative studies of the effects of computerization on the workforce—Zuboff at work sites in several industries including paper and telecommunications, and Vallas and Beck at several paper mills. Vallas and Beck found a reprise of the displacement of knowledge and skill away from workers and toward management and engineers. Zuboff found a more complex process in which workers were initially disoriented by the change, particularly the loss of physical contact with the product and need to rely on indicators rather than direct experience of the process. But in some cases they achieved a new mastery over the high-tech equipment and were able to integrate feedback from it into a new understanding of the work process.

Factories are not the only sites for new technology or forms of organization. Two studies summarized in Part IV were conducted of the effects of office technology. Appelbaum and Albin's study of the insurance industry found that computers could be used in clerical work and claims processing in ways that either enhanced the autonomy of the worker or rendered the work routine and repetitive. A major research project into the effects of computerization on the office, directed by Heidi Hartmann, produced a number of case studies and a summary volume. The chapter summarized here is a thought-provoking analysis of what makes a job good or bad and how various elements of job quality may be affected by technological change.

Technology has effects on individual workers as well as on the organizational framework within which work gets done. One recent concern of researchers has been whether and to what extent computerization has affected the skill content of jobs and how that effect, if any, influences wages by shifting demand for particular skills. After a detailed econometric analysis David Autor, Lawrence Katz, and Alan Krueger found that by virtually any measure, the increase in computer use in the workplace is associated with an acceleration in wage inequality. John DiNardo and John-Steffen Pischke questioned whether this was in fact a real result of computerization or whether the measurement of computer use was capturing the effect of unmeasured variables. They found that the use of writing implements also had a measurable and statistically significant effect on wages; they interpreted the increased payoff to using pencils at work as a spurious reflection of the effect of some other unspecified variable. If such a spurious relationship exists for pencil use, might it appear for computer use as well? DiNardo and Pischke presume that computers are having a profound impact on the workforce, but that the effect on wages is likely to be an indirect one resulting from the development of more complex, information-rich work settings. In the ongoing debate between the two teams of researchers, Autor et al. respond that the statistical evidence shows a strong, direct influence of computerization on wages.

Stephen Barley reintroduces the idea of power, bringing an organizational theorist's point of view to his case of workplace relationships. The final form of any technological or organizational change will depend on the relative bargaining strengths of workers and managers.

What's Missing from This Picture?

What's missing is a sense of connection of work to some larger purpose. For all its inflated aura of destiny, the project of the Industrial Age was progress, in the sense of raising the general level of material prosperity. Material prosperity is best understood as an intermediate goal. Wealth is not an end in itself, but a means to other ends (such as comfort, amusement, security, respect, and so on).

With the advantage of hindsight we can see that much economic growth has not been environmentally sound, has neither been evenly distributed nor securely grounded, and may not have achieved its intended final ends. Along the way technology was used to externalize the environmental costs—both by shifting it onto those whose voices were little heard and by deferring it to the future. That future is now arriving. As the bills come due we may find that progress, as it was understood in the Industrial Age, is inevitably slowed, stopped, or even reversed.

As to whether the prosperity of the Industrial Age has been successful in improving general human well-being—that is a large and difficult question. Aspects of it were addressed in the preceding Frontiers volume, *Human Well-Being and Economic Goals*.[14] At this point, it is enough to say that this is an issue that deserves much more attention than it has yet received within the debates on the issues discussed here. Lean production or the Swedish model? Open or restricted trade? Taylorist organization or workplace democracy? To make social choices that will go in one of these directions or another, we obviously need to understand the causal relationships among the relevant variables, including various management systems, legal regimes, and labor productivity. But such understanding is not enough in itself. We also need to have a clear idea of our final goals. Then, only, will we be able to probe further into the matter of which social choices will lead toward, and which away from the achievement of our goals.

Notes

1. Clark Kerr, John T. Dunlop, Frederick H. Harbison, and Charles A. Myers, *Industrialization and Industrial Man—The Problems of Labor and Management in Economic Growth* (New York: Oxford University Press, 1964), 3.
2. Manuel Castells, *The Rise of the Network Society* (Oxford: Blackwell Publishers, 1996), The Information Age: Economy, Society and Culture, vol. I, 1
3. Kerr et al. (note 1 above), 24.

4. Harry Braverman, *Labor and Monopoly Capital—The Degradation of Work in the Twentieth Century* (New York: Monthly Review Press, 1974)

5. Braverman gives scant attention to the labor process in the then socialist bloc. He briefly mentions that it mimicked the organization, if not the structure of ownership, of work in the capitalist world to achieve the benefits of modernization efficiently, a situation that he considered to be ultimately bankrupt.

6. Kerr et al., 15, 1960 edition as quoted in Braverman, 16. (In the 1964 edition, page 8, the following phrase carries the same meaning without, however, quite the same resonance: "the inevitable structuring of the managers and the managed in the course of industrialization.") In the introduction to the later edition, Kerr and colleagues claim that their most recent research leads them to downplay the influence of worker protest on the evolution of industrial society and to describe a generally collaborative relationship between managers and the managed.

7. Braverman, 156.

8. David F. Noble, *America by Design—Science, Technology and the Rise of Corporate Capitalism* (Oxford: Oxford University Press, 1977).

9. Ibid., Chapter 10.

10. See Barry Bluestone and Bennett Harrison, *The Deindustrialization of America— Plant Closings, Community Abandonment, and the Dismantling of Basic Industry* (New York: Basic Books, 1982).

11. Ibid., 115.

12. Harley Shaiken, *Work Transformed—Automation and Labor in the Computer Age* (New York: Holt, Rinehart and Winston, 1984).

13. Harvey Leibenstein, *The Collected Essays of Harvey Leibenstein. Volume 2. X-Efficiency and Micro-Micro Theory*, ed. Kenneth Button (New York: New York University Press, 1989).

14. Frank Ackerman, David Kiron, Neva R. Goodwin, Jonathan M. Harris, and Kevin Gallagher, eds. *Human Well-Being and Economic Goals* (Washington, D.C.: Island Press, 1997).

Summary of

Sociotechnical Organizational Change: Technological and Organizational Coevolution

by John A. Mathews

[Chapter 4 in *Catching the Wave: Workplace Reform in Australia* (St. Leonards, Australia: Allen & Unwin, 1994), 85–101.]

The history of modern industry has often been written in terms of technological change. This article describes a more complex, coevolutionary model of technoorganizational change: an iterative process in which changes in technology and changes in organization are each spurred by the other, each foreclosing some possibilities to the other, while opening different possibilities.

Technoorganizational Coevolution

Competition among today's firms to define "best practices"—that is, the most efficient and quality conscious production methods—reflects the struggle to shape the newest paradigm in industrial history. A number of authors have noted transformations that have ushered in new production systems. Perez and Freeman[1] identified five major shifts, focused on (1) the factory system, (2) steam power and powered transportation, (3) the use of steel and electricity and the emergence of large corporations, (4) oil-based energy and the rise of mass production, and (5) information technology.

This analysis will make explicit what can be seen in these descriptions, namely that technological change is associated with organizational change. A change in one of these elements of a production system requires adaptations that can spark innovations in the other component of the system. On a small scale, if a new conveyor design links two production processes such as manufacturing and packing, this may foster teamwork between two departments. Teamwork may in turn lead to improvements in equipment. With each iteration several possibilities for adaptive response can coexist, but once a choice is made it will shape future options for change. An examination of the five paradigm shifts noted above sheds further light on this process.

The *factory system,* a major characteristic of the first industrial revolution, was initially an organizational innovation that brought under one roof the pieces of production that had been scattered (or "put out") among rural cottages. This made it easier to coordinate production and to control labor. Note that this description reverses the usual treatment of the industrial revolution as originating with the introduction of water-powered machinery. In fact, it was the concentration of labor that made the development and use of machinery feasible.

In the 1830s the *steam engine* liberated factories from dependence on flowing water. New processes for the production of materials, such as iron and pottery, and new forms of transportation, such as railroads and steamships, increased both the productive capacity and the kinds of goods that could be factory-made. Laws, forms of business organization, and workers' organizations began to reflect industrial rather than mercantile or agrarian interests. "Productivity soared with these innovations, leading to a broader-based regime of accumulation, and the production of wage goods for the new working class from the new factories." [87] Systematic attention began to be paid to innovation as such.

With the development of *electric power,* complex technological systems spread rapidly through urban regions and industries. Inventions in new products and processes brought on a new wave of investment and raised productivity further still. The notion of modernism emerged, identified with the dynamism of machinery. Giant corporations emerged and began to integrate what had been separate, market-based activities. Standardization and production with interchangeable parts set the stage for the mass production industries of the twentieth century.

The fourth paradigm shift has been called an "industrial divide" by Michael Piore and Charles Sabel, who describe it as a "parting of the ways between craft- and custom-based production and mass production." [89] *Mass production* is centered on the standardization of products (and consumer tastes), processes, labor, cost, and accounting methods. It requires mass markets and a consistently high level of consumption. The crisis that could result when these conditions failed was exemplified in the Depression of the 1930s, stemming from a critical shortfall in demand. Momentum was regained after World War II. Mass production and mass consumption were supported by an elaborate institutional regime that included collective bargaining of wages, regulation of both domestic and international monetary systems, social security and other welfare measures, and liberal trade policies. Standardization spread to services like fast food and retailing. This whole system, termed Fordism, had a "golden era" from 1945 to 1968. For the past several years, however, Fordism has been declining, partly because the rigidity of mass production makes it unable to cope with shifting markets and the consequent demand for product and process flexibility.

A new paradigm is now struggling to emerge—the fifth in this industrial series. Its characteristic *information technologies* appear to be best complemented by organizational redesign that can take advantage of the possibility that had been so outstandingly neglected in Fordism: workplace initiative. Flexibility is one of the qualities most sought in today's "best-practice" systems. Information technologies offer this quality because they are programmable and can be adapted to changing product demand and innovative processes. However, these technologies are not compatible with the rigid standardization of mass production systems.

Japanese manufacturers were the first to make the necessary organizational adaptations to the new possibility, in what came to be called lean production techniques. Other adaptations emerged as smaller firms created cooperative clusters or networks (for example, in industrial districts such as Emilia-Romagna in Italy, Baden Wuertemberg in Germany, and the Tokyo-Osaka axis in Japan).

Paradigm Shifts and Diffusion

The idea of a paradigm shift can be found in several schools of thought. The terminology itself originated with Thomas Kuhn's discussion of changes in scientific thought. The Schumpeterian school emphasizes the role of innovation and diffusion of technological developments. Economics links innovation with investment.

With each paradigm shift, new best practices emerge that firms ignore at their peril. In each of our historical cases the leading edge technologies fulfilled three conditions: They could be used in most sectors; they were cheaper than the technology being supplanted; and they could draw on abundant raw materials. Changes that occur in this way are not best understood as technological determinism, but rather as compatible technology and organization jointly forming best practices that outperform competing methods of production. Similarly, with the emergence of information technology, we see the development of new organizational forms that can best exploit its potentials.

This line of argument (which has its critics) implies a mismatch between the new information technology and the older organizational forms that were compatible with the mass production paradigm. Information technology contributes most to productivity and profitability when it is employed in systems characterized by flexibility, responsiveness, and adaptability; therefore the firms that adopt such systems gain a competitive edge. However, the general literature on paradigm shifts leaves open the question of how firms should proceed with the organizational part of this technoorganizational shift. Some observations on relatively successful experiences are summarized below.

Adoption of New Organizational Forms

New models of organization can arise through either of two processes: the creation of new organizations or the transformation of existing ones. Transformation is the more common process, but experts are divided on how to achieve it. One school of thought prefers change from the bottom up—the other from the top down. The former approach is participative, but can lack leadership and direction; the latter is autocratic, but can fail to foster sustainable change, since people may not take responsibility for making the change work.

In fact, most programs of organizational change fail, often because many of those who will be affected see their interests as threatened. The keys to successful change are leadership and involvement. Leadership must demonstrate that losses will be offset by gains, paying close attention to the basic interests of employment security, wages, preservation of skills, and a sense of dignity of worth. "[C]hange works best, resulting in sustainable new structure, when it involves those who have a stake in the outcome." [100] Resistance to change must be taken seriously, its sources understood, and special efforts made to educate and include those who feel threatened. Those affected must feel that the process of change is legitimate in the context of agreed upon rules and principles. Often these principles are established and situated within a framework of industrial relations that provides a familiar arena for negotiation of the conditions and consequences of change.

Large corporations that are in the process of introducing the current "best practices" frequently find that the biggest challenge is to bring on board the middle management and technical personnel who feel threatened by the need to share power. Successful efforts to date have often started with small pilot programs that could give concrete forms to the concept and demonstrate success. A "yeast effect" lets changes on the shop floor work their way up to top management at the point when problem-solving teams require management cooperation to get things done. An important part of the shift occurs when management can redefine itself in a "problem-solving" light, in place of its former identification with "command and control."

The process of technoorganizational coevolution requires a series of choices based on probing and testing the environment. Those firms that appear to have made the transition successfully have become "learning organizations" that can continuously find and institutionalize the strategies and structures best suited to meet their needs.

Note

1. C. Freeman and C. Perez, 1998, "Structural Crises of Adjustment: Business Cycles and Investment Behaviour," in G. Dos et al. (eds.) *Technical Change and Economic Theory* (London: Pinter Publishers).

Summary of

Alternative Models of Production[1]

by Eileen Appelbaum and Rosemary Batt

[Published in *The New American Workplace*
(Ithaca, NY: Industrial Labor Relations Press, 1995), 29–84.]

The breakdown of the mass production model in the industrialized countries has given rise to a number of alternative models of industrial organization. In an effort to help U.S. firms catch up with these new organizational innovations, a comparison is presented of the four leading alternatives to mass production developed by other industrialized economies: Swedish sociotechnical systems, Japanese lean production, Italian flexible specialization, and German diversified quality production.

Swedish Sociotechnical Systems

Driven by efficiency concerns and the desire to humanize the workplace in the mid-1980s, Swedish firms began implementing what has become known as sociotechnical work systems. Sociotechnical work systems are more decentralized and more flexible than mass production mechanisms due to their use of work groups. This trait enables them to be more competitive in the low-volume, high-quality niche markets where many Swedish firms operate.

The work groups, or production teams, that have been most successful regulate themselves internally and are responsible for pacing, coordination, sequencing, and quality control. Some even allocate housekeeping tasks such as distributing work assignments among group members and scheduling vacation time. Production teams are also responsible for process improvements and problem-solving. Wage premiums give incentives for workers to be involved in continuous, often firm-sponsored training. Some groups receive a portion of their pay based on group performance.

The following aspects of the Swedish system separate it from the Taylorist work organization and have increased the efficiency of Swedish firms in several ways: (1) A variety of products can be assembled alternately with the same assembly lines; (2) integrating preventative maintenance and repair functions to work groups reduces downtime; (3) the use of quality controls by work groups increases quality and decreases reworking; (4) short absences by work group members can be covered without the need to find substitutes; (5) group work is more attractive to the labor force; and (6) managers see work groups as facilitators of decentralization and of flattened hierarchies.

Japanese Lean Production

The Japanese lean production model arose from an effort to reduce impediments that cause delays and imbalances in production and force firms to hold on to inventory buffers or work in progress. Examples of such impediments are long changeover times, bottlenecks, machine downtime, and quality defects. To reduce these impediments, the Japanese model teaches statistical process control and problem-solving techniques to workers and uses quality control circles to improve quality.

Quality control circles (QC circles) are small groups of hourly workers who are led by a foreman and meet voluntarily to discuss job-related quality problems. Such an approach has reduced costs and increased productivity, while improving morale, motivation, and self-development among workers. However, QC circles are not autonomous and do not participate in managerial decision-making. Foremen perform and supervise most of the housekeeping duties, although the procedures for these duties are often developed and improved on by the workers themselves. The commitment and capability of workers in these firms is enhanced through pay policies, training practices, and employment security—factors that also render these firms attractive to the external labor market.

In contrast to mass production, the Japanese model makes learning active, is able to increase quality without increasing cost, and supports increases in product variety. Active "learning" techniques include just-in-time inventory systems—which ensure that problems are identified early in the production process and are responded to quickly by workers—and process simplification efforts that examine each step in the production process to remove wasteful steps. These simultaneous quality improvements allow for greater efficiency and reduced cost. In contrast to traditional mass production firms, where increased quality would increase cost, the Japanese system also allows for greater product diversification.

Italian Flexible Specialization

As a response to a turbulent market environment that arose in Italy during the 1970s, the system now called flexible specialization was developed. New market conditions required greater flexibility than was possible under mass production. Flexible specialization focuses on (1) small-scale production of a wide array of goods; (2) small networks of producers that attain efficiency and flexibility through specialization and cooperation; (3) representation of worker interests through strong unions; and (4) governmental support for collective goods and services, thereby reducing costs and encouraging cooperation. Firms in these networks share a great deal of trust and information while still competing with each other for customers. These firms thus have the ability to achieve economies of scope, "an enhanced ability to respond to market-driven changes in product characteristics and marketing requirements." [38] In addition, they have a competitive advantage based on their ability to produce and deliver high-quality products with a degree of varied characteristics quickly.

What sets flexible specialization apart from mass production is its ability to prevent excess capacity. This is due to the collaborative nature of the networks since they enable individual firms to adapt to increasing demand without additional equipment that could prove redundant. Networks also facilitate product innovation and customization that are advantageous in niche markets. Flexible specialization performs best where competition is based more on quality and variety than on price.

German Diversified Quality Production

In the 1970s and 1980s, the German auto industry achieved a good deal of its success from its pursuit of quality-conscious markets where competition focused on quality of design rather than price. To reach that market, German firms employed what has become known as diversified quality production. This approach combined the craft and experience of a highly skilled workforce with the use of microelectronic technology to produce high volumes of a wide array of products for the high-end mass market.

To ensure such flexibility, the Germans put extensive effort into retraining to give the workforce a broad base of skills that could easily be adapted to different tasks. This was combined with microelectronically automated technology that enabled equipment to be adaptable to more than one product. German works councils are credited with making this transition run smoothly by practicing "negotiated adjustment" to new technology and changing market conditions. All of these factors altered the economies of scale that firms had traditionally experienced. Break-even points were met much more quickly and at a smaller volume than before.

Diversified production is different from mass production in that it focuses on skills development and the ability to capture high-end markets where customers are willing to pay for quality.

A Comparison of the Models

Each of the foregoing models confers a competitive advantage over mass production under particular conditions in the world economy. Italian flexible specialization is most advantageous during turbulent market conditions or in niche markets where rapid innovation is key. German diversified quality production excels in producing customized goods at high volumes for high-end markets. In contrast, Japanese lean production has done best at reducing costs and therefore finds it more difficult to function in markets where quality is the key component of competition. Finally, Swedish sociotechnical systems perform best in luxury markets.

All these new techniques use enhanced levels of worker participation, though the type of participation varies widely.

> In general, we can distinguish among employee participation schemes based on whether the participation takes place in parallel structures or affects the work organization or power relations between employees and managers; the level at which the participation takes place—shop-floor, establishment, or strategic firm decisions (implementation of new technology, investment plans, marketing strategies); and whether it is consultative (as most QCs are) or substantive. [79]

In Japanese lean production, participation occurs via parallel structures—in Swedish sociotechnical systems it is substantive. Italian flexible specialization is characterized by informal participation by workers on substantive issues—in German diversified-quality-production participation occurs through works councils that take part in plant-level adjustments and strategic decisions.

Conclusion

There are a number of viable alternatives to the mass production model of industrial organization, and each in particular is suited for different types of markets. U.S. firms have borrowed piecemeal from these models, but full applicability may prove to be difficult. In many cases, institutional and other socioeconomic concerns may stand in the way.

Note

1. This article summarizes research supported by the Sloan Foundation.

Summary of

Integrating Technology and Human Resources for High-Performance Manufacturing: Evidence from the International Auto Industry

by John Paul MacDuffie and John F. Krafcik

[Published in *Transforming Organizations,* eds. Thomas A. Kochan and Michael Useem (New York: Oxford University Press, 1992), 209–225.]

Since the mid-1980s, the International Motor Vehicle Program (IMVP) based at the Massachusetts Institute of Technology has been studying auto manufacturers to find and measure indicators of emerging production methods. These researchers developed the concept of *lean production* to characterize a cluster of techniques that originated with Japanese automakers and that today are being adapted, adopted, and debated around the world.

The Organizational Logic of Lean Production

The recent rapid advance of microprocessor-based technologies raised expectations that lower costs and greater quality would follow for firms that adopted them. These expectations have not been realized. Many analysts have concluded that to maximize the benefit of new technologies, skills and organizational context must be compatible and capable of evolving in concert. Lean production, a concept that emerged from a study of seventy auto assembly plants from twenty-four companies in seventeen countries, improves productivity and quality and "takes as a premise the existence of a skilled, motivated, and flexible work force, following a logic quite distinct from traditional mass production." [209]

Lean production integrates a firm's human resource strategy with its technology strategy. It promotes skill, motivation, flexibility, and problem-solving and continuous improvement activity in the workforce. This model contrasts with mass production technology, which seeks to enhance management control, reduce labor costs, and diminish reliance on the workforce. A key part of the organizational logic of lean production is to minimize use of the buffers commonly found in mass production systems to protect the process as a whole from disruption in one of its segments. Some examples of buffers are utility workers who take the place of absentees, repair stations for managing product defects, and storage of a large number of parts in case of delivery delays. Buffers are costly in terms of additional space, personnel, and inventory. They create slack and mask problems. Lean production relies on an insight first put into practice at Toyota, that disruptions are learning opportunities. "The minimization of buffers, as exemplified by just-in-time inventory policies, therefore serves a cybernetic or feedback function, providing valuable information that can be used for continuous incremental improvement of the production system." [211]

This approach is linked to human resource policies. Workers must be able to identify and solve problems on the spot since there are few reserve parts and few places to hide mistakes. Responsibilities like product inspection are carried out by workers who are trained for multiple tasks and willing to rotate jobs and work in teams. Lean production demands mental as well as physical effort, and workers must be well motivated. To encourage commitment, lean production systems include reciprocal policies such as job security, fewer status barriers, performance-based compensation, and company investment in workers' skills. Paradoxically, lean production is both fragile and resilient. Knowledge that a minor problem can spawn a systemwide disruption creates an incentive to maintain communication and solicit problem-solving skills.

Mass production uses division of labor and specialized equipment to produce high volumes of standardized products. Lean production uses multipurpose or programmable equipment that can easily be switched among several product designs. This provides product variety and speeds up feedback throughout the production process. While there is "a tendency for mass production plants to rely on more specialized equipment and for lean production to use more general-purpose equipment," [214] differences between mass and lean production can persist no matter what type of equipment is used. General-purpose tools in a mass production environment tend to be used in specialized ways, while specialized tools in a lean production environment are modified to increase their versatility. Problem solving is applied to analyze hardware idiosyncrasies and make incremental improvements, a process known as "giving wisdom to the machine." Workers subject their own detailed job specifications to continual analysis.

Research Questions, Methods, and Evidence

Two hypotheses have been investigated and researched at sixty-two car assembly plants. First, lean production (human resource development linked to minimal use of buffers) contributes significantly to high productivity (measured as hours per car for a standard set of production activities) and high quality (measured as assembly defects per car). Second, advanced technology is more effective when coupled with lean production.

Several indices were constructed to investigate these hypotheses. The Production Organization Index is an average of two measures: the Use of Buffers Index, which includes variables like the percentage of floor space for repair stations or the frequency of parts delivery; and the HRM Policies Index, which includes variables for human resources practices and work organization. High scores on the Production Organization Index indicate lean production. Two indices measure technology: the Robotics Index indicates the presence of newer, more flexible technology; the Total Automation Index reflects the percentage of production steps that are automated.

It is commonly believed that high productivity and high quality are incompatible. However, in this sample they are positively correlated, with many plants scoring better than average on both measures and a few considered world class with outstanding scores on both indices. The Production Organization Index and technology indices are significantly correlated with quality and productivity. Buffers and HRM Policies are strongly correlated with each other and contribute almost equally to the organization-productivity relationship. However, HRM Policies are more influential in the organization-quality correlation. Unexpectedly, buffers were found to be less important to quality than to productivity. This suggests that if buffers are minimized solely to cut costs, human resource policies that support problem-solving should be used to maintain quality.

To examine the second hypothesis, the sample was split at the average value on the Production Organization Index into lean production and mass production subgroups. These were then split by the average value for Total Automation, giving four quadrants whose average productivity (hours per car) and quality (defects per car) can be compared:

	HIGH TECH		LOW TECH	
	Mass	Lean	Mass	Lean
Hours	30	22	41	35
Defects	79	49	104	73

As can be seen, the best performing plants on this scale combine advanced technology with lean production.

When plants were arrayed along productivity and quality axes four analytical categories emerged: low productivity–low quality, high productivity–low quality, high productivity–high quality, and world class. Average values for the indices used in this study were calculated for each category. This comparison also indicates that technology has the most beneficial impact on performance when combined with lean production.

Conclusion

High-performance and even world class plants are found both in and out of Japan, so it is apparent that the lean production method is not restricted by cultural factors. However, to move successfully from a mass to a lean production strategy, everyone involved must understand the differences in philosophy between the two work systems. The best education for managers and union officials occurs when they have exposure to lean production through joint ventures or geographical proximity. For production workers, hands-on experience with elements like statistical process control or the job specification process seems to work best.

Two kinds of crises can test the fragility of lean production. When problems in production occur, it will be tempting to restore buffers, but a commitment to problem-solving will strengthen the firm and reduce vulnerability in the long-run. In times of economic downturn, the high-commitment employment relationship can only survive if management makes a good-faith effort to protect the jobs of employees.

Summary of

Toward Post-Lean Production

by Christian Berggren

[Published in *Alternatives to Lean Production: Work Organization in the Swedish Auto Industry* (Ithaca, NY: ILR Press, 1992; paperback edition introduction, 1993), vii–x, 232–256.]

For much of the twentieth century manufacturing has been organized around mass production, a model often termed "Taylorist" after Frederick W. Taylor, the founder of scientific management, or "Fordist," after Henry Ford who built the first mass production factory. Taylor saw work, not as a matter of skill and craftsmanship, but as a series of discrete motions that could be analyzed to generate the most efficient, most easily replicated pattern for accomplishing any task. Ford combined such narrowly specified jobs with a highly engineered environment of mechanical conveyances, specialized equipment for repetitive production of standardized parts, and orderly sequencing of the flow of work. The Fordist factory became one of the emblematic institutions of the midcentury industrial economy and one of the engines of post–World War II prosperity.

Although factory workers participated in the general rise in the material standard of living, their jobs were often tedious, physically exhausting, and devoid of interest, responsibility, or authority. As a whole, the system was slow to adjust to economic cycles or changing social or consumer needs. Since the 1970s there has been much rethinking of the Fordist system. Once again, leading candidates for new manufacturing models emerged in the auto industry.

The Volvo Trajectory

In Japan concern for quality and efficiency motivated the development of "lean production," a model that currently dominates discussion of new work systems. But it is not the only alternative. In Sweden the motivation for change came from a need to reduce the tediousness of factory work and led to experimentation with sociotechnical models stressing compatibility among technology, organization, and the human worker.

Unlike many industrialized countries, during the late 1970s and 1980s Sweden had very low unemployment. Manufacturers faced powerful unions and a shortage of labor. Turnover in manufacturing was high, especially among young people. This placed a particular burden on Swedish automakers because they specialized in high-end export markets that demanded well-made, customized products. Quality, prompt delivery, and flexibility were key to the industry's competitiveness, and these factors required a stable, highly competent workforce.

During the 1970s and 1980s, Volvo and other motor vehicle producers in Sweden introduced several innovations when they opened new plants or diversified product lines. They experimented with work teams and lean production, but serious personnel problems remained. Volvo, faced with "massive discontent with working conditions on the assembly line" [235], made serious attempts at reform, but found changes difficult to implement in older facilities with entrenched management cultures.

Newer Volvo plants were better able to undertake experiments in human-centered sociotechnical design. The Kalmar plant was built in the mid-1970s around ergonomic improvements, team-based production, and technological flexibility that allowed components to be moved easily from one team to the next in the production sequence. Though productivity gains were not quickly achieved, by the mid-1980s Kalmar was Volvo's best operation. However, improvements in working conditions were not as dramatic as expected, and the coordination of separately produced components required expensive, complex systems for in-plant transportation and storage. A new Volvo truck plant opened in 1981 with a compromise between traditional and more integrated processes, giving work groups considerable autonomy. By the late 1980s the product design became more complex, pushing the limits of the system. Management tightened supervision, but at the same time set up a dock assembly shop (in which a team of workers assembled a whole truck) for the most complicated vehicles.

In the late 1980s Volvo opened the Uddevalla plant with the most radical production design yet: fifty work teams, each producing a whole car. Before the plant worked out its bugs, a national recession occurred that made workplace reform a luxury and led to criticism of Uddevalla for poor productivity. Though the criticism sparked performance gains, the company's sales plummeted, pitting Volvo plants against each other for dwindling orders. Management was ambiguous about the "noble experiment," closing the Uddevalla plant in 1993 and Kalmar in 1994. Uddevalla was reopened in 1995, as part of a joint venture between Volvo and a British engineering firm to produce niche vehicles, coupes, and cabriolets.

Performance: Productivity, Quality, and Work Conditions

After working out initial problems, the productivity levels of the Kalmar and Uddevalla facilities were comparable to most European plants, and one or the other outranked many other factories in quality, customer satisfaction, or the ability to respond to design changes and variable market demand. One 1993 model built at Kalmar matched Toyota's Lexus for low rates of customer complaints. Uddevalla developed direct relationships with distributors and by 1992 was producing cars on order for European delivery with a four-week turn-around period.

However, other problems hindered these plants from achieving the same performance levels as the most productive Japanese plants. Volvo products were more complicated and difficult to manufacture than Japanese cars. Some turnover and absenteeism persisted. Volvo generally lacked the tight quality control over its suppliers that is characteristic of advanced Japanese manufacturers. Furthermore, because they performed final assembly only, Kalmar and Uddevalla were the easiest facilities to lop off when the recession hit and sales fell.

Critics claimed that long-cycle production (working on an entire product as a team, rather than repeating fragmented jobs in an assembly line fashion) is a form of "craft nostalgia" that extends the assembly process, without significantly enriching the work experience. However, surveys of workers at several Swedish bus, truck, and auto plants indicate that work content is important for workers and that "[t]he further from traditional line assembly a plant moves, the better the outcomes in terms of variation, prospects for personal growth, the taking of responsibility, and the opportunity to use one's skills." [242] Reports of physical strain and fatigue after work were lowest where work cycles were longest, and workers expressed a desire to work on complete vehicles to relieve monotony. More than just adding tasks, holistic long-cycle assembly increases understanding of the interrelated parts of the vehicle, offers a sense of purpose, and increases opportunities to cooperate, interact, and vary the work pace and position.

This approach contrasts with Japanese lean production, which retains the assembly line structure with an intensification of work effort and precise specification of pace and physical movement. Although problem-solving is encouraged, it is not related to the product or process as a whole, but to the continuous improvement ("kaizening") of fragmented suboperations.

Organizational Choice

Organizational Choice, by E. Trist et al. (1963), claimed that work organization is independent of technology and the work process. However, case studies with a longer time frame show otherwise. Japanese competitiveness and lean production rely on a number of components besides the way work is organized. Equipment and parts suppliers, product design, production, distribution, and customer service are linked in collaborations that reduce development times for new models and set-up times for customized products, thus enhancing quality control over both in-house and vendor-supplied components. However, Japanese working conditions involve intense machine pacing, surveillance of workers, rigid production quotas, mandatory overtime on short notice, and ergonomic deficiencies. While lean production has made important contributions, it is hardly a global "best practice." Japanese auto plants in Japan are gaining a reputation as poor places to work, and dissatisfaction is high. In response to this perception, a new Toyota plant opened in 1991 with worker-friendly modifications.

Toward Post-Lean Production

Driven by a demanding workforce, Swedish automakers demonstrated that an integrated, holistic, dignified approach to production is technically feasible, socially desirable, and compatible with market demands. They made significant ergonomic adaptations to human differences, particularly to the needs of women workers, who make up 40 percent of the industry workforce. Other human needs, such as family obligations, were recognized and accommodated. Unions played an important and respected role in planning and work organization.

Some synthesis between the Japanese and Swedish systems is possible. Collaboration between design and manufacturing would enhance the intellectual content of integrated work processes. Some discipline, for example, in quality control procedures, could improve the Swedish model without excessive standardization. Where the two systems are incompatible, firms need to choose between measuring efficiency solely by worker hours or by consideration of human needs. This can assist unions to develop a critical approach to lean production and governments to support labor market conditions that foster human-centered work systems.

Summary of

Japanese Work Organization in Mexico

by Harley Shaiken and Harry Browne

[Published in *Manufacturing Across Borders and Oceans: Japan, the United States, and Mexico,* ed. Gabriel Székely (University of California, San Diego: Center for U.S.–Mexican Studies, Monograph Series #36, 1991), 25–50.]

Questions about management practices associated with Japanese multinational corporations stem from the success of these firms in the international marketplace. How effectively can these methods spread to other firms and other countries? Are they a holistic system of work organization or simply a catalogue of techniques from which managers can pick and choose? This article investigates these questions at Japanese firms in Mexico, some of which are producing for the Mexican market, others for export.

Transferability of Japanese Management Techniques

Although many globally successful Japanese corporations make use of management practices that have been identified with superior quality and productivity, Japanese manufacturers in Mexico tend not to use these techniques. Interviews with thirty-five managers at thirteen Mexican factories owned in whole or in part by Japanese firms indicate they have little knowledge of Japanese methods. Instead, they retain the classical Fordist system typical of U.S. and Mexican factories that employs minutely subdivided tasks under centralized control. Yet, most of these plants achieved or surpassed their quality and productivity goals, indicating that Japanese methods are less integral to Japanese success than many observers have thought.

On the other hand, the transfer of Japanese approaches to several factories in the United States confirms that Japanese workers are not necessary to make these techniques work. In fact, they are not as deeply rooted in Japanese culture as some have assumed—they appeared after World War II and were not widely implemented until the 1960s and 1970s. Whether or not it is in a firm's interest to use these techniques depends on its strategic vision. A management-centered strategy is most likely to employ Japanese practices to lower costs or improve quality. A process-centered strategy will focus on technological improvements using these practices selectively. A product-centered strategy will use them very little. Although it goes against popular wisdom, one observer notes that these practices "are separable and need not be transferred en masse." [28]

Also contrary to conventional wisdom, in Mexico the higher quality and more advanced technology found in the export-production sector, compared to the domestic-production sector, do not lead to differences in the adoption of Japanese management practices. In factories producing for both markets, managers claimed similar hindrances: Mexican workers were poorly educated and had an incompatible work ethic and culture, and the facilities were too new. Even so in a few cases some Japanese management techniques were in evidence, belying the perception that they cannot be introduced into Mexican factories. In fact, one U.S. automaker uses very similar techniques in an assembly plant in the Mexican interior.

Japanese Management Techniques

Analysts do not completely agree on what makes up the Japanese management style or whether it is significantly better than others, but certain "highly visible techniques" can be identified and the reasons for their deployment or lack of it explored. The facilities studied had between 100 and 4000 union and nonunion workers in electronics, automobile, or small consumer durables production. The research focused on techniques used in U.S. as well as Japanese factories as a check against claims that they were only compatible with a Japanese workforce.

Job Security, one of the most heralded Japanese practices, is actually guaranteed for only about a third of the workforce in Japan, namely those in the largest companies. Many firms do, however, make efforts to avoid layoffs, at least of full-time employees. In U.S. transplants, the record is also mixed, although at a California factory jointly operated by General Motors and Toyota, a no-layoff policy is considered critical to union–management cooperation. In Mexico none of the plants guaranteed job security, although one used reduced work weeks to avoid a layoff. Managers claimed such promises are impractical since turnover is high and workers are always looking for better jobs. In the export sector, firms have generally been expanding. Some use high turnover to adjust to cyclical fluctuations through attrition.

Quality Circles (QC) involve up to 17 percent of the workforce in Japan and consist of small groups that meet frequently to conduct quality control and improvement activities. Workers learn engineering and statistical skills to analyze and improve the design of their own jobs, bringing the practice of scientific management introduced by Frederick Taylor to a more advanced level. In Mexico there was little evidence of quality circles; only 400 out of 12,760 employees were involved in any similar activities. Managers cited lack of interest or education on the part of workers, high turnover, and the newness of their plants as obstacles. In spite of high turnover in the export sector, all three plants with some QC-like groups are *maquiladoras.* In one, managers noted more worker interest than they could provide projects for. In another, participants received a wage raise because other *maquiladoras* were recruiting employees with QC experience.

Work Teams composed of eight to ten workers in one production area have a wide range of autonomy, in some cases choosing their own team leaders and making decisions about job assignments, discipline, training, quality, and productivity. Workers learn all jobs in their area so that assignments can be rotated, which increases the firm's ability to adjust to new processes or changes in product mix. Teams do not require high levels of education or motivation, yet few were in evidence in Mexican plants. Those few had little autonomy, merely imparting a sense of group identity. Little formal cross-training was found, and it did not lead to autonomy for workers.

Kaizen means continuous improvement, both as a philosophical umbrella for all the "uniquely Japanese" practices for improving the production process and as a term for "specific training and methods for hourly workers to participate in improving productivity and quality." [40] At one U.S.-owned export plant in Mexico workers take a 40-hour kaizen course taught by hourly workers covering ergonomics, cost reduction, teamwork, safety, and company philosophy. None of the plants in this study had formal kaizen training, but one export-sector auto plant used kaizen concepts in a campaign to define precise work standards for all operations. This plant sets, and often exceeds, high goals for productivity improvement. Only one Mexican manager outside this plant had heard of kaizen, while Japanese managers recited their usual litany of impediments, introducing kaizen principles only among supervisors and engineers, if at all.

Andon lights allow operators to signal emergencies (red) or problems (yellow). "Surprisingly, some plants welcome yellow lights as an indicator that the line is working at absolute peak efficiency; any further load or speed would bring red lights on and halt the line." [41] Only two assembly lines at one plant in this study fully used the *andon* system.

Just-In-Time Inventory in its ideal form uses nearby suppliers to deliver small batches of parts only when needed. Inside the plant, work passes from one station to another with few buffers of spare parts. JIT requires efficient infrastructure, complex supply systems, and well-coordinated production. Although distance, customs, and poor infrastructure can make JIT difficult to implement in Mexico, one U.S. manufacturer there successfully manages close time tolerances even with international supply lines. Some plants studied hoped to reduce inventory, and one did a substantial amount of planning. Otherwise there was little evidence of JIT.

Peripheral techniques such as *chorei* (short daily meetings), supervisors walking the factory floor, and reduction of visible signs of status improve communications and group identification and keep both workers and managers informed about production plans and issues. Several supervisors in Mexico mentioned regular meetings or insistence from Japanese management that they stay in close touch with operators on the floor (even though none of the Japanese managers were fluent in Spanish). Although Japanese firms are noted for consensus management, Japanese managers in overseas plants tend to be isolated from the process. Many Mexican managers noted a difference from American management styles. Some appreciated it, but some experienced it as interference since "everyone gets his hands in others' business." [45] Other Mexican managers felt excluded and looked down upon by Japanese managers.

Related Issues

Low labor costs and access to the U.S. market were commonly cited reasons for Japanese manufacturers to locate in Mexico. Although turnover is high, especially in the *maquila* plants, only one firm expressed dissatisfaction with its labor force. Of seven unionized plants, only one had turbulent labor relations, though some managers commented on the ineffectiveness of the unions. Compared to each firm's most advanced plants, productivity in Mexican facilities was generally lower, due to less automation, and smaller scale because investments were explicitly made to exploit low labor costs. Quality, on the other hand, was usually nearly as good, as good, or better.

Summary of

The Effects of Human Resource Management Practices on Productivity: A Study of Steel Finishing Lines

by Casey Ichniowski, Kathryn Shaw, and Giovanna Prennushi

[Published in American Economic Review 87, 3 (June 1997), 291–313.]

Innovative work practices such as incentive pay, teamwork, and flexible job assignments are often said to increase the productivity of labor. However, there is continuing debate about both the nature of the effects on productivity in theory, and the extent of the effects in practice. This study analyzes the effects of human resource management (HRM) practices on thirty-six steel finishing lines owned by seventeen companies. It finds that HRM innovations are generally introduced in particular clusters, and that these clusters of employment practices have a greater effect on productivity than the individual practices alone. Thus it is consistent with theories that stress the importance of complementarities among work practices.

Sample and Data

The sample consists of several years of monthly data on each of thirty-six steel finishing lines of one particular type (out of roughly sixty lines of this type in the United States), together with detailed information on technology, equipment, management, and employment practices on each line. Measurement of productivity is straightforward, since each line produces a fixed amount of steel per hour whenever it is running, given the specific engineering specifications of that line. A finishing line can operate continuously around the clock, with only occasional scheduled downtime for maintenance. Productivity is therefore measured as the percentage of "uptime"—the percentage of scheduled operating time that the line actually runs. For the more than 2000 "line-month" observations in the sample, the mean uptime is 91.9 percent, with a standard deviation of 4.4 percent.

The heart of the study is a statistical analysis of the effects of HRM innovations on productivity, or uptime. The productivity equations include as many as twenty-five controls for other features of the lines that may affect uptime, including the age of the line, many technical specifications, the temporary disruption experienced when new equipment is added, and the extent of scheduled maintenance. "Fixed effect" productivity models are also estimated; these measure any gains in productivity within those lines that adopt HRM innovations.

Work Practices and HRM Systems

Fifteen new work practices, or HRM innovations, were examined in the study, including one or more measures in each of the following areas: incentive pay plans, selectivity in recruitment, teamwork, employment security, flexibility in job assignments, skills training, and improved communication between management and workers. In addition, the traditional labor relations variables of unionization (33 of the 36 lines were unionized) and rate of grievance filings were considered.

Several recent theorists have suggested that there are complementarities among new employment practices. Problem-solving teams, for example, may be more effective when adopted in combination with incentive pay—allowing workers to share the benefits of improvements they propose—and employment security—guaranteeing that no one will be laid off if productivity increases. The primary question under investigation here is: Do *groups* of innovative HRM practices increase productivity?

Identifying HRM Systems and Their Effects

The fifteen individual HRM practices are highly correlated with each other; that is, lines that adopt one are more likely to adopt others as well. The patterns of implementation of these practices can be grouped into four HRM systems. Starting with the most traditional, System 4 contains no innovative HRM practices; System 3 adds worker involvement in teams (though usually at a low level of involvement) and enhanced labor-management communications. System 2 includes System 3, and adds extensive skills training and high levels of worker involvement in teams; occasionally one or two other innovations are also present in System 2. Finally, System 1 incorporates innovative HRM practices in all areas, including incentive pay systems, flexible and sometimes rotating job assignments, very selective recruiting practices, and an implicit employment security pledge, as well as all the practices included in System 2. All of the lines employed one of these four systems; some lines changed systems—always in the direction of greater innovation—during the study period.

How large is the effect of differing HRM systems on productivity? Average uptime was 89.9 percent in System 4 and 94.0 percent in System 1, with intermediate values for Systems 2 and 3. However, many other factors that affect productivity varied between plants, so simple averages may be misleading. One of the study's several regression analyses estimates that, compared to System 4, the increase in uptime is 2.5 percentage points for System 3, 4.1 percentage points for System 2, and 7.8 percentage points for System 1. Productivity increases of this magnitude are of great value. Cost data from one small line show the value of each percentage point of uptime to be $28,000 per month. The more innovative HRM systems also increase the average quality of output, making them even more valuable.

Alternative Explanations

Several other explanations could be suggested for the changes in productivity. The gains associated with innovative HRM systems might be due to better management, or individual variation in managerial style and behavior; or to threats of layoffs and plant shutdowns, pressuring workers to work harder; or to worker responses to increases in pay under incentive systems. Controlling for these factors leaves the estimated effects of the four HRM systems roughly unchanged. Including fixed effects for specific plants and lines, or for specific years within the study period, strengthens the effects of the HRM systems.

A final statistical analysis provides the clearest demonstration of the importance of the HRM systems. When variables for individual HRM innovations are added to equations that already include the four systems, there is virtually no additional effect on estimated productivity: The HRM systems appear to incorporate all the available information about the effects of innovative practices. The reverse, however, is not true. Beginning with equations that include the fifteen individual HRM practices, there is a significant increase in explanatory power when variables for the four HRM systems are added.

> The evidence shows that *systems of HRM practices determine productivity and quality, while marginal changes in individual work practices have little effect.* . . . [I]nnovative employment practices tend to be complements, as is proposed in the recent theoretical work on optimal incentive structures. That is, workers' performance is substantially better under incentive pay plans that are coupled with supporting innovative work practices—such as flexible job design, employee participation in problem-solving teams, training to provide workers with multiple skills, extensive screening and communication, and employment security—than it is under more traditional work practices. [311–312, emphasis in original]

If the new systems are so clearly productive and profitable, why do any lines fail to implement them? In fact, all new or reopened lines that started up during the study period did adopt innovative HRM systems. Some (not all) older lines stuck with older practices, due to lack of knowledge, institutional inertia, and investment—by both management and labor—in skills and work relationships tailored to the traditional style of HRM.

Summary of

The Limits of Hierarchy in an Informated Organization

and

The Information Panopticon

by Shoshana Zuboff

[Published in *In the Age of the Smart Machine—The Future of Work and Power* (Basic Books, 1988) Chapters 8 and 9, 285–361.]

An informed workplace is one where automation is not only a source of technological advance but also of new information about the technique, efficiency, and quality of the work process itself. This information can alter the balance of power in the workplace in complex ways. Workers may gain an increased share of responsibility and authority, but if the information potential is left untapped, or captured exclusively by management, the alienation of the worker may intensify.

The Limits of Hierarchy

> A technology that informates can have a corrosive effect on the hierarchical organization of work, but its transformative power finally depends on a series of crucial managerial choices. [285]

Case studies conducted at several establishments in a variety of industries show that when automation is introduced, workers and managers are often confused about their roles and responsibilities. Since information embedded in automated systems can be a key to a firm's competitiveness, people at all levels need to analyze and respond to relevant data. Yet, even with this understanding, managers often fear that information "could be misused or misinterpreted . . . that such data can only be managed by certain people with certain accountabilities and . . . certain skills or capabilities." [289] Furthermore, information leads to questioning, a process inimical to the obedience-based structure of the hierarchical firm. Since it is more difficult to determine if a worker is thinking to his or her best ability than it is to monitor a specific task, a worker must be motivated—not just told—to learn, to solve problems, to think critically. Interpreting data does not appear to be work in the way that manual labor does, so managers sometimes see the new work style as laziness. Workers resent this and often feel pressured to master new technology while still expending the physical energy associated with nonmanagerial work.

Workers who once relied on hands-on knowledge gained during years of experience are now distanced from the production process and dependent on computerized machines for information. After gaining experience with automation, some managers come to question the use of technology to override or displace the skill and judgment of the workforce because they see a need for problem-solving and troubleshooting on the ground. To be fully effective, the new technologies require both in-depth knowledge of the production process and technical mastery of computer systems. After their initial resistance, many workers come to a similar conclusion: They could learn to use information technologies as tools to express their own knowledge.

These conflicts played out in different ways in different firms. At one older plant, lines of authority were sharply drawn and the technological transition reinforced mutual suspicion. Workers felt they were taking on additional responsibility without additional compensation or contractual protection. In another plant supervisors appreciated the need to tap the thinking skills of operators but provoked considerable anxiety by subjecting hourly workers to an elaborate qualifications review. Managers eventually realized that workers' commitment to the firm increased when "they had a real share in the business, an opportunity to learn, and the freedom to inquire without confronting arbitrary barriers of managerial authority." [295]

In an earlier industrial period, scientific management (also called Taylorism) analyzed workers' know-how and transferred it into management functions. If automating a workplace is the only objective, computerization replicates this process by translating workers' knowledge into management-controlled algorithms. An informating strategy, on the other hand, would value learning and could undermine the logic of Taylorism. Knowledge returns to the worker, but in an externalized form. Under a compatible management structure, this knowledge can be widely shared, grappled with intellectually, and transformed into insight that can further expand the information content of the system.

Without a conscious strategy to redistribute authority, neither the productive potential of information technology nor that of employees will be realized. Several studies confirm that technological change must be coupled with changes in organization, attitudes, and culture to make a substantial contribution to a firm's competitiveness. The introduction of new technology is not sufficient by itself to achieve strategic change; however, it can put knowledge and authority on a collision course. As workers increasingly interpret and respond to data, the boundaries between management knowledge and operation techniques blur. The system of management domination becomes increasingly fragile.

The Information Panopticon

During the eighteenth century philosopher Jeremy Bentham designed a Panopticon, a structure (meant to be a prison, but first built as a factory) in which a central observer could watch the activities of every other individual within the structure without being observed in turn. Since an inmate (or worker) cannot know at any one time if he or she is being observed, he or she will remain in a state, described by the twentieth-century philosopher Michael Foucault, of "conscious and permanent visibility that assures the automatic functioning of power. So . . . that the surveillance is permanent in its effects, even if it is discontinuous in its action." [321]

"Information systems that translate, record, and display human behavior can provide the computer age version of universal transparency." [322] Supervision often requires considerable psychological effort and difficult face-to-face engagement to get others to do what the company wants. The transparency of information systems offers supervisors a less stressful alternative, reduces uncertainty, and induces conformity to management expectations.

The capacity to track performance was not generally understood until new systems were in place, but once managers became aware of it they were likely to use it to enhance control. Some wanted to coach those who made mistakes. Others saw it as an opportunity to eliminate dependence on worker-provided logs and reports. No longer could workers who made mistakes fudge the numbers to protect themselves. Decisions about termination, promotion, and discipline, often requiring extensive documentation, could be made more quickly with records from instruments that were almost continuously monitored.

However, if computer monitoring substitutes for supervision, reciprocity between managers and workers deteriorates. As one manager put it, "[t]he system can't give you the heartbeat of the plant; it puts you out of touch" [326] with why mistakes were made or opportunities were missed. Small problems are less likely to be smoothed over with small favors. Even for managers confident of their interpersonal skills, the reduction of uncertainty and psychological stress proved a powerful incentive to transform management assumptions, practices, and behavior.

Ultimately, unlike Bentham's Panopticon, the organizations in this study are hierarchical. Managers who are eager for information about subordinates resist technology that could relay information about their own performance up through the chain of command. They equate control over information with control over their own work and the exercise of discretion, while upper-level executives want integrated, real-time data about the entire organization.

Adapting to Visibility and Shared Information

Some workers felt that computerized systems produced an objective performance measure to offset subjective management evaluations and office politics. However, visibility also evoked a sense of vulnerability and powerlessness, so both workers and managers took steps to reduce the risk of unwanted exposure. Managers tried to control the flow of information upward, while many workers changed behavior to conform with company expectations.

When employee participation at all levels is valued, or interdependence between departments is high, a sense of collective responsibility may develop that tempers the oppressiveness of surveillance. Information becomes a communal resource for making decisions and resolving disputes. Arbitrary management power diminishes in the face of objective data. Under more adversarial regimes, workers may try to beat the system, but the transparency of information technology makes the system harder to bypass, raising their frustration.

If collective responsibility is to become the norm, collaborative relationships and egalitarian access to data must be nurtured. Intellectual and communication skills must be enhanced throughout the organization to enable shared understanding of complex information systems. Just as workers are no longer confined to single task-oriented jobs, managers can no longer command in isolation from their peers, superiors, and subordinates.

Summary of

The End of Skill?

by Stanley Aronowitz and William DeFazio

[Published in *The Jobless Future* (Minneapolis: University of Minnesota Press, 1994), 81–103.]

Computers and automation are pervasive in the workplaces of the last half of the twentieth century. Sociologists of the workplace often view technology in one of two ways: either as destructive of the traditional skills that once gave meaning and control to craft-based work, or as a potentially liberating force that can relieve the burden of backbreaking or tedious labor. The first viewpoint romanticizes the past; the second romanticizes the future. But neither deals with the specific context in which new technology is introduced. All too often cybernetics are used as a cost-saving device, freeing industrial, commercial, and professional workers from toil, but hardly in a liberating way, since their liveli-hood is lost with the loss of work.

Nevertheless, "the computer . . . provides a persuasive case for the claim of the newest technophiles that finally, after nearly three centuries of the rational-ization of the labor process, we can envision the reintegration not only of work, but also of humans with nature and with their own species. . . . [I]n its most vi-sionary form, computer-driven technoculture claims to fulfill the dream of the 'whole' person by healing the rupture between intellectual and manual labor and freeing time for the full development of the individual." [82]

Technoculture and Work

In the early days of computer development following World War II there was a clear sense that what was at stake was the reduction of production costs to be achieved by reducing the cost of labor. Unions were prominent and had won good wages and benefits in key industries, as well as work rules that constrained management on the shop floor. In a well-publicized encounter, the CEO of General Motors asked the President of the United Auto Workers, "Who's going to pay union dues?" The union leader responded, "Who's going to buy your cars?"

By the 1970s the United States faced a changing economic environment. Im-ports increased and the production of many products and components moved offshore. Employment in many mass production industries and heavy industries diminished. For the workforce, this had mixed effects. Work in these industries was tightly controlled and coordinated, paced by the speed of assembly lines and machines. But some sense of solidarity and power remained within the workforce; a disruption in any one part of the production process could quickly affect all of it.

The new technoculture in the workplace that emerged with automation con-tinued the long process of disempowerment. Little or no skill was needed to monitor controls for robots or automated processes. In fact the worker is often monitored in turn by the equipment he or she operates. The potential that computerization offered to reintegrate mental and manual labor was often sub-verted by reinforced hierarchies with a new differentiation among levels of ex-pertise.

Knowledge or Skill?

Harry Braverman argued that the capitalist labor process degrades all workers through techniques of domination and deskills them by separating the concep-tion and planning of production from its execution. The new composition of the workforce involved unskilled or semiskilled laborers working under the direction of engineers and scientists who designed products, machines, and techniques, and managers who supervised and coordinated production. Writers following Braverman often see science and technology as forms of capitalist domination. These forms of control, however, can be contested by workers who struggle to design a science and technology that is not about degradation, but about creativity and freedom. In this way, they can struggle to redesign their world.

Paul Adler is a leading critic of Braverman's perspective. Adler theorizes that technology upgrades, rather than degrades, skill. Technological change is beneficial to most workers, whereas deskilling affects only a minority. As old skills are destroyed, new skills are created. The creation of new skills outweighs the effects of deskilling. "Adler argues that Braverman's notion of skill is based on a romantic view of the nineteenth century craftworker and that skill must be redefined in the context of modern technological advances. . . . " [92]

However, Adler does not take the next step beyond the discourse of skill to recognize that, "[i]n a production process in which science and technology are central, knowledge, not skill, defines the process." [92] This constitutes a fundamental shift from experience as the basis of training and acquisition of skill to formal education as the basis of training and the acquisition of knowledge. Skill could only be attained as a result of a long apprenticeship in a trade. Entry to the craft was controlled by masters who protected their skills through associations (guilds, unions, professions) and carefully selected apprentices who would learn the secrets of the trade and carry it on.

Women were historically denied entry to most crafts and are poorly represented in the skilled trades that remain active, even today when they are entering the workforce in great numbers. "Skill is a male discourse. If women were to succeed, they had to change the field of discourse. . . . High technology created a new knowledge space that is not burdened by the gendered history of skill." [96] Even though high tech is still largely a male domain, it is new and not bound by tradition. Hence it presents an arena in which women can struggle to belong.

Flexible Specialization

Some analysts, however, argue "that computer-mediated work *could* provide unprecedented opportunities for the full development of the operator's knowledge and authority over the labor process . . . [and] a new regime of craft production. For them this is the result of a flexible-specialization, decentralized, community-based, small-batch, skilled-worker production process." [90]

Michael Piore and Charles Sable developed the idea of flexible specialization to describe the change from mass production to a system of innovative, constantly shifting components as the impetus for growth and the rebirth of skilled work. But flexible specialization has contradictory tendencies on the issue of skills. It can displace workers as well as shifting the knowledge base to new groups of workers. The change in industrial structure has been accompanied by unemployment, underemployment, and wage reductions, even in industries where the need for computer knowledge is rising or equipment is becoming more sophisticated.

If flexible specialization is the wave of the future, four crucial questions must be answered. First, does it increase skill levels in postindustrial production regimes? As we have seen, there is little agreement on this point. Second, does it create more jobs? Here it is widely agreed that the answer is no. Instead "flexible automation" means that there are fewer jobs overall, but the remaining jobs require more skill.

The third question is, should there be a return to a skill-based system as in the nineteenth-century craft tradition? This system enhanced exclusion at the expense of innovation and quality. Turning back the clock seems unlikely and undesirable. Finally, is it skill that is being increased in these flexible specialization regimes? Skilled work still exists, but it is increasing only at the margins of new production processes. The logical outcome of future production regimes is a technoscience-based, knowledge-centered labor process.

The computer gives a new dimension to communication, "[b]ut the ethic of knowledge sharing . . . has been seriously undercut by rampant privatization; knowledge is organized on a need-to-know, ability-to-pay basis." [100] Ultimately, it may be concluded that the computer mirrors its masters. Despite being employed by corporations who own the rights to dispose of their inventions, there are some who retain the utopian, even anarchist, impulse to finally bridge the gap between intellectual and manual labor. Whether or not the computer is employed as a way to facilitate the emergence of a democratic workplace is indeterminate from the internal constitution of its technology. The uses and social meaning of computer technology depend on the context within which computer-mediated work is done.

Summary of

The Transformation of Work Revisited:
The Limits of Flexibility in American Manufacturing

by Steven Vallas and John Beck

[Published in *Social Problems* 43 (August 1996), 339–361.]

In theory, post-Fordist work processes achieve flexibility by using new information technologies and less-hierarchical forms of management to respond to rapid changes in product markets. The discussion of post-Fordist regimes is part of a long-standing debate about the relationship between technology and the skill content of production jobs. Drawing on case study material, this article examines the experiences of shop floor workers when new technology and new management practices were introduced. Rather than greater flexibility as predicted by post-Fordism, it finds a trend toward greater standardization and displacement of discretion from craft-based to engineering-based knowledge.

Post-Fordism

Many analysts claim that the post-Fordist restructuring of work was ushered in by a crisis in mass production industries. Disagreement lies in what is driving the crisis (changing product demand or changing technology), and whether the situation marks a return to craft-based labor process or is a movement toward a new integration of mental and manual labor. Increased volatility in consumption patterns makes small-batch production more desirable, while microprocessor technologies make it economically feasible. Adaptable production systems, however, require more discretion and intellectual activity from production workers than what was demanded by the simplified tasks characteristic of mass production.

The postwar period has been marked by debate about whether new technology tends to upgrade or deskill production work. In the 1960s Robert Blauner proposed that automation would free workers from standardized work. A decade later Harry Braverman argued that knowledge of production processes shifted from workers to management, while the work itself became rote and deskilled. During the 1980s several theorists argued that the impact of new technologies would vary according to the social conditions in the workplace. Paul Adler linked the recent interest in a flexible, post-Fordist regime to this labor process debate.

While proponents of post-Fordism make bold claims about its ability to transform the nature of work, critics point to conflicts of interest and of perspective within organizations—conflicts that tend to heighten inertia and may lead to complex, even contradictory results.

Case Studies

This focus on broad-based economic factors, like product markets or technical innovation, can remove the framework of analysis away from the workplace realities the theory purports to describe. To get a deeper understanding of the relations of production as they exist and are experienced at the shop floor level, the authors conducted an extensive qualitative research project based in part on interviews, informal conversations, and observations at four paper mills. The mills vary in size, age, product mix, and locale but are all operated by the same multinational firm. The company recently restructured its production technology and management systems at these four plants and seems receptive to the tenets of post-Fordism.

The mills use continuous process technology to produce pulp from logs, wood chips, and chemicals, spread the pulp on wire frames to dry and finish, gather it on huge rolls, and then cut it into sheets or feed it onto smaller rolls. Before automation, workers were in close contact with their own part of the process and product. They listened to machines, felt the texture of the pulp or the dryness of the sheets, watched color set, or smelled the chemical mix. Knowledge built up over a succession of jobs was closely guarded and used to make decisions about the work flow.

The company's recent innovations involved three principal elements. First, distributed control systems were installed that use computer terminals to represent and control production. Second, total quality management was adopted, including Statistical Process Control (SPC) and team-based management. SPC set up production targets and quantified them as centerline values with confidence intervals within which variance was allowed. And third, systems were installed to facilitate communication and information management. Workers now have more information but little or no direct contact with the process. SPC established decision-making parameters, but reduced workers' discretion. So far teams have only had limited responsibilities. Workers were, and still are, isolated from each other and from an understanding of the overall system of production. Although processes at the wet and dry ends are highly interdependent and sensitive to variations in quality and pace, the development of worker skills and job ladders are organized on a department basis so that communication between processes is difficult and sometimes faulty.

Effects of Change

The changes just described appear conducive to post-Fordist transformations by making information and decision tools widely accessible, while laying the groundwork to allow teams to break down hierarchies and departmental isolation. However, the reality observed at these plants differed from these expectations, especially in three respects. First, process engineers became more important. Not only was the number of engineering positions increased to monitor production, engineers came to fill more and more supervisory jobs, blocking production workers from moving into them. Second, legitimate knowledge came to reside in scientific and engineering discourse rather than worker experience. Engineers derided workers' knowledge as amateurish or superstitious, while workers found it hard to make the transition from direct sensory knowledge of the production process to information equipment and theory-based knowledge. Third, decisions became standardized, particularly through SPC, which set up rule-based procedures around accepted parameters. Ironically, the rules themselves were often based on customary values derived from shop floor experience.

Discussion and Conclusions

The four paper mills under study deviate from the expectations of post-Fordist theory in several ways. While workers' skills have risen as they learned to operate computer-based equipment, their autonomy has not increased and the synthesis of mental and manual labor has not occurred. The hierarchy in the firm has been resistant to change. An explanation for this is not likely to be found in reliance on mass production formulae, as some analysts might suggest, since each plant produces a wide mix of products. Niche production areas were no more likely to adopt flexible work systems than mass production departments.

Two other explanations seem more plausible. First, the larger society offers few resources in support of craft-based production. Second, engineers are situated to gain more than production workers from restructuring initiatives. Workers remain embedded in intradepartmental job ladders. They have job security and protected skills with specialized knowledge (and occasionally use this knowledge to resist the arrogance of engineers), but they remain isolated and less able to compete for larger, more autonomous roles within the mills. Engineers, on the other hand, have a cohesive occupational group, a shared sense of mission, and an expertise validated by the larger culture. They are encouraged in a career path that moves through several areas of the plant and builds knowledge of the production process as a whole.

This research suggests that analysts need to pay more attention to the micropolitical effects of restructuring, particularly in light of the kinds of contradictory impulses observed in these paper mills. Management wants more commitment to quality from production workers, yet has undermined worker discretion. Product markets and technology are important influences on workplace organization, but "under circumstances in which craft knowledge has been defined as a sign of backwardness, and definitions of officially sanctioned knowledge shift to the advantage of engineering discourse, flexible work structures seem unlikely to take root *regardless* of the market or technological conditions that obtain." [356] International comparisons indicate that countries with strong craft traditions are more likely to adopt flexible work systems, while others, like the United States, may end up with a hybrid, contradictory strategy that combines high-tech production with Taylorist organization.

Three suggestions emerge from the research. First, in the context of Statistical Process Control, establishment of norms and acceptable variances could be undertaken by production teams based on workers' knowledge and experience. Second, there is evidence that process engineers who grew up near the plants where they work share ties and allegiances to production coworkers and are more willing to respect craft-based knowledge. Third, opportunity structures should be expanded. Supervisory positions should not be restricted to engineers. Training and job bidding procedures should encourage manual workers to work in other departments and gain more comprehensive knowledge of the plant as a whole.

Summary of

Computer Rationalization and the Transformation of Work: Lessons from the Insurance Industry

by Eileen Appelbaum and Peter Albin

[Published in *The Transformation of Work?*, ed. Stephen Wood
(London: Routledge, 1989), 247–265.]

Computer and information technologies are transforming the production of services as well as goods. One version of this transformation is "computer rationalization"—using computers to introduce or enhance Taylorist principles of work organization. An alternative possibility is to use these technologies to facilitate the integration of tasks and the decentralization of control and decision making. These alternatives, and combinations thereof, are now being tried out in the insurance industry, which faces "a broader range of choices than is suggested by any dichotomy such as craft and flexible resources versus mass production and narrowly specialized resources." [249] This article uses four case studies to illustrate the varied implications of computerization.

Automation and Production Organization

The use of computers in the insurance industry differs from that in other "office" industries, such as government or law, in that it has moved beyond traditional support activities to core production activities. During the 1970s, as insurance firms began to use computers more intensively in key production activities, "[a]utomation eliminated the least skilled clerical jobs, such as mail handler, and upgraded entry-level skill requirements; but it also eliminated the most skilled clerical job, that of the rater who determined the price of the policy." [251] Managers increasingly faced a range of options in distributing tasks between workers and machines, and among workers in different occupations. Actual outcomes lie along a continuum whose extremes may be characterized as "algorithmic" versus "robust" organization.

The goal of algorithmic organization is to increase as far as possible the routinization of work, reducing decision making to a set of self-contained rules (algorithms) that can be implemented by a computer. The result is an increased number of routinized data entry jobs and fewer highly skilled professional jobs. Although algorithmic organization is often held up as the state-of-the-art use of information technology, this turns out to be harder to implement in the property and casualty segments of the industry than in the life and health segments.

The alternative approach, which depends on increasing, rather than reducing, the input of human intelligence, is termed "robust" because it "connotes an organizational capacity to adapt to changing conditions." [255] Insurance production organized in this way moves toward the elimination of unskilled clerical jobs and the reduction of routine data entry tasks. The computer is used to spread skills and decision making down in the organization's hierarchy, while skill requirements in the remaining jobs are increased.

Clerical and administrative support jobs in robustly organized firms require that the workers have a range of skills that had not previously been associated with such work. These include social and communication skills; "managerial skills related to planning, organizing time effectively, thinking more comprehensively about the enterprise, and acting in a strategic manner"; [264] and general computer skills. All of these are transferable across a variety of specific job titles and industries, motivating firms to hire them from the outside rather than developing them along internal promotion mechanisms.

At the same time, an important dividing line between algorithmic and robust types of work organization has to do with the role of contextual knowledge—"the extent to which acceptable performance requires the knowledge of the firm's products, production processes, customers, clients, procedures or regulatory environment." [263] The need for contextual knowledge is reduced as far as possible in algorithmic organizations, where the valued skills relate only to generalized information technology. "The extent of contextual knowledge required for a particular function is generally not technologically determined." [263] Instead, it is a result of management's decisions about how to use technology. That decision is influenced at many points by the fact that much of the workforce in this industry is female. These workers face, on the one hand, employer expectations about being able to hire women at low wages and, on the other hand, prejudices about the skills that can be expected from or can be taught to such a workforce.

Four Examples

A central question in the direction taken by an insurance firm is whether routine data entry is to exist as a distinct job to be performed by a data entry clerk, or whether routine data should be entered as they are generated.

1. Some of the largest insurance firms, such as Prudential, use technology to shift insurance application processing from field offices to large, central-

ized clerical processing centers. In one firm that exemplifies this approach, personal computers are used to price life insurance products, but not to enter data into the firm's database or to process applications. The latter, routinized data entry jobs are performed by low-level employees   often mothers who can depend on their husbands' health and other benefit coverage. The chief benefit to the firm is a saving in compensation and other employee costs.

2.   A different approach is taken by a smaller firm that sells its policies through direct-mail advertising rather than relying on agents. The firm's automated mail handling and filing have eliminated nearly all of the least skilled clerical jobs, as policies are entered on-line, and underwriting and rating is entirely computerized. Meanwhile two new types of highly skilled clerical jobs have been created: customer service representatives and claims representatives. This approach has reduced upward mobility within the firm, as college-educated professionals are hired directly (rather than through internal promotion ladders) into the upper management ranks. It has also reduced the size of the workforce: Within three years, employment at the company's main location shrank by more than one-half, from about 5000 employees to about 2300. Dramatic productivity growth is shown by the ability of this greatly reduced workforce to handle more business than the company had done at its previous peak.

3.   Increasingly competitive market conditions in property and casualty insurance lines led the property-casualty division of one of the largest U.S. firms to turn to computer rationalization to reduce costs and improve efficiency. In marketing its products, the company now relies on independent agents and brokers employed by independent agencies on a commission basis The firm's goal is to reduce its sales force by 90 percent, and also to eliminate most jobs in clerical processing of commercial lines products. Many underwriters' jobs are being eliminated. Those that remain have more responsibility, as they are expected to manage the nominally independent agents in the field. The agent's job has become more professional, but their actual independence is questionable. Hierarchy in this firm appears to imply close monitoring; in the personal lines side of its production, electronic surveillance of clerical workers' keystrokes per minute was considered as a way of increasing productivity. The expected benefits to the company include

1. increased market share in commercial commodity insurance because of improved marketing capability and the ability to tailor policies more precisely to client needs, and to achieve substantial cost savings through the elimination of clerical and most underwriting support jobs for this type of risk. [257]

4. A large, established company that was late in taking automation beyond the mainframe stage has drawn lessons from the experiences of competitors, and "views its goals as a computer-assisted rather than a computerized production process, by which it means that it does not intend to establish clerical processing centers to deal with personal lines of insurance." [257] It has organized an operations unit at each of its forty-two branch offices to provide all clerical support required. As the firm decentralizes, jobs in these operations units span a wide range of skill levels. With skilled clerical jobs increasing there is job mobility within clerical work, but it is no longer possible to move from clerical to professional positions. Decentralization has led to large reductions in home office employment at all levels. The home office now provides support for the branches.

Outcomes and Implications

In the examples of the algorithmic approach shown above, technology is utilized to separate the entry of data from the processing of applications. Removing the latter work to remote locations is an extension of the Taylorist organization of work that began with early computer rationalization. Productivity gains are realized in the period immediately following computer rationalization, but are then exhausted. Firms then find themselves with few options for further increasing productivity or reducing costs. Workers feel increased stress, which shows up in sickness, absenteeism, and turnover.

"In contrast, more robust alternatives proceed by increasing the amount of information available to workers at every level within the organization." [260] Decision making is decentralized and the decision-making capacities of all workers, including clerical workers, are enhanced. The robust organization is designed to promote and value employee learning, flexibility, and adaptive behavior. Often, however, these job characteristics are "accompanied by a loss of autonomy, increased stress and more stringent regulation of working time. Clerical workers who are required to handle clients in a given number of minutes and nominally independent sales agents who are now monitored by company employees are obvious examples." [261] Such a structure includes high investments in human capital and high costs for the required internal communication. However, increased costs per worker are often offset by sizeable reductions in the workforce. The robustly organized firm gains additional competitiveness in rapidly changing circumstances where it can take advantage of its increased adaptiveness.

Thus, it would appear that "the choice of organizational structure reflects managements' evaluation of the trade-off between higher costs in the present and the potential for higher productivity, higher quality, or greater flexibility in the future." This rational calculation tends, however, to be affected by a number of other considerations including uncertainty (such as the difficulty of evaluating future gains); managers' attitudes toward and expectations of a largely female workforce; a distaste for relinquishing control, and/or a distrust of lower-level workers, evidenced, for example, in "[r]esistance to providing training to clerical workers" [262]; the managers' own objectives, their sophistication, and their prior experience with change; difficulty in promoting trust among various segments of the workforce, such as carriers and marketers; the climate created by public policy; and the preferences and influence of workers and unions.

Summary of

Effects of Technological Change: The Quality of Employment

by Heidi Hartmann, Robert E. Kraut, and Louise A. Tilly

[Published in *Computer Chips and Paper Clips,* eds. Heidi I. Hartmann, Robert E. Kraut, and Louise A. Tilly (Washington, D.C.: National Academy Press, 1986), 127–166.]

This article examines the effects of new technologies—especially those associated with information—on the quality of employment. Do such technologies depreciate the work experience through fragmentation, electronic monitoring, and deskilling, or enrich it by increasing task integration and autonomy and upgrading skill acquisition? "These issues are especially germane to women, because as clerical workers, bookkeepers, nurses, librarians, and other direct users of information technology, they are likely to be affected in large numbers. In addition, their relative lack of power in the workplace suggests that if information technology has pernicious effects, they will bear its brunt." [127]

Evidence from Surveys and Studies

The aspects of employment quality that are reviewed here are, first, job content, which encompasses attributes that are intrinsically part of the work; second, working conditions, both physical and social, which influence worker satisfaction; and third, economic considerations, which include the compensation, benefits, security, and promotion possibilities associated with a particular job, occupation, or workplace.

At this time there are inadequate data on which to base quantitative, systematic answers to the questions posed in this paper. On the one hand, some studies have documented situations in which the introduction of new technology coincided with a fragmentation of jobs and a decrease in the skill levels required to do them. Such fragmentation is not necessarily caused by the new technology, but it facilitates an ongoing process of routinizing work concomitant with decreased work variety, reduced challenge levels, and less responsibility. Researchers have also identified cases in which technology incorporates substantive knowledge, leaving less for a worker to know. For example, "[i]n the insurance industry, the skilled work of assigning risks or assessing claims has increasingly been codified into computer software, so that less skilled, less experienced, and less educated clerks can perform the work once performed by skilled clerks and professionals." [137]

On the other hand, if the most routinized jobs in an industry are the first to be automated, the remaining job mix may be of a higher quality. Following this line, some researchers argue that new office technologies can reintegrate jobs that were fragmented for other reasons, and can require more skill. After all, new skills are required to master the technology itself. Automation may also increase worker responsibility and the need for cooperation.

Existing survey research does not directly address the effects of technology on employment quality, while research that studies the relationship indirectly should be viewed with caution. However, existing surveys, which may be used as a point of departure, "suggest that workers who use information technology are generally satisfied with it, because it allows them to do their work better and because it improves the jobs themselves or, at a minimum, does not degrade them significantly." [134]

Getting Behind the Studies

Differing views on the effects of technology are in part a result of "comparisons of experiences at different stages in the evolution of the technology, variations in the uses of the equipment, and differing social and economic circumstances under which new technology is introduced." [139] Another reason for disagreements in the research literature has to do with the level at which work units are analyzed. Part of a job may be rendered less challenging when, for example, it is done on a computer, but the time saved thereby may be used for new, more interesting tasks. Thus the effect on the whole job may be different from, and more positive than, the effect on one particular aspect.

Comparisons become even more difficult when we recognize that, when new technology reduces the overall skill requirement for a particular job, that job may be turned over to a different individual—perhaps a labor force entrant with less employment experience and education—while the incumbent workers may, on the one hand, retire or be laid off—or, on the other hand, they may be transferred or promoted. Obviously, workers' perceptions of the effects of technology will be strongly affected by which of these possibilities eventuate for them.

The subtlety of these issues is captured in the observation that, while "the deskilling of some white-collar jobs may be the vehicle by which less advantaged social groups gain white collar work . . . for the same reason, less advantaged workers may face greater job insecurity because those jobs may be at risk of further deskilling or elimination through new technology." [142]

Overall, the skill requirements for the labor force as a whole depend greatly on the evolution of industries—especially on how the better and worse jobs are distributed among the growing and the shrinking industries. The present state of knowledge does not make it possible to determine which trends are currently dominating. However, it is sure that the changing skill requirements that accompany continuous technological change are bound to produce gaps between workers' skills and job requirements. These gaps are a problem that require attention on their own.

Working Conditions

Three aspects of working conditions will be considered here. The first has to do with the extent of monitoring. New information technology increases the amount of evaluative information that managers can collect and analyze about their workers and that can be used to monitor workers more closely. Whether or not managers choose to do so is a social choice. While productivity monitoring may have positive and/or negative effects, many organizations that have the technical capabilities choose not to monitor their workers on an individual level.

A second area where technology is thought to affect working conditions is the possibility of telecommuting and the electronic distribution of work. Telecommuting is the use of computers and telecommunications equipment to work at home or in other locations away from a conventional, centralized office. Because so little telecommuting occurs, it is impossible to get convincing evidence on whether it is a positive alternative work arrangement for those with home and family responsibilities or simply a continuation of the traditional exploitation of isolated, predominantly female workers. This issue can be illuminated by examining home-based work more generally, in which flexibility in employment is usually gained at the price of lost income.

Another important aspect of new information technologies involves ergonomics—the physical fit between people and technology. Increasing quantities of work time is spent sitting in front of computer terminals, which may cause a number of physiological and psychological complaints. In many cases, however, these technologies are introduced into jobs that would be poor anyway.

These examples do not resolve the questions raised at the outset, but instead point to the importance of management choices in how to introduce and employ new technologies.

The Role of Managers

Two issues dominate concerns about the impact of technology on economic aspects of employment quality: compensation and job security. To the extent that technology increases productivity, workers expect to share in the gains. They also expect to be compensated for specific skills they must acquire to use the new technology and the general education levels that technology-intensive jobs may require. Moreover, employees' fears of job loss and employment dislocation associated with technology can be reduced by a number of employer policies.

Management practices and methods of work can be much more powerful influences on employees' job satisfaction than are the technological tools used to do the job. There is much that an organization with a concern for employment quality can do to introduce technology into the workplace in ways that use it effectively, aid the general welfare of the organization, and enhance employment quality.

However, there are many reasons, including economic conditions, interest group conflicts, and workplace cultures, why managers do not act to maximize the effective and humane use of technology. The limited evidence available suggests that the decision to introduce new technologies is typically dominated by economic considerations focusing on product selection with little or no attention to issues such as employee attitudes, skills, and behaviors or organizational effects.

Given the ubiquity of sex segregation of jobs within firms . . . and the small number of women in managerial positions, many of the managers who make decisions about the technology that women will use have never held a job like the one in which the technology is being introduced. Thus, they are likely to have difficulty identifying both the full range of tasks that the technology needs to support . . . and the full impact that the technology will have on the quality of employment. [152]

The Role of Workers

Worker participation affects employment quality and job satisfaction in two ways. First, it changes the contents of the decisions because it provides a mechanism through which workers' interests are represented. Second, participation may be intrinsically satisfying and may lead to increased commitment to decisions, simply as a result of the process by which the decisions were reached.

Workers cannot simply rely on the goodwill of employers to ensure that technology is used humanely. They need mechanisms to represent their interests in decisions affecting employment quality. This participation can take two basic forms: informal participatory practices, which are the activities, knowledge, and expertise that workers bring to bear on many policies; and formal rights giving workers an explicit role to play in company decision making concerning technology. The two forms are complementary. Regardless of the basis for input, early involvement in the system design process is important, as it allows those involved to influence the nature of the goals that are set.

One of the most effective mechanisms for involving workers in decisions has been for workers actively to propose and then to provide feedback on technological design and implementation. Other mechanisms include legislation and regulation, negotiated collective agreements, and more informal discussion. The effectiveness of worker participation depends vitally on the organizational context in which it takes place and on the procedures through which it is accomplished.

In the United States, worker participation programs have been used primarily in manufacturing companies, generally with union representation. Both in the United States and in Europe unionized workers have negotiated technology agreements that provide mechanisms for union involvement in the implementation of technology in their industries. Because European countries have higher levels of unionization than the United States, their technology agreements have been more elaborate and more effective. Different mechanisms may be necessary in the United States, especially to ensure worker involvement among the highly nonunionized female labor force in service industries.

Summary of

Computing Inequality: Have Computers Changed the Labor Market?

by David Autor, Lawrence Katz, and Alan Krueger

[Published in *National Bureau of Economic Research Working Paper* 5956 (Cambridge, MA: NBER, March 1977).]

The cause of rising income inequality in the United States has been the subject of debate among economists, as well as the general public. Some analysts favor an explanation based on globalization and international trade, in which low-skilled production workers are replaced by imports or outsourcing. Others argue that the decline of equalizing institutions, such as the weakening of unions or the falling real value of the minimum wage, is to blame.

This article argues for a third explanation, maintaining that technological change, in particular computerization, has raised the demand for better educated workers and thereby increased the pay gap based on education. Analysis of census and other data for selected years from 1940 to 1995 shows that the demand for skilled labor did grow more rapidly after 1970 than before, and that educational and skill upgrading in the 1980s and early 1990s was closely correlated with computer use and research and development spending. The association of computers with increased skill levels is statistically robust; many different data sets and formulations point to similar answers. By some measures, the rise in computer use statistically "explains" 30 to 50 percent of the recent acceleration in the demand for skilled labor, which is more than is explained by trade.

Trends in Supply and Demand

Despite the large increase in the relative supply of more educated workers, the college/high school wage differential has grown substantially since 1950. This implies that there has been a large increase in demand for educated workers—and that workers with different levels of education are not perfect substitutes for each other in production. Analyzing data separately for each decade leads to some minor puzzles, particularly in interpretation of the 1970s. Thus there is some ambiguity about the starting point for recent labor market changes. However, over a longer period of time it is clear that the relative demand for educated labor was greater in the 1980s than in the 1960s or earlier.

The widespread adoption of computers is a prime suspect for a recent technological change that could lead to major changes in the demand for skills. Data is available on the percentage of U.S. workers who used a computer keyboard in 1984, 1989, and 1993. The overall figure grew from one-quarter of the workforce in 1984 to almost one-half in 1993. The occupational and demographic groups that experienced the greatest increases in computer use—women, the better-educated, whites, white-collar workers, and full-time workers—also experienced faster than average wage gains. The wage premium associated with using a computer is roughly 20 percent, and increased slightly over the decade. The wage premium for college graduates (compared to high school graduates) grew much faster among computer users than among non-computer users.

Computers and Skill Upgrading

Most of the increase in employment and wages of college graduates since 1970 has occurred within individual industries, not as a result of interindustry shifts. Analysis of data on nearly 200 detailed industries shows that the growth of computer use in an industry is associated with increased employment of college graduates and decreased employment of high school graduates, as a percentage of the industry's workforce. The effect of computers on the employment of high school dropouts is ambiguous, but there are few dropouts employed in high-technology industries in any case.

Did the increased employment of college-educated workers in industries that used computers simply reflect an ongoing trend toward higher skill levels in these industries? That is, were the same industries upgrading their workforces equally rapidly before and after the introduction of computers? To test this possibility, the increase in each industry's employment of college-educated workers in the 1960s, 1970s, 1980s, and early 1990s was separately compared to the industry's change in computer use from 1984 to 1993. Skill upgrading in the 1960s was only weakly related to later computer use; skill upgrading in the 1970s and later periods was more strongly related to rates of computerization. The increase in computer use statistically "explains" about half of the increase from the 1960s to the 1980s in the share of employment and payroll going to college-educated workers.

Capital Intensity, R&D, and Computers

Does the association between computer usage and educational upgrading reflect the specific nature of computers, or could it be a consequence of increased capital-intensity (and complementarity between capital and skilled labor) in general? Again, an empirical analysis confirms the importance of computers in particular. Data on capital intensity, and on several measures of computer investments and other high-technology spending, are available for a group of industries (somewhat more aggregated than the ones used in the previous tests). There is a strong association between an industry's computer capital per worker and its rate of educational upgrading of its labor force. This association is not substantially affected when the analysis includes controls for changes in the industry's overall capital–labor ratio. The impacts of computer capital on skill upgrading are much stronger than those of other components of high-tech capital. However, the effect of total research and development spending on skill levels is significant and increasing, and appears to be nearly independent of the effect of computer use.

A similar analysis can be performed on a data set for detailed manufacturing industries used by other researchers. While it has cruder measures of skill levels, it allows comparison of the effects of computer use and of outsourcing (the latter may be a rough measure of trade effects). Although simple analyses show both factors to be associated with increases in skill levels, the computer effect is much more robust than the outsourcing effect when additional variables are included. The most complete versions of this analysis show that the growth in computer investments can explain roughly one-third of the acceleration in skill levels in manufacturing from the 1970s to the 1980s. On the other hand, changes in import penetration and outsourcing explain very little of the increase in the rate of skill upgrading.

In summary, numerous statistical measures and analyses confirm the association of computer usage with industry skill upgrading, and hence with the rising inequality of incomes. The association of labor market changes is stronger with computer usage than with many other proposed explanatory variables. By various measures, 30 to 50 percent of the labor force upgrading can be statistically "explained" by correlation with computer usage.

Although these conditional correlations of computer measures and the growth in the utilization of college workers . . . may not reflect causal relationships, it is clear that whatever is driving increases in the rate of growth of demand for skilled labor over the past twenty-five years is concentrated in the most computer-intensive sectors of the U.S. economy. [33]

Summary of

The Returns to Computer Use Revisited: Have Pencils Changed the Wage Structure Too?

by John E. DiNardo and John-Steffen Pischke

[Published in *Quarterly Journal of Economics* 102 (February 1997), 291–303.]

Does the large measured wage differential for on-the-job computer use (see Autor, Katz, and Krueger article summarized in Part IV) represent a true return to computer skills, or does it just reflect the fact that higher-wage workers use computers on their jobs? This article examines three large surveys of German workers, finding that the same techniques used to estimate the computer wage premium also show large wage differentials for using calculators, telephones, pencils, and chairs (working sitting down). These wage effects cannot represent payment for skill in the use of such common tools, since those skills are universal in Germany. This casts some doubt on the interpretation of computer-related wage differentials as returns to computer use or skill.

Theoretical Framework and Data Sets

Studies estimating the wage differential for computer use (the authors refer primarily to the predecessor of the Autor, Katz, and Krueger article) have relied largely on cross-sectional data. The results of these studies are indirectly consistent with the view that there is a causal effect of computer use and skills on earnings. However, cross-sectional analyses do not provide direct evidence of any causal relationship; they establish an association between computer use and higher wages but not causation. The interpretation of the computer result as causal would be strengthened, however, if the use of more commonplace white-collar tools was not associated with a similar wage premium.

These studies of tools used are made possible by three detailed West German labor force surveys, conducted in 1979, 1985/86, and 1991/92. Each survey has almost 30,000 respondents, representing a cross section of the employed German population aged 16 to 65. Comparison to U.S. data shows that, while computer use was slightly slower to arrive in Germany, the fraction of German workers using computers in 1991 was close to the U.S. figure for 1989. The occupational and demographic patterns of computer use in the two countries are very similar.

Wage Differentials for Workplace Tools

Analysis of the wage differential for computer use in Germany, with and without controls for education, experience, gender, and other factors, yields results comparable to those for the United States. The German wage premium for computer use is slightly lower. In both countries, the premium increases over time. The similarity is noteworthy since the labor market is more regulated, pay setting more centralized, and the wage structure more compressed in Germany than in the United States.

The German surveys included questions on the use of many other tools. In 1991, 44 percent of German workers used a calculator, 58 percent used a telephone, and more than 65 percent used a pen or pencil at work. About 30 percent used manual hand tools such as hammers, screwdrivers, paintbrushes, and hand-operated drills. The earlier two German surveys also asked how often workers sat down when at work.

Analyzing each tool separately leads to estimates of 9 to 14 percent wage differentials for the use of the simpler white-collar tools and for sitting on the job, compared to the 11 to 17 percent wage premium for computer use. Use of the blue-collar hand tools is associated with a 9 to 11 percent lower wage. Controlling for occupation reduces but does not eliminate the differentials. A 4 to 7 percent wage increase is associated with the use of office tools, even within narrowly defined occupations. Controlling for secondary school grades and for father's occupation has almost no effect on the estimates, noting it is less likely that the tools proxy simply for skill.

Simultaneous analysis of the effects of all white-collar tools finds that each has a significant effect. The computer differential remains among the largest, but the differentials for telephone use and for sitting on the job are also substantial. This means that the other tools do not just pick up the effect of computer use when this variable is not included. The computer effect is increasing over time, while the effects of some of the other tools are decreasing, possibly indicating a changing role for computers in the workplace.

Beyond the Treatment Effect

Discussion of the causal effect of computerization on wages often makes the implicit assumption that it is possible to measure the "treatment" effect of computer use. This term is borrowed from the medical literature, where it refers to the change in outcomes if a person is given a treatment, such as a drug. Clinical trials typically involve random assignment of people to the treatment or control groups, allowing identification of the treatment effect as the difference between the outcomes for the two groups. This is not the same as observing the difference in outcomes between people who have chosen to receive the treatment and those who have not, since choices about the treatment may be far from random.

In the case of computers, there is no possibility of randomly assigning computers to a group of previous nonusers and then comparing their wages to a control group. Even if it were logistically possible, such a study would encounter the problems that computers are of value only in some jobs, and in conjunction with some skills. If people with the appropriate skills seek out and obtain the jobs that use computers, the wage premium could be interpreted as a return to skills. This return was roughly 19 percent in the United States in 1989 and 17 percent in Germany in 1991 (ignoring the controls for all the other factors discussed above).

However, the same logic fails when applied to simpler tools. The basic literacy required for pencil use is essentially universal in Germany, so the estimated return to pencil-using skills should be zero. Instead, pencil use is associated with a 13 percent wage premium, which is difficult to interpret as a return to a skill. Alternatively, the finding about pencils can be taken "as an indication that there is substantial selection in who uses office tools: they are used predominantly by higher paid workers . . . [I]f this type of selection is important for pencils or calculators or telephones, then we should probably expect it to be equally important for computers." [301]

One possible response to this problem is to estimate wage growth for workers who start using a computer for the first time. Empirical results in this area are ambiguous. Even a strong positive finding would not rule out the possibility that computer use is a proxy for some other, unrelated skill or job attribute.

In summary, there is no solid proof of the existence of a computer treatment effect—no evidence that giving someone a computer increases their productivity and wages, holding everything else constant. Computers may nonetheless influence work and wages in many ways. Like other new technologies, the spread of computerization changes the types of work being performed and the skills expected of workers in general. In some cases, computerization of suppliers or customers of a firm may be as important as changes in the technology used by the firm itself. All this can affect the job and the wages of an individual worker, whether or not that worker is using a computer for the first time. "[T]here is no clean link between the influence of technology on wages and the computer treatment effects on workers, even if we can estimate this latter effect consistently." [303]

Summary of

Technology, Power, and the Social Organization of Work: Toward a Pragmatic Theory of Skilling and Deskilling

by Stephen R. Barley

[Published in *Research in the Sociology of Organizations* 6 (1988), 33–80.]

Technological changes in the workplace, such as microelectronics, genetic engineering, robotics, and artificial intelligence, promise to transform not just occupational structure but all of Western society. Two sociological theories have emerged that most influence current notions of how technology alters the organization of work: sociology of automation and deskilling theory. However these perspectives fail to capture adequately the multiple, subtle ramifications of technical change, and tend to view technology as either a physical or a social object. A fuller understanding of technological change would consider both the physical form of a given technology, its relationship to workplace organization, and its capacity to alter the balance of power among individuals or groups in the workplace.

Sociology of Automation and Deskilling Theory

Concern over automation motivated industrial sociologists to systematically investigate technology's implications for work. Early studies focusing on automobile plants reinforced fears that automation would "empty labor of meaning and thereby spawn an ever more alienated workforce. However, once researchers began to investigate other industries, the scenario quickly muddied." [35] The effects of automation varied by industry and type of technology. In fact, under certain conditions, automation might even reverse the alienation characteristic of mechanically paced production.

A theory of industrial evolution emerged from this school of thought. This theory proposed that technology evolved through three stages—craft, machine, and automated production—tracing a U-shaped trajectory with respect to alienation. Workers become more alienated as industry moved from craft to machine-based (and paced) work. Automation first increased alienation levels but, as it became more sophisticated, alienation could actually decline. This placed the burden of explanation solely on the technology itself, a form of technical determinism in which technology would eventually eliminate the very problems it caused.

The critical distinction of deskilling theory is its claim that technology is essentially a social phenomenon—specifically, that automation is a means of wresting control from labor by removing skill and autonomy from the worker and investing it in machines and engineered production processes. This implies that the development and implementation of technology has an intentional aspect, that it is a matter of managerial motives rather than technological imperatives. However, deskilling theorists do not tend to explore the implications of this fully, turning to a kind of social determinism with claims that the need to control labor is central to managerial culture.

These two theories operate with different assumptions and offer divergent visions of the future. Each tradition avoids testing the limits of its claims and instead promulgates a one-sided account of technological change. However, evidence from outside each tradition suggests that technologies rarely enhance or degrade work unambiguously. Because deskilling theory and sociology of automation are ultimately deterministic, neither offers a framework sufficiently flexible to account for multidirectional change in the web of occupational roles.

Technology as a Social Object of Organization

Three uses of the term "technology" have prevailed in social science—apparatus, technique, and organization. "When technology and organization are allowed to share the same semantic domain, it often becomes difficult to decide where technology stops and organization begins." [46] Individuals would tend to describe technology in terms of specific machines or techniques, but technologies are also embedded in a social space and web of meaning.

Technology can serve a symbolic as well as an instrumental purpose. New technology may be adopted to signal that the organization is at the cutting edge or that it is at the same level of technical proficiency as other organizations in its field. Technologies are also molded into social objects as different organizations develop their individual interpretive and behavioral templates. Technologies are usually introduced into settings with a history of customary behaviors and relationships that tend to reshape the new technology to be compatible with familiar practices. Where no preexisting work culture exists to influence the meaning of the technology, technical change appears to proceed more smoothly. New technologies may open new arenas of negotiation, engendering opportunities for social change.

Neither a purely materialistic nor a purely cultural theory of technology is adequate for mapping the implications of technology for the workplace. A more viable sociology of technology will require a hybrid paradigm that might be called "interpretive materialism." Such an approach would direct investigators to start with the particulars of the local context in which a technology is used before attempting to unravel the multiple and often conflicting implications of technology on the organization of work.

The Dynamics of Power

The focus on skill in most discussions of technology and work may be too narrow and may divert attention from social action. In fact, most sociologists of technology do not intend to address issues of skill per se, but rather are interested in how technologies alter systems of power and control. Power can be investigated at many levels of analysis, including individuals, groups, occupations, or organizations, and can encompass concepts of dependency, centrality, prestige, and hierarchy as well as the autonomy and control considered by automation and deskilling theories.

To understand whether a new technology will empower or degrade, it may be studied in the following three contexts—taken separately or in combination:

The attributes of the technology. Some technologies produce codes, systems of signs whose meaning requires interpretation, either as an element of intentional design (medical imaging equipment, radar) or as a by-product (sounds that convey information about the functioning of a machine). The ability to interpret codes may represent a source of power and influence for those who operate or maintain the technology. Eventually, technologies may circumvent codes by translating naturally occurring codes into codes that can be read by a machine—the technology would degrade occupations associated with the old code while empowering occupations associated with the new.

Another technical attribute constraining a technology's capacity to empower or degrade its users is how and how much the signals it produces become inputs for its further functioning. Complex and open systems of feedback should empower, while closed systems—those designed to operate without human mediation or interaction—should degrade occupations associated with their use.

Any technology can be described relative to its departure from an earlier technical order. By reducing human discretion and increasing rationality, incremental innovations deskill specific occupational groups. Radical innovations should empower some occupations while degrading or eliminating others. Occupations spawned by radical innovations experience a temporary advantage until further incremental innovations work to degrade or eliminate them.

The organizational and occupational milieu. Technologies rarely alter power distributions directly, but are instead conditioned by the setting in which they are used. Technologies are more likely to degrade occupations when they are accompanied by reorganizations that rationalize work structure, especially in larger firms. They should degrade work less when they are introduced incrementally rather than radically, and when they are deployed by organizations that emphasize ideological rather than rational control—if one can control the premises behind the action, there is less need to control the action itself. Moreover, technologies less frequently deskill members of occupations that have chosen to professionalize rather than unionize. This is because professionalization builds power by monopolizing expertise and knowledge, while unions have usually ceded to management the right to introduce technology as it sees fit.

The larger socioeconomic environment. Finally, the larger socioeconomic environment constrains an organization's or occupation's actions with respect to technology. Organizations are unlikely to employ technologies that degrade work unless the strategy makes economic sense, and that depends in part on conditions in the product market. Labor markets, in turn, affect the occupation's ability to resist degradation. Idiosyncratic conditions of specific industries also influence whether technology will degrade or empower workers.

PART V

Restructuring Employment: Flexibility versus Security

Overview Essay

by Laurie Dougherty

The nature of work has been changing at a fairly rapid pace (compared to the long reach of human history) since the early days of industrialization. The specific quality and intensity of change associated with the last quarter of the twentieth century brought us to call this volume *The Changing Nature of Work*. Among the many kinds of changes documented in this book, Part V highlights the changes that lend the topic a sense of urgency and imply a radical shift in the structure and quality of employment. We have been living through a time of collective anxiety about the nature of work. This anxiety ebbs and flows with the rhythm of the business cycle and differs from one part of the world to another, but its general focus is on the problems of instability and inequality.

Internal Labor Markets

The period immediately following World War II was marked by prosperity and rising expectations in the United States, as well as rapid material progress in many other parts of the world. One cornerstone of this era was the expectation that a job should be a long-term, well-ordered relationship between a worker and a company. The employee would receive a secure livelihood and the prospect of growth, in income at least, and in personal fulfillment at best. The employer would receive a loyal employee whose productivity would improve over time as he or she became more versed in the particular skills and qualities needed by the firm. While economic theory described the employment relationship as a labor market that matched up buyers and sellers of skills and effort, many employers and employees operated within sets of rules and customs that governed movement from one job to another and kept levels of compensation within certain bounds.

During the mid-1960s, after extensive field studies at a wide variety of establishments and review of other research, Peter Doeringer and Michael Piore estimated that four out of five U.S. workers were involved in *internal labor markets,* their term for these rule-based models of employment.[1] Their interviews and observations revealed several patterns for both blue-collar and white-collar jobs. In manufacturing firms unions often acted as the vehicle for negotiating the rules of the workplace, rules that would typically define the tasks to be performed, establish performance standards, set pay scales, and determine procedures for filling vacancies. In nonunionized settings, rules were set by other mechanisms but fulfilled similar functions: to set up an internal system for allocating human resources.

Employees joined the firm at what Doeringer and Piore called "ports of entry" that were exposed to the external labor market—that is, the economic forces of the larger society. Once the employee gained entry, he or she would progress according to the particular rules and customs of the organization. In unionized settings, seniority often governed eligibility for more desirable positions. In white-collar settings, demonstrated competence and ability to learn new skills enabled employees to move along well-defined career paths. Craft and professional workers might not have long-term relationships with particular enterprises, but the craft or profession organized procedures for allocating work and establishing compensation.

Although internal labor markets are protected from the direct effects of economic forces, they do not operate in isolation from these forces. Over time the set of rules and customs adjust to general economic conditions. More to the point, there are efficiencies that give internal labor markets economic viability—particularly reduction of the costs of recruitment, screening, and training for firm-specific skills.

While Doeringer and Piore approach internal labor markets as an analytical construct within which to investigate problems in the economic theory of labor markets, Sanford Jacoby takes a historical view of the same organizational form. His focus is on "the bureaucratization of employment, since many of the features that define good jobs—stability, internal promotion, and impersonal, rule-bound procedures—are characteristic of bureaucratic organization."[2]

In Jacoby's view the well-structured employment relationship emerged out of a struggle between production-oriented managers on the one hand and unions, social reformers, and personnel managers on the other hand. Production managers saw workers as adjuncts to the goal of getting the product out. These managers wanted the flexibility to adapt quickly to changes in technology and demand. The second group, although coming from a variety of motivations, had a common desire to stabilize the employment relationship. Unions wanted to improve the lives of their members. Reformers had humanitarian sympathies with working people (if not with unions) and fears of radicalism. They also saw opportunities for themselves within bureaucratic institutions. Personnel management brought the reform movement into the firm along with a "middle class belief in the necessity of market intervention, the beneficial effects of rational administration, and the power of the educated expert to mediate and mitigate social conflict."[3]

Although not all enterprises had well-developed internal labor markets or bureaucratic structures capable of producing good jobs and well paved career paths, it was the essence of the American Dream that with luck and pluck anyone could find a port of entry to long-term employment and upward mobility. Beginning in the late 1960s and early 1970s, although Europe, Japan, and other countries in Asia were rapidly catching up to the level of material prosperity evident in the United States, the American Dream began to fade. As suggested in the Overview Essay to Part IV, the reasons for this are complex and controversial. The competition from countries recovering from World War II and later from developing countries was one aspect of this change.

Eileen Appelbaum and Ronald Schettkat offer an explanation based on a dynamic endogenous to economic development with evidence from a statistical analysis of cross-country data on specific industries in industrialized countries. Applying the methodology of W.E.G. Salter[4] who, in 1960, found a positive correlation between high-productivity industries and employment, they find that this correlation turned negative for most industrialized countries by the 1980s. They offer the explanation that in the earlier period of positive correlation, growing productivity leads to lower prices for industrial goods, which generates greater demand leading to more employment. They call this the virtuous circle, which is the defining characteristic of an industrial economy. At some point, however, markets become saturated and price elasticities change. People are wealthier (on average) and have accumulated durable consumer goods. They are no longer so quick to purchase something just because the price drops.

One Day's Footnote Is Another Day's Headline

In a footnote to *Internal Labor Markets and Manpower Analysis,* Doeringer and Piore commented that: "General practitioners, street 'hustlers,' freelance writers, some nonunion craftsmen, and the like operate primarily as unorganized independent entrepreneurs. The best illustration of an unstructured occupational labor market is that of harvest labor."[5] Twenty years later, in 1991, Doeringer was principal editor of a research report: *Turbulence in the American Workplace,* turbulence marked by "downsizings and wrenching readjustments . . . lost jobs and even more widespread career disruptions."[6] *Business Week* proclaimed in a 1986 headline: "The Disposable Employee Is Becoming a Fact of Corporate Life."[7] The term "contingent work" became part of the vernacular.

Public and scholarly interest in the nature and extent of contingent work spurred the U.S. Bureau of Labor Statistics to supplement the February 1995 Current Population Survey (CPS) with questions about contingent work. One analysis of this data conducted by the Economic Policy Institute (EPI) and the

Women's Research and Education Institute (WREI) is summarized in Part V. Because "contingent work" is often used loosely in the media, sometimes broadly including part-time work and sometimes narrowly associated with temporary agencies (which is only one form of contingent employment), the analysts who prepared this report used the term "nonstandard" work to describe a set of specific employment arrangements:

- *Temporary help agency (Temps)*—respondents worked for agencies that supply workers to other companies on an as-needed or short-term basis.

- *On-call*—respondents were in a pool of workers called to work as needed, even if for days or weeks in a row. Some examples are substitute teachers or construction workers hired from a union hiring hall.

- *Day labor*—respondents found work by "waiting at a place where employers pick up people to work for a day."

- *Self-employment*—respondents were self-employed as, for example, shop or restaurant owners.

- *Independent contracting (wage and salary or self-employment)*—respondents "obtain[ed] customers on their own to provide a product or service." Independent contractors include freelancers and independent consultants and may have employees working for them.

- *Contract company*—respondents worked for "companies [that] provide employees or their services to others under contract." Examples include security or landscaping services or computer programming.

- *Regular part-time*—respondents worked for a wage or salary for less than 35 hours per week and were not in any of the above categories.

The categories of *nonstandard* work defined here comprised 29.4 percent of the total workforce in 1995, including 34.4 percent of all women workers and 25.4 percent of men. Some workers, particularly independent contractors and self-employed men, can earn more than workers with similar education in similar standard jobs. Some women prefer nonstandard employment in order to have the flexibility to fulfill responsibilities at home. However, in general, nonstandard work is concentrated in low-waged industries or occupations and often offers inferior pay, benefits, and job security even to workers with similar education performing work similar to those in standard work situations.

While the EPI/WREI report is based on data collected from individuals, Katharine Abraham's article, also summarized in Part V, focuses on employers and their motivation for using nonstandard work, particularly with respect to temporary workers, production subcontracting, and contracting out for business support services. Taking her cue from analysts of internal labor markets, discussed above, she uses the term *market-mediated work* to describe an employment relationship that takes place outside of the firm. Rather than finding or developing skills from within their own employee base, firms look to external labor markets when they experience a need for flexibility in staffing or wages, or a need for specialized services.

Peter Cappelli, in an article summarized in Part V, points out that the global race for competitive advantage has a contradictory impact on the nature of work. On the one hand there is a search for improved performance, which requires the reinforcement of internal, firm-specific attempts to build a committed, loyal workforce capable of agile and intelligent response to evolving technologies and fast-moving global economic forces. On the other hand, there is a frantic search to cut costs and to achieve agility by reducing commitments to the workforce in favor of hiring skills on an as-needed basis.

Part IV explores the first horn of this dilemma, the search for high performance through new technologies and new forms of work organization. Part V explores the second—what Bennett Harrison calls "the devolution of internal labor markets and the erosion of employment security,"[8] what Abramson calls "the growth of market-mediated work arrangements," and what the EPI/WREI researchers call nonstandard work. As Cappelli points out, and the historical view of internal labor markets confirms, this growth of market-mediated work is a matter of rebirth rather than the emergence of an entirely new phenomenon. Market-mediated work at the end of the twentieth century looks similar to employment relationships of the nineteenth century: labor contracting, casual labor, industrial homework, movement from one employer to another in search of better prospects. But it also takes on new institutional forms—the temp agency, employee leasing, the headhunter, the high-tech independent contractor. Surveying some of the same territory in another article summarized in Part V, Paul Osterman comes to a less sharp conclusion. He sees the system of internal labor markets as fraying at the edges but still intact.

Thierry Noyelle finds the growth of less stable forms of employment to be a matter of some concern and calls this a new form of labor market segmentation. He draws on theories of labor market dualism (or segmentation) that parallel the discussions of internal labor markets of a few decades ago, investigating why some kinds of work (and workers) remained outside the walls of bureaucratic firms, with their protective employment relationships. Some jobs were low paid, required few skills, and offered little or no job security. While the early literature on dualism focused on industries (such as fast food) or occupations (such as janitors) as the site of "secondary" labor markets, Noyelle turns to the employment relationship as the point of departure for a new form of segmentation. The detailed analysis performed by EPI/WREI on the 1995 CPS data collected by the U.S. Bureau of Labor Statistics seems to bear out the concept of segmentation. Their findings indicate that, with some exceptions, nonstandard work is inferior to standard work in pay, benefits, security, and prospects for advancement.

One of the ways the trend toward nonstandard forms of work renders work less secure is by distancing the worker from the ultimate source of labor demand through intermediaries like temp agencies or contract firms. This can confound the question of who is responsible for compensation and conditions of work. Manuel Castells and Alejandro Portes relate this process to the shadow world of the informal economy. Some aspects of the informal economy are shadowy because they deal in illicit activity, like drug trafficking or prostitution. Other aspects are simply marginal, like scavenging. A large part of the informal economy is linked directly to the formal global economy; however, it remains shadowy because it takes place beyond the reach of accountability, keeping few records and evading regulation of hours, wages, health, and safety. Firms in the formal economy, even wealthy transnational corporations, search for lower costs and the flexibility to respond to fluctuations in demand. This drive generates a chain of work arrangements on an ever more casual basis. For example, a large factory will outsource a component to a vendor who will contract for smaller parts; those contractors will piece out work to smaller groups or even to individuals. At the farthest reaches of the chain, people often work in their own homes or in fly-by-night sweatshops with no guarantee of work beyond what is immediately available.

M. Patricia Fernández-Kelly and Anna Garcia also investigated the relationship between the formal and informal economies, finding that Hispanic women in the United States often work at the end of the contracting chain, working for low pay under uncertain conditions. It is interesting to compare here a summary from Part III on globalization, in which Hernando Gómez-Buendía describes the particular political conditions that generated a large informal sector in Latin America. Because relatively few Latin American workers are employed in technically advanced, high-productivity industries, and few are eligible for state-provided welfare benefits, a large pool of workers engages in low-productivity employment, often under unregulated conditions.

Industrial home-based work is the final link in this chain of informalization. Unions have traditionally opposed home-based work because, among other reasons, it is difficult to regulate. However, the emergence of new technologies that can transmit information from one work site to another make working at home a viable option for many white-collar jobs. Kathleen Christensen examines this, also increasing, form of home-based work. Most home workers are women, many of whom work at home in order to be available to children or other dependents. With well thought out guidelines concerning performance, hours, health and safety, and child care, home-based clerical work can be a reasonable option.

Martin Carnoy and Manuel Castells also look toward guidelines for coping with the changing nature of work, but on a scale that encompasses the broad range of changes in the relationship between work and economic security at the end of the millennium. They stretch the agenda beyond the particular nexus of firm and employee to consider implications for families, communities, and society at large. They envision a society that organizes its resources around learning, to impart to workers the up-to-date skills needed to meet the challenges of new technologies and rapidly shifting economic conditions. At the same time, a learning society would allow individuals and families to reconfigure their allocation of time to work, leisure, and learning in order to adapt as conditions change and opportunities arise or fade. Carnoy and Castells' report to the OECD offers the hope that families, communities, and the state will be able to build new bases of economic and social support in the face of employment insecurity.

Notes

1. Peter B. Doeringer and Michael J. Piore, *Internal Labor Markets and Manpower Analysis* (Lexington, MA: Heath Lexington Books, 1971). The following discussion draws on Doeringer and Piore's analysis of internal labor markets. The 81 percent estimate is on page 42 and is derived from *Introduction to Labor Economics* by Orme W. Phelps.
2. Sanford M. Jacoby, *Employing Bureaucracy—Managers, Unions, and the Transformation of Work in American Industry, 1900–1945* (New York: Columbia University Press, 1985), Introduction. Quote is from page 2.
3. Ibid., 7.
4. W.E.G. Salter, *Productivity and Technical Change* (Cambridge: Cambridge University Press, 1960), cited in Appelbaum and Schettkat.
5. Doeringer and Piore (note 1 above, 41). Part VIII contains a brief discussion of employment situations with little or no structure or truncated mobility ladders.
6. Peter B. Doeringer, ed., *Turbulence in the American Workplace* (New York: Oxford University Press, 1991), vii.
7. Michael A. Pollock and Aaron Bernstein, "The Disposable Employee is Becoming a Fact of Corporate Life," *Business Week* December 15, 1986, 52–54.
8. Bennett Harrison, *Lean and Mean—The Changing Landscape of Corporate Power in the Age of Flexibility* (New York: Basic Books, 1994), 199.

Summary of

Employment and Productivity in Industrialized Economies

by Eileen Appelbaum and Ronald Schettkat

[Published in *International Labour Review* 134 (1995), 605–623.]

Differences in unemployment rates in industrialized countries since the 1970s are often seen as the result of differences in labor market regulations and institutions. According to this view, highly regulated European economies were unable to respond to changes in the world market, while deregulation in the United States allowed firms to engage in employment expansion as the economy grew. However, endogenous forces may be challenging the traditional positive correlation between productivity, employment, and economic growth. Rather than stifling employment and productivity growth, institutions may now be offering policy options in response to structural changes in the world economy.

Interindustry Patterns of Employment and Productivity Growth in Industrial Society

In 1960, W.E. Salter published his seminal study on structural economic change based on an analysis of productivity growth in twenty-eight British mining, manufacturing, and utility industries. Salter found no systematic relationship between productivity growth in an industry (which he measured as change in output per worker) and earnings growth in that industry. He interpreted this to mean that changes in earnings are not determined by industry-specific conditions, but by factors in the larger economy. Nevertheless, Salter did find a negative correlation between productivity and prices and a positive correlation between productivity and employment. When output per worker rose, the cost of producing the same amount of output fell, allowing for lower prices. As goods became cheaper, demand for them increased, leading to an increase in employment in that industry. In industries where price elasticities for products were high, lower prices could generate dramatic increases in demand, and employment effects were pronounced.

Mass production of household durables was the hallmark of the Golden Age of economic expansion after World War II. A system of positive feedback developed. Markets expanded and economies of scale led to higher productivity, lower prices, and higher employment, which further expanded demand. This was a defining characteristic of an industrial society. Policies that bolstered income when demand slowed effectively kept the system operating. Institutions involved in the operation of labor markets were less important than differences in productivity between industries. Where productivity was low, usually in services, prices rose relative to prices in manufacturing. In some service industries (such as domestic servants or railway porters) demand withered away.

The Post-Industrial Society

By the 1980s, industrialized countries began to experience a reversal in the relationship between productivity growth and employment expansion. Employment in high-productivity industries began to stagnate or decline. Unless employment in low-productivity industries could take up the slack, unemployment was bound to grow. This shift was "caused not by exogenous factors, rigid labor markets, or policy mistakes, though these may exacerbate the problem, but rather by the endogenous development process itself." [611] In accord with Harrod's Law, the absolute value of the price elasticity of goods falls as income rises. In other words, as households become more prosperous, they are less responsive to lower prices; as they accumulate more durable goods, they are less apt to need new ones. Employment thus begins to slow down in those industries in which productivity growth is most rapid. This process "contributed to the end of the virtuous cycle of economic development in industrialized countries. It marks a change that is often, though imprecisely, described as the shift from an industrial to a service economy." [611]

Distribution Effects

OECD data for industries in fifteen countries exhibits this reversal in relationship between productivity[1] and employment, but also confirms the persistence of other patterns noted by Salter—that earnings differences are not correlated with productivity differences between industries, and that productivity gains translate into lower labor costs and lower prices. Further analysis of OECD data comparing labor cost indicators, operating surplus (a proxy for profits), and productivity levels reveal that the share of labor productivity gains declined in many countries during the 1980s. In some of these countries the profit share of productivity gains increased, while in others the productivity of other nonwage components increased.

Alternative Explanations

While the reversal of the relationship between productivity growth and employment in industrialized countries has gone unnoticed, the decline in manufacturing employment has received much attention. A review and extension of these arguments to productivity and employment growth dynamics provides possible alternative explanations for the phenomenon under discussion. Some arguments are:

1. Trade among industrialized countries has led to "deindustrialization." Trade can account for employment losses in countries in which traded sectors are less efficient than they are in the trade partner. Trade cannot, however, account for the negative correlation that exists between employment growth and productivity growth in industries located in OECD countries.

2. Since the early 1970s, less industrialized countries engaged in trade have experienced an increase in the growth rate of exports from newly industri-

alized countries (most of which go to industrialized countries), and a decrease in the growth rate of exports from industrialized countries. However, estimates of employment impact on the industrialized world are too
low to account for the decline in manufacturing, nor can they explain why
the reduction in employment is greatest in industries with high productivity growth. Adrian Wood, in his 1994 book *North–South Trade, Employment and Inequality,* claims that the greatest reduction of employment in
industrialized countries is occurring among low-skilled manufacturing
workers. This is because industry is shifting toward more capital intensive
(presumably more productive) employment activities, and/or firms are investing in more labor-saving technology as a defense against competition
from low-wage countries. These effects may be accurately described, but
they do not explain the negative correlation between employment and
productivity growth. The outcome of this shift in the composition of labor
and capital is still not clear. If firms defensively turn to labor-saving technology, the impact on employment will still depend on the price elasticity
of demand, as explained above.

3.   Some analysts claim that in mature (nonagricultural) economies the shares
     of services and manufacturing in real output remain constant over time,
     while their rates of productivity growth diverge. However, one recent
     study shows an increased role for demand factors in U.S. output shares,
     while other studies indicate that the share of services in real output is
     growing faster than the share of goods. Both are consistent with the analy-
     sis given here that demand elasticities for manufactured goods change as
     industrialization progresses.

4.   The negative relationship between productivity growth and employment
     could mean that industries, as they are defined in this analysis, have sub-
     markets with different patterns of productivity and demand that are
     masked by industry averages. Though individual firms within an industry
     may differ in productivity growth, the differences evaluated here occur *be-
     tween* industries. In this case, higher-productivity firms will survive and
     lower-productivity firms will not. The more productive firms will expand
     supply to compensate, and employment in the industry will still depend on
     demand elasticities.

Conclusion and Policy Options

Industrialized countries have shifted from an industrial to a postindustrial
model. While some have argued that exogenous changes in wage and price-set-
ting behavior caused this shift, these two variables exhibit the same relationship
to productivity under both regimes. Instead, the shift is shown to be the result

of factors endogenous to the process of development itself. As incomes rise, demand is less responsive to the decrease in price that accompanies productivity growth; in other words, as households accumulate consumer durables, the demand for new ones declines.

In the long run this shift may reverse the relationship again if new products are introduced that are capable of setting off a new "virtuous cycle." Information and communication technology may be the key. Although their full potential is not clear, public policy can increase the capacity to diffuse and incorporate new technologies. In the short run, however, it appears that employment growth will remain confined to services. Countries might choose policies that can increase productivity in services, perhaps through teamwork or shared income arrangements, or they might choose to promote inefficient, low-wage activities. "But these are social and political choices on which economists can lay no special claim and on which, like other citizens, [each] gets just one vote." [622]

Note

1. Productivity is defined as real output per employed person, except for the United States, where employment is based on full-time equivalents and includes the self-employed.

Summary of

Nonstandard Work, Substandard Jobs: Flexible Work Arrangements in the United States[1]

by Arne L. Kalleberg, Edith Rasell, Naomi Cassirer, Barbara F. Reskin, Ken Hudson, David Webster, Eileen Appelbaum, and Roberta M. Spalter-Roth

[Published by Economic Policy Institute and Women's Research and Education Institute (Washington, D.C.: 1997), 1–94.]

With the presumed growth of nonstandard work arrangements in the 1980s and 1990s, the media forecast the dissolution of employment stability and a new, more entrepreneurial economy in which workers bounce from job to job, engaged in cut-throat competition for short-term, project-oriented work. This reinforced the popular perception that nonstandard work is inferior to full-time regular employment and is undertaken by those who cannot find better jobs.

To better understand the reality, the U.S. Bureau of Labor Statistics added questions about contingent work to the February 1995 Current Population Survey (CPS).[2] Using the BLS data, it is possible to investigate several aspects of the quality of nonstandard jobs and the motivations of those who hold them. This study is a comprehensive analysis of these data.

Characteristics of Nonstandard Jobs

The term contingent work has become loosely associated with both employment instability and nonstandard employment relationships. For example, a temp worker may work short-term assignments at a variety of firms (reflecting instability) but be employed by the same agency throughout (reflecting a stable employment relationship). This report uses the term nonstandard work to highlight work arrangements other than regular, full-time ("standard") jobs.

In addition to part-time workers, nonstandard workers include employees of temporary help agencies, on-call workers, day laborers, self-employed persons, independent contractors (who may be self-employed or work for a wage or salary), and contract workers. (See Table V.1.) Nonstandard jobs tend to be more insecure than regular full-time employment, lasting for only a short time or for the duration of a project, and may terminate with little or no notice.

Table V.1. Workers, by Work Arrangement

Work Arrangement	All	Women	Men	White	Black	Hispanic	Other Race
Regular part-time	13.7%	21.3%	7.1%	13.7%	13.2%	13.8%	14.1%
Temporary help agency	1.0	1.1	0.8	0.8	1.9	1.3	1.0
On-call/Day labor	1.6	1.7	1.5	1.5	1.7	2.5	1.7
Self-employment (independent)	5.5	4.8	6.1	6.3	1.5	3.2	5.5
Contractng WS (independent)	0.9	0.9	0.9	0.9	0.7	0.8	1.0
Contracting SE	5.6	3.7	7.3	6.4	2.4	3.3	4.2
Contract company	1.2	0.8	1.6	1.2	1.1	1.3	1.7
All nonstandard	29.4%	34.4%	25.4%	30.8%	22.4%	26.2%	29.2%
Regular full-time	70.6	65.7	74.7	69.2	77.6	73.7	70.9
All	100%	100%	100%	100%	100%	100%	100%

Source: Author's analysis of February 1995 Current Population Survey. From Kalleberg et al., *Nonstandard Work, Substandard Jobs: Flexible Work Arrangements in the U.S.*, Economics Policy Institute and Women's Research and Education Institute, 1997. Reprinted with permission.
Abbreviations: WS is wage and salary; SE is self-employment.

The Quality of Nonstandard Jobs

All types of nonstandard work, on average, are inferior to regular full-time work. Nonstandard jobs pay less than regular full-time jobs to workers with similar characteristics and educational qualifications. The wage penalties for nonstandard workers are due, in part, to the nonstandard arrangement and, in part, to the industry, occupation, or general quality of the jobs typical of these types of work arrangements.

Comparing wages among standard and nonstandard workers with similar personal and job characteristics shows a majority of nonstandard workers, including 81 percent of women in nonstandard jobs, are paid less per hour than workers with similar characteristics in similar regular jobs. This group includes part-time work, female on-call and self-employed workers, and male temporaries. A second group of nonstandard jobs, which includes female temps and male on-call workers, pays wages similar to regular employment, but this group employs only 4.4 percent of nonstandard workers. A third group of nonstandard jobs pays better than similar standard jobs and includes contract workers, independent contractors, and self-employed men. This category holds a little over one-third of all nonstandard workers, but nearly two-thirds of the men in nonstandard jobs.

Wages are not the only criteria for evaluating the quality of jobs. Compared to regular workers, workers in nonstandard jobs are also far less likely receive benefits. Only 12 percent have employer-provided health care compared with over two-thirds of regular full-time workers. Workers in nonstandard jobs are also more likely to be in jobs that offer less security. About 18 percent of both men and women in nonstandard jobs have jobs of uncertain or limited duration, three times the proportion of workers in standard jobs. Although information on work histories is limited, what there is lends little support to the often-expressed hope that nonstandard work will offer a gateway to a better job. It does lend support to the suspicion that the downsizing wave of the early 1990s moved some workers from more secure to less secure work arrangements.

The proportion of black and Hispanic workers in nonstandard jobs is less than the proportion of white workers in such jobs, but blacks and Hispanics are in poor-quality, temporary, on-call, or day laborer jobs at a higher frequency than whites and less often in the more lucrative self-employed or independent contracting positions.

Why Do Some People Work in Nonstandard Jobs?

Nonstandard work employs 29.4 percent of all workers, 34.4 percent of female workers, and 25.4 percent of males. Although these jobs are often inferior to regular full-time jobs, some analysts claim that many employers and employees prefer the flexibility of nonstandard work arrangements. Flexibility can reduce a firm's costs by employing workers only as needed, and by replacing secure, well-paying standard jobs with poorly paid nonstandard ones. Flexibility can help workers balance work and family responsibilities. However, if flexible jobs are poor-quality jobs, family circumstances may force some workers to take jobs they would not want otherwise.

Motivations for taking a nonstandard job can be either voluntary or involuntary. Involuntary reasons reflect the inability of the worker to find a more preferable standard work arrangement under existing labor market conditions. Voluntary motives further divide into two categories: family and other voluntary. A worker who might otherwise prefer a standard job may choose a nonstandard work arrangement to accommodate family obligations. The "other voluntary" category reflects a true preference for some kind of nonstandard work or some other reason such as health, partial retirement, or student status.

For men voluntary reasons for nonstandard work generally correspond to the quality of the job. Men who are independent contractors or self-employed are well compensated and often prefer this type of arrangement. Men in temporary jobs usually claim they could not find regular full-time work. Relatively few men cite family reasons. Women are far more likely to express a family-based reason, particularly women with children who work in regular part-time jobs. Even women in the relatively well-paid independent contractor category are more likely than men to offer a family reason for this choice.

Policies to Improve Conditions for Nonstandard Workers

Some types of nonstandard work offer an attractive combination of good pay, flexibility, and autonomy; but most nonstandard jobs are insecure and poorly paid with few benefits. Women often accept such jobs in order to have time for family responsibilities. A number of policies have been proposed that would improve conditions in nonstandard jobs directly, or make standard employment better able to accommodate the needs of families.

For example, the Equal Pay Act, which prohibits discrimination on account of race or gender, should also require equal hourly pay for similar work under any type of work arrangement. Nonstandard workers should receive the same benefits as standard workers on a prorated basis. Health insurance and pensions should be made portable when workers change jobs, or universally provided through a tax-funded system. When nonstandard work involves dual employment relationships—such as a temp agency or contractor providing employees to a client firm—labor law should be amended to clearly designate each firm's legal responsibility for health, safety, and other regulated conditions of work. Programs such as unemployment compensation and the Family and Medical

Leave Act should eliminate eligibility rules that leave out some nonstandard workers. Flexible options, such as variable starting and quitting times, would enable more workers with family responsibilities to undertake full-time employment.

Notes

1. This article summarizes research supported by the Ford Foundation.
2. The February 1997 Current Population Survey updated these data.

Summary of

Restructuring the Employment Relationship: The Growth of Market-Mediated Work Arrangements

by Katharine G. Abraham

[Published in *New Developments in the Labor Market*, eds. Katherine G. Abraham and Robert B. McKersie (Cambridge: MIT Press, 1990), 85–120.]

In market-mediated relationships, firms look outside to find the labor and skills thay need, rather than hiring workers onto their own payrolls. The use of market-mediated employment arrangements appears to have grown from the mid-1970s to the mid-1980s. The paper focuses on three specific types of such relationships: the use of *temporary worker*, *contracting out*, for business support services, and *production subcontracting*. An important finding is the differences among these in the reasons that they are attractive to firms—especially their roles in buffering change. The paper considers the factors that could confer advantages on firms who turn to market-mediated employment realtionships, and seeks evidence on whether these factors have increased in importance.

Trends in Market-Mediated Work Arrangements

The coverage and importance of internal labor markets seemed to increase over much of the twentieth century. Internal labor markets use administrative rules to allocate and compensate labor. This can reduce the costs of recruiting and screening employees, and allows firms to incorporate training and rewards for good performance into long-term employment relationships. If skills are specific to the firm or industry, long-term employees will become more productive and more valuable. If employees value stability, they may work for a lower wage in return for stable employment.

During the period examined in this study (1972 to 1986), the trend toward stronger employer-employee attachments slowed while the use of market-mediated work arrangements increased. Direct evidence concerning the extent of market-mediated employment is limited but allows some inferences to be drawn. Although their methodologies are not directly comparable, both the U.S. Bureau of Labor Statistics (BLS) monthly payroll survey and the Bureau of the Census (BOC) five-yearly Census of Service Industries show that employment in the business services industry grew much faster than employment overall. This category contains a number of specialized services, ranging from computer programming and data processing to janitorial and mailroom services, which are good candidates for market-mediated work arrangements. The business services industry also includes personnel supply services, of which temporary help is a large component.

From 1972 to 1986 personnel supply services employment expanded at an annual rate of 11.5 percent (as compared to total nonagricultural employment, which grew at an annual rate of 2.2 percent). From 1982 to 1986 the temporary help industry grew at almost 20 percent a year, bringing employment in this sector to around 800,000 people—nearly up to the level of the automobile industry, and significantly above employment in the manufacture of computers and semiconductors. Beyond the agencies specializing in supplying temporary help, a reasonable guess is that "the aggregate employment of all types of temporary workers averaged something over 1.5 million people" during 1986. [91]

A survey of businesses conducted on behalf of the Bureau of National Affairs (BNA) was designed to fill in some of the gaps in other data sources. About 90 percent of responding firms used some form of short-term employment, through direct short-term hiring, agency temporaries, or on-call workers. These forms of work increased the total hours worked in these companies by about 1.4 percent. The survey was useful in investigating whether the growth in employment through temporary help agencies offset declines in other functionally equivalent work arrangements. The answer appears to be that, at least between 1980 and 1985, there had "been across-the-board growth in the use of market-mediated work arrangements." [92]

Reasons for the Use of Market-Mediated Work Arrangements

There are three possible reasons why employers may prefer market-mediated work arrangements. The first involves *staffing flexibility*. Firms that use market-mediated work arrangements may be able to adjust the quantity and skill mix of labor to changing conditions while protecting regular employees. Since internal labor markets generally involve some investment in selecting and training long-term employees, these employees are likely to be kept on the payroll even during slack periods to ensure that they are available when needed. If fluctuations in demand are expected, there is an incentive to keep the core of regular employees small and use supplemental staff on an as-needed basis. This can save on labor costs even if short-term workers earn higher hourly wages or are less productive than regular employees.

If seasonal or cyclical fluctuations are being absorbed by the business services industry, relieving other firms of the strains of demand fluctuations, this should be reflected in the relative variation in employment levels in personnel supply services, which is dominated by temporary help agencies. "[P]ersonnel supply services employment . . . is so strongly seasonal and so strongly cyclical as to lend support to the conclusion that agency temporaries are filling a buffer role for user firms." [99–100] By contrast, neither the seasonality nor the cyclicality of demand appears to affect the use of subcontractors.

The second employer motivation involves *wage flexibility*. Firms may look to the outside labor market to circumvent some wage constraints imposed by internal labor markets. The relevant wage constraints may include union contracts or efficiency wages—higher wages paid to induce greater effort or lower turnover. Moreover, workers' ideas about equity may limit employers' ability to pay some workers within the firm high wages while paying others low wages. While a firm may pay efficiency wages for essential or highly skilled jobs, it may choose to by contracting out peripheral activities like cleaning. However, workers' ideas about equity may also generate morale problems if there are large wage differences within the firm. "Moving work outside the internal labor market permits the firm to take advantage of low market wage rates for certain types of work without violating internal equity constraints." [96]

To fully understand the role of wage flexibility, it is necessary to compare not only wages and benefits but also the productivity levels of long-term and short-term employees. Where there are intermediaries such as subcontractors or agencies, fees and markups need to be compared to a firm's own overhead expenses when doing the work in-house. Though data for such a complete analysis are not available, data that have been obtained from employer survey responses indicate that lower wages and benefits are important motivations for contracting out low-skilled work. In contrast, these are generally not the main reasons for the use of temporary workers.

The third possible employer motivation reflects a need for *specialized services* that cannot be economically provided in-house. This figures prominently in employers' reports of why they use outside contractors, particularly among those who contract for administrative support services.

Why Have Market-Mediated Work Arrangements Increased?

While this article cannot examine all possible explanations for the recent increase in market-mediated work, evidence may be adduced for several possible causes. One is increased variability in product demand. Since the early 1970s there has been an increase in macroeconomic volatility. Exchange rates have fluctuated, producing uncertainty in export markets. Product life cycles have become shorter, requiring more frequent adjustments of equipment and labor.

Another motivation may be greater costs of hiring and firing employees. There is some indication that it is more expensive for U.S. firms today to adjust the size of their workforce. Antidiscrimination legislation may restrict the ability of employers to dismiss or lay off employees, as they may be vulnerable to charges of race, sex, or age discrimination. A few court cases have further restricted the ability of firms to dismiss employees at will, holding that in some cases there are implicit contracts that obligate the employer to fulfill assurances made to their employees. Explicitly short-term arrangements would circumvent these constraints.

Finally, there is evidence that during the 1970s and 1980s there was a significant widening of wage sectoral differences, which may have created an incentive for high-wage firms to contract work out to firms with lower wages.

Conclusions

The BLS and census statistics, together with other survey data, add up to a picture in which employers have quite different motivations for the different sorts of market-mediated work arrangements in which they engage.

Temporary employment—including both agency temporary employment and hiring of temporaries onto organizations' own payrolls—is the only category of market-mediated work for which buffering regular employees from fluctuations in demand appears to be a primary employer motivation. For business services requiring relatively low skills, wages, and benefits in the business service sector appear to be substantially less generous than elsewhere in the economy, and employers appear quite likely to view savings on labor costs as important in their contracting-out decisions. Labor-cost savings are also cited as important by a substantial fraction of organizations that subcontract production work. The ability of contractors to provide specialized services that cannot be economically provided in-house has been conspicuously absent from popular discussions of market-mediated work arrangements. It is therefore all the more striking that so many organizations cite contractors' special expertise as a reason for their contracting-out activity. [110]

It is a mistake to lump together all of the market-mediated arrangements discussed here under the single heading, "contingent work." Only temporary workers, who absorb the pains of demand fluctuations, should be so labeled.

Summary of

Rethinking Employment

by Peter Cappelli

[Published in *British Journal of Industrial Relations* 33 (1995), 563–602.]

During the mid-1990s interest in workplace change turned to concern and even anxiety over signs that customary employment relationships were breaking down. One company after another downsized or reengineered costs, pressuring others to do the same to stay competitive. Secure jobs and predictable career paths were seen as relics of bureaucratic corporations too big and too rigid to meet the challenges of a fast-moving economy. But in fact, employment stability is a relatively recent phenomenon, while the trend toward more subcontracting, contingent work, decentralized decision making, and increased worker autonomy is reminiscent of labor market conditions in the nineteenth century. The reappearance of less permanent forms of work indicates a weakening of the internal labor markets that emerged in the early twentieth century.

Pressures in Support of Internal Labor Markets

Internal labor markets are "formal arrangements for managing employees in large firms . . . that (have) buffered jobs from market pressures." [563] In *Internal Labor Markets and Manpower Analysis* (1971), Peter Doeringer and Michael Piore argued that internal labor markets developed for efficiency reasons. They encouraged the long-term attachment of employees so that firms could identify and promote good workers, invest in the development of needed skills, and reap the benefits of well-trained, loyal employees. The transaction costs of recruiting, negotiating rewards, and measuring and monitoring performance were reduced. Sanford Jacoby argued in *Employing Bureaucracy* (1985) that internal labor markets developed when reformers and unionists pushed to improve and stabilize working conditions and production planning, particularly in wartime.

This internal labor market system was based on the principles of scientific management and included narrow job descriptions, on-the-job training, extensive supervision, job security that increased with seniority, and standardized pay scales that ensured that shareholders, not employees, bore the brunt of business risks. Internal job ladders offered security and upward mobility in exchange for loyalty and performance. The arrangement maintained needed skills within the organization.

Pressures Against Internal Labor Markets

During the 1980s and 1990s, competitive pressures reduced the benefits of internal labor markets while increasing the burden of fixed costs. New accounting practices encouraged cost reduction. Deregulation, international competition, and stockholder pressure squeezed profits, while a wave of leveraged buyouts left many businesses with high-interest debt. Changing consumer preferences called for shorter product-development cycles and rapid obsolescence. This required flexibility and the ability to accommodate change, reducing the viability of standardization, bureaucratic decision making, or long-term training trajectories. Unions, government regulators, and human resources theorists—advocates for labor market stabilization—lost influence. Employment regulation unwittingly stimulated evasive activity—for example, changing hourly workers to salaried status to exempt them from overtime pay.

Subcontractors, temp agencies, and employee leasing outfits took on more of the burden of compliance with labor and antidiscrimination laws. These agents also reduced hiring costs and expedited the search for appropriate skills, while the orderly progression to better jobs within the firm began to erode. With the spread of computers the information and control functions of middle managers diminished, and employee teams took on decision-making and monitoring functions. Unions, which generally negotiated systematic pay grades and seniority-based job ladders, were in decline. Rapidly changing products and technologies meant that skills could quickly become obsolete or inappropriate.

Evidence of Change

Adequate data about the extent of these trends is difficult to obtain, but several studies indicate that firms are, in fact, relying less on internal labor markets and more on contingent work, and are contracting out work that could be done in-house. Over half the firms surveyed in one study had at least one high-performance work practice, with work teams or quality circles the most common.[1] Such practices give wider responsibilities to workers, the need for layers of supervision is then reduced, and the system of narrowly defined duties and clear job ladders breaks down.

In the early 1990s, many companies reduced employment without reducing output. As compared with earlier layoffs, this wave of "downsizing" affected older and more educated employees, particularly white-collar workers. Overall, permanent job loss rose because workers were not recalled after business cycle layoffs. Job tenure (length of time with one employer) for men seems to have declined—a trend most evident for less educated men and older white men who once had previously been well protected by internal labor markets. Tenure for women, however, increased because fewer women now quit their jobs to marry or have children.

Wage structures are also changing. Internal labor markets could insulate compensation from external market forces by relating pay to the firm's need to motivate employees and allocate skills. However, wages are becoming more

linked to supply and demand for particular occupations. Inequality between occupations in the same firm is growing since some occupations will command a
higher wage than others. Variance in earnings for individuals increased from the
1970s to the 1980s. The payoff to working for one company for a long time is
falling; workers who changed jobs frequently received almost the same increase
in earnings during the 1980s as those who remained at the same job over ten
years. A dramatic indicator of the shift of responsibility from employer to employee is the trend away from defined benefit pension plans, in which a retiree
receives a predetermined benefit level according to years of service, to defined
contribution plans in which employers contribute to each employee's retirement fund (often a 401K plan).

Internal labor markets maintained an implicit contract: security and predictability in exchange for commitment and performance. This important norm
of reciprocity was broken when long-term service was no longer rewarded.
Public opinion surveys report less optimism about personal success in the 1990s
than in the 1960s. A sense of duty has given way to a view that work should be
a source of personal satisfaction—though job satisfaction and commitment have
both declined sharply. Downsizing has had profound effects on the morale of
employees who remain with a firm, although firms often experience productivity increases and cost decreases because employees are afraid of being the next
to lose their jobs. In contrast, top-level managers report satisfaction with the results of restructuring and seem unconcerned with declining morale.

Contradictions and Social Implications

Recent trends in employment relations present several contradictions. Team
work requires "idiosyncratic skills that both demand training and are difficult to
replace." [591] A firm investing in training wants employees who will stay and
return the benefits of their higher skills to the company; however, attachment
to firms is weakening. Employees prefer to develop skills that are transferable to
other firms and employers want employees who bring skills with them when
hired, but worker mobility discourages employers from providing such skills.
Furthermore, now that many work activities are carried out by cross-functional
teams, simple entry-level jobs and clear job ladders that offered new workers a
place to start are disappearing. Temp work now serves as the point of entry for
many workers who seek permanent employment.

Low morale has not yet caused a decline in productivity because workers fear
job loss, but problems will emerge in the long run, especially when reduced
commitment coincides with team-based organization and less supervision. One
solution is to rely on peer pressure to enforce work effort; another is to peg
compensation even more closely to performance. Over time expectations will
adjust to changed conditions, but this will have wide social implications. Work-

ers will have to take on more responsibility for their own training and career development. If income continues to become more variable, financing patterns and lifestyle decisions may change. College education and home ownership, which require steady income to repay long-term debt, will be difficult to achieve.

Ultimately, society as a whole will need to make available education and training opportunities if employers are reluctant to make these investments and if employees are unable to pay for them. This poses a question of distributive justice, since employers are the ones gaining the most from the changes in the workplace. Tighter labor markets could tip the balance in favor of employees, but rising volatility in wages, corporate structures, and morale still presents a serious challenge for firms, workers, and society at large.

Note

1. See P. Osterman, "How common is workplace transformation and how can we explain who does it?" *Industrial and Labor Relations Review* 39 (1994), 173–88; cited by Cappelli, 574.

Summary of

Internal Labor Markets: Theory and Change

by Paul S. Osterman

[Published in *Labor Economics and Industrial Relations,* ed. Clark Kerr (Cambridge: Harvard University Press, 1994), 303–340.]

Traditional economic theory held that the labor market acted as a high-turnover spot market where at least one side of the market—either employers or employees—saw few advantages in maintaining stable employment. In the 1950s, 1960s, and early 1970s, however, the rival Internal Labor Market (ILM) theory gained acceptance. ILM theory argues that labor markets tend to be made up of distinct noncompeting groups, while a "port of entry" separates work within the firm and from the external labor market. Labor markets inside the firm are governed by a unique set of rules and actions unlike those found in conventional markets. This essay presents the development of ILM theory since its inception, and offers an integrative theory of how ILMs evolve.

Changes in the ILM Model

The internal labor market model generally described in the literature from the mid-1940s to the mid-1970s was based on unionized workplaces, characterized by strict job classifications, seniority, grievance procedures, and so on. Beginning in the 1970s, as firms modified past practices in order to improve performance, to keep unions at bay, and to cope with changes in the economy (including high economic volatility, technical change, and increasing education levels of workers), a competing model of the ILM emerged. The new model, stemming from the American nonunion sector and from the spread of Japanese factories transplanted to the United States, stressed direct communication with workers, team production, and quality circles.

Such changes in the nature of firms and the economy have posed the following challenges to ILM theory: (1) Are ILMs still relevant, or are they breaking down? (2) Are the traits of ILMs changing? (3) What is the degree of variation in the structure of ILMs in similar industries in different countries?

Reasons why ILMs might be losing importance include such trends as white-collar and managerial layoffs, the rise of the contingent and temporary workforce, and the rise of regional networks (rather than single firms) for the stages of careers. Recent Current Population Survey data on length of job tenure reveal that ILMs are still quite significant, but are deteriorating at the edges. While ILMs are of greater relevance for women, for men there has been a "nontrivial" drop in the fraction of middle-aged workers who hold long-standing employment relationships. It is also clear that there has been an increase in contingent employment. Some firms seem to offer security to a core labor force, then surround the core with peripheral employees. However, it remains to be seen if the loosening of relationships with a portion of the labor force can explain the recent trends in job tenure.

There is evidence that the rules that govern ILMs are indeed changing. Many firms are organizing work around more flexible job boundaries, with greater attention to training, more communication with the labor force, performance-based pay, and in some cases enhanced job security. Firms that have been found to adopt these measures are those that have close links to international markets, were part of larger organizations, used high-skill technology, emphasized quality rather than price competition, and valued employee well-being. While transformations of this kind in the United States mimic those of Japan, it is interesting to note that outside the auto industry, many Japanese-owned plants in the United States show little resemblance to Japanese management models.

In short, ILMs are much more open to question than they have been in the past. Firms are now using a number of ILM systems that range from the standard union model to models that mimic those of Japan. Variation exists across nations, even among firms that operate similar product markets.

Understanding How Internal Labor Markets Evolve

A variety of conceptual frameworks have been used to explain the existence of ILMs, including performance-based models, social process models, and external environment models.

Performance-based models propose that ILM rules are determined by calculating the configuration that will produce the most output. This category includes three subgroups. The first two are found in the economics literature. The oldest theory, supported by evidence of wage returns on job tenure, holds that ILMs lower the cost to the firm of training and retaining skilled workers. More recently, economists have claimed that ILMs are more efficient because they reduce transaction costs, resolve principal-agent problems, and maintain job stability through the use of efficiency wages. A third performance-based model comes from industrial relations, human resource management, and organizational sociology. Unlike economists who tend to focus on control through fear of unemployment or loss of wage premiums, these groups tend to emphasize that ILMs induce greater worker commitment by increasing employee identification with the goals of the firm. Increased commitment leads to more effort, more attention to quality, lower turnover, and so on.

Social process models can be passive or active. ILM rules may result from the inertial impact of customs and norms that are part of a firm's history and accumulated sense of what is appropriate, or they may be an outcome of political contests for power within the firm.

External environment models propose that ILM structure is influenced by external factors as obvious as government employment and wage policies, or as subtle as differences in educational or cultural systems. The external environment may also act through channels of imitation. According to some sociologists, institutions may seek legitimacy by imitating powerful actors in their environment.

An Integrative Theory

Performance systems, social processes within the firm, and the influence of the external environment can be integrated into a dynamic theory of the evolution of ILMs. The performance impulse is the impetus for change in ILM structure. To fully understand this change, performance must be viewed in a much broader sense than can be found in the economics literature. Performance-based changes in ILMs are simultaneously influenced by norms, customs, politics, mimicry, and the external environment.

Performance concerns have certainly driven the adoption of workplace innovations such as team production and quality circles. The economic explanations that focus on control, however, are not adequate. Efforts to improve quality may lure employers to improve control over the labor force, but many observers of Japanese and European ILM models emphasize employee cooperation and commitment more than control. It has been argued that commitment is a subtle form of control grounded in psychology rather than in economic principles. Nonetheless, it appears that commitment is a truly distinctive dimension of performance, separate from control. At the same time there is a fine line between the two concepts, and ILMs may achieve the best gains by operating in each realm. While performance can explain the changing nature of ILMs, it can also explain how ILMs are fraying at the edges. It is possible that there are many circumstances where the traditional forms of work organization is superior and cheaper.

While performance considerations are very strong, changes in ILMs have also occurred because of customs, norms, and political considerations. The time and compromise involved in union acceptance of work rule changes is but one example of such cases. Finally, the evolution of ILMs is also a function of aspects of the external environment.

Summary of

Toward a New Labor Market Segmentation

by Thierry J. Noyelle

[Published in *Skills, Wages, and Productivity in the Service Sector* (Boulder, CO: Westview, 1990), 212–225.]

In a market environment where both small and large firms are confronted with far greater competition than in the past, fewer firms can now hide behind oligopolistic arrangements. In contrast, the very nature of skills is increasingly at the basis of segmentation, at least for the segmentation between core and skilled contingent workers. Where skills are somewhat generic and demanded by a broad array of firms, workers who can supply them increasingly are likely to be organized on a contingent basis; where skills remain highly firm specific, their supply is likely to remain internalized among a group of core workers. A major issue is how fast these two groups are growing relative to the third group, low-skilled, contingent labor. [223]

Advanced economies are undergoing a transformation, due in part to the rapid growth of service industries compared to the rest of the economy. The transformation is also linked to the reorganization of labor markets into a dualism between "core" and "contingent" workers. An earlier form of dualism in labor markets, where some employees had long-term security and access to internal career ladders while others did not, was based on sharp differences between the oligopolistic and competitive sectors of the economy. Today the dualism is no longer defined by economic sectors, but by the roles and skills of particular types of workers within a company—with a growing tendency for each firm to have both core and contingent employees.

Changing Labor Demand

Most important in changing the structure of markets has been the intensification of competition, due principally to deregulation and rising internationalization of the economy. Each of these factors has tended to make industries less oligopolistic. One example is the department store industry; the shift to new, suburban locations and the rise of discount department stores pried open retail markets to a host of newcomers. Another is consumer banking, which lost its monopoly over small savers as mutual funds and other investment vehicles became available.

In many industries, market concentration continued based on the reality of economies of scale and scope, but the removal of oligopolistic or regulatory barriers (which had restricted prices, products, or geographic service areas) intensified competition. New information technologies, especially computers, have transformed the demand for labor by raising the potential for developing new products and for reorganizing the division of labor. Examples include bank credit cards, airline reservation systems, and parcel tracking systems. "Production workers are decreasing in numbers while the remaining labor force is increasingly needed either to sell, to assist customers, or to develop new products, new markets, and new strategies. The upshot is considerable upskilling and a shift toward activities that demand high levels of technical expertise." [215]

Another important factor is "vertical disintegration," which means that firms stop doing some functions internally and begin buying them as needed on the open market. This has occurred in large part due to intensified competition. As companies lose their monopolistic "rents" they can no longer afford to pay more to have a job done internally instead of buying it externally. An example is the U.S. motion picture industry. Studios used to have long-term contracts with everyone involved in the process, but today they negotiate contracts for each project. Increasingly, successful firms specialize in particular market segments, buying related functions externally.

The use of contingent labor—a labor force that employers can use flexibly with respect to fluctuations in product or service demand—has grown rapidly.

There are four principal forms: seasonal part-time, permanent part-time, temporary, and independent individual contracting. Temporary work has grown most dramatically, from 20,000 people employed by the temporary agency industry in 1956 to over six million people who now work as temps for some part of a given year. While the roots of expanding contingent work are largely in the industry changes discussed above, changes in labor supply have also played a part.

Changing Labor Supply

Although about one-quarter of part-time employment is involuntary (with the percentage growing slightly in recent years), part of its growth is due to changes in labor supply, including more women and school-aged youth in the workforce, more two-earner families, and higher educational levels among employees. Between 1965 and 1985 the fraction of working-age females who were employed rose from 36.7 percent to 54.5 percent. In addition, between 1965 and 1985 the proportion of all adult households with two wage earners rose from 47 percent to 70 percent. Industries such as department stores and supermarkets introduced short-hour shifts of four or fewer hours daily, to accommodate women with children, older workers who want to work shorter hours, and youth.

Rising educational attainment has made the labor supply much more varied in terms of levels and types of education. For example, of people between ages 25 and 29, in 1965 only 20 percent had some college education, while by 1985 this figure had risen to 45 percent. An external labor market that can provide workers at different levels of preparedness allows firms to avoid internal training costs and to dismantle internal job ladders. This has made it more difficult for people with less formal education, such as clerks, to rise gradually to higher ranks in corporations.

Beyond Industrial Dualism

Labor markets have been restructured into three principal segments: core workers, skilled contingent workers, and low-skilled contingent workers. The number of core employees—those with permanent, secure jobs, who enjoy opportunities for mobility within the firm—has fallen greatly. Today it is often restricted to only a select number of professional and managerial workers. Other specialized professed professionals are commonly hired on a contingent basis.

A second, rapidly growing group consists of skilled contingent workers, including such occupations as nurses, accountants, lawyers, systems analysts, and computer programmers. Such workers are often driven by their own professional goals rather than criteria set by one company. This may lend them to choose a variety of job assignments in order to improve their professional expertise. Turnover in such jobs is quite high, and the firm's commitment is short term. Employers have a decreasing role in organizing this part of the labor market, while professional organizations and employment agencies take up the slack.

Finally, there are the low-skilled workers. Contingent hiring arrangements for such employees has always been a part of the labor market. But in recent years there has been a rapid decrease in the number of low-skilled workers included in the internal labor market, as companies shift them to a more insecure status, and a larger proportion have only part-time employment.

Differences from Earlier Segmentation

From the 1920s to the 1960s a dichotomy emerged in the U.S. economy between a "core" of mostly large firms and a peripheral economy of mainly small employers. The core, including many giant industrial corporations, tended to be oligopolistic, where profits and employment were relatively secure. Peripheral firms faced more intense competition and volatile demand for their products. The labor market reflected these conditions, with workers having far better long-term prospects for higher wages and promotions than those employed by small companies.

Where skills are somewhat generic and demanded by a broad array of firms, workers who can supply them increasingly are likely to be organized on a contingent basis; where skills remain highly firm-specific, their supply is likely to remain internalized among a group of core workers.

Conclusion

In recent years the burden of unemployment has fallen most heavily on low-skill workers. It may simply be that U.S. society is eliminating such jobs faster than society can cope. But it can also be argued that the failure to deal satisfactorily with the mismatch between job requirements and the skills of workers reflects problems in our educational and training systems.

Summary of

World Underneath: The Origins, Dynamics, and Effects of the Informal Economy

by Manuel Castells and Alejandro Portes

[Published in *The Informal Economy: Studies in Advanced and Less Developed Countries,* eds. Alejandro Portes, Manuel Castells, and Lauren Benton (Baltimore: Johns Hopkins University Press, 1989), 11–37.]

"History is full of surprises." [11] The informal economy, long considered incompatible with advanced, institutionally rich capitalist economies, is making a comeback in developed and less developed regions. In fact, informalization appears to be characteristic of recent economic trends—horizontal networks rather than vertical bureaucracies; subcontracting rather than union contracts; and the expansion of entrepreneurship, cash economies, barter transactions, and casual labor markets. This article explores the nature of the informal economy, its causes and effects, and its integral relationship to the formal economy.

What Is the Informal Economy?

The informal economy is a common-sense notion with moving social boundaries that is best understood as a process, rather than an object. It is both flexible and exploitative, productive and abusive—"above all, there is disenfranchisement of the institutionalized power conquered by labor in a two-century-old struggle." [11] Although most people in the informal sector are poor, some informal entrepreneurs achieve high incomes. Despite images in the collective consciousness, the informal economy is not the survival activity of destitute, marginal people. Rather, "[i]t is a specific form of relationships of production, while poverty is an attribute linked to the process of distribution." [12] Either a street seller in Latin America or a Silicon Valley moonlighter can manifest its central characteristic; "it is unregulated by the institutions of society, in a legal and social environment in which similar activities are regulated." [12]

The informal economy exists only in relation to an institutional framework; in a perfect market economy, all activity would be informal. What is new is the growth of the informal sector at the expense of formal work relationships. Informal activity does not rein back economic development—it constitutes a novel social trend. Sweatshops may be an old form, but their reappearance after a long period of institutional control marks a new form redefined in the context of prior institutional regulation. The disregard for regulation may affect the status of labor (evading social benefits or minimum wages), conditions of work (neglect of health and safety), form of management (fraudulent activity or un-recorded cash payments), or criminality of the product or service itself (involvement in the drug trade). This article is concerned with the unregulated production of otherwise licit goods and services.

The Reality and Structure of the Informal Economy

The informal economy is universal. It is found at different levels of economic development. It is heterogeneous in form and has apparently grown in recent years. There are serious measurement problems involved in trying to define and analyze informal economic activity, since it often takes place below the threshold of government recording requirements or is deliberately clandestine to avoid regulatory burdens. However, researchers using a variety of methods and data from both aggregate statistics and field studies have found an increase in conditions favorable to informal activity or their persistence in the face of economic development.

Although the informal economy is heterogeneous in form, three common aspects merit attention. First, there is the *systemic connection to the formal economy.* "The specialized networks formed by unregulated enterprises free large firms from the constraints imposed upon them by social control and institutional norms." [26] Often there is a two-tier economy in which boundaries vary with political winds and changes in social unrest. "There are actually two intertwined processes at work: the decentralization of large corporations into semiautonomous units and the informalization of as many of these units as possible, so that to the benefits of flexibility are added the advantages of unregulated activities in a regulated environment." [26]

Second, there are *characteristics of labor.* Labor tends to be downgraded, receiving less in wages and benefits or to working under worse conditions than formal sector workers. The downgrading of labor is not random but depends on circumstances (such as immigration status, minority group membership) that allow companies to enforce their demands. Here, too, boundaries can shift—if structural unemployment rises, a formerly well-paid union worker may end up as a pirate cab driver, while immigrant workers can move to the forefront of labor militancy. "The informal economy evolves along the borders of social struggles, incorporating those too weak to defend themselves, rejecting those who become too conflictive, and propelling those with stamina and resources into surrogate entrepreneurship." [27]

Third is the role of *government attitudes.* Governments generally tolerate or even encourage the informal economy as a vehicle to absorb social conflict, reduce unemployment, or provide economic incentives. Informalization "is often the expression of a new form of control characterized by the disenfranchisement of a large sector of the working class." [27]

Causes and Effects of Informalization

Precise causes of informalization differ with each society, but field researchers have identified several common themes. The first is a reaction to the power of unions, most often on the part of business, but in some cases by workers who feel that unions defend their own interests at the expense of the unorganized. Businesses also use informalization to avoid state regulation, taxes, and social legislation. International competition particularly affects labor-intensive industries, and moving work underground is one strategy for reducing labor costs.

In many developing countries, industrialization occurs under conditions that preclude enforcement of state-sponsored regulations. Industries like those in the Mexican maquiladora zone would be likely to go elsewhere if standards were upheld. And, in many countries, the economic crisis of the mid-1970s left millions of people in such harsh living conditions they were willing to accept whatever avenues out of misery they could find. While many arrangements are marginal, flexible, and ad hoc, "[t]he small scale and face-to-face features of these activities make living through the crisis a more manageable experience than waiting in line for relief from impersonal bureaucracies." [29]

Informalization also contributes to a decentralized model of economic organization. The national, vertically structured corporation is no longer the final stage of industrial evolution. Networks are the emergent form, and, while not all networked firms are informal, networks are a congenial form of organization for informal relationships.

The effect of informal organization on productivity is contradictory. Because a substantial part of the informal economy is in services and because its manufacturing technology is less advanced, labor productivity tends to be lower. But the reduction of bureaucratic overhead means that the productivity of capital may become higher. The best known effects are the reduction of labor costs (particularly the indirect costs of social benefits), payments to the state, and constraints on hiring and firing.

Besides these economic effects, there are social effects caused by the disintegration of collective processes surrounding work. Organized labor loses ground politically and becomes defensive about its position in the formal economy, since it is split off from workers outside of it. Workers' consciousness fragments along age, ethnic, and gender lines. Heterogeneity of work and social conditions becomes the norm, blurring the class structure. "Thus, the woman sewing at home for a 'friend of the family' who is a middleman selling to a commercial intermediary of a large department store, cannot be socially equated, nor does she equate herself, with a garment factory worker." [31]

The boundaries of the informal economy vary with different contexts and historical circumstances, but the general trend is sustained by powerful forces. However, this is not the whole story. Some production and distribution processes require stability and long-range planning. Social forces in unions and official bureaucracies resist informalization. New generations of workers may mobilize to control the economy, or the state may see fit to intervene. Whether or not a new social contract will emerge is unclear, but "a return to the vertical, centralized, assembly-line model of production is unlikely in the medium term." [33] The question remains whether informalization and decentralization will proceed uncontrolled or will be brought under regulation.

Summary of

Informalization at the Core: Hispanic Women, Home-Based Work, and the Advanced Capitalist State

by M. Patricia Fernández-Kelly and Anna M. Garcia

[Published in *The Informal Economy—Studies in Advanced and Less Developed Countries,* eds. Alejandro Portes, Manuel Castells, and Lauren A. Benton (Baltimore: Johns Hopkins University Press, 1989), 247–264.]

It may seem contradictory to observe that informal economies are growing in industrialized countries during the latter part of the twentieth century. However, informal activities, such as sweatshops, unlicensed factories, and home-based work, are proliferating despite the focus on large-scale industries in the modern world system. This article examines two factors that have enabled informal economic arrangements to flourish in parts of the United States: the actions of state and federal government agencies, and the presence of immigrant women. Los Angeles and Miami, sunbelt cities with large Hispanic populations, appear similar, yet they exhibit very different patterns of industrial development, immigration, and insertion of new working populations into the labor force. In both cities the informal economy is thriving, but in different ways and for different reasons.

Economic Informalization and the State

The informal economy is a fluid process involving investors, workers, and state agencies. Researchers do not agree on how to define or evaluate it, but for the purpose of this discussion four points should be highlighted. First, informalization is not a marginal phenomenon driven only by the survival needs of the poverty-stricken. Multiple links exist between the strategies of the poor and the unregulated operations of modern industries. Subcontracting is an important connection that allows large producers to lower costs, spread risk among several subcontractors, and avoid unions. Second, informalization is not an aberration or remnant of preindustrial production, but a recurring phenomenon tied to the changing relations between capital and labor and changing competitive conditions. Third, informalization is a counterweight to, and sometimes intended to weaken, organized labor and formal labor relations. And fourth, the informal sector includes entrepreneurs who often act as middlemen, organizing informal labor and linking it to the formal sector.

While analysts also disagree on the relationship between the state and the informal sector, some simple assumptions can be dismissed. States are not simply passive reflectors of socioeconomic or political processes. At the same time, the consequences of state action cannot always be assumed to be what the state intended. In a federal system like that of the United States, authority is dispersed among several branches and levels of government, often leading to contradictory policies and practices that leave spaces for informed responses in times of crisis or to meet an upsurge in demand.

Three general and overlapping factors play a role in the growth of the informal sector: legislative changes, enforcement challenges, and the different and often contradictory agendas of government agencies. The role of legislation can be illustrated by the historical development of industrial regulation of home-based work. Federal wage and hour law, in effect since 1938, bans homeworking in several industries, particularly in the garment and textile industries. Yet the electronics industry, which did not exist when the law was written, developed through the extensive use of homeworkers. State modifications to federal regulations, and exemptions like the rule that workers who must care for dependents may be allowed to work at home, mean that the application of laws is uneven and open to interpretation. Enforcement is often constrained by small budgets or driven by political agendas either to protect illegal operations or to make an occasional dramatic show of force. Finally, government agencies may have incompatible mandates. For example, departments that regulate wages and hours have different definitions of an employee, independent contractor, or self-employed person than the IRS. Generally, under protective labor codes, employees have certain rights and employers have certain obligations. Definitions establish who is eligible for such protections and who must furnish them. The IRS is only concerned with employment relations for the purpose of ensuring that one party or the other pays the appropriate employment-based taxes. The IRS category of statutory worker, one who is employed but not working on the employer's site, opens a loophole for the employment of homeworkers.

Labor Market Insertion Patterns of Hispanics

While manufacturing employment for most ethnic groups fell in the 1970s and 1980s, the employment of Hispanic women increased. In the New York, Miami, and Los Angeles areas, 35 percent of women in the manufacturing sector are Hispanic, with a much higher proportion working as operators, fabricators, and laborers. An especially high share of women in textile and garment machine operator positions are Hispanic.

The apparel industry in California dates to the late nineteenth century. The industry experienced an upsurge in the 1920s when runaway shops sought to evade unions in New York and grew again when the rise of the movie industry established Southern California as a fashion center. By the mid-1940s there were 28,000 garment industry workers in the Los Angeles area, a number that more than doubled by the mid-1970s. The industry has recently come under heavy pressure from imports forcing it to cut costs and adapt frequently and rapidly to changes in consumer tastes. The pattern of Mexican immigration meshes with the desire of producers to take advantage of low-cost, more flexible, informal labor relationships. Mexican women have a long history in the garment industry, and manufacturers are able to draw on a continuous stream of new immigrants. Many immigrants from Mexico arrive alone, without community support and without the legal status that would bring them under the umbrella of protective labor laws. Over one-third of women in the garment industry are heads of households. In many cases, working at home allows them to look after their children at the same time.

In Miami, the garment industry remained small until the late 1960s and early 1970s. The wave of Cuban immigration that followed the Cuban revolution provided a labor force of women eager to maintain middle-class incomes for their families and men who were willing to act as middlemen between employers and the workforce. In addition, the area was home to many retired garment industry executives from New York who saw an opportunity to set up new businesses in Florida. For many Cuban women, working at home became a way to achieve control over their own work schedules or accommodate their husbands' wishes that they not work outside the home. Since Miami does not have the same continual influx of immigrants that Los Angeles has, and since men in the community form the conduit for labor contracting, the garment industry faces labor shortages that enable women workers to assert their preferences for homework.

> The comparison between different experiences among Hispanic women in two social settings shows that involvement in informal production can have entirely dissimilar meanings depending on the type of incorporation into the labor market. The examples considered should reaffirm the importance of studying the underground economy as an uneven and richly variegated spectrum, rather than as a homogeneous phenomenon resulting from the interaction of standard economic factors. [262–267].

Summary of

Reevaluating Union Policy toward White-Collar Home-Based Work

by Kathleen E. Christensen

[Published in *Women and Unions—Forging a Partnership,* ed. Dorothy Sue Cobble, Chapter 10 (Ithaca, NY: ILR Press, 1993), 247–259.]

Industrial homework was originally concentrated in manufacturing industries. Because home-based work is difficult to monitor and regulate, homeworkers were often caught in exploitative situations. In the 1990s, homework presents a more complicated picture. In certain industries, garments and electronics for example, home-based manufacturing can still be found and may even be increasing. However, most homeworkers are now in service positions, often in white-collar jobs ranging from "the high-priced telecommuter to the harassed and overworked data-entry pieceworker." [247] The majority of those who work exclusively in the home are women, either self-employed or working part-time. The type of homework that offers the most scope for abuse is that in which the worker is labeled an independent contractor. This article gives an overview of the character of modern home-based employment, along with "a proposal for policy directions, not only in the sense of how unions can organize homeworkers but also how they can best represent their interests." [246]

Home-Based Work: Motives and Types

The public discussion on home-based work indicates that it is preferred by mothers with children at home, but 1985 figures from the Bureau of Labor Statistics show that 43 percent of women who work at home do not have children. These women are working at home because they have recently reentered the workforce or are nearing retirement, need extra income, or must care for an elderly relative. The types of home-based work also vary widely and include a broad array of working arrangements, from self-employed workers to independent contractors and traditional company employees.

Self-employed workers are those who are in business for themselves and have autonomy in the marketplace. Women-owned businesses are the fastest growing small business segment, and many self-employed women work at home. *Independent contractors* are, for tax purposes, also defined as "self-employed" by the firms for which they work; however (as discussed below) this is frequently a fiction. *Company employees* who telecommute or otherwise work from home retain the rights and privileges of in-house employees. They receive similar pay and benefits and are eligible for training and promotions. Telecommuting is not yet common among U.S. firms, but where it is offered it is often seen as a strategy for attracting and keeping valuable employees who prefer flexible schedules.

Macroeconomic and Legal Conditions Affecting Homework

Two macroeconomic trends help to explain the current work environment. One is the history of downsizing, mergers, and acquisitions that so profoundly affected U.S. firms during the decade of the 1980s.

> In fact, between the beginning of 1980 and the end of 1987, the Fortune 500 companies reduced their work forces by 3.1 million, going from an aggregate of 16.2 million employees to 13.1 million. This type of internal labor market turbulence has prompted many companies to rethink their overall staffing attitudes and practices. . . . Many companies now treat their personnel in much the same manner as they do their inventories, striving for a just-in-time staffing strategy . . . just sufficient to meet current demand. [248]

Many U.S. firms have responded to the need for flexibility by creating an ad hoc two-tiered workforce. The first tier comprises core employees who are on company salary and have relatively secure job tenure, opportunities for training and advancement, and health and pension benefits. The second tier includes self-employed independent contractors, temporaries, or casual part-timers. Many of these worked for the company as core employees before the upheavals of the 1980s.

The situation of so-called independent contractors is often illegal as well as disadvantageous. They have little independence, often working under the pressure of strict quotas and turn-around times, and sometimes obliged to sign contracts that prevent them from simultaneously working for any another employer. Yet they have none of the job security of core employers, nor do they have benefits such as paid sick leave and vacations, health care, or pension plans. "They become responsible for paying their own social security (FICA) taxes. They operate entirely out of the mainstream of the company, so they are not in the pool of candidates considered for job advancement, skill upgrading, or retooling. They often work in both isolation and ignorance of other workers. They rapidly become second-class corporate citizens." [250]

The criteria in the Internal Revenue Code that are most often applied to determine whether an individual has the status of employee or of self-employed independent contractor define the latter as those who have made some investment in equipment or capital, skills that allow them to compete in the marketplace, and control over the execution and timing of work, and who do not work for only one employer over a long period of time. The large number of "independent contractors" who cannot be so described are entitled to the rights and protections accorded by law to company employees. "[A]ccording to these common law criteria, many women doing clerical work at home are being hired fraudulently as independent contractors." [251]

A second macroeconomic trend is of more relevance to the company employees who retain their status as core employees while working at home. This option is generally conceived as a concession on the part of the employer, designed to attract and retain the best workers in the face of a dwindling supply of workers trained for jobs that require education and technical skills. This supply squeeze is seen in a recent survey of more than 700 human resource executives, as described in *The Wall Street Journal*, 1989:

> . . . 43 percent report problems finding qualified executives; 66 percent cite difficulties finding technical help. . . . In order to attract workers, the study finds, higher wages are being offered by 58 percent of these companies, tuition aid by 52 percent, and better health benefits by 31 percent. All of these recruitment incentives are costly. Some firms are turning, therefore, to less expensive incentives such as flexible schedules, which include professional part-time, job sharing, and telecommuting as effective tools for recruiting and retaining the employees they want. [252]

It should be stressed that the seller's market described here refers to workers from the educated middle class.

Union Policy Directions

> The critical question regarding white-collar work at home is not what can be done to stop it, but rather for whom it is advantageous and under what conditions? . . . it tends to work best for the company employee who preserves all the rights, privileges, and federal safeguards, such as workers' compensation and unemployment insurance, that are part of employee status. It can also work for people who genuinely want to be in business for themselves and who choose to incubate their business at home for a certain period of time in order to minimize the failure rate of small businesses. It works least well for workers hired under questionable independent contracting conditions. Given this, what directions can unions pursue regarding people who do white-collar work at home? [253]

Unions have traditionally opposed home-based work because of its potential to undermine negotiated pay scales and working conditions. However, the new forms of homework must be viewed differently. Self-employed workers often participate in guild-type associations that approximate some of the benefits of union membership. Self-employed workers and independent contractors could be included in organized unions as associate members, thereby gaining benefits, training, and a voice to advocate for their interests. Independent contractors would especially gain from an affiliation that could advise them of their rights, lobby to improve their legal status, and bargain with employers on their behalf. Access to these workers is not as difficult as might be feared, especially since many are affiliated with a single employer and can communicate through computer hookups. Other, less vulnerable self-employed workers would benefit significantly from access to affordable health insurance and reduction of the isolation of homework.

Only one local union, the Wisconsin State Employees Union, has negotiated a contract that covers home-based workers. The University of Wisconsin's Hospital and Clinics entered into the contract because the hospital needed more transcribers than could be accommodated on-site. The contract specifies performance and security criteria as well as working conditions, and each home site is inspected by a labor–management committee. Although the program is small, it has been successful and offers a good model for structuring the employment relationship for home-based workers.

Since 1989 the Internal Revenue Service has made greater efforts to enforce the distinction between employee and self-employed contractor. This should strengthen the potential for unions to provide appropriate protection to homeworkers.

Summary of

Sustainable Flexibility: A Prospective Study on Work, Family, and Society in the Information Age

by Martin Carnoy and Manuel Castells

[Published as Vol. 5, No. 29 of the *OECD Working Papers* (Paris: OECD, 1997).]

While flexibility, a hallmark of the Information Age, enables businesses to respond to rapidly changing conditions and markets, it can also wreak havoc on human life and society. Tension between the flexible, networked global economy and the need for economic security can best be resolved if the basis of security shifts from permanent jobs to learning-centered social institutions.

The Transformation of Work and Employment

Information technologies and globalization have complex effects. Information technology both creates and destroys jobs, deskills and reskills the workforce. It reverses the salarization of work and the socialization of production that have been typical of the industrial era in favor of decentralized management, individualized work, and customized markets that fragment work and segment societies. Globalization increases competitive pressures on industrialized economies, but it also opens new markets for goods and services. Outcomes depend on the interplay between institutions, firms, and labor force characteristics. Existing social welfare systems, meant to smooth out occasional interruptions in employment, are inadequate when instability becomes the norm.

Flexibility and networking are facilitated by information technologies and have become key elements of the transformation of work. Flexibility means constant adaptation to changing products, processes, and markets; it requires higher skill levels as increased autonomy and responsibility are vested in the workforce. Networking, a form of organization well suited to fluid conditions, operates internally among levels and actors in firms and externally among firms.

Since firms often adjust by reducing hierarchies and displacing labor, microlevel activity is volatile. Yet, at the macroeconomic level, research shows no significant employment problems emerging from technological change; some countries even report modest net employment gains. The OECD 1994 *Job Study* concluded that unqualified generalizations are unwarranted "because positive and negative effects do not coincide either in time or in space; adjustment takes time, and industries and types of workers that will benefit from technological change are different from the ones that lose from it. Also, institutional and systemic factors affect the capacities of countries to efficiently generate employment through development, acquisition, and diffusion of technologies."[1]

Worldwide trade, investment, and resource exploitation are centuries old. What defines the new global economy is the ability—recently achieved with the advent of computer-based communications, machines, information systems, and transportation—to conduct core, strategic activities in real time on a planetary scale. Labor markets are becoming more interdependent with segmentation of work across borders. Global trade favors skilled workers in developed countries, but their unskilled workers face competition from low-wage developing countries.

Although institutional constraints vary, flexible work is increasing in OECD countries, forming a *core labor force* of information-based managers and analysts, and a *"disposable labor force* that can be automated and/or hired/fired/offshored, depending on market demand and labor costs." [16] Flexibility pushes many individuals into contingent or self-employment positions, or segments of firms under outsourcing and subcontracting agreements. Flexibility can eliminate benefits, job security, and career path—it can also supplement primary jobs, adjust work sharing among household members, and encourage gender equality. The key is to harness flexibility with the least social cost.

Social Crisis

The transition to the information society is characterized by various forms of crisis under different institutional arrangements. In Europe unemployment is widespread, particularly among youth (except in Germany). Many workers leave the labor force by the age of fifty-five; worklife is shrinking even as life expectancy is increasing. Even though only 40 percent of a man's life is spent in full-time employment, social policy is still organized around work. The United States, which created millions of jobs (with high-skill jobs growing faster than low-skill jobs), still experienced an average weekly earnings decline of 18 percent from 1973 to 1993. Households maintained living standards only by sending additional members into the labor force. Income inequality in the United States is the highest of any industrialized country, with more families (particularly those headed by women) in poverty, along with other signs of social disorganization, such as addiction, crime, homelessness, and violence.

In Japan, despite the recent economic slowdown, unemployment for the core labor force is low; however, this affects only 30 to 50 percent of the workforce, while temporary and part-time workers (mostly women) absorb fluctuations in labor demand. Redundant workers at large companies are often sent to smaller firms in the same supplier networks (*keiretsu*). In times of economic difficulty the government subsidizes employment and companies retrain core employees. Nevertheless, the growing integration of Japan into the global economy will make it harder to protect workers. It is already more difficult for young workers to enter core positions.

Everywhere these crises disrupt the institutions on which society depends: the family, the community, and the state. This removes psychological, social, and financial supports and deepens the crisis in a vicious cycle that is difficult to break without a general overhaul of the relationship between work and society. "Developing individual work flexibility and creativity while creating the conditions for sustained productivity and social cooperation is the historical dilemma posed by the current transformations of work and workers." [24]

Critique of Current Policies

OECD countries employ three strategies in response to the crisis in work. The U.S. neoconservative model promotes decreased state regulation and increased labor market flexibility, relying on the family and voluntary organizations to reproduce values such as honesty and diligence, which are essential for productivity. While a dynamic private sector is necessary in a competitive environment, proponents wrongly assume that deregulation alone can increase both employment and wages. They do not connect declining wages and increasing inequality with stresses on family structures. They also ignore the limited resources available to voluntary organizations and the divisive effects that selective distribution of these resources can have on civic life.

Under the Keynesian welfare state, as found in Europe, government investment in infrastructure and support for consumption generates employment. This model worked when a few highly industrialized economies had well-defined national markets large enough to support a cycle of productivity and wage growth that produced revenues sufficient for new private sector investment and for the public provision of health, education, and social insurance. The competitive environment of the late twentieth century diminished the ability of the state to raise revenues, leading to budget deficits and cuts in social spending. Many elements of the welfare state are worth preserving, but its grounding in secure, lifetime employment is no longer sustainable.

The work-sharing model, most actively promoted in France, assumes that technology destroys jobs and that remaining work must be redistributed in a shorter work week. In the short run this strategy may preserve jobs when a firm is restructuring, but it has not proven to be effective at creating jobs. Significant employment growth would require the flexibility of part-time, less permanent work. Without a redefinition of the relationship of work to the social context, work sharing cannot stem the present trend toward a two-tier structure of better and worse jobs. Right now "human investment benefits (health care, educational and training opportunities, pension funds, access to child care services)" [31] are linked to full-time employment. This job-centered approach means that without full-time employment for all, equity cannot be achieved.

Alternative Strategies: In Search of Security

Each of these strategies has its own shortcomings, but one flaw afflicts them all: the failure to recognize that the work system is changing "away from permanent jobs as the locus of work toward a complex network of learning institutions, including the workplace, families, and community schools." [26] Though this will not create more jobs by itself, such a learning network "provides the basis for greater productivity, greater equality, and the reintegration of individualized citizen-workers." [33] Flexible information-based systems of work reward workers who have higher skills and the ability to learn and adapt to change. A society that institutionalizes lifelong learning will develop workers who are able to match these requirements. In a learning society, workers may periodically withdraw from the workforce to enhance current skills or learn new ones, relieving pressure on employment or translating new knowledge into self-employment.

Families, schools, communities, and the state will play important roles in a learning society. Families will not only be production or consumption units as they were in the past, but also investors in human capital. At times one adult may be the main source of support while others in the family attend school or start up a new business. The education of children will be an important focus of family activity and of community resources, a center from which other social networks may emerge (as in a program in Bologna that brings elderly citizens back into the classroom).

Schools will also need to address the kinds of learning needed in an information-based society. More and more workers will need not only the higher-order problem-solving skills now taught in postsecondary schools, but also the skills to work together in teams that are cooperative, innovative, and internally motivated and managed. Education will need to foster the ability and motivation to learn and to teach within cooperative frameworks. As the lifespan reorients around learning, schools should expand their domain to include all elements of human experience, from early childhood development to parenting and networking skills to retraining in the face of new technological and social needs to preparation for involvement in community activities.

The state has a long tradition of involvement in education and should participate with households and learning networks by providing educational services, school-to-work transition programs, and service activities linked to training opportunities or tuition remittances. The state can support adult learners with income, benefits, or child care while they go back to school. Such policies can provide a hedge against the risks inherent in a flexible job market, both supporting families and individuals in times of transition and preparing them to meet new challenges.

In many OECD countries the military has been an effective and widely accepted training program and, particularly in the United States, has been a force for equalizing skills and opportunity for youth. "Properly organized, other forms of service . . . could be a valuable and valued apprenticeship, combining skill acquisition, an enhanced sense of self through helping others, and learning in a cooperative work environment with other young people from diverse backgrounds." [48] When government absorbs the cost of education and the dissemination of information, small firms and networks of firms benefit as well as individuals, becoming better able to compete against large corporations.

"Society pays an enormous price when it allows the market alone to set incomes." [51] The state can develop policies that promote solidarity, equality, and cooperation to mitigate the harsh effects of extreme individualization and competition. These policies should begin with a focus on universal enhancement of capabilities rather than entitlements, equalizing learning for all children, and expanding its reach over the lifespan. But this will not solve all problems that citizen-workers face, particularly during this period of economic and social transition. Not all older workers can easily acquire new skills, nor should they be forced into low wage jobs. Early retirement and community service are options, as well as adult education and tax incentives to employers. A solidarity policy will maintain and strengthen efforts to guarantee a minimum income—minimum wage, unemployment insurance, antipoverty programs, and social security programs that vary inversely with need.

Note

1. OECD, *OECD Jobs Study—Facts, Analysis, Strategies* (Paris: OECD, 1994), 164; quoted by the authors, 13–14.

PART VI

Emerging Patterns of Industrial Relations

Overview Essay

by Kevin Gallagher

From the perspective of workers, the changes in the workplace that are addressed in this volume raise many questions. What are labor's goals? Should labor be working to expand democracy in the workplace? To secure employment and equity throughout the entire workforce? Or to contribute to a firm's productivity and take home a paycheck? Are these goals mutually exclusive? And finally, *who* should be working *for* labor?

Until recently, trade unions throughout Western Europe and North America were viewed as major actors in the struggle for democracy in and out of the workplace. They were considered the benefactors of a long development paralleling the history of industrialization. Industrial relations scholars built a sizable literature that pointed to the integrated effects of unions and predicted harmonious economic development based on balancing interest group representation and stable labor–management relations. Is this still the case?

One group of articles summarized in Part VI reviews how trade unions are responding to the changes occurring in the workplace and suggest how unions might respond to them in the future. Another set of summaries looks abroad to works councils and producer cooperatives as possible alternatives to the traditional union model.

What Do Unions Do?

The Labor movement has won substantial gains for workers in the past—in the words of a recent bumper sticker, "the people who brought you the weekend." It is common, if perhaps ungrateful, to ask what unions have done for us lately. Looking forward, can unions also enhance productivity and reduce workplace inequality? The traditional *monopoly union model* of neoclassical economics would say no. This model sees the union as maximizing a utility function (based on the wages and employment of its members) subject to the constraint of a labor demand curve. Unions will continually demand more pay and secure employment for their members. The model thus views unions as slowing a firm's response to declines in demand, and hence delaying the firm's hiring decisions—once hired, union members are harder to fire. In sum, costs will be higher and profits and productivity will be lower under such regimes. A theme that recurs throughout this volume is that such a simplistic formula seldom represents the real world.

In striking contrast to the monopoly view is the Richard Freeman article summarized in Part II of the volume. Now a classic, the article applies Albert Hirschman's exit-voice concept to the industrial relations of the firm. Freeman's model asserts that, by addressing job issues with the employer through the expression of "voice," the need for "exit" is reduced. Consultations between unions and management can reduce quits, lower hiring and training costs, and encourage investments in human capital. Testing this theory on four large sets of U.S. workers, Freeman found that profits and productivity were enhanced where unions gave workers a "voice."

Part VI begins with a summary of work by Francine Blau and Lawrence Kahn, showing that unions can reduce the extent of wage inequality within the workplace. They conducted a comparative analysis of the inequality of the distribution of male wages in the United States and in nine other developed countries, where unions are relatively larger and more powerful. They found that wages are most compressed in unionized settings and that the difference between the United States and the other countries is located almost entirely in the lower half of the wage distribution. The most persuasive explanation of these patterns is the presence of centralized bargaining institutions in the European nations. That is, powerful unions seem to have pulled low-wage workers upward toward the median income, while having surprisingly little impact on wages above the median.

If unions enhance democracy and productivity while simultaneously reducing inequality, why are unions on the decline?

How Management Changed

The employment relationship is changing throughout the developed world as employers, workers, unions, and governments adapt to greater international competition and technological change. Managers around the world are constantly experimenting with different employment practices with the hopes of increasing productivity and market share, or simply staying alive. Richard Locke and Thomas Kochan, in the next article summarized here, generalize four recent patterns of change in industrial relations: (1) Decisions about employment, wage bargaining, and so on are increasingly being made at the individual firm level; (2) decentralization is accompanied by a search for greater flexibility in the organization of work; (3) there is a rising premium on skills and an emphasis on training and retraining workers; and (4) unions are facing new challenges and declines in membership as industries restructure, the workforce changes in composition, and the average size of enterprises declines. In another article, Kochan recognizes that the backdrop for these developments is an increasingly conservative political environment and the decreasing effectiveness of labor laws as a deterrent to employer resistance to union organizing campaigns.[1]

Many of the new forms of flexible work organization involves varying degrees of employee participation and workplace committees. Such systems occur in firms and sectors with and without unions. These new work arrangements consist of systems such as quality circles, employee teams, gain-sharing plans, training programs, and information-gathering forums, in addition to employee ownership programs and worker representation on corporate boards of directors. While some of these systems could be merely the latest management fad, the next article summarized here, by David Levine and Laura D'Andrea Tyson, finds that participation programs are starting to show a positive effect on productivity. These authors categorize participation schemes into three categories; consultative participation (such as quality control circles), substantive participation (often involving work teams), and representative participation (such as worker–management committees and employee representatives on boards of directors). Substantive participation has a positive effect on productivity in most studies; the results for other forms of participation are ambiguous. Levine and Tyson conclude that a successful program must have elements of profit sharing, job security, measures to increase group cohesiveness, and guaranteed individual rights to workers. However, conditions in the product, labor, and capital markets may discourage firms from adopting industrial relations systems that allow for such participation.

During President Clinton's first term of office, the United States Departments of Labor and Commerce set up a "Commission on the Future of Worker–Management Relations." The commission was asked to address what new methods or institutions could enhance workplace productivity through worker–management cooperation and employee participation. The commission heard testimony, conducted and commissioned surveys, and so on. During the testimony, Bruce Carswell, Senior Vice President of GTE and Chairman of the Labor Policy Association said:

> The message that we would like to leave with you today is that our nation can
> no longer afford to view the employment relationship as American workers and

management competing with one another in a zero-sum game. Instead, we need to create a partnership among empowered employees, government, industry, and unions, such that everyone is playing on the same team in pursuit of mutually beneficial objectives.[2]

In short, management is attempting to take the "voice" idea to market.

What Should Unions Do Now?

How should trade unions, the historical vanguards of workplace democracy, respond to this changing environment? Some say that new forms of work organization are the latest attempt by management to increase control over the production process and therefore argue that they should be rejected. Others see them as an opportunity to increase union bargaining power.

The decline in union membership in the United States has been quite dramatic. In 1954, over 30 percent of all U.S. workers were union members. By 1996 that number dropped to 14.5 percent. This has been attributed to international trade, occupational and sectoral shifts, and the emergence within manufacturing sectors of new high-technology industries that employ high percentages of white-collar workers and technical workers. Unions have been unsuccessful in responding to this decline because of their "association with rigid internal labor markets, their lack of any significant institutional presence in external labor markets, their inability to influence decisions in strategic management or to take wages out of competition, and the instrumental and work-place specific nature of union membership in the United States."[3]

Because of their reduction in power, unions are more and more being left out of new participation programs. The exclusion of unions from these work systems has led some unions to be very skeptical of them. Some authors go on to say that unions are therefore acting rationally when they are involved in rejecting such changes, and that a return to more radical measures is needed.[4]

A recent report by the AFL/CIO stated: "It is unlikely in the extreme that . . . management-led programs of employee involvement or 'empowerment can' sustain themselves over the long term." It is certain that such systems cannot meet the full range of needs of working men and women.[5]

At the same time, recent research has begun to show that, when worker participation programs are coupled with union involvement, both workers and management reap higher benefits. A study of a large sample of Michigan firms found that firms with work teams and unions performed 35 percent better than those without unions (performance was measured as value-added net of labor cost per employee). The authors add that, compared to nonunionized settings, unionized workplaces provide greater insurance that a serious hearing will be given to employees' ideas in participation programs.[6] Another, more recent, large-scale study sample found that unionized firms with practices that promote joint decision making with incentive-based compensation have higher productivity than similar nonunion plants.[7]

Findings of this type have led some to rally behind the idea of reforming the union movement. Since the management community has exhibited a consensus that greater flexibility and greater employee involvement are necessary, unions could work to help forge these participation programs rather than resist them.[8]

In an impassioned article summarized in this section, Joel Rogers adds that unions can again contribute to democracy if they expand their scope. Unions, in his view, could serve better if they aimed at career security rather than job security. This could be done in part by providing all workers with the advanced training they need. Also, unions should press industry and government to establish uniform conditions of compensation and employment. This twofold strategy will appeal to firms because employers will benefit from an increasingly skilled labor pool, and because they will be more willing to offer good pay and working conditions if they know that their competitors must do the same. Rogers goes on to argue that unions would have more power and be more effective if they sought more control over production decisions, were more spatially and sectorally coordinated, centered around markets, not firms, and played an active, independent role in politics.[9]

The question is, can such reform ever happen here? Rogers says that in small pockets it already is, citing a hopeful local example in Milwaukee, Wisconsin. It is too early to tell whether, as Rogers hopes, this will not just be an isolated incident, but the beginning of a trend.

What Else Could Be Done?

A common conclusion is that the traditional union alone is not sufficient to represent workers and expand workplace participation in the economy of the twenty-first century. The rest of the articles in Part VI explore two other types of work arrangements that might serve as models for the future: works councils and producer cooperatives.

Works Councils

These changes may require forms of representation and participation that resemble European works councils more than American-style collective bargaining. There is an active and lively debate underway, both with the union movement and among managers and other industrial relations professionals and researchers, concerning the wisdom and viability of these new forms of participation, roles for unions, and models of organizational governance.[10]

Survey data indicate that 30 to 40 million American workers without union representation would like some form of representation, and some 80 million workers, many of whom do not approve of unions, nevertheless wish for some independent voice in their workplace.[11] What other options are available? While works councils have been in existence for a very long time, they have recently reemerged in the U.S. industrial relations literature as a possible alternative and/or supplement to the traditional union model. Found mostly in Europe, works councils, which can operate alone or as complements to trade unions, are representative bodies elected by all workers at a workplace, including union members, white-collar, and supervisory employees. These councils, sometimes mandated by law, institutionalize worker rights to information and consultation on the organization of production and, in some cases, codetermination of decision making. In addition to institutionalizing worker input, works councils also often enforce state regulation of the workplace in such areas of occupational health and safety. They are seen as being able to extend their reach beyond the unionized sector while supplementing the work that unions already do. The key distinction between works councils and unions is that the former have information and consultation rights only.[12] The most extensive and best known councils are in Germany; others of particular merit are in the Netherlands, Spain, Greece, Italy, and France.

That works councils can be an important form of democratic participation is evident from workers' involvement in them. In Germany works council representatives are elected every four years on a nationwide election day, when there is a regular turnout of 90 percent. Furthermore, councils promote workplace democracy by changing the relationship between workers and their superiors. Works councils provide employees with a secure institution from which to raise concerns and complaints without fear of sanctions.[13]

Management and union responses to works councils are mixed. Employers have favored works councils "to the extent that councils give them access to reasonable worker representatives who were not outsiders—that is, not full-time union officials—and in the hope that councils would foster worker loyalty to the firm by stressing their shared interest with the employer in the firm's success in the marketplace."[14] Unions are at times suspicious that council membership will lure employees into rubber-stamping business decisions that they actually have no capacity to affect. Also, works councils are feared to "crowd out" traditional unions. On the other hand, in Germany, unions benefit from works councils because the councils make it possible for workers to be represented in vital nonwage interests. Works councils also provide union recognition and are used by unions to recruit new members.[15] While it has been shown that the likelihood of works councils substituting for unions is very low in Europe, unions still resist this form of work organization in the United States and Great Britain.

An economic analysis of works councils is presented in the summary of an article by Richard Freeman and Edward Lazear. With an eye to the possible use of works council in the United States, the article develops modeling techniques to address whether works councils require external institutional mandating, outlines the requirements for a council's ability to communicate productivity-improving information between workers and firms, and examines what might go wrong in a works council setting. It has been argued that the strengthened trust within a works council setting will lead to greater productivity in these firms. Such claims have yet to be demonstrated empirically.[16]

Producer Cooperatives

The ultimate form of participation is a firm owned and controlled by workers. Such producer cooperatives are rare in reality, but the concept has given rise to a steady pool of both theoretical and empirical literature. If cooperatives are such a good idea, why don't we see an increase in this type of work arrangement? To what extent could they be a promising alternative to current industrial relations?

In a sweeping review article on the subject, John Bonin, Derek Jones, and Louis Putterman canvas the recent proliferation of theoretical and empirical findings on producer cooperatives (PCs). Their article, summarized here, is restricted to industrial cooperatives in developed countries where workers have formal decision-making power over the firm's operations. Even with this arguable narrow definition of a PC, there is a broad diversity of PC experience. Italy has the largest PC sector, accounting for 2.5 percent of all nonagricultural employment nationwide. Other countries with considerable numbers are France and Spain (particularly the much discussed Mondragon case), the United Kingdom, and to some extent Sweden and Denmark. As will be discussed a little later, the U.S. plywood industry in the Pacific Northwest also has a long history of cooperatives.

In theory, the absence of workplace hierarchies in PCs may allow greater productivity through cooperative problem-solving and informal social pressure supporting higher levels of effort. In addition, a feature of many PCs, profit sharing, has been identified as a factor contributing to productivity in conventional firms. On the other hand, some theorists argue that because worker-owned enterprises will attempt to maximize average earnings per worker, rather than conventional profit maximization, PCs may tend to decrease employment following an upward demand shift. (Articles summarized here discuss and refute this theoretical claim.)

An article by William Bartlett, summarized in Part VI, compares PCs with private firms in Italy, finding that the PCs provided more tranquil labor relations, with no strikes, low quit rates, and fewer and lower-paid managers. The

PCs also offered greater employment stability, paid comparable wages, and achieved higher productivity despite lower capital-to-labor ratios.

Similar results were found in the case of producer cooperatives in the U.S. plywood industry. Producer cooperatives in the plywood industry in the Pacific Northwest date back to 1921. By 1950 almost 25 percent of the industry's output came from cooperatives. In 1986, it was estimated that the cooperatives' share of plywood production was almost 50 percent. Studies of these cases have found that a cooperative is more likely to adjust earnings and less likely to adjust employment in response to price changes than is a conventional firm.[17]

If PCs have remained a productive force for such a long time, in this era of turmoil in industrial relations, why are there so few PCs in industrial market economies? Bonin's survey of the literature concludes that

> The explanation of the relative scarcity of PCs lies in the nexus between decision making and financial support. Worker control requires (at least partial) worker ownership for incentive reasons but the latter conflicts with the worker's desire to hold a relatively low-risk, diversified portfolio. External financiers with no direct control of company governance will not commit significant funds without receiving a substantial premium to reflect the risk involved. Hence, worker controlled PCs have difficulty finding the internal sources and competing with conventional firms for investment funds.[18]

The final article in this section, by Herbert Gintis, shows how democratic firms in general suffer from these obstacles. In addition to the differential access to credit and capital markets outlined above, workers and stockholders also have divergent interests with respect to risk. He argues that owners can induce desired risk behavior more effectively through incentives to a few managers than through a wide distribution of incentives to its members. According to Gintis, the most successful remedy for this problem would be to repair the failures in labor and capital markets that prevent workers from launching democratic efforts within firms.

Where to Go from Here?

Labor and management can be seen as actors who are either fundamentally at odds with each other, or else harmoniously joined together in their shared interest in productivity. Much of the literature falls between these two positions. When looked at more closely, it can be divided into a literature that argued for a democratic workplace for democracy's sake, and a more recent literature about employee participation for productivity's sake. Future research will have to ask the question: Can these two goals be compatible or are they necessarily in conflict?

Notes

1. Thomas Kochan and Kirsten Wever. "American Unions and the Future of Worker Representation," in *The State of the Unions,* eds. George Strauss et al. (Madison: Industrial Relations Research Association, 1991), 368.

2. Commission on the Future of Worker–Management Relations "Fact Finding Report" (Washington, D.C.: United States Department of Labor, United States Department of Commerce, 1994), 32.

3. Kochan and Wever (Note 1, above).

4. Arndt Sorge and Wolfgang Streeck, "Industrial Relations and Technical Change: The Case for an Extended Perspective," *New Technology and Industrial Relations,* eds. Richard Hyman and Wolfgang Streeck (New York: Blackwell, 1988).

5. *The New American Workplace: A Labor Perspective.* A Report by the AFL/CIO Committee on the Evolution of Work (Washington, D.C.: AFL/CIO, February 1994).

6. William Cooke, "Employee Participation Programs, Group-Based Incentives, and Company Performance: A Union–Nonunion Comparison," *Industrial and Labor Relations Review* 47, 4 (July 1994), 597.

7. Sandra Black and Lisa Lynch, "How to Compete: The Impact of Workplace Practices and Information Technology on Productivity" (forthcoming).

8. See Kochan and Wever (Note 1, above), 377.

9. A focus on markets would allow the union to represent the peripheral workforce described in the Part V—part-timers, members of temporary agencies, those in subcontracting arrangements, and so on.

10. Kochan and Wever (Note 1 above). See also Michael Piore, "The Future of Unions," in *The State of the Unions,* eds. George Strauss et al. (Madison: Industrial Relations Research Association Series, 1991).

11. One example of findings like this is Henry Farber and Alan Krueger, "Union Membership in the United States: The Decline Continues," in *Employee Representation: Alternatives and Future Directions,* eds. M. Kleiner and B. Kaufman (Madison: Industrial Relations Research Association, 1993).

12. Joel Rogers and Wolfgang Streeck "Workplace Representation Overseas: The Works Councils Story," in *Working Under Different Rules,* ed. Richard Freeman (New York: Russell Sage Foundation, 1993), 98.

13. Ibid., 105–106.

14. Ibid., 103.

15. Ibid., 117.

16. John Addison has attempted to use the exit-voice model to analyze works councils in Germany, but found little effect. See John Addison, Kornelius Kraft, and Joachim Wagner, "German Works Councils and Firm Performance," in *Employee Representation: Alternatives and Future Directions,* eds. B. Kaufman and Morris Kleiner (Madison: Industrial Relations Research Association, 1993), 305–335.

17. John Pencavel and Ben Craig, "The Empirical Performance of Orthodox Models of the Firm: Conventional Firms and Worker Cooperatives," *Journal of Political Economy* 102, 4 (1994).

18. See Bonin et al., "Theoretical and Empirical Studies of Producer Cooperatives: Will Ever the Twain Meet?" *Journal of Economic Literature,* 31 (1993), 1316.

Summary of

International Differences in Male Wage Inequality: Institutions versus Market Forces

by Francine Blau

[Published in *Journal of Political Economy* 104, 4 (1996), 791–837.]

Many economists have written about the recent trend toward increased wage inequality, which has occurred in most industrialized countries. Equally important, however, are the large and persistent international differences in the level of inequality. In particular, the distribution of wages is much less equal in the United States than in western Europe. This article presents a detailed comparative analysis of the inequality in the distribution of male wages in the United States and nine other developed countries in the 1980s. It finds that the difference between the United States and other countries is located almost entirely in the lower half of the wage distribution, and argues that institutional rather than market forces offer the most persuasive explanation of these patterns.

Institutions and Inequality

The mechanism by which market forces affect the distribution of wages is simple and familiar. Greater inequality in one country rather than another could result from either supply or demand factors. That is, there could be international differences either in the distribution of valuable skills in the labor force or in the patterns of demand for (and hence payment for) particular, scarce skills. However, the empirical analysis discussed below finds that these factors, as best as they can be measured, are of only secondary importance in explaining the actual international variations in inequality.

Institutional factors affecting wage determination have more complex effects. The United States has the lowest level of unionization among the major developed countries. This could lead to greater inequality of wages in several ways. First, unions raise their members' wages relative to other workers; the union/nonunion wage gap is much larger in the United States than elsewhere. Second, union contracts reduce the variation in wages within the unionized sector of the labor force. This sector is smaller in the United States, and the more variable, nonunionized sector is larger. Third, collective bargaining in the United States is more decentralized—thus bargaining does less in the United States than in Europe to reduce the variation in wages among unionized workers. Industrywide collective bargaining agreements in several European countries set nationwide minimum pay standards. In addition, union and government policies in some countries explicitly seek to raise the wages of the lowest-paid workers. Several of these factors suggest that the U.S.–European difference should be particularly evident at the bottom of the wage distribution—which is exactly what the data show.

Wage determination is far more centralized in other developed countries than in the United States. Sweden and Norway have had a single nationwide agreement between the employer association and the major union federation (although there has been some recent movement away from this pattern in Sweden). Austria and Italy have nationwide collective bargaining agreements covering entire industries or groups of industries; Germany has similar agreements on a statewide basis. Australia has government tribunals and compulsory arbitration that set wages for most workers. Switzerland and Britain have less centralized wage determination than many other European countries, but more multiemployer contracts, and a higher degree of unionization, than the United States. In several European countries, the union movement has pushed explicitly and somewhat successfully for pay scales that raise the relative position of the lowest-paid workers.

Data and Results

The heart of the study is an empirical analysis of micro data on individual workers from the United States and nine other developed countries, for various years in the 1980s. To increase comparability, the sample is restricted to male wage and salary workers aged 18 to 65. Other work by the same authors has examined international comparisons of the gender gap in wages, finding similarities in the patterns of male-female inequality and of inequality within the male workforce.

One summary measure of inequality is the standard deviation of wages—it is largest for the United States, with Australia in second place and the European countries all noticeably more equal. More information about the shape of the wage distribution can be obtained by examining the ratios (or differences in logarithms) between the 10th, 50th, and 90th percentiles of each country's wages.

The ratio of 90th percentile to 50th percentile wages is 1.7 for the U.S. The average 90/50 ratio is also 1.7 for the other nine countries in the study.[1] The 90/50 ratio, in fact, is greater for Switzerland (the highest in the study, at almost 2.2), Britain, and Hungary than it is for the United States. Thus the pattern of inequality in the upper half of the wage distribution does not distinguish the United States from other developed countries.

On the other hand, the distinction is quite clear in the ratio of 50th to 10th percentile wages. This ratio is 2.8 in the United States compared to an average of 1.6 for the other nine countries. The 50/10 ratio was 2.1 in Australia and

1.8 or less in all the European countries. The United States has a much greater degree of inequality, therefore, in the lower half of the wage distribution.

How much of the difference between the United States and other countries is due to the distribution of skills, or due to the rate at which skills are paid? For the standard deviation of wages, only 6 percent of the difference, on average, is due to a less equal distribution of education and work experience in the United States, and 15 percent is attributable to less equal average payment for these skills. Nearly four-fifths of the difference is due to "residual" inequality—the greater variation in the United States is the treatment of people with the same skills. For the 50th/10th percentile ratio, focusing on the lower half of the distribution, 43 percent of the difference between the United States and other countries is due to America's less equal distribution of education and experience—only 4 percent is due to difference in the relative payment of these skills. More than half of the difference is still "residual" inequality. (In the upper half of the labor force, the U.S. distribution of education and experience is more equal than that of the other countries.)

A number of other statistical analyses tell similar stories. For example, a detailed correction for international differences in the distribution of occupations and industries suggests that low-skilled workers should in general fare *worse* relative to the middle in other countries than they do in the United States. This effect points in the wrong direction and cannot explain the opposite, observed pattern of smaller low-to-middle skill differentials outside the United States.

Testing the Effects of Institutions

Several authors have produced rankings of countries with respect to the degree of centralization in their wage-setting procedures. An average of these published rankings yields an index of centralization. Not surprisingly, the index shows the United States to be the least centralized of the ten countries in the study. This index is strongly correlated with both the standard deviation of wages and with the 50th/10th percentile ratio; it is not, however, significantly related to the 90th/50th percentile ratio. This provides clear statistical evidence of the importance of institutions in explaining the international patterns of inequality.

If centralized wage-setting institutions increase the relative wages of workers at the bottom of the skill and income distribution, those workers may have fewer employment opportunities. With the cost of low-skilled labor raised above its free-market price, the demand for such labor may drop. An examination of the employment/population ratios for low-, middle-, and high-skill groups shows that higher-skilled workers are more likely to be employed in all countries—but the gap between employment rates for the middle- and low-skill groups is greater in continental Europe than in the United States, Britain, and

Australia. Europe's more egalitarian wages for low-skilled workers may come at the expense of fewer job opportunities for this group.

It is sometimes suggested that the government is an employer of last resort for unemployed, low-skilled workers. However, in the countries in this study, the government workforce is relatively skilled, and there are no clear patterns of international variation in the skill level of public employees. If European governments attempt to compensate for their relatively greater unemployment of low-skilled workers, it appears that they do so indirectly through policies such as training programs and subsidies for relocation, not through direct public employment.

Note

1. These are the antilogs of the logarithmic data in the study's Table 1.

Summary of

Participation, Productivity, and the Firm's Environment

by David I. Levine and Laura D'Andrea Tyson

[Published in Alan Blinder, ed., *Paying for Productivity* (Washington, D.C.: Brookings Institution, 1990), 183–243.]

How does employee participation in decision making affect productivity? Global competition has spurred interest in this question, especially in light of the strong performance of Japanese and other companies with participatory industrial relations. This article examines the effect of participation on productivity, concluding that the theoretical relationship is ambiguous, while the empirical literature finds a usually positive, often small, effect. It then identifies features of a firm's management and human resource systems that are needed to sustain employee participation, and discusses the effects of the external economic environment on the firm's decision to introduce such features.

The Theory of Participation

The standard economic theory of the firm suggests that owners will be opposed to employee participation. Agency theory implies that owners must provide incentives to motivate managers to act in the owners' interests. The greater the number of decision makers, the more expensive and inefficient such incentives become. However, if participatory arrangements motivate workers to create more ideas, to share their knowledge of the work process, and to encourage productive behavior of fellow workers, the result may be an increase in efficiency—and even an increase in managerial control.

Still, the question of how to motivate workers remains unanswered. All firm members would be better off if everyone worked hard, yet there is always a temptation for an individual to reduce effort. Any one worker can be a "free rider" if everyone else continues to work hard. The result can be a noncooperative solution that is individually rational for each worker, but far from optimal for the firm or workers as a group.

Participation can support a cooperative strategy where group interaction and peer pressure maintain the optimal level of work effort. In fact, it may actually change the goals of workers, bringing them closer to the goals of the firm. Such a discussion leaves conventional economic theory behind. Other social sciences have explored these topics, but unfortunately have not found definite consistent relationships between participation, morale, and productivity.

The Empirical Evidence

Participatory workplace arrangements can be grouped into three broad categories. *Consultative participation* solicits workers' opinions and suggestions, but reserves all final decision-making power to management. Quality control circles are the most common example of consultative participation in the United States. *Substantive participation* gives groups of workers, such as work teams, power to make decisions in selected areas. *Representative participation* gives workers as a whole formal representation through workers' councils, joint labor-management committees, and employee representatives on company boards of directors. In contrast to substantive participation, representative participation may encompass a broader range of issues, but give workers more diluted influence—perhaps only an advisory or informational role—on the issues that are discussed.

An extensive survey of the empirical literature on the link between participation and productivity reaches several general conclusions. Consultative participation is not likely to achieve lasting improvements in productivity; most studies find that the half-life of quality circles is less than three years. On the other hand, substantive participation has a positive effect on productivity in most studies, though some have found only a weak or statistically insignificant effect. It can be hard to separate the effects of participation from other workplace innovations. Representative participation can improve performance when it is part of a package of participatory policies. When introduced alone it may improve labor–management relations but has little effect on productivity.

Studies of worker-owned firms and cooperatives usually find that both participation and ownership have positive effects on productivity. It is dangerous, however, to extrapolate these results to conventional firms. The analysis presented below suggests that the effects of participation are likely much smaller in conventionally owned and organized firms.

Four Requirements for Participation

Since the evidence suggests that participation can have positive effects on productivity, why don't we see more of it? Four characteristics are required for successful participatory systems. The external economic environment may discourage firms from adopting these characteristics.

First, some form of *profit or gain sharing* is a key element of participatory systems. There are many different ways of linking some part of worker compensation to a measure of profitability or group productivity. Profit sharing is required for a sense of fairness and commitment; without it, workers will feel it is unfair that they do not share in the benefits generated by their cost-saving ideas. Payment based on group performance gives workers incentives to maintain norms of high effort and monitor each other—and to cooperate in the work process.

A second essential characteristic is job security and *long-term employment relations*. Workers are unlikely to help increase efficiency if they fear that doing so may jeopardize their jobs. Long-term commitments also encourage workers to develop the skills and the workplace relationships that allow more effective, productive work.

A third category, *measures to increase group cohesiveness*, includes narrowing differences in wages and status, and payment based on group rather than individual performance. Large firms with successful participatory arrangements tend to pay relatively egalitarian wages, in part to induce cohesiveness within the workforce.

Finally, participatory systems usually provide *guaranteed individual rights* to workers. For example, a just-cause dismissal policy, specifying the grounds on which a worker can be fired, helps foster a sense of fairness and trust, which are vital to participation.

Participation and the External Environment

Even if participatory workplaces are potentially efficient, conditions in the product, labor, and capital markets can discourage firms from adopting an industrial relations system that allows participation. The more variable the demand for the firm's product, the more expensive it is to guarantee long-term employment. When the business cycle is pronounced, employers find it profitable to use cyclical layoffs. This sets up a feedback mechanism, since cyclical layoffs amplify business cycle fluctuations—making it even more costly for other firms to maintain long-term employment and worker participation.

Labor market conditions affect the profitability of participation systems in several ways. When unemployment is high, the traditional approach to labor discipline, based on the threat of dismissal, is relatively cheap (as explained in "efficiency wage" theories, Part II). However, when unemployment falls, traditional labor discipline becomes more expensive, and a participatory system of motivation and incentives becomes more attractive.

Similar considerations apply to wage differentials: If wages are generally unequal, so that star performers are paid large premiums in other firms, then participatory firms that try to maintain egalitarian wage schedules will tend to lose their best workers. But if wage differentials are narrow at all firms, the participatory approach to motivation can lead to efficiency gains without the risk of losing the best or highest-skilled workers. Likewise, it is easier for a firm to maintain just-cause dismissal policies if all other employers do. If only one offers such policies, all the least-motivated workers will want to work there, creating an adverse selection problem.

Capital market conditions also influence the viability of participatory arrangements. Conventional lenders are biased against reliance on the intangible trust and motivation that are crucial to participatory firms, and may evaluate such firms' prospects in an unduly negative manner. This and other capital market problems can be minimized if participatory firms develop close relationships with their investors.

Brief case studies of participatory firms in Japan and Sweden suggest that both countries have enjoyed product, labor, and capital market conditions that favored participation. The four characteristics required for successful participatory systems are present in both cases (though in Japan, only about 30 to 40 percent of the labor force is employed in the larger, participatory firms). These success stories can be contrasted with other environments in which market conditions have discouraged participation. There are several implications for public policy to promote participation. Desirable policies include maintenance of high and steady aggregate demand; promotion of long-term employment relations and just-cause dismissal policies; measures to lengthen managers' and investors' time horizons; and more research and dissemination of information on workplace participation itself, to make the option more familiar and acceptable.

Summary of

Conclusion: The Transformation of Industrial Relations? A Cross-National Review of the Evidence

by Richard M. Locke and Thomas Kochan

[Published in Richard Locke, Thomas Kochan, and Michael Piore, eds., *Employment Relations in a Changing World Economy* (Cambridge: MIT Press, 1995), 359–384.]

Industrial relations are changing throughout the developed world, as unions, employers, and governments adapt to greater international competition. The result is an increasing diversity of employment practices, making it difficult to identify clear trends and patterns of change. Part VI is the conclusion of comparative international study of industrial relations, seeking to describe, explain, and generalize from the contemporary changes in employment practices.

Reviewing the Evidence

A brief review of the evidence (presented in earlier parts) identifies four common patterns of change in industrial relations. First, decisions about employment, wage bargaining, and other aspects of industrial relations are increasingly moving toward the individual enterprise level. In the past, most European countries, and Australia, had centralized industrywide or nationwide systems of bargaining and negotiations, to a far greater extent than in the United States. Even in the U.S., however, industrywide pattern bargaining occurred in major unionized industries. Changes have occurred in some of the countries with the most centralized industrial relations, such as Sweden, Australia, and Italy, all of which have moved to industry or enterprise autonomy in bargaining. Movement toward decentralization occurred throughout the 1980s in the United States and the United Kingdom, as former bargaining patterns declined.

Second, decentralization was accompanied by the search for greater flexibility in the organization of work. Strict European hiring rules have been bent to allow employers greater discretion in picking new employees. Youth, part-time, and/or temporary employment has risen sharply in Italy, Spain, Norway, the United Kingdom, the United States, Germany, and Japan. Linked to changes in hiring practices are internal efforts at reorganization, including use of teamwork, quality circles, job rotation, flexible hours and work assignments, and other innovations.

Third, there is a growing premium on skills, and a corresponding emphasis on training and retraining of workers. In Canada, Australia, and France, national governments have launched substantial worker training programs, while major reforms to enhance vocational training have been adopted in Britain,

Spain, Norway, and Sweden. Performance- and/or skill-related pay systems have likewise grown in importance in many countries.

Fourth, unions are facing new challenges and declines in membership, as industries restructure, the workforce changes in composition, and the average size of enterprises declines. The challenge has been greatest, and the decline in membership steepest, where labor laws are least favorable and business and/or government are most opposed to unions, as in the United States, Britain, and France. But similar, though less pronounced, declines in union membership have occurred in Japan, Australia, Italy, and the private sector in Canada. In some countries—Italy, the United Kingdom, Norway—new types of employee associations have emerged to challenge the role of established unions.

While there are common trends, there are important institutional differences between countries as well. For example, employer efforts to reorganize work are often resisted by unions in the United States, where reorganization may threaten job security, but welcomed by unions in Germany, where jobs are more secure. However, the employers' search for flexibility, in varied forms, can be seen throughout the industrial world.

Cross-National and Cross-Firm Variations

The pressure for flexibility arises within differing national contexts. At one extreme, in countries such as Japan and Germany, flexible, team-oriented work systems were already relatively common, and new practices introduced in recent years are only incremental changes. At the other extreme, where work has traditionally been organized along more rigid Taylorist lines, as in the United States, Australia, Britain, and Canada, there has been much greater pressure for fundamental transformation in employment practices. There are also differences within countries. Not surprisingly, new practices are most often adopted in new or completely reorganized plants, and in industries where the pressures of international competition are strongest. Many innovative work practices remain new and fragile. Only in Japan and perhaps Australia is there strong government support for the new, flexible approaches to industrial relations.

Innovations in work practices and worker–management cooperation are not likely to be sustained when workers fear that increases in productivity will lead to losing their jobs. Unfortunately, demands for innovation have been increasing in recent years while job security has been decreasing almost everywhere. Employment security is generally much stronger in continental Europe, Scandinavia, and Japan than in the United States or Britain, though in some cases, such as Japan, Italy, and Spain, the protection available in the primary labor market does not extend to employees of small firms.

Continuous training and staff development is the best route to employment security in a changing world, yet it is unfortunately rare to find firms thinking this way. An alternative, common in America, is to shrink the number of full-time career employees and rely on subcontractors or contingent workers for a growing number of tasks. This can accentuate gender, racial, and ethnic divisions among workers, leading to conflict (and to a diminishing number of "good jobs"). The same problems and pressures will arise elsewhere. Japan has faced an especially acute adjustment crisis in the 1990s, and will be under continuing pressure to change, perhaps threatening the lifetime employment system now common in its large firms.

Real-wage gains have slowed, particularly in the United States. Moderate growth has continued in Japan and several European countries. Inequality of incomes has increased within most countries, most dramatically in the United States. Countries where centralized wage-setting structures remained in place—Germany, Norway, Japan—saw little if any rise in inequality. The United States is exceptional among developed countries in the weakness of its unions and of its worker training programs. These factors combined with very decentralized wage determination help explain why the United States leads the developed world in the recent growth of inequality.

Current Tensions in Employment Relations

All countries exhibit an uneasy coexistence of cost-cutting and high-value-added competitive strategies. Cost-based strategies can lead to a downward spiral of wages, working conditions, and labor standards, in an adversarial atmosphere. High-value-added strategies are preferable in normative terms; it is important to explore the factors that support this choice.

Most firms engage in both strategies, sometimes sequentially. For example, in the United States in the early 1980s, many industries laid off workers and demanded concessions from unions, More recently, the same industries have made efforts to cooperate with employees in improving quality, productivity, and labor–management relations.

> The low-cost response to market pressures and changes appears to be most frequent in countries with weak institutions, low levels of unionization, decentralized bargaining structures, and a limited government role in labor market affairs. Again the United States is the extreme case, followed closely by Britain. [374]

Cost-cutting may confer a short-run competitive advantage, but exerts a perverse social externality in the long run. It becomes riskier for firms to make long-term investments in upgrading skills, pushing a country toward a low-wage, low-skill equilibrium. Pressure in this direction is affecting even the countries with the strongest institutional constraints on the market.

As the benefits of flexibility and innovation emerge, there is the potential for polarization between jobs that are based on the new practices and those that are not. "This not only makes it more difficult to sustain commitment to value-added strategies at the micro level but also exacerbates the divisions among different groups within society." [375] A clear example of the resulting problems has appeared in the U.S. petrochemical industry, where cost-cutting efforts led to a growing number of less experienced, nonunion contract employees doing high-risk jobs—and to increased rates of accidents and injuries among these workers. Only recently have new training programs and upgraded labor standards addressed this problem.

It is ironic that unions are declining in influence and membership, just when a strong employee voice is increasingly needed in corporate and industry decision making. Yet a simple revitalization of unions is unlikely to occur. What new or modified mechanisms can effectively represent worker interests? Germany's works councils provide one important model; Australia's "managed decentralism" of labor relations, standard-setting, and training programs suggest another.

The "bottom line" is that there is indeed a transformation of employment practices underway around the world. While there are common themes that affect all countries, there are also historical factors that create different conditions in different locations.

> [T]here is not a single natural response to increased market competition. Nor are the variations observed simply random deviations from a single market-determined result. Instead, employment relations are shaped in systematic and predictable ways by institutions that filter these external pressures and by the strategies of the key actors. [382]

Summary of

Microchips and Macroharvests:
Labor–Management Relations in Agriculture

by Robert J. Thomas

[Published in *Workers, Managers and Technological Change*, ed. Daniel B. Cornfield (New York: Plenum Press, 1987), 27–45.]

Since the 1960s the United Farm Workers have called several strikes and consumer boycotts to bring attention to the poor working conditions faced by agricultural workers in the U.S. Southwest. During the same period, adoption of mechanical options has been rapid in some cases and slow in others. This unevenness is related to the struggle between employers and unions for control over agricultural labor markets and working condition as well as to the changing structure of the industry in the Southwest.

Political Economy of Agriculture and Unionization

Since the 1960s the agriculture industry in the U.S. Southwest has been an arena for political and economic ferment. Growers, plant breeders, and electrical engineers have collaborated in attempts to rationalize fruit and vegetable growing. While impressive technological innovations have been achieved—including plants bred to withstand mechanical harvesting and machines fitted with sensors to detect signs of ripeness—diffusion of these technologies has not been straightforward. Many employers rely on a low-waged labor force, As long as the labor force continues to be replenished by new waves of immigration, employers have little incentive to mechanize. The United Farm Workers have engaged in a protracted struggle to organize field workers to improve their pay and working conditions. At the same time an industry that was once family farms has been reorganized by large industrial enterprises that saw agriculture as an investment opportunity.

Immigration Policy and Farm Worker Organizing

Historically union organizing in the fields of the Southwest faced great obstacles. Employers were well organized through the American Farm Bureau Federation, which maintained implacable hostility to unionization and successfully fought attempts to bring farm workers under the National Labor Relations Act of 1935. At local levels, in communities economically dependent on agriculture, growers used the police or vigilantes against union organizing.

From 1880 to about 1940, agriculture was organized around small farms producing for local markets. Skilled family labor was sufficient for most operations except during planting and harvesting seasons. The labor market for unskilled seasonal labor was a political construction, shaped by producers' influence on immigration policy to ensure a supply of unskilled labor "willing to travel in search of employment, and willing to accept meager wages . . . which would be available when needed for short periods but which could be jettisoned when unneeded." [32]

From 1942 until 1965, the Bracero Program formalized recruitment of cheap seasonal labor through contractual arrangements between U.S. grower associations and the Mexican government. The Kennedy administration dismantled the Bracero Program in 1965, but farm labor remained outside the National Labor Relations Act. Eligibility rules for state unemployment benefits gave agricultural workers little choice but to move on when the season ended. Few citizens, even among the growing urban unemployed, were attracted to work in the fields, while a loophole in immigration law allowed emergency increases in immigration during labor shortages. Bracero labor was replaced by "green card" and undocumented Mexican labor.

Structural Change in Agriculture and a New Union Approach

After World War II the structure of the industry changed as agricultural production became more concentrated in large farms. In some cases mechanization took hold. Some enterprises were susceptible to union challenges. Large firms like Tenneco, Purex, Coca-Cola, and Schenley built marketing networks, links to fertilizer producers, vast landholdings, and technical advances that increased the costs of entry and eroded the position of small growers. Advertising created brand-name associations for many agricultural products, both processed (such as Campbells soups or Gallo wines) and unprocessed (such as "Sunkist" inked on orange skins). Concentration and scale stabilized employment practices, concentrated workers, and made them easier to organize. The high visibility of brand-name producers and their exposure in many product markets made these firms ripe targets for consumer boycotts.

The United Farm Workers (UFW), headed by Cesar Chavez, adopted a nontraditional, community-based effort that offered a credit union, insurance, and other member services to create bonds within the fragmented workforce. It leveraged the growing concentration and changing structure in the industry to exploit pockets of stability and promote consumer boycotts of well-known producers. Grape production in Kern County, California, provided one of the few opportunities for year-round work in agriculture. The scale of the industry (a large proportion of the country's grape output) and the meticulous pruning and weeding required in the off-season enabled workers to settle in the area and commute from farm to farm. As farms became larger, workers remained with one company for longer periods of time.

An early UFW strike against grape growers, sparked by members' refusal to cross picket lines put up by Filipino workers, succeeded in bringing workers in protest together, but failed when employers imported strikebreakers from Mexico. The UFW turned to a consumer boycott, turning it into "a biting economic weapon. Through effective public relations, an emphasis on nonviolence, dramatic pilgrimages, highly publicized fasts, Chavez and the UFW made the plight of the farm worker much more visible." [39]

Boycotts in the wine grape, table grape, and lettuce industries faced different circumstances, but eventually made inroads in winning representation and securing contracts. In the wine industry, where large corporations like Schenley were involved, boycotts of brand-name products were effective, and the UFW built a base around contracts with several large wine producers. Table grapes mainly come from medium-sized producers and are not sold by label, but a protracted education campaign induced consumers to substitute other fruits for grapes. The boycott paid off for the UFW after a long and bitter struggle. In the lettuce industry, there were mixed results. Lettuce has few substitutes, but some large producers were vulnerable in other product markets, leading three to sign contracts. However, smaller growers resisted the UFW.

These victories proved tenuous. Employers resisted contract provisions or began signing contracts (often "sweetheart deals") with other unions, most prominently the Teamsters. Still, the UFW emerged as the most influential agricultural union by the late 1970s. They achieved substantial increases in wages and benefits, an Agricultural Labor Relations Board to enforce labor law, widespread representation, and a system of hiring halls and seniority that undermined the exploitative labor contract system. But agricultural employment still remains less attractive than other sectors, and mechanization has begun to reduce the number of workers in the fields.

Challenges for Labor Relations: Two Cases

The UFW has had little success in mediating the impact of technology. Employer decisions about labor-displacing technology are influenced by cost and managerial control. "These are, of course, the points on which the UFW and other farm labor unions find themselves hung: The more successful they are as economic and political agents, the more likely it is that companies will attempt to eliminate them as obstacles to organizational performance." [42] Illegal immigration also poses challenges to any attempts to improve workers' conditions.

Production of tomatoes for processing was a major, very labor intensive part of postwar agriculture. The University of California created a mechanical harvester and a tomato able to tolerate it, but growers only became interested after the termination of the Bracero Program cut the unlimited supply of cheap labor. Employment dropped from 50,000 to 18,000 in just a few seasons. Another drop in employment occurred during the late 1970s when electrooptic sorting reduced the number of workers per harvesting machine from twenty-five to only five or six.

In the head lettuce industry, private and public sources also combined to develop new technologies. The industry was slow to mechanize, but the UFW was active in organizing lettuce workers. Lettuce is sold directly from the field to supermarkets and institutions, so growers have developed durable links with buyers. Large growers are well capitalized and able to grow lettuce year-round by operating in several areas, reducing dependence on price fluctuations. When the Bracero Program ended, the industry raised wages to attract workers. Citizens did not move into the back-breaking work, but undocumented workers did. So, paradoxically, the lettuce industry is both highly unionized and highly populated by undocumented workers too vulnerable to offer effective resistance. "Employers, not surprisingly have been quite adept at whip-sawing the UFW with the issue of undocumented workers and the threat of mechanization." [45]

Summary of

Alternative Forms of Work Organization Under Programmable Automation

by Maryellen R. Kelley

[Published in *The Transformation of Work,* ed. Stephen Wood
(London: Routledge, 1989) 235–247.]

Programmable automation (PA), the use of computers to coordinate the operation of machines, is a new technology for batch manufacturing processes. There is much debate over how this technology will affect the social organization of work. Some hope that the microprocessor applications of PA will play a seminal role in restoring U.S. competitiveness in the world economy.

Post-Taylorist theorists such as Poire and Sabel[1] portray PA as a flexible form of automation that will flatten bureaucratic hierarchies within firms and require collaborative, skill-enhancing forms of work organization. In contrast, labor process theorists, building on the work of Braverman's deskilling thesis and often taking the old, strict Taylorist approach as their starting point, see PA as the latest attempt by management to increase its control over the production process by reducing its dependence on worker's skills.

This article draws on a study of U.S. manufacturing plants of various sizes that are using microprocessing PA systems. It concludes that neither a post-Taylorist nor a labor process (strict Taylorist) description adequately characterizes the trends in work organization that are associated with PA. As an alternative framework for analysis, post-Taylorist theories identify possibilities for worker-centered control over programmable automation. This article extends the post-Taylorist approach, discovering a reality of PA control that is shared between white-collar and blue-collar workers.

Alternative Forms of Organization for Programming Tasks

Machines in batch manufacturing were conventionally operated by blue-collar workers. With PA, machines are directed by a computer program, leaving open the important question: Who controls the programming? The predictions of labor process theory, assuming a strict Taylorist approach, would expect programming to be performed by engineers and managers, centralizing work organization by shifting the locus of control from blue-collar workers to management.

By contrast, post-Taylorist (or postindustrial) theorists would suggest that firms could distribute programming responsibilities widely among blue-collar workers to gain flexibility and flatten the occupational hierarchy within the firm—an outcome that may be called "worker-centered control." Another possibility, "shared control," emerges when control over programming is shared between white-collar and blue-collar workers. In both of these more contingent approaches to the distribution of control, the firm gains flexibility by decentralizing programming while maintaining a hierarchical chain of command.

Of the nearly 477 establishments surveyed in 1987, 44.8 percent use shared control and 31.2 percent use worker-centered control. Only 24 percent could be described as strict Taylorist (blue-collar workers have no responsibility for programming). However, the strict Taylorist establishments tend to have more employees, so that the number of workers in manufacturing occupations operating under the Taylorist approach rises to 38.8 percent of the sample. In establishments with the shared control form of work organization, 40 percent of machine operators wrote programs on a regular basis. In contrast, 62 percent of the worker-centered groups of PA machine operators were found to write programs regularly. These findings are contrary to the "labor process" hypothesis that the main function of PA is to enhance managerial control.

Factors Influencing the Organization of Work

Work organization in facilities using microprocessing PA develops as a function of three interconnected variables: organizational size, industrial relations, and the technical requirements relating to product variety and to volume of output. This research supports the expectation that unionization (the leading industrial relations variable) correlates with a tendency to rely on the strict Taylorist model, while large firms tend to separate programming from operating work roles. The interaction of these two factors may be exemplified by two statistics: (1) In unionized plants with 1000 or more workers, there is less than a 4 percent chance that control over programming will be exclusively worker-centered. (2) In an average-size firm with no union there is a 50:50 chance that programming will be shared between blue-collar and white-collar workers.

Contrary to these findings, labor process theory might imply that unionized workplaces have an advantage in attaining PA operating responsibilities for their members. However, the conventional collective bargaining approach appears too weak to counter management's power to reorganize work roles when new technology is introduced. In the U.S. industrial relations system, management can avoid bargaining over wages and work rules by creating entirely new specialized technical occupations outside the bargaining unit composed of blue-collar occupations. Thus the chances of worker-centered control are, in fact, smallest in unionized plants. Even shared control is significantly lower in plants that are unionized than in those that are not.

Organizational structure and technological capability appear to be independent dimensions. The likelihood of finding a Taylorist approach to the way programming is controlled depends on organizational, not technical, factors. Regarding the technology variable, the major advantage of PA is "a gain in efficiency when many different small-batch runs are to be carried out with the same equipment." [245] Flexible specialization theorists argue that this advantage can only be fully exploited when the workers who perform other machining functions also write the programs. This is only partially true. Data from this study show that plants that differ widely in both batch size and product variety. A more applicable version of the flexible specialization hypothesis would be restricted to a "combination of specialization in very small batch production (a median batch size of fewer than ten units) and a large array of product types (more than fifty different parts of products)." [245] Plants with such a high degree of technical flexibility have about the same chances of having either a worker-centered approach or a shared-control over programming.

Conclusion

Across a broad spectrum of U.S. industries, the modal approach to work organization under microprocessing PA appears to be shared control. With shared control, neither the strict Taylorist form, as described by labor process theorists, nor the worker-centered approach, depicted by post-Taylorist theorists, holds true. Instead, a certain degree of programming by workers is permitted while the organizational hierarchy is maintained.

The debate has been miscast as a controversy over a "technological imperative allegedly driving management's approach to the organization of work." [246] This article reveals, however, that no technological imperative exists. Rather, the degree of centralization of control over programming responsibilities is a joint function of organization size, industrial relations, and technical factors.

Note

1. Michael Poire and Charles Sabel, *The Second Industrial Divide* (New York: Basic Books, 1984).

Summary of

A Strategy for Labor

by Joel E. Rogers

[Published in *Industrial Relations* 34, 3 (July 1995), 367–381.]

Despite the importance of unions to democracy and a well-ordered economy in the United States, it is obvious that organized labor has been in decline in terms of membership, clout, and public opinion. This article offers suggestions for a strategy to revive labor by examining the general conditions for successful union organization and then presenting a stylized model of "traditional union-ism" to contrast with the recommended alternative. An example of the alternative model's operation is discussed, and the gains that might follow from its wider adoption are considered.

How Unions Win and Lose

> Unions advance when they put forth practical programs of action that (1) ben-
> efit their members or potential members; (2) solve problems in the broader so-
> ciety—often, problems for capitalists, on whose well-being the rest of the soci-
> ety unfortunately depends; and (3) by doing both these things achieve the
> political cachet and social respect—as carriers of the 'general interest'—needed
> to secure supports for their own organization. [368]

In the New Deal and postwar era, unions achieved these conditions by functioning as the redistributive agent of the working class, translating particular
worker demands into general interests. This particular strategy is now less pos
sible, however, since its most important organizational preconditions have been
undermined.

These preconditions included the existence of a national economy sufficiently
insulated from foreign competitors; large, lead firms dominating industry clusters and providing ready targets for worker organizations; and a more or less de-
terminate working class, whose distinctiveness and integrity was assured by the
leveling organizations of mass production. They have since been replaced by
economic internationalization, a worldwide reorganization of production, and
workforce heterogeneity.

It is hardly surprising, then, that even the strongest unions are on the defensive. To survive and prosper in the new restructured system, they need to create and occupy a place analogous to their old one. For example, unions can
serve members' interests by aiming for career security rather than job security
and by providing all workers with the advanced training and counseling they

need and want, services rarely provided by employers or by government. This will ensure worker power in the more fluid, less fixed structures of the modern labor market.

Even if skills are made more versatile, careers independent of particular firms are impossible if workplace standards are so diverse as to be barriers to worker mobility. Therefore, unions should also press industry and government to establish and meet uniform conditions of compensation and employment. Unions have unique capacities to perform this role, combining first-hand knowledge of workers "needs" with the institutional ability to enforce uniform standards.

The interests of firms are advanced by this twofold strategy of new model unions—first because employers will benefit from an increasingly skilled labor pool, and second because they will enjoy advanced forms of cooperation and comparability across firms in the face of growing decentralization.

Just as in the old system, unions can play an economic role that both advances their members' interests and solves economywide problems beyond the capacity of any one firm. Organizationally, this will require them to be attentive to a wider variety of worker interests, and to be defined more by geographic region than by economic sector. It is also vital that unions extend the reach of worker power, seeking government support for generic baselines for worker representation.

The reemergence of unions as innovative, moral, and rational agents of general social benefit will reward them with a greater degree of political capital, stemming from a greater degree of identification in the eyes of the general public. This suggests a basis for a new political role for unions, locally and nationally, as advocates for the legislated social protections and supports needed to ensure equity as well as innovation.

The Old Model and the New One

Union activity in the United States remains largely defined by a series of practices that comprise a distinct model of "traditional unionism." To prosper in the new order, unions must abandon this model. The traditional union model was characterized by four basic elements.

First, unions were narrowly focused on simply providing services to members. Organizing expenditures stagnated or declined. Where new units were targeted for organizing the goal was simply to win an election and secure a contract. Where organizing failed to achieve majority support within a limited time frame, it was generally abandoned.

Second, unions stayed clear of issues involving control of production. They did not typically seek to take responsibility for steering the firm's product strategy or organizing the inputs necessary for preferred strategies. Since unions were in a weaker position than employers, such assumption of responsibility was seen as promising only responsibility, never power, and blurring the distinctions between "us" and "them" critical to maintaining solidarity among workers.

Third, organization centered around specific firms or employers and was not centrally coordinated. Collective bargaining agreements were generally negotiated on a firm-by-firm and, often, plant-by-plant basis. Contract administration was highly decentralized, with wide variation in agreements across sites. Within regional labor markets, little effort was made to generalize wage or benefit norms beyond organized employers. Efforts at multiunion bargaining, much less organizing, were infrequent. Murderous jurisdictional disputes were not.

And fourth, unions were unconditionally aligned with the Democratic Party, while showing open disdain for independent politics. Political work was also heavily skewed toward national, rather than state or local, government.

This model functions poorly in the present climate because service provision is extremely expensive, while the absence of workplace or political activism means there is no way to engage the membership. Together these conditions inhibit a union's organizational capacity. Economic restructuring has made employer decisions decisive for member well-being. Unions can no longer afford to ignore control of production. But achieving influence requires coordination on a sectoral basis, not just within individual firms.

Within local and regional markets, the defense of unions is unthinkable without substantial local political power. Obtaining the necessary local and statewide political power requires forging alliances between unions and a range of community groups and populations, which would frequently defy the conventional strategy of the Democratic Party.

Imagine, then, the traditional model turned on its head.

First, the unions would organize everywhere. Imagine a union movement that took the development of grassroots organizing capacity—among rank-and-file members, stewards, local unions—as its maxim, building on the one great strength labor still has: the loyalty of its people. The organizer would be an on-the-scene, full-time union activist without service responsibilities. It then becomes possible to contemplate truly long-term campaigns and a clearer focus on the real goal of organizing—to build the union presence in the workplace.

Second, the unions would seek to control production. This power could then be used to bargain for more power in decisions further back in the production chain. In the United States, coordination across firms to supply the needed inputs for advanced production is something that unions are uniquely positioned to provide. Imagine, then, a labor movement that offered itself as another force of production—but only to employers prepared to share power in decision making and to comply with specified wage and production standards.

Third, unions would be spatially and sectorally coordinated, centered around markets rather than firms. However, this simply cannot be done by a single union. Imagine, then, a labor movement that devised joint organizing strategies for entire economic sectors and for regional labor markets. It would be natural for regional labor bodies to assume supervision of such organizing.

And finally, the unions would be independent in their politics. Imagine a labor movement that was governed in its political endorsements and supports not by party label, but by the values and priorities of those seeking its help. Imagine too that labor invested heavily in developing its own capacity to shape the terms of political debate and action, focusing more on membership training, internal candidate recruitment, the development of precinct-based labor-neighbor political machines, and ongoing work with progressive caucuses of candidates elected. This effort is most feasible in local and state politics where costs are cheaper, the immediate relevance of office is greater, and the vast majority of politics is nonpartisan. It would again be possible for labor to help set, and move, the public agenda.

Could It Happen Here?

Is it possible to imagine unions adopting this new strategy? In fact, certain elements are already appearing, albeit in modest, isolated examples. One place where the new strategy is most advanced is in Milwaukee, Wisconsin. The city's central labor council has revived itself as the key arena of cross-union coordination on all manner of organizing campaigns, solidarity activities, and joint political work. Among its activities is leadership of a labor–community coalition. A group of unions and local employers have established a sectoral training consortium in manufacturing. The agreement is now being extended to the suppliers of consortium members, while the standards of the training are increasingly taken over by the local technical colleges. Unions have taken leadership in the design and administration of one-stop shopping centers for the delivery of labor market services and income assistance for dislocated workers. With strong labor leadership, an independent political arm has been formed and has successfully run a range of candidates for state and local office on its pro-labor platform. Broader goals are also now being contemplated.

If union leadership took examples like this seriously and targeted their efforts and expenditures to make such configurations stronger and more widespread, unions could then reemerge as carriers of the great popular political message of our time: that human values should be imposed on the economy, and that the way to do that is to mobilize the people themselves as a force of production and social authority. Labor would have the wherewithal to take a leading role in a new national future.

Summary of

An Economic Analysis of Works Councils

by Richard B. Freeman and Edward Lazear

[Published in *Works Councils: Consultations, Representations, and Cooperation in Industrial Relations* (Chicago: University of Chicago Press, 1995), 27–50.]

Works councils exist in a variety of forms, but all serve the central function of establishing a group of worker representatives (however selected) who facilitate honest communication between workers and management, and who provide workers an avenue for consultation on certain decisions. While this rarely extends to co-determination (the German model being the outstanding exception), the requirement for consultation in itself may be a source of bargaining power.

Works councils may operate as supplements or complements to trade unions. Some firms have supported them as alternatives to unionization. In the United States, in the early part of this century, works councils covered 10 percent of the workforce in several major industries. They quickly lost popularity among managers, or workers, or both. In the 1920s most vanished from the United States. However, they continue to play a significant role in Europe.

This article draws on a combination of interviews and abstract modeling techniques to address several questions:

> Do councils require external institutional mandating, as in most of Western Europe, or can they be expected to arise from voluntary managerial decision making? When will councils communicate productivity-improving information between workers and firms? What are the benefits and costs of giving councils co-determination rights over some decisions? What can go wrong in a council setting and what arrangements might minimize the risk of poorly functioning councils? [27–28]

Works Councils: Mandated or Voluntary?

The value of works councils for workers depends importantly on the long-term benefits that result when cooperation and two-way flows of relevant information strengthen the firm and increase its profitability. This value can be reduced if the firm is determined not to share such gains with the workers, or if other changes (such as reduced employment security) shorten the workers' time horizons.

As institutions that give workers power, councils can affect the distribution as well as the amount of the firm's surplus. The greater the power of works councils, the greater will be workers' share of the economic rent—and the greater the likelihood that firms will oppose them. The social optimum regarding the amount of power given to councils can be expected to lie somewhere between the preferences of labor and management. Thus, if works councils are to fulfill their social potential they must be mandated by institutions (presumably government) outside of the firm.

Communication

> Management may misinform workers about the situation of the enterprise when it sees workers' gains as owners' losses. Knowing that management can use information strategically, workers may disregard what management says even when it is truthful. [33]

Firms are especially likely to be generous with financial information when times are bad and an exceptional work effort is needed for the firm's survival. Because workers may not believe this (a firm could "cry wolf" to motivate workers' efforts simply to increase profits), councils need to be designed to overcome asymmetries in information between labor and management. They also need to overcome differences in education and in "language," to enable the council members especially, but also the rest of the workers, to understand financial and business terms and ways of presenting information, and to communicate, for example, with accountants.

The socially optimal situation produces the maximal average utility for the workers when they have full information about the state of the firm. Full information allows them to respond flexibly by working extra hard in bad times and at a normal pace in good times. The firm's gains from such a situation are, however, less than the overall social gains; so the firm will voluntarily disclose information less frequently than is socially desirable. Hence it may be necessary to mandate councils' access to certain kinds of information—such as the enterprise's financial condition and its business plans—on a regular basis, not only in times of crisis.

Councils can improve the incentives for workers to provide information, and also affect worker-to-management communication by filtering the information through the workers who are on the councils. However, for workers to communicate truthfully with management they need reassurance that the information they provide will not further empower the firm to resist sharing economic rents. Thus the communication function of works councils will be enhanced when the councils effectively give workers some control over the use of information they provide.

Representation on Councils

Works councils, as forms of representative government, must consider how well the subset of the population (works councilors) reflects the preferences of the whole population (workforce). When there is a large majority on a particular issue a large council is more representative and will communicate preferences more accurately. However, when there is a near-even split of opinion the danger is increased that the council will favor the minority. In fact, there are diminishing returns to increasing council size. Adding members improves the accuracy of information from workers when there is a strong but not overwhelming majority, but adds little accuracy when the workforce is nearly evenly divided or unanimous over an issue.

Different countries and settings have produced a variety of means of filling the council membership. In some cases blue-collar workers may elect white-collar workers as their representatives. In others (for example, Belgium) counselors must be selected from union election slates. A significant issue is how to achieve minority representation on specific issues. Proportional representation is a partial, but imperfect, solution. An alternative possibility is to select councilors randomly (like a jury), with the option that a randomly selected delegate will have the right to appoint a willing alternate from the same age, gender, or otherwise defined group.

Consultation and Co-Determination

An essential feature of works councils is that they possess consultation rights over some categories of firm decisions. This implies a cost to the firm in preparing for and participating in meetings, as well as through delays in action. However, consultation can increase profitability when workers alone, or the combination of workers and managers talking together, can discover or create solutions to company problems that would not have been found otherwise. "The essence of co-determination is teamwork." [44]

Consultation is not always useful. Benefits must be weighed against costs—especially the costs of delay. Because most managers are keenly aware of these potential costs, outside of Germany co-determination rights are generally accorded only with respect to decisions on which management is likely to be neutral. However, firms may thereby lose important benefits that would come with the enhanced job security that results from the German-style works council. Additional job security induces workers to take a longer-run view of the firm's prospects. Secure workers value company profits because profits reflect future worker compensation. One would expect workers in enterprises with strong works councils to have greater loyalty to their firm than workers in other firms.

Works councils are most likely to increase enterprise surplus when they have limited but real power in the enterprise. Many important questions remain unanswered, but the foregoing analysis suggests the value of paying serious attention to the design of council-type arrangements that might fit decentralized labor systems such as those of the United States or Britain. There are potential net social gains from works councils. To realize these gains, the rules governing councils must be written carefully, creating realistic bounds on the power of both labor and management, and fitting appropriately within the broader labor system.

Summary of

Theoretical and Empirical Studies of Producer Cooperatives: Will Ever the Twain Meet?

by John P. Bonin, Derek C. Jones, and Louis Putterman

[Published in *Journal of Economic Literature* 31
(September 1993), 1290–1320.]

In recent decades, as the number of worker-managed firms, or producer cooperatives (PCs), has increased, economists have engaged in extensive theoretical and empirical analyses of such enterprises. However, theoretical and applied studies tend to approach the subject in different terms, often making incompatible assumptions about the institutional structure of PCs. This article reviews and compares the theoretical and empirical literature on PCs, addressing four related questions: Do PCs and comparable conventional firms (CFs) make different decisions about employment, output, and prices? Does the internal organization of the PC affect worker motivation and productivity? Does the assignment of property rights in many PCs lead to underinvestment? Finally, why do so few PCs exist in developed market economies?

The scope of this article is restricted to industrial cooperatives, where workers have formal decision-making power over the firm's operations, in developed countries. Even with this somewhat restrictive definition, there is a broad diversity of experience with PCs. Italy has the largest PC sector, accounting for 2.5 percent of all nonagricultural employment nationwide. Other countries with substantial numbers of PCs include France, Spain (particularly the Mondragon group of cooperative enterprises), the United Kingdom, and to a lesser extent Sweden and Denmark. In the United States, the plywood industry in the Pacific Northwest has a long history of cooperatives, as do a scattering of other smaller industries. The size of cooperative enterprises varies, but most are quite small. The average Italian PC has fewer than 20 workers, while some have exceeded 2000. Profit-sharing arrangements, limits on salary inequalities, hiring of nonmember workers, and provisions for the sale of shares by departing members all vary widely between countries, industries, and individual firms.

Employment and Output

The earliest theoretical analyses of worker-managed firms reached the paradoxical conclusion that an increase in the price of the firm's output would lead to a reduction in employment and production. Subsequent studies have shown that this result depended on an oversimplified picture of a PC's labor supply. More careful analyses of the incentives facing cooperative members imply that PCs will expand employment and output in response to an increase in output prices. However, all such models show that, if a PC is maximizing potential dividends, or value added per worker, it will be inefficient, employing fewer workers, paying them more, and producing less than the optimum amount.

Such theories have been difficult to test empirically. Long data series are available for the U.S. plywood cooperatives, but several of the studies using this data rely on problematical estimates of production functions, which are heavily dependent on the appropriateness of the measure of the capital stock. There is no empirical evidence of short-run inefficiency or negatively sloped supply curves. PCs do appear more likely than CFs to vary wages, and less likely to vary employment and output, when prices change. That is, the plywood cooperatives act as if they are interested in maintaining stability of employment, as well as maximizing value added per worker, contrary to the simplest theoretical models of PCs. The few empirical tests using data from other countries have failed to demonstrate any clear differences in the response to price changes by PCs and comparable CFs.

Incentives and Productivity

The disjuncture between theory and evidence continues in the analysis of productivity. Theoretical studies have explored the extent to which different payment schemes can efficiently elicit effort from workers. Some have concluded that incentive problems make it more efficient to maintain a hierarchical firm in which the owner is responsible for monitoring labor. "However, shirking by workers is never reported as a concern in studies of real-world PCs; observers report that workers monitor each other successfully in cooperative organizations." [1302–1303] The absence of workplace hierarchy, in fact, may allow greater productivity through cooperative problem-solving and informal social pressure supporting high levels of effort. One feature of many PCs, profit sharing, has been identified as a factor contributing to productivity increases in conventional firms.

Empirical studies have examined the relationship between productivity and worker participation. Most studies are restricted to PCs alone, due to data limitations. Within the world of PCs, there are quantifiable variations in the extent of worker decision making, profit sharing, and collective ownership. The clearest empirical result is that these variables, as a group, have a positive effect on productivity. The effects of the individual variables differ from one study or country to another. Profit sharing appears to have the strongest effect on productivity, especially in French and Italian PCs.

In contrast, studies that compare PCs and CFs, or use mixed samples, often find no significant productivity gains from cooperative organization. There are several difficulties in interpreting this finding. Among U.S. plywood firms, the most profitable PCs have converted to conventional ownership to allow worker-owners to sell their shares on the market (because these shares had become unaffordable for new workers). If such conversions of the most profitable PCs are common, the productivity of surviving PCs will be biased downward. Moreover, comparative studies often use a simple dummy variable to indicate PC status, missing the potentially crucial variation among PCs in the extent of worker participation.

Lacking a clear theory, it is difficult to identify causality in the relationship between productivity and participation. For example, greater reliance on profit-sharing plans may increase productivity—or greater productivity may mean that there are more profits to share. Better theories and better comparative data sets are both badly needed.

Investment and Finance

Do PCs underinvest, compared to CFs? If (as is usually the case) worker-owners do not receive the full market value of their shares of the company when they leave, they have an incentive to prefer immediate payout of dividends over reinvestment of profits in long-lived capital goods. The worker is sure of receiving the profits from reinvestment only for as long as he or she remains at the firm, and cannot capture the expected value of future profits on departure. So if there is a chance of leaving before an investment has paid for itself, then the worker is better off receiving dividends that can be invested elsewhere.

In theory, such worker-owners might prefer external financing of the optimal level of investment, combined with high payout of internally generated funds as dividends. However, there often are limits on the availability of external financing for PCs. Outside investors typically have less control over management in a PC than in a CF, and may demand increased risk premiums, or refuse to lend at all.

Some theories of PC investment decisions imply that PCs will operate under conditions of increasing returns to scale—likely a sign of inefficiency, since they could lower average costs by expanding. However, empirical tests in several countries fail to support the idea that PCs exhibit increasing returns to scale in practice. Simpler data comparisons provide mixed support for the hypothesis of underinvestment by PCs. While U.S. plywood PCs, and Italian and Danish PCs, have lower capital-to-labor ratios than comparable CFs, the reverse is true for Swedish PCs. In the Mondragon PCs, capital-to-labor ratios are not lower, and are rising faster, than in comparable Spanish industrial firms. Here the existence of a strong cooperative bank, as part of the Mondragon group, may make a difference.

Formation and Survival

The final question is the most important, and the hardest to answer: Why are there so few PCs in industrial market economies? This involves both the formation and the survival of PCs. Some PCs are formed to rescue failing CFs, but most are created from scratch, based on preferences for democratic decision making and/or concerns for employment security.

The business cycle has contradictory effects on PC formation. In periods of expansion workers have greater assets to use in business formation, and may be less risk-averse and more interested in improved or participatory working conditions. However, in recessions the formation of PCs may be an appealing alternative to unemployment or relocation in search of jobs. Empirically, there is no significant relationship between the unemployment rate and the rate of PC formation, but there are waves of PC formation that are somewhat longer than the business cycle.

PCs disappear either through failure or through conversion into CFs. The degree of institutional support is crucial—Mondragon PCs have almost never failed. Several studies find that PCs have better survival rates than comparable CFs, with some tendency for PCs to concentrate in unusually cyclical industries where protection against employment fluctuations is an important goal. Case studies suggest that there have been waves of conversions of U.S. PCs into CFs, but little is known about the causes of such conversions.

"One explanation for the almost-complete mismatch between theory and empirics in this area is that the factors influencing the formation and survival of PCs cannot be separated from the topics in the preceding three sections." [1315] The authors' best guess, which needs to be confirmed through further study, is that

> [T]he explanation of the relative scarcity of PCs lies in the nexus between decision making and financial support. Worker control requires (at least partial) worker ownership for incentive reasons, but the latter conflicts with the worker's desire to hold a relatively low-risk, diversified portfolio. External fi-

nanciers with no direct control of company governance will not commit significant funds without receiving a substantial premium to reflect the risk involved. Hence, worker-controlled PCs have difficulty finding internal sources and competing with CFs for investment funds. [1316]

Summary of

Labor-Managed Cooperatives and Private Firms in North Central Italy: An Empirical Comparison

by Will Bartlett, John Cable, Saul Estrin,
Derek C. Jones, and Stephen C. Smith

[Published in *Industrial and Labor Relations Review* 46, 1 (1992), 103–118.]

There has been extensive theoretical discussion of the expected performance of private businesses that are owned and managed by their workers. At the same time, there have been many empirical analyses, usually case studies, of cooperative enterprises in practice. This article attempts to bridge the gap between the two bodies of literature, first reviewing the theoretical discussion and then testing it against a survey of the actual comparative performance of worker co-ops and traditional companies in two regions of Italy in 1986/87.

Predictions from Theory

The academic literature begins with the assumption that worker-owned enterprises will attempt to maximize average earnings per worker, rather than conventional profit maximization. As a result, the theory predicts that cooperatives will tend to decrease employment following an upward demand shift, both in the short-run and possibly in the long-run. On the other hand, some authors argue that co-ops tend to have ties to the local labor market and will thus seek to maximize employment as well as income per employed worker.

Regarding wages, some have argued that co-ops will pay higher wages than private companies whenever profits are high, since worker-owners will be quick to reward themselves. However, especially in young co-ops, worker-owners may also choose to limit wages in the short-term in order to invest for future growth. Co-ops may also choose to ensure that employment is stable by sacrificing current income to prevent layoffs.

Economic theory seems to suggest that how many hours of work each worker chooses to do should depend on the reward systems within the cooperative. If all workers share equally in the enterprise profits, then average hours worked will be relatively low because of the "free rider" problem—everyone gets the benefits of extra work by any individual.

Some writers argue that co-ops that finance their investment with internal funds will be undercapitalized, for two reasons. First, workers will only want to tie up their capital internally for as long as they expect to be with the co-op. Second, workers will not want to invest if they can get a higher rate of return through alternative investments.

Authors disagree over the level of efficiency of worker co-ops versus traditional companies. Some believe they will be less efficient because there is no one with an incentive to monitor work performance. Others argue that employee participation can reduce socially wasteful conflict in the workplace through reduced supervision costs and higher levels of worker commitment, leading to higher productivity. In addition, co-ops may also yield gains in other social objectives, such as work satisfaction for their employees and responsibility to their communities in terms of social and environmental impacts.

Characteristics of the Sample Firms

Worker co-ops are spread throughout Italy, both geographically and across industries. For this study, the geographic area was limited to two regions, Emilia-Romagna and Tuscany, which between them have 14 percent of the nation's co-ops. The sample was limited to companies involved in light manufacturing, and included 49 cooperative and 35 private firms. Companies were selected by matching co-op and private firm characteristics in terms of size and sector (mainly metalworking, clothing, and woodworking). Co-ops averaged 92 employees each, private firms 118 employees.

Among the co-ops there were 18 firms in metalworking, 11 in textiles and clothing, 13 in woodworking, and 7 in other fields. About two-thirds of the co-ops had been founded from scratch, with the remainder formed from failed private companies. The co-ops formed from scratch tended to be older and bigger, and paid slightly higher wages, than those that were conversions.

Arrangements for members' investment and repayment differed from one co-op to another. However, contrary to the expectations in some of the theoretical literature, very little of the profits were paid out as dividends (only 7 percent on average in Tuscany, and 5 percent in Emilia-Romagna). Most profits were reinvested, perhaps in part because dividends are taxed more heavily than reinvested profits.

One of the clearest contrasts between the co-ops and the profit-making firms is in their customer base. The co-ops had a much higher share of their sales going to local governments. Meanwhile, the privates were far more export-oriented, selling about 40 percent of their output outside of Italy, compared to 16 percent for the co-ops.

Empirical Findings

The survey included both a questionnaire, completed during a face-to-face interview at each firm, and collection of economic and financial data from company records for the prior five years (1981–1985). In the survey, companies reported on their own perceived objectives. They were asked to rate the importance of increased sales, creating jobs, and increased incomes (profits) on a scale of one to five, with one being "not important" and five "very important." The mean scores showed no significant differences between the co-ops and private firms in their rankings of sales (4.5 for both groups) and job creation (3.2 for both). Only on increasing incomes was there a statistically significant difference, with rankings of 3.7 for co-ops and 4.2 for privates.

Differences in wages and salaries between the two types of firms were not statistically significant for unskilled and skilled workers, nor for supervisors. Most firms operated in fairly competitive markets, so that hypotheses about the distribution of excess profits in co-ops were not relevant to this study. Both co-ops and private firms tended to follow the well-established union wage rates for their industries. Salary differences for white-collar workers were slightly significant, averaging 14 percent higher in the private firms. However, the salary differences for managers were large and significant, averaging 60 percent higher in private enterprises. Overall hourly labor costs did not differ significantly between the two groups.

Employment was slightly more stable in the co-ops. This was shown both by usage of the government employment insurance system, which was lower for co-ops, and by variation in actual employment levels over time. From 1981 through 1985, employment in the co-ops fell by about 7 percent while dropping by 20 percent in the private firms. The survey provided no support for the theoretical hypothesis that due to the "free rider" problem, levels of work effort might be lower in co-ops; instead, co-op workers averaged 4 percent more hours than those in private firms.

The labor force structure of the two groups differed in significant ways. The proportions of men and women were similar on both, as was the average length of tenure with the firm. But there was a substantially higher proportion of unskilled workers in the co-ops, and a much lower percentage of managers (3.9 percent for co-ops and 8.9 percent for private firms).

Surprisingly in terms of theory, co-ops and privates had similar attitudes toward investment criteria. Just over half of both used a simple "payback period" as the criterion for evaluating investments and used approximately the same number of years for payback (4.5 years). The two types also did not differ significantly in their sources of finance, with each relying on internal sources for about half total funding. Balance sheet data does show a substantially higher level of fixed assets per employee for privates than co-ops.

Several measures of productivity showed results greatly favoring the co-ops. The ratio of value added per employee and value added per hour were both about one-third higher in the co-ops; the ratio of value added to fixed assets was more than 50 percent higher in the co-ops. The higher labor productivity did not result in the payment of higher wages, but may have benefited the worker-owners through payment of dividends and interest on loans made by members to the co-ops.

Industrial relations measures favored the co-ops, which had no strike activity, compared to 40 percent of the private firms, which experienced strikes during the five years. Co-op quit rates were significantly lower, and absenteeism was only half as high, as in the private firms. Co-ops also tended to provide more training opportunities, with the proportion of workers in training courses twice that in the privates (2.7 percent versus 1.1 percent). Private firms took no advantage of training opportunities offered by local governments and the European Community, while 1.2 percent of co-op workers were involved in such programs.

In summary, the co-ops in this study, compared to private firms, provided more tranquil labor relations, with no strikes, low quit rates, and fewer and lower-paid managers. The co-ops offered greater employment stability, paid comparable wages, and achieved higher productivity despite lower capital-labor ratios. These findings confirm some theoretical predictions, while contradicting others. Of course, they remain somewhat speculative since they are based on a single study.

Summary of

Financial Markets and the Political Structure of the Enterprise

by Herbert Gintis

[Published in *Journal of Economic Behavior and Organization* 11 (May 1989), 311–322.]

Why in a democratic society are so few firms structured along democratic principles? A good part of the answer relates to differential access to credit and capital markets and the divergent interests of workers and outside stockholders with respect to risk. (Mathematical proofs of these propositions are appended to the original article.)

Financial Markets and Firm Structure

Most economic activity takes place in firms in which management is accountable to outside creditors and stockholders, not to those engaged in the firm's day-to-day activities (the firm's employees, called "members" here to emphasize the potential for democratic governance). Conventional wisdom holds that the hierarchical division of labor in most firms is not compatible with participatory decision making, and that democratic firms cannot control opportunistic behavior. However, this confuses the organization of the firm, which incorporates efficiency goals, with its political structure, which addresses accountability. Even in a firm in which authority resides with the members, those members can delegate authority to management in the interests of efficient operation. Conversely, since factor markets are imperfect, conventional firms are as likely to misallocate resources as democratic ones.

Worker-*owned* firms tend to be scarce because of the unique problems of obtaining adequate financing. Capital markets diversify risk, whereas financing through members' equity concentrates risk—both their jobs and their savings become dependent on the same enterprise. Workers are not generally wealthy and find it difficult to raise sufficient equity by themselves. Furthermore, when they go to borrow, their lack of equity means they are turned down for loans or must pay relatively higher interest rates for borrowed funds. However, full worker ownership is not necessarily the only path to economic democracy. Even a firm that is financed through external equity and credit markets can be run in a democratic fashion, that is, "accountable to its members according to some reasonable notion of political representation," [311] and should, in theory, be able to attract capital in financial markets if it is operated in a competitive fashion.

In reality, even with an efficient management structure, a democratic firm will lack access to equity markets on a par with conventional firms. Potential stockholders, who can diversify risks through equity markets, usually prefer relatively high levels of risk at any one firm in hopes of large returns. Employees, on the other hand, who are more concerned with keeping their jobs, would be less willing to make risky decisions if the decisions were in their hands. Since risk behavior is difficult to observe and enforce, stockholders would have to offer costly incentives to induce levels of risk acceptable to them. In a firm with a democratic decision-making structure, these inducements would have to be offered to the majority of members, but in a managerially controlled firm inducements can be limited to only a few managers.

If an economy that can foster rapid innovation—thereby engendering more risk—is dynamically superior to more conservative regimes, then the challenge is to devise mechanisms that can preserve competitive financial markets without reinforcing antidemocratic biases.

Modeling Risk Behavior

To focus on the availability of equity, certain assumptions are made—namely, that debt levels, product and factor prices, and production possibilities are the same for all firms. Members remain employed unless the firm fails. If the firm fails, wages will be paid up-to-date but workers will be unemployed thereafter. Creditors will receive the liquidation value of the firm. In the case of success, stockholders are the net benefactors. In this model, the only choice variable is the level of risk, with the implication that higher risks yield higher returns to investors. For workers, employment has a present value and job loss has a cost. These can be evaluated for various levels of risk. Even if workers have assets, unemployment insurance, or alternative employment, job loss has a positive cost. Several propositions follow from these assumptions.

1. If members prefer to minimize the risk of bankruptcy, but stockholders prefer higher levels of risk, outside stockholders will be better off if members also own stock.

2. The level of risk chosen rises with the degree of member ownership. A decline in the cost of job loss means that workers can tolerate higher risk and outside stockholders can tolerate more democracy in the firm.

3. Under some circumstances it is in the stockholders' interest to give stock to firm members, in order to make them share the stockholders' attitudes toward risk. The higher the cost of job loss, the greater the stock transfer that is required to achieve any given change in firm members' preferred risk levels. This explains one reason why owners prefer hierarchical management: It is obviously cheaper to give stock to a few top managers, rather than to a majority of employees. In the hierarchical firm, the top managers are the only firm members whose risk preferences matter.

Conclusion

"Our analysis may strike the reader as a mere gloss on the venerable argument that the democratic firm allocates risk inefficiently because it does not maximize profits, and is shunned by competitive financial markets because it is inefficient." [317] However, equity markets are imperfect even with respect to traditional firms. This analysis suggests that firm members and owners have different interests in the choice of risk, and that owners can induce desired risk behavior more effectively through incentives to a few managers than through a wide distribution of incentives to members.

A democratic society presumably wants to expand democratic participation in the economy if that does not conflict with standards of liberty, efficiency, innovation, and growth. However, simply guaranteeing financing to circumvent competition and increase performance is not being advocated here. Indeed, policy makers are no better at assessing a firm's risk behavior than stockholders. A strategy of taxes, subsidies, and regulations that offset the advantage of traditional firms also reduce overall risk-taking in the productive sectors of the economy. This may result in suboptimal levels of innovation—even more so for democratic firms. Thus the most successful policies may be those that repair failures in labor and capital markets.

In the labor market, work intensity and quality cannot be contractually enforced. This leads to unemployed labor and excessive job loss even in equilibrium, making democratic firms even more conservative toward risk. The market fails to provide insurance against job loss if workers' performance cannot be controlled or if job loss is not a threat. This leaves insurers to face a moral hazard, since less-employable workers are more likely to seek insurance. Public policy can act in favor of tight labor markets, unemployment compensation, and retraining in a way that would render the democratic enterprise competitive and socially efficient.

In capital markets, the risk behavior of financial resource managers cannot be contractually specified, so both capital and credit are rationed according to access to equity. This is a vicious cycle since it is difficult for many individuals with insufficient equity to advance without borrowing first. Since ownership sharing improves the position of firm members relative to passive investors and creditors and also raises the firms' optimal risk level, public policy should provide a source of credit to members of democratic firms.

PART VII

Difference and Diversity in the Workplace

Overview Essay

by Laurie Dougherty

Work is an important part of personal identity. For many it offers an opportunity to express talent or fulfill the need for achievement. Even where the work itself is not intrinsically interesting or rewarding, the ability to earn a livelihood contributes to one's independence and self-esteem. As William Julius Wilson points out in his recent book *When Work Disappears,* work can also have an effect on group identity, exerting a collective sense of fulfillment, achievement, or purpose, while the lack of work, when widespread, leads to disorganization and deterioration of community institutions.[1]

Conversely, identity has a powerful influence on the workplace. The role of group identity, particularly race, gender, and ethnicity, is a vital interest for many researchers. The summaries in Part VII reflect that interest. Because the world of paid employment has been dominated and defined by men, and in most developed countries by white men, the efforts of women and minorities to prosper in that world are marked by a consciousness of difference. All too often difference is met with prejudice, discrimination, and hostility. But difference can add diversity, creating a more textured workplace culture and introducing fresh points of view.

During the nineteenth century biological explanations of differences between human beings held sway, based on attempts to link essential differences of intelligence or character to superficial differences in skin color or other aspects of physical appearance. These attempts have been discredited and today we look to historical factors for understanding. While it is true that one is born a man or a woman into a particular racial or ethnic group (or mixture of racial/ethnic groups), the meaning attached to race, gender, or ethnicity is an artifact of culture, tradition, and social, economic, and political interaction. Work is one of the major building blocks in the construction of difference.

Racial Interactions: Identity, Ideology, and Economics

Michael Omi and Howard Winant distinguish between racial awareness, formed in each historical period through interaction with "structural and cultural dimensions" of the larger society, and racism that offers ideological support for the dominance of one group over another. They describe early American history, from the European conquest through the era of slavery, as a "racial dictatorship" in which "most nonwhites were firmly eliminated from the sphere of politics."[2]

Three consequences followed from the imposition of racial dictatorship: American identity was defined as white; the color line became the fundamental division in the United States; and opposition and resistance infused the consciousness of nonwhites. "The dictatorship elaborated, articulated, and drove racial divisions not only through institutions, but also through psyches, extending up to our own time the racial obsessions of the conquest and slavery periods."[3]

As W.E.B. Du Bois pointed out, even white people with little income or status share in "a public and psychological wage" that improves both the self-esteem and the social treatment of whites as compared to blacks.[4] David Roediger takes up this theme in *The Wages of Whiteness*. As wage labor became more prominent throughout the nineteenth century, workers of European descent first identified themselves as free laborers and not slaves, a distinction that transformed into an identification as white workers and not black.[5]

In *The Declining Significance of Race*[6] William Julius Wilson proposed that stages in race relations in the United States were associated with different economic regimes. During the time of slavery, plantation owners practiced a paternalistic form of racial oppression. The Civil War was followed by a brief period of democratization in race relations; but with the end of Reconstruction, black people's attempts to achieve economic and political parity with whites were met with Ku Klux Klan violence and state-imposed segregation in the South. In the North race relations were more complex, with competition for jobs a key element in racial conflict. White workers often used emerging forms of labor organization to exclude blacks, while employers often used black workers as strikebreakers. Wilson argues that this divergence of interest between labor and management prevented a strong unified movement against blacks from coalescing in the North.

As more black workers moved into industry in the period between the two world wars, unions began to include them. The Congress of Industrial Organizations (CIO), in paticular, adopted an inclusive approach to labor organization, in contrast to the exclusionary craft-based approach of the American Federation of Labor (AFL). During the post-World War II economic boom, black workers achieved a substantial presence in unionized manufacturing employment. With the Civil Rights movement of the 1950s and 1960s, which broke the grip of legalized segregation, more and more African-Americans went to college and moved into the expanding white-collar labor market. Wilson goes on to say that with the entry of many blacks into these forms of employment, and the subsequent growth of the black middle class, racial distinctions lessened in importance and class distinctions became more prominent as determinants of life chances for black people. Poor and uneducated blacks were increasingly marginalized. Their situation deteriorated to the point that Wilson called them an underclass, isolated from the general prosperity of the postwar United States and from the rising fortunes of the expanding black middle class.

Mobility

Still, for African-Americans in the middle class the path is not smooth. As Jennifer Hochschild points out in her 1995 book, *Facing Up to the American Dream*,[7] the movement of black Americans into the middle class coincided with a change in upward mobility trends beginning in the 1970s. Overall, incomes began to polarize: "More middle-class Americans fell into poverty and fewer poor people rose after 1980 but . . . more middle-class Americans became rich and fewer rich fell into the middle class after 1980 than before." Faced with increasing economic insecurity at the moment of their own rising aspirations, many middle-class African-Americans became disillusioned with the American Dream, which, as Hochschild formulates it, hinges on success. Success is supposed to be within reach of everyone, resulting from individual actions and abilities and tightly bound with virtue and self-image. Yet middle-class black Americans are acutely aware that success often hinges on economic and political forces beyond their control.

In "The Making of the Black Middle Class"[8] Sharon Collins maintained that federal government initiatives "stimulated and enforced" the growth of the black middle class, from Franklin D. Roosevelt's executive order mandating fair employment in civil service, to the 1964 Civil Rights Act, the establishment of the Equal Employment Opportunity Commission, and provisions for affirmative action and minority set-asides. In the private sector, according to Collins, employers often met the expectations of equal opportunity by hiring minorities into human resources or EEO compliance departments.

In an article summarized in Part VII, Collins reported on a series of interviews with African-American executives in Chicago in the mid-1980s, finding that this labor market niche has the paradoxical quality of limiting mobility for minority group members while purporting to enhance the position of minorities within corporations. Many of her interviewees occupied positions directed toward improving corporate relationships (or the corporate image) in minority communities. However, these positions, such as Equal Opportunity Officer, or

Community Relations Director, while commanding impressive titles and perhaps even impressive compensation, often served as a sidetrack or even a dead end to the career paths of the men and women who held them. These jobs were off the beaten path to the centers of corporate power. Their occupants tended to lose out on promotions and to underdevelop the skills and internal networks needed to move into the revenue producing positions that led to the top.

The results of Collins' interviews resonate with the results of a detailed econometric study by John Bound and Richard Freeman, also summarized here. They analyzed data on young men (since their situations reflect current labor market conditions, not the results of seniority or past experience). A decade of rapid labor market gains by African-American men reached a peak in the mid-1970s, with a few years of approximate racial equality both among young male college graduates nationwide and among young men in the Midwest regardless of education. The rapid growth in the proportion of African-Americans graduating from college may have exceeded the growth in demand for their labor.[9] Indeed, most young male college graduates, black and white, worked in education and public administration in the 1970s. These jobs were hard hit by public sector cutbacks in the 1980s and 1990s. While such jobs are still important, a growing proportion of male college graduates work in the private sector, where racial inequality is more pronounced.

The problems of mobility for black men are not confined to executives. For young black men without a college education, the notable labor market gains in the Midwest were linked to the fortunes of heavy industry, which went into decline after the 1970s. In the 1970s, 40 percent of young black men in the region worked in the heavily unionized durable goods manufacturing sector, but only 12 percent did so in 1989.

If manufacturing and the public sector were no longer providing opportunities for young black entrants to the labor force, Chris Tilly and Philip Moss ask if the evolving labor market tends to disadvantage young black men. Their interviews with employers in several industries, indicate that the demand for "soft skills" is increasing. Soft skills fall into two general categories. The first is similar to Arlie Russell Hochschild's concept of emotion work, described below. It includes the relational skills necessary for working with customers, coworkers, and supervisors. Some managers associated relational skills with the ability to learn and acquire "hard skills" (such as basic math and language and technical skills). The second category of soft skills is motivational, involving characteristics such as attitude or dependability.

The more importance managers attributed to these skills, the more they (including some black managers) were likely to look on young black men with disfavor. Some of these impressions are based on a realistic appraisal of black men who "act tough," but some of the impressions reflect stereotypes gathered from the media or cultural misunderstandings based in their own experience. While some respondents attributed problems to innate failings of black men, others took responsibility for a mutual breakdown of communications or felt that the desirable characteristics could be taught or fostered by appropriate training and management practices. Moss and Tilly conclude that public and private sector policies that encourage appreciation for diversity and training in appropriate workplace behavior can reduce the disadvantages young black men face in today's labor market.

However, code-switching, the process of switching back and forth between two styles of language and behavior, may be difficult for some to master. As Wilson points out, in the chapter of his most recent book summarized in Part IX, years of disinvestment in inner-city communities have produced a culture of alienation from, and often hostility to, the norms and practices of white society, including the idiom and disciplines of the workplace. Even those who do not internalize these attitudes and want to participate in the wider society may display "ghetto-related behavior" in order to fit in. To succeed at work and survive at home, young African-Americans must often become bicultural.

The challenge of bicultural fluency is not only a matter of switching on and off the behavior and argot of street kids. Ella Louise Bell reported on "The Bicultural Life Experience of Career-Oriented Black Women,"[10] based on interviews with highly motivated black women. She found two basic patterns: "Assimilation requires blacks to conform to the traditions, values, and norms of the dominant white culture. . . . Compartmentalization, the alternate behavioral response, occurs when blacks establish rigid boundaries between the white and black life contexts." [462] Many respondents valued both parts of the bicultural experience, but many also experienced stress, social marginality, and identity crises, including conflicts over core values, affiliations, and life roles.

Gender Roles in the Workplace

Women in general experience conflicts over values, affiliations, and roles when they enter the workplace. Many of these conflicts are involved with the relationship between women's traditional role in the home and women's involvement in market-based work. Of course it is impossible to avoid the biological reality that women bear and nurse children. However, many feminists argue that the fact that women all too often are forced into dependency and denied a role in public life is not a matter of biology, but of the historical playing out of a patriarchal agenda.

Alison Jaggar, in *Feminist Politics and Human Nature*,[11] links several ways that women struggle for liberation to differing visions of human nature. Her taxonomy may be debatable, but her insights are interesting. According to Jaggar, liberal feminists take their cue from the Enlightenment concept of a dualism between the rational activity of the mind and the irrational activity of the

body. Jaggar maintains that the goal of liberal feminists is to overcome the unfair projection of the irrational onto women, thereby overcoming the privileged
position of men in society. Their strategies tend to focus on gaining access and
equality for women in arenas of public life such as business and politics. Other
feminist schools of thought, according to Jaggar, reject Enlightenment dualism
and are more willing to engage intellectually with the biological and social
processes for the reproduction of human life and society. Radical feminists focus
on the patriarchal control of women. Marxist feminists assume the standpoint
of the working class and hope for the victory of the working class over the bour-
geosie to dissolve all forms of oppression, including the traditional patriarchal
division of labor between men and women. Socialist feminists, with whom Jaggar herself most closely identifies, hold that the standpoint of women (which includes both commonalities and differences in experience) is necessary to a fully
adequate theory of human nature—one that excavates the reality obscured by
male-dominated worldview and that offers a more comprehensive analysis of a
gendered human society. The issue of what happens to the care of home and
family when women move into the marketplace is explored further in Part VII
of this volume.

Women's experience of gender roles is not a monolithic one, however.
Wealthier women may employ less privileged women for household chores and
even for nursing their children or caring for sick or elderly dependents.[12] These
working women, in turn, must make other arrangements for their children. In
a rural subsistence economy, women may produce goods for local markets and
make substantial contributions to household production of food, fuel, and
clothing as well as doing domestic chores and caring for children. Depending
on the cultural context, this may mark a dual burden for women with no gain
in status, or it may win for women a share in household or community power.[13]

Niches

Although labor markets of the modern industrial era bear little resemblance to
earlier economic systems, differences along racial, ethnic, and gender lines persist. The summaries in Part VII explore some of the dimensions of race, gender,
and ethnicity as they are related to the changing nature of work. One of the key
points to be examined is the disproportionate concentration of men or women
or members of particular racial or ethnic groups in certain job categories. The
idea of labor market queues, originally proposed by Lester Thurow,[14] offers a
model of how employers rank the desirability of prospective employees using
group identity as a factor of evaluation.

Both employers and applicants have queues, or ranking systems, for their
preferences. Employers rank candidates, while candidates rank occupations—
and these queues interact. Labor market queues have three characteristics:

order, size of the relevant pool of jobs or applicants, and intensity. An employer with an intense preference for white men for a particular job category will choose white men until the pool is exhausted even when there are better qualified women or minorities. If the pool of preferred candidates is smaller than the number of jobs that need filling, then members of other groups will have a chance of getting hired. If the intensity of preference based on group identity characteristics is low, then any qualified candidates will have a good chance of getting hired.

In an article summarized in Part VII, Barbara Reskin and Patricia Roos apply the concept of queuing to gender in the labor market. A number of factors can influence employer preferences for men or women, including customary notions about the appropriateness of certain jobs for men or for women, stereotypes about the fitness of men or women for certain types of jobs, or perceptions of the productivity of a group's members based on experience with or hearsay about individuals in that group (statistical discrimination). Some employers may be reluctant to antagonize male employees by introducing women into the workplace.

Since the 1970s, many of these obstacles to the employment of women have broken down and women have entered many occupations in large numbers. Factors such as equal opportunity laws, the rapid growth of the service sector, and the emergence of managers with more enlightened attitudes changed the order, shape, and intensity of gender queues. The proportion of women in many occupations expanded rapidly. In a few cases, the occupation shifted from mostly male to mostly female.

Often this shift reflected interaction with the job queues formed by men and women. Some occupations became less desirable to men, either because new opportunities were opening up, or because changes in technology or other conditions of work made particular occupations less desirable to men. For women, though, the niches that men abandoned often represented a better opportunity.

Although she does not make particular reference to queuing, Arlie Russell Hochschild, in a chapter from her book *The Managed Heart*, summarized here, describes the process by which women more often than men are slotted into workplace roles where "emotion work" is a major occupational characteristic. Hochschild defines emotion work as the work of producing a particular emotional state, such as gratitude or fear, in a customer, client, or coworker. Flight attendants, for example, attempt to produce gratitude among passengers, while bill collectors produce fear among delinquent debtors. There is a tendency for women to be more prominent among flight attendants and men to be bill collectors, since women are considered to be more nurturing and men to be more authoritative. In general, however, women are considered to be both more emotional than men and better able to manage their own emotions and to manipulate the emotions of others. According to Hochschild, about half of the jobs that women do in the United States and about a quarter of the jobs that men do involve emotion work.

In another summarized article, Marilyn Power and Sam Rosenberg point out that young women often begin their work lives in service sector jobs that are poorly paid, but which offer easy entry and flexible hours. However, white women are much more likely than black women to move into occupations with better earnings potential. Following a cohort of women service workers 18 to 28 years old in 1972 interviewed by the national Longitudinal Survey of Young Women, the authors found that by 1988, 74 percent of white women had moved into other categories of employment, but only 47 percent of black women had done so.

Overall statistics from census data (not just those women who entered service sector jobs at an early age) show the proportion of black women in service work dropped from 60 percent in 1960 to 26 percent in 1994. In 1960 only 20 percent of white women workers were in the service sector, dropping to 17 percent by 1994. However, few women of either race moved into highly paid male-dominated occupations.

Women in the Global Workforce

In 1970, Esther Boserup noted that the economic role of women is often marginalized during the early years of industrial development as production moves out of home and community and into factories. After a period of adjustment, women's participation in the industrial labor force will begin to rise, tracing a U-shaped pattern over time.[15] According to Nilüfer Çagatay and Sule Özler, in an article summarized in Part VII, the imposition of structural adjustment policies by global financial institutions to manage debt reduction in many developing countries has altered this pattern, drawing women into the industrial workforce earlier in the development process. On the one hand, these policies encourage export-oriented production as a way to acquire foreign currency for debt repayment. The export sector employs women disproportionately for the hand-assembly of goods like small household appliances, electronic components, toys, and garments. On the other hand, structural adjustment often demands austerity in government programs, resulting in employment instability and higher prices for essential goods and services. Under these conditions women may need paid employment to supplement or stabilize family incomes.

The particular choices women make are linked to large-scale forces in the global economy. Ching Kwan Lee draws on both feminist analysis and labor process theory to explore differences in management practices in two factories, one in Hong Kong and one in Shenzhen in the People's Republic of China. These factories are in the same company, both employ women production workers to perform similar work, and some managers travel frequently between them. Yet control over production is different in each plant. Ching attributes this to differences in the intersection of gender and power in each plant.

In Shenzhen, young women seek opportunity in rapidly industrializing urban centers, but employment depends on maintaining connection to networks rooted in their home communities. Within the Shenzhen factory in this case study, discipline is rigidly applied and these networks serve as a mechanism of control. Young women remain in a similar relationship to their elders, particularly male elders, as they would at home. In the Hong Kong factory, on the other hand, older, generally married women work in a less rigid environment. Manufacturing is declining in importance and workers are moving to more promising sectors. However, for these women it remains a congenial niche, and their family responsibilities are accommodated within reason as an inducement to stay.

Humor reinforces labor and gender relationships. In Hong Kong, teasing by supervisors and among the women themselves reinforces their matronly status. This status accommodated and humored by supervisors and a limited amount of self-management is allowed. The women workers, whose primary identification is with their family role, feel sorry for male supervisors whose identity and livelihood is tied up with a dying industry. In Shenzhen, teasing, like other ways of relating at work, such as sharing breaks, tends to take place among people from the same village or region, reinforcing the networks that structure the expanding labor market. Conditions in the two labor markets and traditional attitudes toward women, as matrons or as maidens, influence the organization of work at the shop floor level.

The summary by Saskia Sassen-Koob focuses on the relationship between labor market niches and patterns of female migration. Many women migrate to accompany or follow husbands who move in search of work. However, women themselves are increasingly being recruited into the labor force in both developing and developed countries, so that distinct patterns of female migration are discernible. The growing integration of the economy on a global basis encourages a series of migrations on the part of women from industrializing countries. The growth of international investment in export platforms in developing countries draws young women from rural areas into export manufacturing jobs in urban industrial centers. With this emigration and a shift from subsistence to export agriculture, the social and economic structure of rural communities has been disrupted.

Although it appears paradoxical, the same countries experiencing an expansion in employment are also experiencing emigration to developed countries, in particular to the United States. Although only a small percentage of women work in the export manufacturing sector, a point made by Lourdes Benería in an article summarized in Part III, the export sector is influential in generating migration patterns in developing countries.

There is high turnover in export manufacturing due to poor working conditions and to employers' preference for young women as employees. Older workers are let go, and there is a continual drawing in of new workers. High employment and high unemployment coexist. The movement of young women into the cities in search of employment has a disruptive effect on their home villages, encouraging more young men to migrate and making the rural areas less likely to draw women back. Although Sassen-Koob does not devote much space to agriculture, in the early part of this article she seems to give equal conceptual weight to export agriculture as a disruptive element on traditional patterns of work, also setting migration in motion, particularly of men. Finally, the presence of multinationals brings Western material culture into people's field of vision, acting as an inducement to emigration. Change in the countryside and turnover in the cities is a push factor to migration within developing countries. The foreign presence is a pull factor to immigration into developed countries. Within developed countries themselves, the service economy has produced a bifurcated labor market able to absorb immigrant workers: A highly paid professional and technical workforce demands specialty goods and services produced by low-wage service workers.

Conclusion

The image of the worker as "the man in the gray flannel suit" or the hard-hat construction worker, an image that is essentially male and white, is giving way to the reality that men and women of all races and nationalities perform work that is productive and necessary. In trying to understand which economic factors fulfill human needs and which ones threaten them, one of the greatest challenges is to balance respect for diversity against the danger of discrimination based on differences (whether real or perceived). Striking this balance has important implications for how effectively and productively we make use of our human resources. It also has important implications for the extent to which people from all parts of our diverse population are able to make use of their talents and fulfill their aspirations. As work changes, so do we.

Notes

1. William Julius Wilson, *When Work Disappears* (New York: Alfred A. Knopf, 1997). A chapter from this book is summarized in this volume in Part IX.
2. Michael Omi and Howard Winant, *Racial Formation in the United States: From the 1960s to the 1990s.* (New York: Routledge, 1994).
3. Ibid., 66.
4. See the discussion of W.E.B. Du Bois, *Black Reconstruction in the United States,*

1860–1880, in David Roediger, *The Wages of Whiteness: Race and the Making of the American Working Class* (London: Verso, 1991).

5. Roediger, note 4 above, Chapter 3.

6. William Julius Wilson, *The Declining Significance of Race—Blacks and Changing American Institutions* (Chicago: University of Chicago Press, 1980).

7. Jennifer Hochschild, *Facing Up to the American Dream—Race, Class and the Soul of the Nation* Princeton, NJ: Princeton University Press, 1995).

8. Sharon M. Collins, "The Making of the Black Middle Class," Social Problems 30, 4 (April 1983), 369–382.

9. This would suggest the existence of a labor market queue, as described later in this essay, for educated black men. Black women who graduated from college continued to find jobs and experience rising incomes.

10. Ella Louise Bell, "The Bicultural Life Experience of Career-Oriented Black Women," *Journal of Organizational Behavior* 11, 6 (November 1990), 459–477.

11. Alison M. Jaggar, *Feminist Politics and Human Nature* (Savage, MD: Roman & Littlefield Publishers, Inc., 1988).

12. See Alan R. Meyers, "Global Development and Personal Dependency: The High Cost of Doing Well," *World Development* 19, 1 (January 1991), 45–54 for a discussion of the employment of immigrant women from developing countries to care for elderly and disabled dependents in developed countries.

13. See Teresa L. Amott and Julie A. Matthaei, *Race, Gender and Work* (Boston: South End Press, 1991), Chapters 1 and 2.

14. Lester Thurow, *Poverty and Discrimination* (Washington, D.C.; Brookings Institution, 1969). Cited in Reskin and Roos.

15. Esther Boserup, *Women's Role in Economic Development* (New York: St. Martin's Press, 1970). Cited in Çagatay and Özler.

Summary of

Queuing and Changing Occupational Composition

by Barbara F. Reskin and Patricia A. Roos

[Published in *Job Queues, Gender Queues—Explaining Women's Inroads into Male Occupations,* eds. Barbara F. Reskin and Patricia A. Roos (Philadelphia: Temple University Press), 29–68.]

Since 1970 a number of occupations have shifted in gender composition, in some cases going from an almost all male to an almost all female workforce. A dual queuing process effectively models labor market dynamics. "Job queues and labor queues govern labor market outcomes: employers hire workers from as high in the labor queue as possible, and workers accept the best jobs available to them. As a result the best jobs go to the most preferred workers, and less attractive jobs go to workers lower in the labor queue; bottom-ranked workers may go jobless, and the worst jobs may be left unfilled." [30]

Labor Markets as Queues

In trying to understand why there are higher rates of unemployment for blacks, Lester Thurow in *Poverty and Discrimination* characterized the labor market as a queue in which employers rank their preferences for hiring different racial groups. Employers then offer the most desirable jobs to workers at the top of the queue. Whites are generally the preferred group and, according to this hypothesis, black workers only get jobs in particular occupations when there are no more white workers available. Queuing can also be used to analyze differences in gender concentration in occupations. Since workers also have preferences for certain occupations, labor and job queues interact, resulting in an uneven, but also unstable, distribution of men and women across occupations.

A labor market queue is not a simple matter of absolute preference. Queues have three structural components, each of which may differ depending on employers, workers, or changing circumstances. Ordered elements are definitive characteristics of a queue that establish which jobs are most desirable and which group is favored for the best jobs. The shape of a queue reflects the absolute and relative size of its elements. If a preferred group is larger than the number of good jobs, some members will have to take less desirable jobs, but if the preferred group is smaller than the number of good jobs, then workers farther down the queue will be able to get better jobs. The intensity of preference determines how much group membership overrides other considerations. An extremely racist employer would choose even a poorly qualified white employee over any black candidate. Another employer might choose well-qualified black workers after the pool of well-qualified whites was depleted. An employer with weak racial preferences would give any well-qualified candidate a fair chance at obtaining a good job.

Changes in the size of subgroups or in the number of jobs in an occupational category can create a mismatch that places members of a less favored group into good positions or forces them out. For example, during wars when the supply of men available for civilian jobs or war production decreases, women gain access to those positions, "but each time men have come marching home from military service, employers have restored the prewar sex (and race) composition of most occupations." [35]

How Employers Rank Workers and How Workers Rank Jobs

Economics generally holds that workers are ranked in terms of potential productivity; however, such economic rationality is inadequate to explain gendered labor queues. Custom can dictate that some jobs are appropriate for men while others are meant for women. Since an individual's productivity is difficult to predict, proxies such as education or experience are often used. Stereotypes about men and women (that men are more mechanically inclined or that women have higher turnover rates) contribute to the use of group membership as a proxy. Some employers fear that resistance from male employees to women entering the workplace will be disruptive. Although women are paid less than men, even within the same occupations, less cost-sensitive employers may pay a premium for male workers. Male business owners and managers may also exhibit a bias in favor of men in order to maintain male privilege and power both in the workplace and in society.

Workers' preferences for jobs are based on characteristics such as compensation, status, autonomy, security, interest, working conditions, and opportunities for advancement. These characteristics may have different weights for different people, but a number of studies indicate that men and women generally value similar characteristics in occupations, particularly with respect to income and prestige.

Women's Inroads into Men's Occupations

After 1970 a number of occupations began to recruit or retain women in disproportionate numbers. This feminization reflects changes in the structural features of queues. Rapid expansion of the service sector outran the availability of qualified men. Employers began to recruit from less advantaged groups and to provide training to increase productivity. Accordingly, women's share of employment grew most in fast-growing occupations. Nevertheless, some desirable high-growth jobs that were easy to enter, such as carpentry and truck driving, experienced no shortfall in male candidates and the percentage of women in these occupations barely grew. Growing occupations that experienced high turnover rates also feminized rapidly, in some cases flipping from mostly male to mostly female. Labor shortages in professional occupations increased incentives to extend educational opportunities to new groups. In expanding occupations, job security and opportunities for advancement also grew, reducing resistance from men.

Several occupations went through similar feminization in the 1970s, but for reasons other than dramatic growth. Some jobs dropped lower in men's job queues because more desirable opportunities opened up to them. For women, however, these jobs often represented a step upward. Feminization often accompanied technological change that altered the division of labor, changed working conditions, or reduced skill requirements. Insurance adjusters, who had primarily been men working in the field with a lot of autonomy and good chances for advancement, faced cost-cutting pressure when the financial industry was deregulated. When these jobs became computerized, standardized, and more like routine clerical positions, their earnings potential fell. Men dropped out of these jobs, and women took their place.

In several feminizing occupations, earnings declined compared to the labor force as a whole, while the payoff per year of education also suffered a relative decline. In some occupations the proportion of full-time, year-round jobs dropped. In other cases economic fluctuations or changing government regulations altered the wage structure of particular jobs. Changes in skill requirements or declining job security, occupational prestige or opportunities for advancement made certain jobs less attractive to men. In the book publishing industry, for example, when marketing considerations overrode literary concerns, the prestige and autonomy of editors eroded, and men left the profession.

The Changing Shape and Intensity of the Labor Queue

For several reasons employers began to rerank men and women in the 1970s. With women's liberation, women challenged discriminatory practices in employment and education. Antidiscrimination regulations made it more expensive for employers to queue on a gender-specific basis and these costs often outweighed the benefits of placating male employees. As women increased their education, proved themselves to be as competent as men, and increasingly entered the workplace due to labor shortages and affirmative action pressure, employers began to recognize the absence of productivity and cost differences between men and women workers. Some researchers believe that skills in many feminizing occupations shifted in favor of stereotypically female tasks such as routine clerical work or the emotion work of dealing with customers. However, most jobs include both stereotypically male and female aspects that can be easily manipulated to justify employer choices.

In many cases men abandoned jobs because they became relatively less desirable. Women, however, also entered job niches that were not threatening to men. Finally, new managers brought new values and different priorities to employment choices. Younger managers and new employment arrangements such as franchising and the advancement of women into management positions deconstructed tradition-bound centers of bias.

"This analysis leaves unanswered a key question: Why should women move into occupations that men have rejected in favor of greener pastures? The answer is simple: because they are preferable to most female occupations." [61] Even while declining relative to male jobs on average, the occupations that feminized during the 1970s still paid better than traditional female occupations. However, these shifts in the job queue would not have produced such pronounced changes in employment patterns without the labor shortages or external pressures that also affect employers' construction of labor queues.

Summary of

Between the Toe and the Heel—
Jobs and Emotional Labor
and Gender, Status, and Feeling

by Arlie Russell Hochschild

[Published in *The Managed Heart* (Berkeley: University of
California Press, 1983), Chapters 7 and 8, 137–184.]

When an organization seeks to create demand for a service and then deliver it, it uses the smile and the soft questioning voice. Behind this delivery display, the organization's worker is asked to feel sympathy, trust, and good will. On the other hand, when the organization seeks to collect money for what it has sold, its worker may be asked to use a grimace and the raised voice of command. Behind this collection display the worker is asked to feel distrust and sometimes positive bad will. In each kind of display, the problem for the worker becomes how to create and sustain the appropriate feeling. [137–138]

Two chapters in *The Managed Heart* describe emotion work. Chapter 7 describes different types of emotion work; Chapter 8 analyzes why women are more apt to be engaged in emotional labor than men, particularly if it involves showing deference. Occupational data (presented in the book's appendix) indicate that about one-third of all workers in the United States do some type of emotion work. "This means that one-third of all workers experience a dimension of work that is seldom recognized, rarely honored, and almost never taken into account by employers as a source of on-the-job-stress." [153] One-fourth of the jobs held by men and one-half of the jobs held by women involve emotion work.

Between the Toe and the Heel

Flight attendants and bill collectors represent the extremes of emotion work. "The project of the flight attendant is to *enhance* the customer's status, to heighten his or her importance. . . . Every act of service is an advertisement. In contrast, the final stages of bill collecting typically *deflate* the customer's status, as the collector works at wearing down the customer's presumed resistance to paying." [139] These workers are trained to view the customer in ways that accord with their own sympathetic or nonsympathetic behavior. Passengers become guests or children, while debtors are loafers or cheats. Apart from training, both jobs probably attract people with personal qualities compatible with the position. Careful screening of flight attendants assures that the appropriate qualities are present, while high turnover does the same for bill collectors—those who don't like the work quit. Even so, workers interviewed in both jobs spoke of curbing their feelings in order to perform. "In both, supervisors enforce and monitor that curbing, and the curbing is often a personal strain." [146]

Many jobs requiring emotional labor lie between the extremes of flight attendant and bill collector. They are found in occupational categories ranging from professional to clerical and service work. Although emotional labor is generally directed outward toward members of the public (by diplomats, nurses, waiters), it can also operate internally, as in the relationship of a secretary to an executive. Cashiers and salespeople need to "produce short bursts of niceness many times a day," [150] while others, such as psychiatrists or social workers, must develop deeper relationships with clients. Emotion workers may face conflicting demands. Some parents expect day care workers to focus on education while others want warmth and nurturing for their children. Part of the job for lawyers and doctors is to produce emotional states, such as trust or calmness.

The three criteria used to define emotion work are: (1) The worker has contact with the public; (2) the worker must produce an emotional state, such as gratitude or fear, in another person; and (3) training and supervision enable the employer to exercise some control over the workers' emotional activities. Some of the workers just described supervise themselves, and so do not fit the third criterion.

"[T]he question of how work affects the workers feelings is far broader than the question of whether that work calls for emotional labor." [154] For example, many jobs place an emotional burden on workers, demanding that they suppress feelings of frustration or anger, without necessarily requiring them to produce an emotional response in others as a product.

Middle-class families are the training ground for emotion workers, through a system of personal control that elicits desired behavior in children by means of emotional appeals, such as by using "It would mean a lot to me" statements. [157] Middle-class children learn that feelings, their own and those of others, are important and are to be monitored and controlled. In contrast, working-class families are more apt to use positional control in which rules and status are the basis for controlling behavior.

Gender, Status, and Feeling

Both men and women do emotion work, but its impact is more important for women than for men—important in different ways, since women are considered a subordinate social stratum with less access to money, power, authority, or status. Several consequences follow. For example, "women make a resource out of feeling and offer it to men as a gift in return for the more material resources they lack." [163] Women tend to specialize in mastering anger and aggression in favor of being nice, while men more often engage in aggressive tasks, while mastering fear and vulnerability. Women have a weaker status shield against the feelings of others, so that female flight attendants, for example, might find themselves easier targets of verbal abuse than male attendants. "[F]or each gender a different portion of the managed heart is enlisted for commercial use." [163–164] More often, women use beauty, charm, and relational skills, while men use anger and threatening behavior. The capacities that are, in these ways, offered up to the public are capacities from which the individual is in danger of being estranged.

Women are considered more emotional than men, but they are also regarded as better able to manage emotion and to command feminine wiles. Studies indicate that women adapt more to the needs of others and are more likely to cooperate than men. Are these passive characteristics gender-specific? "Or are they signs of a social work that women *do*—the work of affirming, enhancing, and celebrating the well-being status of others? . . . [M]uch of the time, the adaptive, cooperative woman is actively working at showing deference." [165] This is a form of what Ivan Illich calls "shadow labor" that does not quite count as labor, but is needed to get other things done. A number of psychological studies show that qualities expected of or associated with women include warmth, supportiveness, gentleness, awareness of others' feelings. "As for many others of lower status, it has been in the woman's interest to be the better actor." [167]

Racism shares certain patterns with sexism, but in marriage "the larger inequities find intimate expression." [169] Close relationships between men and women require the disguise of subordination that may lead women to seek equality assertively in limited domains. On the other hand, women are expected to carry cooperative, nurturing qualities into public life. "The world looks to women for mothering, and this fact silently attaches itself to many a job description." [171]

Jobs in large organizations requiring personal relations skills are growing in number, so the emotion work of status enhancement has been made more public, systematic, and standardized. Public contact positions often mean public service jobs that are ranked at the bottom of the scale of desirable positions, probably because people in service jobs are more dependent on and at the mercy of others. Women in public contact jobs receive less deference than men, and their feelings carry less weight. An observer of the British Civil Service described a "doctrine of feelings" [172] in which consideration for other's feelings in matters of employment increased with personal rank. Women, however, experience this as another double standard. While men in public life express anger or passion with no loss of credibility or worth, "women's feelings are seen not as a response to real events but as reflections of themselves as 'emotional' women." [173] Women lack a status shield for protection from the feelings of others and are more exposed than men to rude speech or tirades against the company they represent. Women in positions with much public contact effectively become shock absorbers for discontented customers.

Men and women are expected to fulfill the different fictive biographies that customers bring with them. During an interview, a male flight attendant commented that passengers often ask if he plans to go into management, while a female flight attendant said she is often asked why she is not married. Passengers also assume that men have more authority than women regardless of age, and both male and female flight attendants were observed to act accordingly, with men more confident and women more deferential in passenger interactions.

Any job raises issues of demarcating where the job ends and the self begins. For women in high public contact jobs like flight attendants, there are also other identity issues. A woman might actually be motherly and/or sexually attractive, but on the job she may use these qualities to win regard. These behaviors are also partly the result of corporate engineering—company emphasis on appearance and demeanor—so that many women become estranged from the role of the woman they play at work, an estrangement that often leads to psychosexual dysfunction. This division can be a defense of the real self against the stresses of work, but it can also destroy a healthy sense of wholeness.

Summary of

Race, Class, and Occupational Mobility: Black and White Women in Service Work in the United States

by Marilyn Power and Sam Rosenberg

[Published in *Feminist Economics* 1 (1995), 40–59.]

Service sector occupations have historically been a major source of employment for black and white women in the United States. These jobs are typically low paid and offer few promotional opportunities, but their easy entry and flexible hours attract women of all types. Figures indicate, however, that black women experience considerably less occupational mobility than white women working in this sector.

This study seeks to explain these differences as a function of race, class background, child-bearing, and initial occupational category.

Methodology and Measures of Occupational Mobility

The study relies on a sample of women polled by the National Longitudinal Survey of Young Women (NLS) who reported working in service occupations in 1972 and in the same or a different occupation in 1988. The sample includes 261 white and 135 black women who were between eighteen and twenty-eight years old in 1972 and who were employed at least one week in both 1972 and 1988. Rather than limiting itself to conventional regression analysis, the study uses descriptive statistics and "an exploratory, storytelling approach, which more effectively illuminates the complexity of the interaction of gender, race/ethnicity, and class in the lives of women." [48]

For the purposes of the study, occupational mobility was measured in two ways: by occupation and by wage ranking in 1969 and 1988. Occupations were classified according to one-digit census occupational categories. Jobs were ranked by mean earnings for full-year women workers in the 1970 census, the three-digit census occupational categories, and creating an index ranking from 1 to 15.

Findings

Historically black women have been confined to the lowest level of manual occupations, especially domestic work, farm work, and unskilled factory jobs. However, black women achieved dramatic improvement in the postwar period, through movement out of service and into professional and clerical occupations. In 1960, 20 percent of white and 60 percent of black women were in service occupations. By 1994, the rate had fallen only slightly for whites to 17 percent, but by more than half for blacks to 26 percent. However, this study suggests that among women from 1972 to 1988, white women enjoyed a much greater level of occupational mobility than black women beginning in the same sector (see Table VII.1).

In 1988, 74 percent of the 1972 cohort of white women had left service work, while only 47 percent of blacks had moved into other categories. For whites, 24 percent had moved into the first two, and most prestigious, census categories of professional and managerial workers, while the same was true for only 15 percent of blacks.

However, few women of either race were able to enter the relatively highly paid male-dominated occupations. For those women who left service work, the

Table VII.1. 1988 Occupations of White and Black 1972 Service Workers [44]

Occupation	White	Black
Professional, technical, and kindred	23.0%	11.1%
Managers, officials, and proprietors	11.5	3.7
Clerical and kindred	24.5	15.6
Sales workers	3.8	1.5
Craftsmen, foremen, and kindred	1.1	0.7
Operatives and kindred	8.4	11.8
Private household workers	1.5	5.9
Other service workers	24.5	46.7
Laborers, including farm	1.5	2.9
Total	99.8%	99.9

largest single shift was into "clerical and kindred" jobs (24 percent of whites and 16 percent of blacks), which are relatively low-paid positions. Of the women who obtained professional and technical jobs, half became noncollege teachers or nurses.

In addition to their place in a major occupational category, the sample participants were also ranked according to their incomes at the beginning and end of the study period according to the earnings ranks described above. The ranks ranged from 1.0 for earnings between $0 and $2,000 to 15.0 for incomes between $15,000 and $16,000. As of 1972, white women had a mean rank of 2.75, while blacks averaged 2.36. By 1988, the mean for whites had risen to 4.85, a gain of 2.10 ranking points, while blacks rose to 3.91, a gain of only 1.55 ranking points. Accordingly, not only did white women begin work at higher earnings levels than black women, but the income gap between both groups also grew over sixteen years.

These results "suggest that service work may be more likely to serve as a temporary occupation for young white women who are preparing themselves for better jobs, while for black women service is more likely to become a long-term job category." [44]

Children, Education, and Class Background

Women's responsibilities to care for children greatly affect their ability to participate in the paid workforce and pursue strategies for job advancement. Access to financial and other resources can reduce the degree of conflict between the demands of family and work life, an especially important issue to note given that on average black women are likely to have fewer resources than white women.

Within the sample group, black women were also more likely to be limited by family responsibilities than white women because they had more children and began having children earlier. In 1972, blacks had an average of 1.48 children each, while whites had only 0.65. By 1988, black women had 2.96 children on average and white women had 1.99. Additionally, black women were much more likely to be single parents. In 1972, 56 percent of blacks and 84 percent of whites reported being married.

Although the presence of children did not affect the earnings rank of women in 1972, having children that year is associated with lower mobility in future years. By 1988, white women who had children in 1972 had achieved an earnings rank of 4.5, while those who did not have children in 1972 rose to 5.1; for black women, the numbers were 3.7 and 4.2 respectively.

The white women in the sample had higher levels of educational attainment (measured by grade level completed) than blacks both in 1972 and 1988, with the size of the gap remaining constant over time. Whites had 12.0 years of education completed in 1972 and 13.0 years by 1988; blacks had only 10.8 and 11.9 years respectively. In addition, the white women were significantly more likely to be attending school while working in 1972: 24 percent of white service workers compared to 16 percent of black service workers were in school. Further, while both black and white women benefited from additional schooling, black women's upward mobility was considerably lower.

Class background is also crucial in young women's opportunities for job advancement. In this study, class is measured by the occupations of the women's fathers. Of the white women's fathers, 42 percent were in better-paying professional, managerial, and craftsmen occupations in 1968 (when the NLS survey began), while only 9 percent of blacks' fathers were similarly employed. Meanwhile, 36 percent of black fathers were in the lower-paying operatives and service workers categories compared to only 19 percent of the fathers of white women.

The study also suggest that young white women were employed more often than black women in service jobs that allowed for greater flexibility to pursue educational options. As of 1972, 24 percent of whites were waitresses compared to only 8 percent of blacks. Furthermore, 12 percent of whites were "private baby-sitters" who often enjoyed flexible schedules. Only 6 percent of black women worked as baby-sitters, while 22 percent report being "private household" workers and 8 percent chambermaids. Hospital attendants, a job that usually calls for more rigid scheduling requirements, accounted for 14 percent of whites and 23 percent of blacks

Conclusion

The sample of participants used for the study were in the same occupational category in 1972, were of the same age group, and were living through the same social and economic changes of the 1970s. Yet, a complex intertwining of race, class background, and family status can be used to explain the different levels of occupational mobility achieved by white women and black women. This finding brings into question "the meaningfulness of cross-sectional analysis of occupational distributions" and of statistical studies that treat the effects of race and gender oppression as simply additive. Instead, race, gender, and class background must be viewed as important analytical instruments that allow for the examination and consideration of vastly different life experiences.

Summary of

Black Mobility in White Corporations: Up the Corporate Ladder But Out on a Limb
by Sharon M. Collins

[Published in *Social Problems* 44 (February 1997), 55–67.]

Even after several decades of political and social pressure for diversity, few blacks have advanced to top-ranked decision-making positions in white-dominated corporations. Neoclassical and social structural theories are usually considered opposing explanations of such labor market outcomes. This study, however, indicates that they can be interactive, with human capital mediated by the managerial division of labor.

Framing the Issues

Federal legislation arising out of the civil rights movement of the 1960s and 1970s pushed predominantly white corporations to increase the number of African-American managers. By the early 1990s, however, few had moved into top positions. Many talented and ambitious African-Americans were assigned to positions related to minority issues. These jobs often carried impressive titles and were well compensated, but they removed their occupants from the centers of corporate power and actually eroded the skills needed for decision-making positions.

Neoclassical theories (human capital theory) and status attainment theory found in sociology argue that "economic progress among blacks is a color-blind function of supply-side characteristics such as education, ability, and individual preference." [56] Lack of progress is thus a matter of poor attitude, ability, education, or preparation. Structural theories in contrast, hold that job characteristics can foster or inhibit progress and that white men are more likely to hold jobs with advancement potential. This study found, however, that human capital and the structure of the professional opportunity acted together to shape career paths.

Racialized and Mainstream Division of Labor

This study interviewed seventy-six of the most successful black executives in major Chicago-based corporations in 1986. Their experiences suggested two categories of jobs. *Racialized* jobs, such as affirmative action or urban affairs positions, are those that specifically relate to minority communities whose purpose is to reduce discrimination in employment practices or to enhance the company's image among minority customers. *Mainstream* jobs relate to the firm's total constituency and generally involve profit-centered activity such as sales, finance, or operations. Mainstream jobs form the pipeline to senior-level strategic careers.

One-third of the subjects had held only mainstream jobs, 16 percent had held one racialized job, and about half had held two or more racialized jobs. For comparison, twenty white Chicago-area CEOs were asked if they had held racialized positions. Only one said yes, and only as a temporary, part-time assignment. Although the career patterns for black and white managers were different, African-Americans did not have different educational levels than senior executives. Furthermore, almost half of those in racialized positions began their private-sector careers in mainstream jobs. Some blacks who were moving up the corporate ladder were heavily recruited by superiors to fill positions that would improve a firm's relationships with minorities.

Racialized jobs were often initially attractive with good pay, ample expense budgets, and prestigious titles. Racial unrest in the 1960s and early 1970s put occupants of these positions in the spotlight and offered them a sense of purpose and value to the company. In some cases, black employees saw these jobs as the only way to secure management positions.

Mobility or . . .

As their careers tended to stagnate, blacks in racialized positions saw themselves as caught in "a kind of a golden handcuffs trap" [60]. Sixty-four respondents employed in the private sector since 1972, long enough for a clear career trajectory, present a career typology: twenty-four had *mainstream* careers with no racialized jobs; twenty-two had *mixed* careers with mostly mainstream jobs, but at least one racialized job; and eighteen had *racialized* careers with a majority of racialized jobs.

Respondents with racialized careers advanced less than those with mainstream careers. Those with mixed careers, most of whom had had only one or two racialized jobs, had career patterns similar to those with mainstream careers. Respondents with racialized careers perceived limitations to advancement and described their own jobs as "dead-end" and "money-using" positions rather than "money-producing" positions. [60] They were far less likely than those with mainstream careers to expect promotions, either with their current employer or on the open job market. White executives also perceived blacks in racialized jobs as out of the running for advancement.

. . . Marginality?

Not only do racialized jobs deflect people from the direct route to top positions, "they underdevelop the talents and skills that corporations value, and therefore marginalize the job holder." [61] Blacks in racialized positions performed a valuable function, buffering the corporation during periods of racial turmoil. But this function had little applicability to mainstream positions. As one urban affairs director, formerly in sales, put it, "I was just their spook who sat by the door, and I understood that . . . and I charged them well for it." [62] These managers were not given responsibilities beyond those relevant to minority communities and did not engage in the normal progression of activities that would broaden their experiences and skills. An affirmative action manager would recruit blacks, but not whites, and would not gain related experience, for example, in labor relations, that was needed for promotion to senior personnel positions. In a similar vein, someone who positioned the firm's products in minority communities would not gain more general sales or public relations experience in the process.

Success in racialized positions prolonged these managers' career segregation, undermining their value in mainstream corporate functioning. Those who tried to move to mainstream functions or departments were stymied. While they became well-connected to minority communities, they lost touch with the company's internal networks. Several were stonewalled in their attempts to find better career opportunities. Some were priced out of the market for the lower-level mainstream positions for which they qualified; some who moved into mainstream positions could not effectively compete.

Interaction of Human Capital and Structure

Human capital and occupational structure are not independent of one another. Rather, the job structure represented in this study fostered human capital deficits. Human capital theory may explain the supply of black managerial talent that enabled these firms to meet antibias pressure, but it cannot by itself explain who succeeded in rising to positions of power and who did not.

The study has several implications. First, aggregate-level data, without reference to job characteristics, cannot explain black progress or lack of it. Second, inequality can be manufactured within the work process itself. Well-educated African-Americans can be concentrated in positions without profit-centered responsibility, deskilled, and eased out of the running for top positions. Third, structural explanations correspond to conflict perspectives or status frameworks in sociology. Seen through this lens, racialized career construction serves several purposes. Under pressure to incorporate minorities, white managers hoped to minimize minority "impact on organizational culture and structure" and to protect themselves from new competitors for high-level positions. [65] Racialized jobs met these goals efficiently. Accordingly, though the number and visibility of African-Americans in managerial positions increased, the pool of black managers able to compete for powerful mainstream careers diminished.

Summary of

What Went Wrong? The Erosion of Relative Earnings and Employment Among Young Black Men in the 1980s

by John Bound and Richard B. Freeman

[Published in *Quarterly Journal of Economics* 107 (February 1992), 201–232.]

"From the mid-1960s to the mid-1970s black Americans made large gains in the labor market relative to whites . . . [but] the era of relative black economic advance ended in the mid-1970s." [201–202] Thereafter, racial earnings and employment gaps widened rapidly for male workers. This article explores what went wrong beginning in the late 1970s, based on the annual Current Population Survey and other data on individual workers. The analysis focuses on young men (defined as those under twenty-eight and less than ten years out of school) because they are more affected by current labor market conditions. Older workers are protected to some extent by seniority and the accumulation of human capital.

The changes since the 1970s can be attributed to a variety of factors, including the economic decline of inner cities, the loss of manufacturing jobs, the fall in the real value of the minimum wage, and the decline in union membership for those with less education. The declining relative position of black college graduates may reflect the weakening of affirmative action, occupational downgrading, the decline in government employment, and the huge increase in the ratio of black to white college graduates.

Dimensions of Change

Among young men, all major categories of blacks suffered earnings and/or employment declines relative to comparable whites in the late 1970s and 1980s.

For young men as a whole, the racial earnings gap (controlling for education) narrowed rapidly from the mid-1960s to the mid-1970s, then began to widen. The employment rate, or ratio of employment to population, also showed a widening gap at many levels of education and experience. For example, for men with twelve years of education who had been out of school for five years, the black employment rate was 9 percentage points lower than the white rate in 1973, and 15 points lower in 1989.

The decline was particularly steep for two groups: those in the Midwest with high school education or less, and college graduates nationwide. In these groups, the racial earnings gap had essentially disappeared in the mid-1970s; in fact, in 1975, young black men were earning 8 percent more than whites in the Midwest, and 6 percent more among college graduates. By 1989, blacks were earning 19 percent less than whites in the Midwest, and 16 percent less among college graduates—a remarkably rapid change.[1] In contrast, among high school dropouts nationwide, there was no significant increase in the earnings gap (which remained substantial throughout the period), but a rapid increase in the employment-rate gap.

Explaining the Trends

To assess the importance of potential explanatory factors, regression analysis was used to estimate the time trend in racial earnings gaps with and without additional factors. The starting point was the trend found when controlling only for education and experience. Subsequent regressions also controlled for location, industry, occupation, union membership, and the real value of the minimum wage. In most cases the inclusion of these additional variables reduced the magnitude of the time trend, thus "explaining" some of the worsening position of blacks. The regression analysis explains 62 percent of the trend in the earnings gap for all young men, 72 percent for those in the Midwest with high school degrees or less, and 41 percent for college graduates.

For the Midwest, by far the most important factor was the change in industries in which blacks were employed. Other significant effects were due to changes in occupation, union membership, and the value of the minimum wage (industry and union membership are highly correlated, and therefore their effects overlap). In the 1970s over 40 percent of young black men in the Midwest were employed in durable manufacturing. By 1989 this had fallen to 12 percent, a drop of 28 percentage points. For young white men in the Midwest, the comparable drop was just 10 percentage points. Controlling for education and industry, the unionization rate for young black men was 10 percentage points higher than for whites in the Midwest and the Northeast in 1973, but no higher than for whites by 1989. The decline in the real minimum wage had only a modest effect in the Midwest; it was much more important in the South, where many young workers were at or near the minimum wage.

The causes of decline were somewhat different for black college graduates. Changes in occupation were the most important, though changes in industry also mattered. In the 1970s, 68 percent of young black college graduates, and 69 percent of comparable whites, were in professional and managerial jobs. By 1989 these figures had fallen to 46 percent for blacks and 59 percent for whites. These declines—22 percentage points for blacks, 10 for whites—are very similar to the declines in the percentage of college graduates working in education and public administration,[2] suggesting that cutbacks in public sector employment may have accounted for much of the change. The ratio of black to white young college graduates grew rapidly in the 1970s and 1980s, perhaps reflecting increased equality of educational opportunity. Thus the supply of black college graduates may have grown faster than the demand.

Three Other Possibilities

Three other possible explanations are often suggested for the widening racial gaps of the 1980s. First, unmeasured labor market skills of young blacks may have deteriorated due to poor schooling, family breakdown, increased drug use, or other factors. This is difficult to maintain in the face of the evidence. Black students' standardized test scores rose slightly relative to whites in the period; and older cohorts of black workers, whose skills were presumably established in earlier, better times, suffered declines in earnings relative to whites that paralleled those of young workers. The survey data used as the basis for statistical analysis in this article is unlikely to include serious drug users.

A second possibility is more serious. The tremendous increase in crime among young black men may have caused some of the erosion in employment of black high school dropouts. Statistical analysis using a different data set allows estimates of the effects of a criminal record on the probability of employment for young high school dropouts. A history of incarceration had a highly significant effect, reducing the probability of employment by 21 percentage points in 1983 and 17 points in 1988. Having being on probation, but never having been incarcerated, caused 16 and 11 percentage point reductions in the employment probability in the two years. Less serious records (only convicted or only charged) caused smaller, and usually not statistically significant, reductions in employment.

Census and Justice Department figures imply that the percentage of young (ages 18 to 29) black male high school dropouts in prison or jail at some time during the year rose from 7 percent in 1980 to 20 percent or more (one estimate suggests 26 percent) in 1989. Since there is turnover in the incarcerated population, even more have criminal records. The surge in the number of young blacks with criminal records did not begin until the 1980s. Using the estimates presented here, this could account for 71 percent of the declining employment rate for young black high school dropouts from 1979 to 1989. The employment rate for young white high school dropouts remained roughly constant in this period, and the number with criminal records was comparatively small.

A final factor that is not captured in the statistical analyses is the change in the government's role, particularly the weakening pressure for affirmative action. Past studies have shown that the rise of affirmative action contributed to the increased relative earnings of black college graduates in the late 1960s and early 1970s. Correspondingly, the decline of government effort and expenditure on affirmative action in the 1980s undoubtedly allowed the relative decline of black college graduate earnings. This occurred at a time when other analysts have suggested that the overall distribution of earnings was becoming wider (less equal). This widening differentially hurt blacks both because they began at a lower point in the distribution and because they were losing the government support that had helped them move up in earlier times.

Notes

1. Calculated from Table 1, p. 209. There and throughout the original article, comparisons are expressed in "log points," or differences in natural logarithms, which are roughly equal to percentages for small differentials, and slightly greater than percentages for bigger differentials.
2. The share of young black college graduates working in education and public administration fell from 38 percent in the 1970s to 17 percent in 1988/89, a 21-point drop; the comparable decline for whites was from 28 percent to 14 percent, a 14-point drop.

Summary of

"Soft" Skills and Race: An Investigation of Black Men's Employment Problems

by Philip Moss and Chris Tilly

[Published in *Work and Occupations* 23 (August 1996), 252–276.]

Compared to young white men, young black men earn a lower hourly wage and have a higher rate of unemployment. These gaps were closing until the mid-1970s, but subsequently began to widen again. Among several other factors associated with these trends are changing skill needs, especially a growing requirement for "soft" or social skills. Defining soft skills as "skills, abilities, and traits that pertain to personality, attitude, and behavior rather than to formal or technical knowledge," in 1991 and 1992 the authors conducted fifty-six face-to-face interviews with employers in four industries in the Detroit and Los Angeles metropolitan areas. The interviews focused on hiring practices relating to entry-level jobs requiring no more than a high school diploma. The goal was to investigate "how and why employers formed negative assessments of the soft skills of black men and why employers sought increased levels of soft skills in entry level jobs." [255]

The Growing Importance of Soft Skills

Performance in service jobs is affected by the worker's ability to relate well to customers. In many other contexts an individual's productivity depends strongly on relationships with coworkers and with managers. The acquisition of "hard skills" (reading, arithmetic, and more technical skills) can in some cases be linked to relational skills.

The employers surveyed in this study focused attention on two clusters of soft skills. The first category is related to Hochschild's concepts of "emotional labor"[1] and focuses on the ability to interact with customers, coworkers or supervisors. Interaction involves "friendliness, teamwork, ability to fit in, and appropriate affect, grooming and attire." [256] The second category is motivation, which includes characteristics such as "enthusiasm, positive work attitude, commitment, dependability, and willingness to learn." [256]

The employers surveyed were aware of the growing importance of soft skills, frequently attributing the trend to competitive pressures that are driving up the importance of customer service, quality, and teamwork. Most included soft skills on their list of the most important hiring criteria, and almost half put soft skills in the first place on that list. By comparison, the picture was more mixed for hard skills, with some new requirements (such as computer literacy) offset, in part, by occasional comments about the declining need for hard skills (as among sales clerks). The most marked trend was a growing emphasis on customer service and customer relations.

Soft Skills and Race in the Eyes of Employers

The growing emphasis on soft skills disadvantages black male job applicants. Given that perceptions of soft skills depend on cultural definitions, employer assessments are likely to be affected by cultural differences and racial stereotyping. Assessment of a potential employee's soft skills (in a prehiring interview, say) is inevitably subjective and is therefore an easy conduit for racial discrimination. Most respondents (well over 80 percent in three of the sectors studied) identified the interview as the most important source of hiring information. The exceptions are public sector agencies, some of which make efforts to downplay interviews or eliminate them altogether, precisely because of the racial bias they can inject into the hiring process.

Employers in the sample who placed "the greatest emphasis on soft skills were those most likely to have negative views of black men as workers." [260] This assessment by employers may be divided into three parts: stereotype, cultural difference, and accurate perception of the skills of black men.

Employers have formed their perceptions of black men from experiences with employees, applicants, and the media, and from experiences outside work. Some of these attitudes reflect stereotypical views or generalizations from subgroups, such as black men in prison. However, the amount of detail in some responses indicates that some of the negative employer comments were based on real experiences. Other researchers also report that many young black men from inner cities act tough, stressing skills they have developed to survive in dangerous environments. However, these behaviors are not likely to be reassuring (indeed, they are not developed to be reassuring) to employers, coworkers, and customers.

Regarding interaction with customers or coworkers, employers had two main concerns: Black men were seen as defensive, hostile, or having a bad attitude; and black men were considered difficult to control and sometimes intimidating to white supervisors. When cultural differences between young black men and customers, coworkers, or supervisors contributed to problems in interaction, some respondents saw this as a mutual problem, but white respondents were more apt to see it as a failure of young black men to communicate well. "This conforms with the view expressed in focus groups by young, inner-city, Black and Latino men, that code-switching—being able to present oneself and communicate in ways acceptable to majority White culture—is the most important skill needed to find and keep a job." [268]

A large minority of respondents felt that black men lacked motivation, calling them lazy or irresponsible, and blaming such characteristics for high turnover rates. Many other respondents claimed not to see differences in work ethic between racial groups. However, a substantial majority, whether or not they specifically questioned the work ethic of black men, "agreed with the idea that immigrants have a stronger work ethic than native-born workers." [263]

Employers often lumped interaction and motivation together by use of terms such as "attitude," tending to assume that this is innate. Sociologist William Julius Wilson has identified these attitudes as a product of poor neighborhoods. However, several respondents noted that interaction skills can be taught, while others argued that motivation is in important ways endogenous to the workplace. Employees respond to workplace norms, and effective management can foster motivation.

For instance, two Los Angeles warehouses in the same industry in the same Latino neighborhood, but with different management practices and different pay schedules, had very different experiences with turnover, employee attitudes, and gang-related problems. The employer with the more productive and stable workforce offered a higher than normal wage, along with rules for employee behavior that were intelligently geared to the need, for example, to downplay gang affiliations.

Conclusions and Remedies

Competitive pressures are driving the growing demand for soft skills, but since employers often perceive black men as lacking in these qualities, firm restructuring leads to greater racial inequality. However, public and corporate policies can improve labor market outcomes for black men. During a recession employers can screen for the skills they need rather than achieving the desired skill mix through training. Macroeconomic policies that reduce unemployment will enable more black men to be hired. Affirmative action, minority contracting, and community economic development are microlevel programs that can improve job prospects for minorities. "[T]here should be a high payoff to programs that teach code switching to assist inner-city Blacks in bridging the cultural divide with employers." [271]

At the company level, diversity training and management practices that motivate workers can improve the work experiences of young black men. Several respondents noted that team-based management reduces interaction problems. Minority-owned suppliers, evident in the auto parts industry, are often committed to recruiting in minority communities. Recent initiatives for skills development, particularly from the U.S. Department of Labor, emphasize both the importance of soft skills and the fact that they can be learned.

Additional research is needed to substantiate (or refute) the findings presented here. If they are valid, then more research is needed to understand how employer stereotypes are formed, what real cultural differences exist, how worker or manager retraining can bridge gaps, and how to modify trends to avoid further disadvantages for young black men.

Note

1. See summary in Part VII: Arlie Russell Hochschild, *The Managed Heart* (Berkeley: University of California Press, 1983), Chapters 7 and 8, 137–184.

Summary of

Feminization of the Labor Force: The Effects of Long-Term Development and Structural Adjustment

by Nilüfer Çagatay and Sule Özler

[Published in *World Development* 23 (November 1995), 1883–1894.]

Many researchers have found that women's labor force participation rates respond to changes in the level of economic development. These changes can be examined in a single country over time or in cross-section studies comparing countries at different stages of development. It has been hypothesized that structural adjustment policies imposed by The World Bank and International Monetary Fund have drawn more women into the labor force in industrializing countries. This econometric study separates the general level of development from the impacts of structural adjustment to analyze the effects of each on the feminization of the labor force.

Feminization of the Labor Force

As countries move through stages of economic development, the labor force participation rate (LFPR) of women goes through characteristic changes illustrated by a U-shaped pattern—first declining, then rising. Originally, development analysts thought that development and women's entry into paid employment would occur in concert. However, in 1970, E. Boserup argued that women are marginalized in the initial stages of industrialization and their share of the labor force declines. Men have better access to education and technological training, prompting productivity differences between men and women and hence employer preferences for men. As urbanization increases and home-based production is replaced by factory-based production, women find it more difficult to combine productive activity with reproductive responsibilities (care of home and children). This is witnessed in the downward segment of the U-curve. Over time, women adjust to more extensive industrialization. Their educational levels rise, fertility rates fall, domestic labor becomes commodified, and the labor force becomes feminized as women's share of employment rises, forming the upward segment of the U-curve.

This historical pattern can also be seen in cross-section data comparing countries at different stages of development. Most research confirms the U-shaped relationship with phases of economic development. However, this general pattern contains differences mediated by demographic, cultural, and ideological issues. For example, the highly feminized labor forces in Eastern European countries reflect the socialist commitment to women's economic engagement. On the other hand, Islam and Catholicism are often perceived as impediments to women's labor force participation.

Shorter term macroeconomic policies also affect labor markets, particularly structural adjustment programs that combine stabilization and trade reform policies. The impact on women's labor force participation is related to two effects. First is the expansion of the export sector, which tends to be feminized in developing countries. Export-oriented industries, which are generally labor-intensive, using unskilled labor for which women have a comparative advantage, pull women into the labor force. Global competitive pressures can also favor women who receive lower wages than men. However, where more skilled labor is required or mechanization is greater, defeminization may occur.

The second aspect of structural adjustment that can lead to an increase in women's labor force participation rates is the worsening of the income distribution that generally follows, since women are often pushed into the labor market to make up for falling family incomes.

Empirical Investigation

Using pooled World Bank data from 165 countries for 1985 and 1990, variables were constructed to represent the effects of trade openness and income distribution on women's labor force participation rates. The ratio of exports to GNP indicates trade openness. The income share of workers in manufacturing industries is an estimation of income distribution (though data for all industries was not available). Other variables included the log of GNP, investment levels, inflation as an alternative indicator of income distribution, demographic characteristics, and the presence and intensity of World Bank and International Monetary Fund structural adjustment programs. Geographic regions were used as controls or to test alternative model specifications.

Results

The results confirm a robust relationship between women's labor force participation rates and economic development—the feminization U-curve—modified by demographic and cultural or ideological factors. After controlling for the feminization U-curve, the structural adjustment hypotheses were also confirmed. Women's labor force participation increases under structural adjustment through both the push factor of worsening income distribution and the pull factor of increased openness to export trade.

Summary of

Engendering the Worlds of Labor: Women Workers, Labor Markets, and Production Politics in the South China Economic Miracle

by Ching Kwan Lee

[Published in *American Sociological Review* 60 (June 1995), 378–397.]

This case study focuses on the experiences of women working for the same company, but in different factories—one in Shenzhen, in China's fast-growing Guangdong province, and the other in Hong Kong. The study explores the very different shop floor relationship regimes in the two factories, drawing on both feminist analytical methods and theories of production. Each approach can be reconstructed in light of the other and in view of the specific labor market circumstances that shape power relationships at these two work sites.

Gender and Production Politics

Feminist theory argues that gender is socially constructed and is a constituent dimension of power relations, including workplace relations. Much recent feminist analysis relies on investigations of particular settings to draw out an understanding of how gender is constructed. This empirical approach "begs for theories that can explain commonalities and differences." [379] Theories of production politics, particularly those in the Marxist tradition, attempt to explain power relationships in the workplace and can be reconstructed to encompass gender.

The two plants chosen for this study offer examples of distinct factory regimes, which might initially be classified as despotic (Shenzhen) and hegemonic (Hong Kong) according to Michael Burawoy's theory of production politics as described in *Manufacturing Consent* (1979) and *Production Politics* (1985). A despotic regime is marked by rigid rules and punitive enforcement. Workers are dependent on wages, and wages are linked to performance. In a hegemonic regime, state-provided welfare and regulation free workers from wage dependence. Management objectives are achieved with worker consent.

The two factory sites studied, however, reveal deviations from Burawoy's theory of production politics, stemming from the characteristics of production workers at each site. The workers in Hong Kong, mainly middle-aged working mothers, lack alternatives to wage labor and receive few benefits or protections from the state, conditions that should give rise to a despotic regime. Yet they work in a congenial atmosphere that accommodates their need to fulfill obligations at home. At the Shenzhen site, the young, single women workers can return to agrarian life in their home villages as an alternative to wage labor. This circumstance should foster a hegemonic regime, but the workers are still subjected to despotic control and punishment that imposes the discipline required for industrial work. "Managers do not see the need for despotism in Hong Kong because the manufacturing jobs are declining and women workers desperately want to cling to their factory employment. In Shenzhen, despotism is possible because the state allows it and there is an ample supply of cheap labor. Despotism is also necessary because workers have not acquired the discipline of industrial work." [380]

Burawoy's theory of production politics also needs to be supplemented with an understanding of gender. "Matron workers" in Hong Kong and "maiden workers" in Shenzhen represent different cultural ideas about women and constitute different labor markets. Yet in each case gender is mutually constructed by management and workers, and is considered an important part of the way that "shop-floor power relations are conceived, legitimized, naturalized and criticized." [380]

Localistic Despotism and Familial Hegemony

Rather than "institutional reflections of capitalism's historical tendencies," [382] factory regimes are negotiated orders that simultaneously embody both management domination and the collective resistance of workers. The two patterns of production politics defined here—"localistic despotism" in Shenzhen and "familial hegemony" in Hong Kong—were composed of management strategies for control and workers' subjective responses to economic realities.

The Shenzhen factory was very regimented. Fines were imposed for absence (even for documented illness or leaves with permission). Meals were furnished, but took place on a strict schedule. Overtime was mandatory, with little advanced notice. Compared to rural labor under a hot sun, workers preferred factory work but resented the control of their time and their inability to plan free time. The most resented penalties were the fines for absenteeism.

Local networks, based on home villages, counties, or the distinction between northern and southern China offered introductions to employers, places to stay, loans, and other assistance in emergencies. These networks also operated inside the workplace, from influencing hiring and promotion decisions to extending petty favors such as longer bathroom breaks, getting water, playful gestures, teaching new skills, or helping with work backlogs. In some cases, local networks, through the agency of male or elder kin, enforced factory discipline on maiden workers—for example, exposing and defeating one woman's strategy to get leave to visit home, and preventing another from quitting to take a higher paying job. Despotic control was thus both tempered and reinforced by local networks.

Despite its harshness, the work experience had different, more liberatory meanings for the young women workers than for their male kin or supervisors. Working meant a chance to escape from arranged marriages, to date freely, to widen their prospects for marriage, to take classes during periods of low overtime, or to save money for education or for starting a small business once they were married and settled into adult life.

In Hong Kong, the atmosphere of "familial hegemony" meant that control was covert and was exercised by winning the consent of the women production workers. Women shared meals informally, were allowed to be late or to take off a few hours on occasion to attend to family business, and, under the direction of their female line leaders, often swapped components of their jobs to balance workloads. Family life dominated conversations and family references were common in the nicknames workers had for each other and for managers.

Both management and workers used si-lai, a Cantonese expression for a domineering matron, to describe women working in the Hong Kong plant. For managers it meant that women considered work secondary to family responsibilities and were concerned that their femininity and reputations not be jeopardized. Allowing women to fulfill their duties at home and to adopt a familiar and domineering demeanor at work cajoled them into good performance. Women themselves identified with si-lai. Although they accepted the role of men as principal breadwinners, they knew that if they had time for further training they could move into management. Foremen were pitied for their personal stake in a declining industry. Family roles gave women leverage with which to resist certain management demands.

The State, Labor Markets, and Managerial Autonomy

Differences in state intervention and regulation do not explain regime differences between the Shenzhen and Hong Kong factories. In neither case does the state constrain management autonomy. Although some reforms were instituted after labor unrest in 1967, Hong Kong's minimalist state offers little in the way of welfare support or restriction on the power of employers that would free workers from the need to work. Unions are weak and collective bargaining is rare. In Shenzhen, management autonomy was maintained by close clientalist relationships with state agencies through the medium of gifts and entertainment.

In the Asian context, community resources, whether based in local networks or families, are more important than the state in defining labor markets and determining work conditions. In Shenzhen, localistic networks were used to manage the recruitment of young women from the enormous floating population of migrant workers that resulted from agrarian economic reform. Despotic control was seen as a necessary form of discipline because of their youth, peasant mannerisms, lack of industrial experience, and mobility from company to company in search of better jobs. In Hong Kong, the labor market was tight, workers had long tenures with one company, and were dependent on families for support. These conditions encouraged a familial environment based on workers' consent. Because the communal institutions of localistic networks, kin, and families "mediate the supply of women's labor for factory work and provide the means for maintaining women workers' livelihoods, management and workers share an interest in incorporating these institutions into shop-floor practices, thus producing two different factory regimes." [394]

Summary of

Notes on the Incorporation of Third World Women into Wage Labor through Immigration and Offshore Production

by Saskia Sassen-Koob

[Published in *International Migration Review* 18 (Winter 1984), 1144–1167.]

Labor-intensive production of agricultural and manufactured export goods in industrializing countries has expanded since the 1970s, as has emigration from developing countries to the United States. Both trends are drawing Third World women into the wage labor force on a massive scale, but the trends are theoretically puzzling since emigration normally accompanies a lack of employment growth and opportunity in the country of origin.

Employment of immigrants and offshore production are functionally equivalent ways for firms in developed countries to secure a low-wage workforce and avoid organized labor. This article indicates that, "The same set of processes that has promoted the location of plants and offices abroad also have contributed to a large supply of low wage jobs in the U.S. for which immigrant workers are a desirable labor supply." [1145]

Industrialization and Female Migration

The redeployment of labor-intensive production to certain Third World locations created a significant demand for labor in those countries. Why then did these same countries also experience high rates of emigration? A chain of relationships can be traced from industrial growth through its employment impacts to its cultural-ideological effect on people.

Because internal consumption markets are limited, access to world markets, supported by foreign direct investment, accounts for most of the new industrial growth in developing countries. The export sector in developing countries involves agriculture and manufacturing, both of which induce internal migrations, but with different patterns, particularly for men and for women. Differences in migration can also be discerned between Latin America, the Caribbean, Asia, and Africa. In general, large-scale commercial agriculture displaced small farmers, creating both a rural labor supply and an increased demand for low-wage labor. However, much of this demand occurred on a seasonal basis only. Rural unemployment, migration from one rural area to another, and migration to the cities all increased. Men sought work either in commercial agriculture or in industrializing urban areas. Some women remained in the countryside and others sought work in the cities.

Export manufacturing also increased the demand for labor, concentrated it near transportation and services, and promoted ancillary employment in industries such as packaging or construction. This growth in export manufacturing should have absorbed displaced rural labor. Instead it drew new segments of the population into the labor force, mostly young women who would not have entered the wage labor market so suddenly if industrialization were more gradual. Unlike earlier forms of modernization, which introduced capital-intensive forms of production and favored male employment, export manufacturing is labor intensive and employs women in large numbers in industries as diverse as garments and electronics.

Although export-led growth increased employment, it did not do so in a stable way. The mental and physical fatigue produced by jobs in export industries led to high turnover. This suited employers' preferences for younger women. Many women who went to work in these industries eventually became unemployed. This constant turnover of employment sustained the migration of young women to the cities, a phenomenon that also proved disruptive of the local economies in communities from which they came. Households were left without a traditional source of labor. Young men were left without partners or a role in the feminized export sector; as described above, they were often displaced from traditional employment in agriculture.

Several factors have converged to transform internal migration into emigration, a phenomenon echoed by research evidence that indicates that recent migrants have a higher tendency to migrate again. Unstable employment means that high levels of employment coexist with unemployment. "Incipient Westernization among [export] zone workers and the disruption of traditional work structures combine to minimize the possibility of returning to communities of origin." [1151] Contact with foreign workers in export zones provides information about potential destinations and a sense of familiarity with other countries. After this exposure to Western culture, workers are even less likely to return home. Migrants are receptive to the image of the United States as a land of opportunity, an image enhanced by the productive activity of U.S. firms in foreign export zones producing for the U.S. market.

Labor Demand and the Absorption of Immigrant Women

The supply of jobs in the developed world has been restructured in such a way as to increase the demand for low-wage labor, in particular female labor. Several analysts have noted a trend, confirmed by census data for various occupations and industries, toward a polarization of income. A shift from manufacturing to services increased the proportion of jobs that are low paid, while the fastest growing service industries concentrate jobs at the high- and low-wage ends. Many high-tech production jobs are low-wage, while some older manufacturing industries (such as furs, garments, and footwear) suffered job downgrading when the work was moved to nonunion sweatshops or homework settings. Computerization upgraded or downgraded many middle-income jobs.

These trends may be even more intense in the major cities that receive most immigrants, since new-growth sectors concentrate in major cities—particularly producer services with almost half its jobs low-waged. Globally dispersed production requires centralized administration, which is also concentrated in major cities. The sheer concentration of people (residents, workers, and tourists) in large cities induces a proliferation of small, low-cost service producers that need a low-wage, nonunionized workforce to be competitive. Downgraded manufacturing jobs are concentrated in major cities near available workers and design centers so as to be responsive to consumer demand for specialty goods.

This demand for specialty goods reflects the other end of the polarization effect. The expansion of high-income jobs itself increases the demand for low-wage workers. "Behind the gourmet food stores and specialty boutiques that have replaced the self-service supermarket and department store lies a very different organization of work." [1155] Compared to the capital-intensive nature of middle-income suburbs that rely on transportation, appliances, self-service shopping for mass-produced goods, and household labor, high-income households rely on hired staff and consumption of specialty products and services that are labor-intensive to produce and deliver.

This expansion of demand for low-wage workers coincides with the expansion in immigration, centered in the major cities of a few states. Just over half of legal immigrants are women. Their labor force participation rates are lower than those of immigrant men or native women, but their concentration in certain occupations (operatives and services) and industries (garments, textiles, food, and social services) is high. Immigrant women form both a labor supply on which the downgraded manufacturing sector relies heavily and a labor pool for many service jobs historically typed as women's jobs.

Conclusion

Studies of women migrants usually focus on family roles and the effects on gender of migration to industrialized countries. This study suggests a new approach whereby a connection is made between female migration and the current capitalist world economy. Although many women migrate domestically or internationally with their husbands or families, fundamental processes are forming both a supply of women migrants and demand for their labor within export industries in Third World countries as well as within low-wage industries and occupations in the United States.

PART VIII

The Household Economy and Caring Labor

Overview Essay

by Neva Goodwin

At the heart of the issues to be taken up here is a tension between the work that women do through the market, for pay, and the kinds of unpaid work that women have traditionally done outside of the market. There are three leading, legitimate, and often conflicting goals regarding the relationship between women's market and nonmarket work: (1) The goal of equalizing female and male access to market earnings; (2) the goal of ensuring that the important parts of the work traditionally assigned to women will continue to be done, somehow, by someone; and (3) the goal of fairness in the overall distribution of work of all types.

Goal (1) was long regarded as a purely feminist agenda. Within recent decades, however, it has become accepted by large numbers of both men and women, including many who do not regard themselves as feminists.

With respect to goal (2) we will focus especially on domestic labor. This is the work that makes "home" a place where children are nurtured and socialized, and where both children and adults are physically and psychically nourished and refreshed, enjoy much of what makes life worth living, and develop their potential as individuals and as contributing members of society.

This essay will emphasize the importance of the work done by women that is at present unpaid. In the industrialized world this includes domestic labor as well as an overlapping, but not identical, category of "caring labor." The latter includes all work that meets the needs of relatively helpless groups such as the sick, the indigent, children, and the elderly. The quality of this work depends on human compassion as well as practical assistance. In all societies most of this "caring labor" is traditionally done by women—whether or not it is done through the market. In developed countries, where much of this work has been marketized, the resulting jobs remain gender-stereotyped and generally receive low status and low pay. The other, better compensated work options now increasingly available to women, as a result of progress in attaining goal (1), raise concerns about women's continued willingness to perform unpaid domestic chores or poorly paid, low-status caring labor.

When considering the possibility that the socially critical domestic work is receiving less attention than is desirable, it is important to avoid blaming women, or asking the female half of the human race to make sacrifices to rectify the situation. In the United States, in particular, the difficulty of simultaneously achieving the first two goals has set up conditions of cognitive dissonance. While gender equality has gradually been gaining wider acceptance, those individuals who were most likely to draw attention to the conflict between women's domestic roles and their achievement of economic parity were the ones who were committed to maintaining the traditional, inferior status of women. At the same time, many of those who were most committed to equality between the sexes have simply ignored the conflict between goals (1) and (2).

The third goal, fairness, has recently become a focus of concern, in part as a result of ignoring the conflicts between the first two. Even while the issue of fairness is gaining attention, for most people the more urgent concern is still the fear that some of the domestic labor on which society most critically depends is being neglected. Its urgency and emotional impact can be seen in the questions, *Who Pays for the Kids?* (the title of a book by Nancy Folbre)[1] or "Who'll care for the dependent elderly?" (raised in the article by Allan Meyers summarized here). Many people worry about how (if at all) child care is being organized; or about the increasing numbers of mentally incompetent people who appear to be without care or a home; or about how our own needs in old age will be taken care of. As an example, the 1995 *Human Development Report* states that "[w]omen's vital social functions for maintaining families and communities . . . become only too visible when juvenile delinquency rates rise, the elderly are left to die alone or cultural traditions wither."[2]

Our first step toward grappling with the tensions between the three competing goals will be to situate the household economy and caring labor in a larger context of economic activity.

An Overview, with Competing Interpretations

In 1995 the annual *Human Development Report* of the United Nations Development Program (UNDP) took gender disparities as its central issue. This is an issue that must begin with definitions and measurements, since so much of women's work has tended not to be included in formal quantifications of economic activity.[3] What is typically left out includes not only women's traditional, domestic roles but also other unpaid activities, of both women and men, in production done for household use, for the benefit of the community, or for exchange in the informal sector.[4] Globally, the report found that only slightly more than half of the total time spent on economically productive activities is being reported in the standard System of National Accounts (SNAs) and included in conventional income measures such as GDP. Reviewing a sample of thirty-one countries, the report summarizes:

> Of men's total work time in industrial countries, roughly two-thirds is spent in paid SNA activities and one-third in unpaid non-SNA activities. For women, these shares are reversed. In developing countries, more than three-fourths of men's work is in SNA activities [while developing country women again devote two-thirds of their time to non-SNA work]. So, men receive the lion's share of income and recognition for their economic contribution—while most of women's work remains unpaid, unrecognized and undervalued.[5]

This is a fascinating new area of empirical research. However, the UNDP itself cautions that many measurement problems remain to be resolved before precise, reliable international comparisons can be made. The limited data now available suggest that total work time, per adult, in developing countries is about 20 percent greater than in industrial countries. The latter, of course, have a larger percentage of their population out of the labor force—either in school or retired. (Both of these fractions continue to increase, as schooling is extended later in life, and as life expectancy extends ever farther beyond retirement age.) With respect to two countries with some of the best data on work time, Norway and the United Kingdom, the UNDP found that:

- There has been a decrease in total work for the population as a whole as well as for both women and men.

- Men's and women's contributions to total work are becoming more equal. . . .

- There is also a tendency toward equalization of men's and women's contributions to both SNA and non-SNA work, more so for SNA work.[6]

That description is what many people would expect to see as the result of economic growth. An optimistic view might hope that such trends will spread to all nations of the world, if they just stay on track with the project of modernization. Among the alternative, more pessimistic views, an interesting one is provided by economist Shirley Burggraf, who focuses on what will happen if women, as well as men, actually behave as they are described in conventional economic theory.

Economic rationality is normally said to consist of an individualistic, selfish, and competitive drive to maximize the satisfaction of personal wants and preferences. Burggraf anticipates that women who enter the competitive arena will have markedly less time for unpaid domestic work as well as for poorly paid caring occupations. In adapting to the prevailing norms, women will undergo attitude changes, becoming less willing to sacrifice opportunities for career advancement and financial security for the sake of children or others who need nurturing care. Burggraf believes that a combination of opportunities, pressures, and cultural belief is already bringing about such changes.

> There is an emerging economic actor the world has never seen [before]: a rational, independent and informed female who understands the concept of opportunity cost and who can act accordingly. . . . Given what the market says about the relative value of doctors, lawyers, managers, engineers, plumbers, and mechanics versus housewives, teachers, and social workers, it is a safe prediction that as women increasingly exercise their choices with the same kind of economic rationality that many men do less and less time and talent will be invested in society's caretaking functions.[7]

Should we be looking forward to a world in which the male work profile increasingly looks like the female profile? Such a world has been made possible by rising labor productivity. (That, in turn, has a complex relationship with a more troublesome factor: unemployment.) Or should we, rather, be fearing a world in which women compete in careers designed by and for men, and no one is left to take care of the children, the elderly, and the quality of domestic life? In considering these issues we will look, in the next summary, at the question of how women divide their time between paid and unpaid work.

Women's Labor Force Participation

Lourdes Benería discusses global changes in women's labor force participation and in women's work in the home. Her analysis is supportive of the widely held impression that modernization implies an increase in the hours of work that women offer through the labor market. However the details, and even the direction of the trend, vary by decade and by location, as women resort to what Barbara Lobodzinska refers to as "the old survival techniques" that are called into play in hard times, when "the preservation of the family becomes an undisputed priority for women." [Lobodzinska, in the article summarized here, p. 520] The difficulty of even knowing the facts is illustrated by Benería's example of two contrasting figures for the Dominican Republic. The 1981 census reported the labor force participation of rural women in the formal economy as 21 percent. A 1984 survey, including informal sector activities and subsistence production as well as formal employment, revised this figure to 84 percent. [Benería, p. 1553]

Regional diversity shows up clearly when we look at female participation in the paid labor force as a percentage of male participation. Ruth Sivard has provided such data for the population aged 15 to 64 in 1985, when the region that came by far the closest to parity in this respect was Eastern Europe. The labor force participation of women was 90 percent that of men.[8] In the same year in North America the female labor force participation rate was less than 65 percent that of men. In the Far East it was nearly 60 percent of the male rate. In Western Europe and Oceana, less than 55 percent; in Africa and South Asia, around 45 percent; and in Latin America and the Middle East, around 30 percent.

These generalized figures become more revealing when they are compared with a more detailed look at a single country. Claudia Goldin's book, *Understanding the Gender Gap,* provides an excellent historical portrait of women's participation in the labor market in the United States.[9] Goldin refers to a U-shaped process extending across the last two centuries, in which the market activity of adult women declined to a low point (between 1910 and 1920) and then rose.[10] In this picture, women (especially those who, out of extreme poverty, would accept very bad working conditions) were drawn out of home production into the paid labor force in the early phase of industrialization. As the process of industrialization continued through the nineteenth and into the early twentieth centuries, its benefits begin to be more widely felt in terms of rising income. It then became feasible for more women to assume the roles we may dimly remember from past generations: It was a mark of status and (presumably) a source of comfortable living for family members when the wife could be a full-time homemaker.

The more recent rise of the second arm of the U represents a renewed entrance of women into the labor force in response to a number of factors, including shifts in demand toward the service sector (which employed more women) and technological change.[11] Supply-side variables included increased female education and improved workplace conditions that made market work more attractive. In particular, reduced hours made it more feasible for women to combine paid work with domestic responsibilities, at the same time as the latter were reduced by decreased family size. A variety of other factors strengthened women's motivation to earn an income. These include the rise in divorce, as well as family expectations for material improvement that raced ahead faster than the pay increases of a single earner.

In the early part of the twentieth century, the assumption about female workers was that they were young and not yet married. In fact, "three-quarters of all female workers in 1900, and more than one-half in the (nonwar) years prior to 1950, were single."[12] Although public discussion of the social consequences of married women in the labor force began in the 1920s, the actual numbers involved at that time were small. "Even as late as 1940 most young married women exited the labor force on marriage, and only a small minority would return to the labor force."

It was after 1950 that there was an explosion in the labor force participation and attachment of married women in the United States, increasing by 10 percentage points in each subsequent decade. The proportion of women aged 25 to 34 years old who worked full-time, 50 to 52 weeks a year, went from 39 percent in 1966 to 55 percent in 1986. The percentage of mothers with children younger than a year old who were in the labor force went from 32 percent in 1977 to 52 percent in 1988. Today, more than 70 percent of all U.S. mothers are in the labor force.[13] As summarized in a work of the Population Reference Bureau,

> A dramatic transformation in labor force expectations of and for women had occurred in a generation. As a nation, we are concerned with the unsettled issues arising from that revolution: What will bolster the institution of marriage as husbands' and wives' role become more similar than dissimilar? Who will properly care for our children if all the adults in the family are in the paid labor force?[14]

Attempts to understand trends through historical comparisons are complicated by dramatic changes in the kinds of activities, or their relative weight, that are included in the category of unpaid domestic work. For nineteenth-century Americans, weaving and clothes-making were among the important domestic activities. Within modern homes the former persists only as a rare hobby, and the latter is moving toward a similar status. The sense of loss or threat that lurks behind the second goal laid out in this essay is not based on a wish for home-made clothes. Nevertheless, these comparisons are mentioned because those who are concerned about the performance of essential domestic work often write or speak as though referring to some better "olden time." In the United States that image is probably rooted in circumstances special to the first half of this century. It was then crystallized and idealized in 1950s movies and TV shows, just at the time when the real shift began—of married women into the labor force.

Unfair Burdens

The story just told is not a simple one of substituting hours of paid work for hours of unpaid work. At least in part, the effect has been additive. The result is generally longer work hours put in by women. These are the result both of predictable, routine forms of work as well as of episodic demands imposed by illness, other emergencies, and the years in which mothers are caring for young children while also making other economic contributions to the family. This includes the woman who is breast-feeding, preparing infant foods, and carrying a child on her back while working in the fields or walking to fetch water. It also includes the mother who juggles getting the kids to day care or extracurricular activities while fitting in the grocery shopping and other domestic obligations around the demands of a nine-to-five (or longer) job.

The latter dual role—the one most likely to resonate with readers of this book—probably does not require longer hours of work than the role of the frontier wife and mother, who made many household items, grew and processed much of the family's food, and could purchase few of the educational and other services that we take for granted. This does not mean, however, that it should be accepted as the way things have to be. Indeed, as noted by Lotte Bailyn (summarized here) and others, the Scandinavian countries have shown that it is indeed possible to express society's valuation of caring work by committing a significant proportion of total resources to paying for its performance.

Focusing on the United States, authors such as Arlie Hochschild, Nancy Folbre, and Juliet Schor (all represented in Part VIII) have addressed in various ways the unfair burden of women who carry a disproportionate share of unpaid domestic work along with market employment. Schor notes that even when women are employed they still spend about two-thirds as much time on domestic work as women who do not have market employment; also, that the average amount of time spent on domestic work by the latter has remained virtually unchanged throughout this century—in spite of the introduction of appliances advertised as time-saving. The implication of her article is that there are still significant efficiencies to be gained through social and mechanical innovations designed specifically to reduce housework. Arlie Hochschild, by contrast, expresses concern about the introduction into domestic life of a cult of efficiency, in which family time is parceled out in a Taylorist fashion because parents are experiencing a "time famine," as companies compete for loyalty and time against what she calls "corporate America's local rival—the family." The "third shift" described by Hochschild is the additional effort now required to control the damage—especially to children—that results from the time bind faced by women and men who are working a first shift in a paid job and a second shift at home.

Women who try to have both a career and a domestic life pay a variety of prices. In general, women still face the prejudices and difficulties that are the object of the first goal mentioned in this essay: Equality of job opportunities, and equal pay for equal work, are both still hard to achieve. This point will not be much discussed here, as it will be a major issue for the next Frontier volume, on economic power and inequality. In passing, however, we may note the strong correlation between the types of work that women do in the market and the types of work that receive low pay and low status. It has often been noted that when women enter and become predominant in formerly high-status professions, the status and pay for those jobs declines. There are also numerous examples of women taking the jobs that are avoided by men because of their lower pay and status.[15]

A subtler point about the devaluation of women's work is found in Nancy Folbre's article, 'Holding Hands at Midnight': The Paradox of Caring Labor," in which she addresses the general topic of caring labor, including those aspects that are performed through the market (such as nursing, community work, or teaching). (Note that this subject is also taken up in the Hochschild summary,

"Between the Toe and the Heel," in Part VII.) Folbre focuses especially on those predominantly female jobs that have a "caring" component, and examines a variety of explanations (neoclassical and institutionalist economic, as well as psychological or anthropological explanations) for this nexus of characteristics. She contrasts two feminist economist positions: (1) that "women must be willing to enter traditionally male occupations and compete more aggressively with men in order to improve their positions" (Folbre, 1995, 84), versus (2) that "an emphasis on rewarding caring has somewhat anti-market implications, simply because the market does not elicit caring." (Ibid., 85) She concludes:

> Feminism has played an important role in challenging the patriarchal family, helping establish new rights for women and children and demanding anew definition of family commitments that goes beyond traditional, hierarchical and necessarily heterosexual models. How ironic it would be if progress on this front were neutralized by an individualism so extreme that it renders the best of family values obsolete. An economy based purely on the pursuit of self-interest doesn't leave much room for love. . . . (Ibid., 86–87)

Summaries in Part VIII by Francine Blau and Ronald Ehrenberg as well as Folbre's other summarized article, "Children as Public Goods," describe the real cost, in terms of career development, for a woman to being married and having children.[16] This cost has risen steeply in this century, for a number of reasons. Folbre stresses that in earlier times, women, lacking high-wage alternatives to domestic labor, faced a lower opportunity cost. For both women and men the out-of-pocket cost of raising children was lower because children left the dependency stage earlier, the costs of provisioning and education were lower (these costs have hugely increased with the increasing complexity of society), and children might begin to contribute to the family economy by age five or six. Modern parents, by contrast, continue to provide significant support to their children at least through high school, often through college, and even beyond. In the past children not only provided labor in the parent's business (especially in agricultural societies); they also supplied a home, food, and care for parents who could no longer provide for themselves.

The Cost to Society: Market Equality versus Domestic Responsibility

Changing realities in the last area mentioned—the expectation that children will act as insurance for their parents' old age—are described in the last article summarized here, by anthropologist Allan Meyers. Meyers tells of a personnel shortage in long-term care for individuals with disabilities (especially the elderly), noting that "the industrialized countries have come to rely increasingly upon immigrants (documented and undocumented) and refugees, mainly women from developing countries, to meet their dependency needs." [Meyers, 49] However, this case rests mainly on a dramatic growth in dependency (as the population ages and medical advances can increasingly save the lives of those afflicted, by birth or accident, with severe disabilities), and only secondarily on a reduction in the willingness or ability of developed-country populations to meet those needs. Meyers poses the urgent question: If currently less developed countries pursue the path of modernization, following the demographic trends of the industrialized countries, who will take care of their dependent elderly populations?

On the parameter of child care, a careful time-use study from the early 1970s noted that "female employment reduces the time spent with children by slightly more than one third."[17] The fear that the necessary domestic work traditionally associated with women will simply not get done receives some support from demographic trends. A decline in birthrates below replacement level is already evident in a number of western—and increasingly, also, eastern—European countries.[18] This is consistent with the "economic woman" argument, that a cost-benefit calculation goes against motherhood.

A recent study by Jonathan Gershuny and John Robinson (summarized here) does not dispute that market work is in conflict with domestic work, but reports more complex findings. The time that women spent on domestic chores (other than child care) in the United Kingdom and the United States dropped overall between the 1960s and the 1980s, with the timing of sharp drops in each country coinciding with especially rapid increases in paid labor force participation. However, when these authors separately analyzed two groups—women with, and women without, paid jobs—they found that in both countries each group has *increased* the time devoted to child care, a finding that is open to a variety of interpretations.

In general, at least over relatively short time periods (a few decades), and within single countries or fairly homogeneous regions, it appears that paid work is in competition with unpaid work and reduces the time available for the latter.

Prescriptions and Policies

The complex of problems addressed in this essay includes the following facts: There is much important caring work to be done in the world; women who take formal employment are likely to have less time available for unpaid work; and the existing situation in most of the world, in which women carry a dual burden of caring and earning, is inequitable. Even less acceptable is the idea that history should be rolled back and women should leave the world of paid work. The following is a short list of alternative possible responses.

1. *Socializing the costs of caring labor.* This is what has, in fact, been under-
    taken in social welfare programs in virtually every modern nation. The
    question is not whether this is a good idea, but how far to take it. The
    menu of possibilities includes public support for maternity programs in-
    cluding nutrition, health, and training for motherhood; a vast variety of
    other kinds of public health programs, relevant to all ages and segments of
    a given population; nursing homes, home-visiting services, Meals-on-
    Wheels; public child care (day care, nurseries); publicly supported educa-
    tion from kindergarten through graduate school; and so on. As noted ear-
    lier, this solution has been taken farthest in some northern European
    countries, where, it could be argued, the conflict between the first and sec-
    ond goals listed at the start of this essay has been virtually eliminated. In
    Scandinavia and the Netherlands a variety of caring activities are recog-
    nized as socially valuable, and a collective decision has been made to allo-
    cate significant public resources to paying people to perform these tasks
    within socialized facilities. As an example of the backwardness of the
    United States in this respect, "[a]ll industrialized countries except the
    United States provide family allowances based on the number and ages of
    children to allow mothers to choose to stay home."[19]

2. *Shifting activities out of the family into other social institutions.* This ap-
    proach may or may not be included under the first option above, depend-
    ing on whether or not the alternative institutions are publicly supported.
    Much of this has already happened in industrialized countries. For exam-
    ple, education is increasingly left to schools, counseling is available from a
    variety of specialized professions, and care for the sick can be purchased
    through nursing homes or other market arrangements. As Meyers points
    out, the limits of this solution may have already been reached in the area
    of elderly care, as long as society's valuations of these caring activities re-
    mains unchanged. Likewise, if schools are to take on more than their pre-
    sent roles, they will need more personnel, with some different kinds of
    training, and more funds to attract qualified people into these positions.
    Many other institutional solutions, as long as they are not socialized (such
    as quality care for individuals born with severe mental or physical disabili-
    ties), will remain out of reach for all but the wealthy.

3. *Workplace policies to make it easier for people to fulfill the requirements of
    both work and home.* This is related to the two previous options, but de-
    pends more on action taken at the firm level and usually has consequences
    for the cost of doing business. Decades of experience now make it clear
    that when such policies are applied to women only, they can be a two-
    edged sword. For example, parental leave, when applied more to women
    than to men, can provide humane relief from some of the most acute pres-

sures of juggling motherhood and career, but with the unwanted effect of dampening women's career prospects. (This point is brought out in the summaries by Baylin, and by Francine Blau and Ronald Ehrenberg.[20]) Less obviously gender-related policies include employer flexibility with respect to options for part-time work, work performed at home, and similar moves that were described in Part V. As we saw there, while these options can have many advantages they can also help to create a "mommy track" or, sometimes, to shift the balance of power away from the worker, toward the employer.

4. *Privatizing the benefits of caring labor.* As discussed earlier, nearly all of the economic incentives that used to exist for parenting have evaporated. Are there ways of tying some benefits to successful parenting without creating perverse incentives? As an example, some additional retirement bonus might be awarded to the contributing parents of each child who successfully completes high school. This is a thought-provoking but problematical proposal.[21] A less problematical example of privatizing the benefits of caring labor emerges in proposals to subsidize family home care for the elderly, based on the savings to society over nursing home or hospital care.

5. *Changes in living design.* Some aspects of domestic labor may still be open to simplification or reduction in time requirements via improved materials, technologies, and social systems (clothes that don't require ironing, automated shopping and delivery services, and so on). Other aspects might become a lesser burden through deeper social change. Suggestions along this line include communitarian living arrangements as suggested, for example, by Hilkka Pietila (summarized here).

6. *Changes in cultural expectations, with special attention to gender roles.* Most proponents of this approach (including a majority of the authors summarized here) stress the desirability of reexamining how males are socialized, to make it more acceptable for men and boys to share in caring labor. This usually includes deemphasizing aggressive, competitive behavior. A major change of this sort would include a reevaluation of what really matters in life, and what are the deepest sources of pleasure and satisfaction. This possibility might, for example, move some individuals in the direction of the voluntary simplicity movement, where a consciously directed reduction in wants reduces the time required to earn a living and increases the time available for living. If men and women were to share equally in cultural changes of this nature, they would have more freedom to reconsider the individual gains that come from participating in caring labor. An overall increase in "leisure" (nonpaid-work) time would also make it easier to negotiate a fair division, between men and women, of the less appealing aspects of caring labor.

Most of the articles summarized in this part of the volume contain prescriptive comments, with more frequent reference to prescriptions (3) and (6) than to the others. But this is clearly not an either-or matter. Each of the six categories of response appears to have limits in how much it can accomplish; however, synergies among several of them could enlarge their limits. As is so often the case, it seems that any possible effectiveness of each approach is likely to be enhanced if some or all of the others are present.

Overall, examination of the literature in this area is encouraging. It would be good if there were more public debate than now exists in this country regarding the proposed categories of prescription, but there is cause for cautious optimism in the fact that, across a fairly wide political spectrum, none of them appears to be out of bounds for consideration. Regarding the three goals with which we started, substantial progress has been made in putting them all on the table together, in spite of the difficulties in their simultaneous resolution.

Notes

1. Nancy Folbre, *Who Pays for the Kids?* (London: Routledge, 1994).

2. UNDP, *Human Development Report* (New York: Oxford University Press, 1995), 98.

3. The UNDP's definition of "economic activities" was governed by a "third-person rule": an activity qualifies as economic if it would be possible to hire someone else to do it. For an interesting critique of this rule, see Himmelweit, "The Discovery of 'Unpaid Work.'"

4. In an article summarized here Lourdes Benería identifies four types of productive work that are largely unrepresented in formal accounts of national wealth: subsistence production, informal paid production, domestic work, and volunteer work. Women play a larger role than men in all of Benería's categories. The first of them, which includes agriculture as well as provisioning activities such as the collection and transportation of water and fuel, is likely to be the dominant category of unpaid work in rural areas of the Third World. Because of the focus of this book on the industrialized world, we have not attempted to cover the work issues that are especially related to subsistence production.

5. UNDP (note 2, above), 88.

6. Ibid., 94.

7. Shirley P. Burggraf, *The Feminine Economy and Economic Man: Reviving the Role of Family in the Postindustrial Age* (Reading, MA: Addison-Wesley Publishing Company, Inc., 1997), 22–23.

8. Ruth Sivard, *Women, A World Survey.* (Washington, D.C.: World Priorities, 1995). This reflects simply the number of people who had paid jobs. The 1995 UNDP estimates suggest that, if the comparison were made on the basis of hours worked in the formal labor force, women may in fact contribute more than 100 percent of the male average of formal labor hours. Lobodzinska's article provides a closer look at how these figures should be interpreted, in terms of women's experience and status at work and in the home.

9. Claudia Goldin, *Understanding the Gender Gap: An Economic History of American Women* (New York: Oxford University Press, 1990).

10. For a similar U-shaped curve in other countries, see the summary in Part VII by Nilufer Cagatay and Sule Ozler.

11. Goldin (note 9, above) puts forth an interesting thesis on the role of technical change:

> As a general proposition, technological advances are accompanied by an increase in the female intensity of an industry or a sector of the economy. Where technological change has been greatest from 1890 to 1980, as measured by total factor productivity increases, women's employment share relative to the average in the economy has increased the most. . . . Although technological change does not always lead to the replacement of male workers by females, the instances of men replacing women because of technological change are few compared with those of women replacing men. [94]

12. Ibid., 175. The next two quotations are from the same source, pages 95 and 216.

13. Article by Barbara Vobejda in *The Washington Post* Jan. 26, 1998, A04. The article notes that, of the children under five whose mothers work, 43 percent are cared for by relatives (including fathers and grandparents), 29 percent are in organized child care centers, and 21 percent are cared for by a baby-sitter or nanny.

14. Suzanne Bianchi and Daphne Spain, "Women, Work, and Family in America," in *Population Bulletin* 51, 3 (Washington, D.C.: Population Reference Bureau, Inc., December 1996), 3.

15. Cf. ibid. pages 20–21; also Lobodzinska, summarized here. There is a strong improving trend with respect to these problems: "Between 1980 and 1994, the ratio of women's to men's earnings among full-time, year-round workers, the most commonly used barometer of gender wage inequality, increased from 60 to 72 percent." [Bianchi and Spain (note 14, above), 24.] At the same time, the improvement in the status and pay of jobs open to women—the approach toward achieving goal (1) (equal work and equal pay)—is creating the pressures described below on goal (2) (that household and caring work not be neglected).

16. See also Jane Waldfogel, "The Price of Motherhood: Family Status and Women's Pay in a Young British Cohort," *Oxford Economic Papers* 47 (1995), 584–610.

17. Philip J. Stone, "Child Care in Twelve Countries," in ed. Alexander Szalai, *The Use of Time: Daily activities of urban and suburban populations in twelve countries* (The Hague: Mouton; publication of the European Coordination Centre for Research and Documentation in the Social Sciences, 1972), 263. Note that the reference here is to full-time employment (7 to 8 hours a day). While the average figure cited here seems to hold over a good many different circumstances, there is more variation in the overall consequences for women's time use as they enter the market. A particularly close analysis was given to a comparison of time use in three cities, in the United States, Yugoslavia, and Poland. In the U.S. city studied, unemployed housewives were "relatively speaking, the most privileged as far as amounts of free time were concerned," enjoying almost six hours of nonwork time per day—"about an hour more than the average employed man." In Poland housewives and employed males each had a little less than five free hours per day. In Yugoslavia housewives had just a little more than three hours of free time, compared to four hours for employed men. The reduction in leisure time for women in the three cities when they took employment was as follows: in the United

States, 2 hours reduction, to 4 hours leisure time; in Poland 1.5 hours reduction, to 3.5 hours leisure time; and in Yugoslavia 1.5 hours reduction, to 2.5 hours leisure time. In the latter two cases the reduction in leisure time would have been even more dramatic if the researchers had included the women's approximately one hour reduction in sleep time. [Ibid., 270–272]

18. While the total fertility rate in the United States has hovered at or just under 2 percent, most of Europe is considerably below this. The total fertility rate "was lowest in Italy and Spain (1.2) in 1996, with Germany, Greece, Latvia and Romania close behind with an average of 1.3 children. Fertility in many European countries has declined since the 1970s despite policies designed to promote childbearing, including subsidized maternity leave and family allowances for each child." [Bianchi and Spain (note 14, above), 39.]

19. Ibid., 41.

20. See also Heike Trappe, "Work and Family in Women's Lives in the German Democratic Republic," in *Work and Occupations* (Beverly Hills, California: Sage Publications, 1996).

21. This is an adaptation of a far more extreme proposal by Shirley Burggraf (note 7, above), to make all social security payments to parents dependent on their children's earnings, while nonparents would be expected to save for their own retirement out of the funds they had not spent on raising children.

Summary of

Introduction to *Gender and Family Issues in the Workplace*

by Francine Blau and Ronald Ehrenberg

[Published in *Gender and Family Issues in the Workplace,* eds. Francine D. Blau and Ronald G. Ehrenberg (New York: Russell Sage Foundation, 1997), Chapter 1, 1-19.]

Women have been moving into the workplace in ever greater numbers over the last half of the twentieth century. Shortly after World War II women began entering (or returning to) work in midlife as their children became older. Recently more women with young children are also working outside the home. Both the workplace and the household are changing in response. This article is the introductory chapter to a book that examines several aspects of the intersection of work and family in the United States, along with policy implications.

Gender Gaps

Since the 1970s, women have been moving into traditionally male professional and managerial positions. Nevertheless there is still significant occupational segregation (the tendency for men and women to work in different kinds of jobs). Women remain heavily concentrated in "female" jobs or face a "glass ceiling" that limits access to the highest levels of success. Large majorities of both men and women polled by *Fortune* magazine in 1995 agreed that "male-dominated corporate culture" poses a significant obstacle to women. [3] Few women hold top-level positions in business, higher education, or government.

It is especially difficult for women with children to gain equality in the workplace. While mothers hold jobs in increasing numbers, few women have managed to have both families and successful careers. College-educated women early in the twentieth century faced a clear choice: marriage or career. In the decades after World War II their experience was similar to that of less educated women: taking jobs after their children had reached school age or older. This was not, however, a pattern compatible with career development. In recent decades many women expressed a desire to "have it all"—career and family—but reversed the sequence, hoping to establish careers before starting a family. Yet, according to one study, even under a broad definition of career, only 22 percent of women who graduated from college between 1966 and 1979 had both family and career by the late 1980s.

With women having, on average, fewer weeks of full-time work over the course of the year than men, by the 1990s annual earnings for women appear to have stalled at around 70 percent of men's annual earnings. However, the hourly pay comparison has improved more: weekly earnings for women working full time in 1995 were 76 percent that of men's, compared to 61 percent in 1978. According to one analysis of wage determinants, marriage (absent children) has a positive effect for men and a smaller but still positive effect for women. However, while the effect of children is neutral or positive for men, it is negative for women, even after controlling for education and experience. Even while the average wage gap between men and women steadily narrowed, a comparison of 30-year-old workers in 1980 and 1991 found that mothers' wages only grew from 60 percent to 75 percent of men's wages, while non-mothers nearly closed the gap, rising from 72 percent to 95 percent of men's wages. "Thus, the relative disadvantage of mothers compared with others increased." [9] These results imply that efforts to address the gender wage gap should focus especially on the issues that confront parents in the labor market. The articles in the volume introduced here deal especially with three such issues: parental leave, the length of work-hours required by employers, and the gender of supervisors. The article on the last of these three topics did not lead to clear conclusions.

Parental Leave

Parental leave takes different forms in different countries. In the United States, the last industrialized country to mandate family and work policies, the Family and Medical Leave Act of 1993 requires firms with fifty or more employees to offer up to twelve weeks of unpaid leave to meet family responsibilities. In many

European countries, longer leave periods are the norm and often include income support. While parental leave can reduce the conflict between work and child care for parents of infants, parental leave that is too well supported can increase inequality in the labor market. Although fathers as well as mothers are eligible for family-oriented benefits in many countries, generally it is the mother who stays home with young children. If she extends her leave to the point that she misses opportunities for advancement or her skills become obsolete, her position in the labor market will fall short of its potential.

On the other hand, short parental leaves (in excess of actual maternity leave, which is a medical benefit) can improve women's chances for career success. A woman who might have quit a job in order to spend the first months at home with her newborn child can, with parental leave, return to a job in which she has begun to build a career. Every employer has unique routines and tasks that can only be learned through on-the-job experience. If a woman quits, these skills will go unrewarded when she reenters the job market. If the previous job was particularly well-suited to her qualifications and preferences, she may not find such a good fit elsewhere. She will lose job satisfaction, while two employers and society at large will be poorer for the less efficient use of her skills.

The Rat-Race Equilibrium

Even if, after bearing a child, a woman returns to the same position with the same career potential, she still faces difficult choices in balancing the time devoted to work and to family. Many careers do not brook balance—they demand total commitment. They may even operate under a "rat-race" regime in which working longer hours is not only a matter of getting more done (with commensurate rewards in pay and promotions), but is a signal to employers of hard-to-measure qualities such as ambition and motivation. Even a person who prefers shorter hours may work long hours in the early stages of a career, hoping to gain a powerful position with more discretion over work and family choices. To defeat this agenda and screen out all but the most dedicated (or workaholic) employees, a firm may set performance requirements extremely high.

This rat-race hypothesis is a controversial one, but it does highlight the fact that equality is not easy to achieve, and policies can have unintended consequences. Firms that initiate flexible hours will attract more than their fair share of less-committed employees, a situation that economists call adverse selection. If a firm provides child care assistance so that all employees can work long hours, but working long hours remains the hallmark of a top-level performer, then those who hope to succeed will have to work still more to overtake the rest.

Implications for Policy

> Given the changes in women's roles within the family that potentially affect all family members, attaining greater gender equity in the labor market requires addressing the issues that arise from shifts in gender roles in the family. Chief among them is how workers of both sexes can more effectively mesh their home and work responsibilities. [3]

For some advocates of maternity leave the paramount goal is to allow the development of healthy, secure bonds between infants and their mothers. Others are more interested in the economic benefits. Family leave policies that fall into the middle range of those now in place (in Europe as well as in the United States) seem to serve both goals. However, given existing cultural habits and expectations regarding male and female family and work roles, as the policies go toward the more generous extreme, there may be a trade-off between the immediate economic and the child-welfare effects.

Some economists have expressed concern about the impact of mandated family leave policy on economic efficiency. However, longitudinal analysis of a number of macroeconomic indicators in several countries shows little or no direct economic effect from moderate levels of parental leave. Indirect improvements to economic efficiency are expected by those who see such policies as making up for market failures related to externalities or adverse selection. For example, if young children receive better care from parents than from other care givers, the child's improved health and adjustment to social norms will reduce medical, schooling, and other costs to society as a whole—a positive externality for which parents may be unwilling to bear the full cost. An adverse selection issue arises in the possibility that firms offering parental leave could disproportionately attract employees who were likely to take it, unless government levels the playing field by requiring all firms to offer this benefit.

Citing research that indicates that the mother's employment has no negative effect on children over a year old, advocates for gender equality claim that extended leave reinforces the traditional division of labor between men and women, and disadvantages women in the workplace. From this point of view, child care subsidies are the preferred public policy option.

Workplace policies that encourage men to take on more household responsibility would shift the balance of equity not only in the home, but also in the workplace. Even if corporate culture continued to favor those who commit to very long working hours, if men shared equally in family work, the penalties for shorter employment hours would no longer fall disproportionately on women.

Fundamental to an assessment of these and other policies is the requirement to develop "appropriate social and employer policies to meet the needs of workers with family responsibilities." [19]

Summary of

Historical Changes in the Household Division of Labor

by Jonathan I. Gershuny and John P. Robinson

[Published in *Demography* 25 (November 1988), 537–552.]

In the last half of the twentieth century, as women have rapidly moved into the paid workforce, there has been concern about how women's traditional responsibilities in the home will be fulfilled. One possibility is for men to increase their share of time spent in household work. This article reviews data on time use, especially in the United States and the United Kingdom, to evaluate changes in patterns of household labor time for men and women.

The Household Time Debate

Contemporary discussions of women and housework tends to present a pessimistic portrait of women as trapped in low-status household chores because of their role in social reproduction—maintaining the family for societal continuity. This role means that women have less time and energy to devote to paid work than men have. "With power in modern societies increasingly defined by position in the paid labor market, therefore, women's housework responsibilities perpetuate their inferior status." [537] Empirical analysis of time budgets confirms that women do indeed bear the lion's share of responsibility for work in the home. However, this research is mainly reported on a cross-sectional basis, which cannot capture changes over time. When these studies are compared historically they show declining gender differentials. Women's share of domestic work is decreasing while men are doing more.

Why, then, the pessimism? There is, first, the observation that women who enter paid work still retain significant home responsibilities. Note has also been taken of cases in which household technology improves the quality of housework without reducing the time spent doing it. Cross-sectional studies comparing women with and without access to domestic technology, countries at different stages of development, and countries in different periods of technological development, have suggested that the time spent on domestic work is constant or, counterintuitively, may even increase with greater access to technology.

These observations are contested by an analysis that couples a new look at older data with more recent survey evidence. The results show that time spent by women in at least some kinds of household work has, in fact, declined in recent years.

Methodology: Behavioral versus Compositional Change

"The basic measures of time use in this article are derived from time-budget surveys in which the respondents report all their daily activities within a structured diary format." [539] Time diaries have been shown to be reliable methods of self-reporting, easy for respondents to use, and able to capture periods when more than one activity is going on. The time diary data analyzed here was collected in the United Kingdom in 1961, 1973/74, and 1983/84 and in the United States in 1965/66, 1975, and 1985. The analysis focuses on activities of the 25 to 49 age group to achieve greater standardization and reduce the effects of demographic shifts affecting older and younger groups (such as longer education, later marriage, or early retirement).

At first glance, the data suggests that time spent in child care is increasing in the United Kingdom but decreasing in the United States, while time spent by women in routine domestic work is declining in both countries. It is important to investigate whether these changes simply reflect structural shifts—women moving from the household to the paid workplace—or changes in family structure. If working women generally spend less time in routine household chores than full-time homemakers do, when more women move into paid employment, average time spent on routine chores will drop. This would represent a change in the structure of women's time rather than a change in the behavior of women in similar circumstances.

The pessimistic view holds that there is a core amount of household work from which women cannot escape, whether or not they work outside the home. Interpretation of the data as a structural shift is consistent with this view. It could simply mean that more women are moving toward this inescapable core. This issue can be analyzed by distinguishing the effects of more women working outside the home, on the one hand, from the reality, on the other hand, of whether each category of women (with and without paid employment) are spending less time in housework.

Statistical techniques (such as shift-share analysis) were used to decompose structural and behavioral effects. Examination of the data and a literature review from several social sciences indicates that involvement in paid work (full-time, part-time, or none) and family status (no children at home, at least one child under 5 years old, or children 5 to 18 years old) are the most relevant structural variables. To examine the behavioral variables, household activities were divided into four categories: shopping and related travel; child care; routine domestic chores like cooking and cleaning; and odd jobs like pet care or gardening. (The last category was not evaluated due to problems with the U.K. data.)

Changes in Unpaid Work Time

Between the 1960s and 1980s, both countries witnessed an overall drop in the time women spent in routine domestic chores. "Does this really reflect a change in behavior or merely a change in the structure of the population? In the United Kingdom, most of the reduction took place during the 1960s and early 1970s. In the United States, most of the reduction happened during the later 1970s and early 1980s. In both countries, then, the major reduction in core housework took place over the period that women's participation in paid work increased most." [544]

There is also a compositional change that shows up in the details: women with children reduced their time spent in routine domestic chores, while women with no children increased housework time somewhat—although the absolute amount of time remained less than for women with children. These changes were virtually identical in the two countries. Shift-share analysis indicates that 90 percent of the reduction in time spent on domestic work in the United Kingdom was due to behavioral change, while in the United States 60 percent of the reduction can be attributed to behavioral change. A second type of share analysis indicates that the time women spend in routine household chores has been dropping and the time spent by men has been increasing. However, the absolute amount of time men spend is still well below that spent by women.

Share analysis of the time spent in child care reveals more similar patterns in the United States and the United Kingdom than the raw data would indicate. Once the large increase of women in the United States into paid work is accounted for, there is an increase in child care time for both U.S. and U.K. women. This may reflect changing norms (Dr. Spock-inspired child-raising practices) or a perception that children need more protection from crime or traffic. It could also be an artifact of the research. In earlier surveys attention to a child may have been reported as a secondary activity while the mother was doing laundry or other chores. More recently, child care may be identified as the primary activity while an automatic washing machine runs in the background.

British women have dramatically increased shopping and related travel behavior, compared to only a slight reduction in the United States. This may reflect an increase in purchasing power and the introduction of self-serve markets to the United Kingdom at a later period than in the United States, where such facilities predate the survey period. Time spent in both child care and shopping by men in the United States dropped slightly, while it increased for men in the United Kingdom.

A final form of analysis, variance decomposition using multiple classification analysis, was applied to the U.S.–U.K. surveys as well as to data for four other countries: Canada, Denmark, Norway, and Holland. Across all countries and all studied decades, women spent an average of 214 minutes per day in routine domestic work, while men spent 27. Of most interest, though, is the effect of structural components and the change in behavior over time. Working outside the home reduces the time women spend on housework. On average, for each 100 minutes in paid work there is a 31-minute drop in housework. The reduction for men is much smaller. Women with children spend more time than average on housework, while women with no children spend less time than average. Children have little or no effect on the amount of time men spend on housework.

Overall, it appears that the time women spend on housework in the United States and the United Kingdom is falling, even when structural changes are accounted for, while the time spent by men is increasing (but at a slower rate). Similar trends exist in the four other countries examined. Patterns of change for child care and shopping are more mixed, but absolute amounts of time devoted to these activities by men and women are on converging paths.

The reduction of women's time in these activities may be variously explained by the movement of women into paid work, the low status and unpleasantness of housework, support for gender equality from women's movements, and the diffusion of household technology, where time-saving effects of new appliances like dishwashers and microwave ovens may be apparent only over the long-term. However, there is not enough evidence on which to draw firm conclusions about causal relationships. Based on the evidence presented here, a less ambitious assertion can be made—"that it is the trends that we have outlined— the declining totals of domestic work, with a marginal redistribution from women to men—rather than the previously assumed constancy of domestic work over historical time, that constitutes the facts to be explained by theorists of domestic production." [551]

Summary of

Accounting for Women's Work:
The Progress of Two Decades

by Lourdes Benería

[Published in *World Development* 20 (1992), 1547–1560.]

Women's work has been persistently underestimated in statistics and national income reporting. Accordingly, the contribution of women to the economic life of households, communities, countries, and, indeed, the global economy as a

whole has neither been appreciated nor adequately considered in economic decision making. This article reviews the theoretical constructs and methodologies involved in data collection and analysis and reports on the progress made
over the past twenty years.

Cause and Consequences of Underestimation

Historically, statistics for national income accounting, economic analysis, and
planning have been geared toward market activities and trends. In capitalist
economies the market is the core of economic activity and the dominant framework for understanding it. According to the 1954 International Conference of
Labor Force Statisticians, labor force participation and production are related
to work "for pay or profit." However, there is a growing realization that market transactions do not capture all economic realities and are particularly inadequate for understanding much of the economically relevant work that women
do.

Four areas have been identified where productive work occurs but is largely
unaccounted for: subsistence production, informal paid production, domestic
work, and volunteer work. Both conceptual issues and measurement methods
have diverted attention from these sectors. The first two suffer from measurement problems, while the latter two expose more conceptual difficulties in recognizing that women do, in fact, engage in economic activity.

Subsistence production was recognized as a critical component of national income accounting by statisticians who developed these systems in the late 1940s.
The omission of subsistence production meant that less-developed countries
appeared poorer than they actually were and that growth rates were artificially
elevated when this activity moved into the formal market. In an effort to change
this, the U.N. and several countries began to develop new estimation methods.
In 1966, labor force statisticians adopted a new definition of the labor force as
"all persons of either sex who furnish the supply of economic goods and services," whether they are engaged in market transactions or not.[1] Measurement
problems still existed. Women's contributions were often not separated from
family labor totals. Variations in measurement criteria across countries and lack
of clear specification of what constitutes subsistence production particularly affect the understanding of women's work. Women are so highly involved with
work in the home, the line between subsistence production and household production is difficult to draw.

Informal paid work is recognized as economic activity by virtue of being re-
munerated, but is by definition hidden from or beyond the scope of available
data collection methods. The informal economy is unstable, precarious, and unregulated. Part of it is underground. The high level of participation by women
means that underestimation undermines efforts to understand women's eco-

nomic contribution and the conditions of women's work. So far efforts to collect data have been on an ad hoc basis. However, the U.N. has developed guidelines and carried out several pilot projects combining microeconomic surveys with macroeconomic data.

Domestic work is not considered a substitute for market activity, yet there is a joke among economists that GNP goes down when a man marries his housekeeper—since she no longer transacts with him for a wage. Domestic work often blends into subsistence production, particularly in developing economies (processing food, hauling wood or water, making clothes or pots). In higher-income countries domestic work incorporates self-help projects like construction or repairs, which could otherwise be purchased through the market. Domestic work is difficult to measure and to compare with market work. However, and despite skepticism among some analysts, these difficulties are not insurmountable.

Volunteer work also involves women disproportionately. In the mid-1980s, women in New Zealand pointed out that money contributed to charity, mostly by men, is tax deductible, while contributions of time, mostly by women, are not. Volunteer work is generally directed outside the family, but lines can blur when family members benefit from community volunteer efforts. Some women in countries with austerity programs imposed by structural adjustment packages have set up collective kitchens that blend volunteer, domestic, and subsistence activities.

Recognition of the economic value of unpaid and unrecorded work presents a more accurate picture of reality, acknowledges the contributions of women more fully, and provides a more comprehensive measure of welfare. These are subjects of quantitatively large significance. Estimates of the value of unrecorded activities have ranged from one-third to one-half of GNP as now measured. To be effective, human resource and output planning and policy must consider all relevant economic activity. A full understanding of household dynamics, savings, consumption, and labor force patterns is not possible without information about the paid and unpaid work of women.

Progress Report

Progress has been made along several lines of inquiry in the conceptualization, specification, and measurement of unpaid and unrecorded work and the elaboration of theoretical frameworks for analyzing the household and relating household production to market production. In 1982, labor force statisticians aligned the definition of the economically active population with the U.N. definition that incorporates subsistence production. Next came efforts to standardize and clarify the specification of tasks. Some analysts proposed multiple specifications for different purposes. This discussion is ongoing and systematic within the U.N. and among academicians and women's organizations. It has resulted in further revision of the definition of economic activity and in changes in the Standard Classification of Occupations. Although recent formulations are broad enough to encompass previously unconsidered economic activity, in practice the focus is still on the market rather than on its contribution to welfare.

Neoclassical, feminist, and Marxian authors have devoted attention to household dynamics by taking up topics like the sexual division of labor, the social construction of gender discrimination, or the importance of household labor for the reproduction of the labor force. A different theoretical discussion asks whether household and market production can be aggregated for accounting purposes even though home-based labor is not subject to the same competitive pressures or productivity standards as market-based work. (Some researchers counter that inefficient households would fail to achieve their purpose—to survive and subsist.)

Progress has been made on two methodological fronts. One is more accurate collection of country-level data, marked by revisions to regular census and survey vehicles, and targeted surveys in several countries. The other is the development of a variety of estimation approaches and tools. The main approaches revolve around input (valuation of labor time spent in household production) or output (imputation of market prices to goods and services produced in the home).

Input valuation generally uses one of three estimation methods: (1) *global substitute*—measuring the cost of a hired domestic worker; (2) *specialized substitute*—measuring the cost of specialized workers for each domestic task; and (3) *opportunity cost*—measuring the wage a household member would command if he or she worked in the market. Output valuation requires detailed information about the price each household good or service would have on the market and the costs of inputs. Each method offers insights and drawbacks. For instance, if a woman must walk farther to fetch the same amount of water, an output method would reflect the constant amount of water, while an input method would reveal the woman's increased effort.

Statistical Information: Objectives, Problems, and Purposes

Many obstacles remain before reliable and relevant data can be collected on a consistent basis. These challenges generally stem from a lack of awareness, resistance to change, technical problems, or costs. Solutions begin with an analysis of existing methods, a review of definitions for substance and clarity, greater attention paid to technical issues in survey research, sensitivity to cultural issues, and proper training and supervision of data collection workers.

How would accurate and relevant data on women's economic activity be used? Several applications have been mentioned above, but there are also other uses: to enhance indicators of the condition of women; to improve research and analysis of women's activity; to shed new light on the historical record of women's activities in the home (which often provide unacknowledged economic benefits); or to better understand the relative weight of domestic work in relation to GNP. These issues will gain importance as sentiment builds among researchers to shift national accounting "away from the goal of measuring goods and services exchanged through the market toward providing more sophisticated indicators of social welfare and human development." [1558]

Note

1. International Labor Office, *International Recommendations on Labor Statistics* (Geneva: ILO, 1976), cited by the author, 1548.

Summary of

Women's Employment or Return to "Family Values" in Central-Eastern Europe

by Barbara Lobodzinska

[Published in *Journal of Comparative Family Studies* 27, 3 (1996), 518–543.]

Women in the former Soviet Union and in Eastern Europe face many confusing changes, often involving conflicting values. Not only do they face the transition from socialist to capitalist economies, and from authoritarian to democratic government—they must redefine their own roles in relation to work, family, and their own self-image and aspirations. To further complicate this transition, the ideology of socialism, which proclaimed equality for women, was not fully implemented in the day-to-day reality of women's lives.

Under socialism, as under capitalism, women often worked two shifts: one on a job, the other at home. However, under socialism, the expectation that women would work in a paid job was much higher and many economic institutions were organized around that expectation. Now that those institutions are being taken apart, women are reevaluating the rewards to working outside of their family responsibilities, and the realistic options for getting good jobs in a volatile economy.

Ideology versus Reality

> Socialist ideology claimed 'equality for all' as a token taken for granted. Women were indoctrinated that the road to universal equality is outlined by achievement of justice for all workers (men and women alike) in the process of their victorious struggle against the exploiting owners of the means of production (not associated with men). Women were not expected to distinguish their own specific needs and issues . . . because only through being a worker (preferably in the heavy industry) they had a chance to achieve equality. [339]

Although equality was the official doctrine, many women found themselves in an inferior position, working in monotonous, low-status jobs while bearing most, if not all, of the responsibility for maintaining home and family. Many managers believed that women were good at these tedious jobs and ill suited to work requiring creativity, adaptation to change, technical skill, or managerial responsibility.

In Poland, Hungary, and Lithuania women may have achieved a higher average level of education than men, but they were more focused on the humanities, teaching, social sciences, and medicine, as opposed to the vocational and technical tracks followed by men. With men expected to be the primary breadwinners, and female earnings averaging only 70 percent of their husbands, women's occupational choices were less oriented to personal career considerations. Many women accepted low-skilled white-collar and service jobs that could flexibly combine the roles of wife, mother, and employee. Often a predilection for less-demanding work compatible with responsibilities in the home was instilled in girls early in life by their own families. Where women did move into skilled positions formerly dominated by men, like teaching or medicine, those professions lost status.

Unemployment and Motivations for Employment

"[W]omen are regarded by many in the former socialist countries as the primary losers under the new circumstances." [536] As Central and Eastern European countries moved toward market economies, unemployment became a problem. With jobs scarce, women were often consigned to less attractive ones. To the extent that family and mother's benefits still exist, they make women more expensive, and therefore less desirable as employees.

In some ways, socialism had fulfilled its ideals about working. Since every able adult was expected to work, wages were set with the expectation that families would have two incomes and many benefits were tied to employment, including generous benefits for mothers. Economic reality along with social pressure thus obliged nearly all women to work outside the home. Nevertheless, family roles remained central to their choice of employment. However, researchers have long noted that women often have other, more personal, reasons for working. They may wish for financial independence, or want to pursue particular interests, or want to be involved in activity and relationships outside the home. A survey of unemployed women in Poland in the early 1990s discovered that nearly half defined an occupation as "a source of satisfaction," while 22.5 percent saw it as "a chance to utilize own abilities and qualifications," and only 18.1 percent sought an occupation as "a source of high income." [529] One indication that women have aspirations beyond financial need is that women have been steadily increasing their skills and education, even though, under the egalitarian ethic of socialism, higher education does not result in much higher pay.

A large survey of occupationally active women was carried out in Poland in 1987 and again in 1991, both before and after the emergence of the market economy. When asked to choose among several possible lifestyles, the largest group of respondents (about one-third, in both phases) thought women "should work, but [should expect] to interrupt work in order to take care of the children, to aim for family partnership relationships, to favor harmonious family life over own career advancement." [353] The next largest group (about 23 percent) preferred full equality with men both at home and at work. However, when the group that was willing to work only if it didn't interfere with the family is combined with respondents who felt that home and family should be women's primary (or only) occupation, three-quarters of all respondents in both phases weighed in on the side of putting family first. The percentage of women who would choose a successful career even at the expense of the family was negligible.

Women's values did not change radically after the fall of socialism. The majority of women hoped to find some combination of work and family responsibility. The central goal, now as before, was the preservation of the family. However, the economic changes have left many families struggling for survival, without accustomed health and family benefits or even a job. "Many signs indicate that in the past, combining family and occupational roles was burdensome and not rewarding enough for women." [34] Unemployment, however, is no solution. Housing shortages and reduced incomes mean overcrowding and lack of privacy.

Return to "Family Values"

Women's concerns, pushed to the background, are generally ignored by politicians and political activists. Religious organizations that have taken up the cause of the family encourage a return to traditional family values, favoring strong marital relationships and rejecting divorce and abortion. The back-to-home tendency has been much publicized, but in reality the trend is complicated by a reaction to the mandatory nature of work under socialism. Women now are evaluating work, not under pressure to meet a "politically correct" ideal, but with consideration of realistic options for getting good jobs and the real burden of their domestic obligations. Under socialism, women were told they had already achieved equality, but behind the ideology a very traditional, patriarchal set of values kept women in a second-class, and overburdened, role.

Under capitalism, the challenge will be for women to achieve equality under more competitive and entrepreneurial conditions, requiring new technical skills. The conditions for job equality must include upgrading of machinery and other work-related equipment to Western standards, which, among other things, have effectively abolished the employment advantage of strong (male) musculature. To achieve equal treatment and full participation of women, it is also necessary for men to recognize that children are important to them as well as to their mothers, and to learn to communicate and cooperate at home. Women need role models and an understanding of how discrimination limits their prospects. The conflict between motherhood and employment was camouflaged in the past by small family size and low-pressure jobs. Now it is possible to face this conflict more openly. But for women to change their situation men must also change their ways of thinking, and there must be changes in the legal basis for gender-stereotyping in jobs.

Summary of

Changing the Conditions of Work:
Responding to Increasing Work Force Diversity and New Family Patterns

by Lotte Bailyn

[Published in *Transforming Organizations,* eds. Thomas Kochan and Michael Useem (New York: Oxford University Press, 1992).]

The Industrial Revolution ushered in a gendered division of labor, between specialists in breadwinning and specialists in caretaking. Although this is no longer held up publicly as the norm, women still retain primary responsibility for many caring activities in the home sphere.

> More than half of all mothers with children under one are now in the paid labor force. . . . Today, less than 10 percent of families follow the pattern of a husband at work and a wife at home caring for the children. . . . [A study] has

found that between two and three of every five employees are having problems managing the often conflicting demands of jobs and family life. . . . Yet the structure of the workplace is still geared to the assumption that workers can commit all their energy and time to their employment. [188]

A potential crisis is brewing in the United States. As firms translate the need for global competitiveness into requirements for higher worker productivity, workers are under pressure to work longer and harder. The losers are the nation's children as well as other individuals (for example, the elderly) and community organizations that have traditionally depended on unpaid, caring labor, especially from women.

Policy Options

A comparison with Sweden casts the U.S. situation into sharp relief. In both countries women have been encouraged to enter the formal labor force, but U.S. policies apparently assumed that this massive change would occur without causing or requiring any other adaptations. By contrast, the Swedish commitment to enabling women to have jobs was accompanied by a serious effort to change gender roles, primarily by urging men to increase their involvement with child care and other family responsibilities.

Rather than looking to the Scandinavian welfare model, U.S. policy makers have tended to hold up Japan's example of a more participative and committed workforce—without, however, recognizing the salience of the accompanying Japanese institutional norms, such as the support that nonworking wives give to their husbands careers and families and the reciprocity of loyalty between firms and workers. Ignoring institutional context, U.S. policy has held up the ideal of "gender-neutrality," even in areas such as pregnancy leaves (by subsuming them under disability provisions) and custody decisions in divorce cases. Yet the consequences of pregnancy and motherhood, as well as of divorce, are far from gender-neutral.

Policies at the firm level have fallen into two categories. One is arrangements by employers that are designed to accommodate the family needs of workers. Examples are on-site day care or other provisions to assist workers in acquiring family services. In effect, this response attempts to ensure that employees will be able to give more time to work. This, however, is not really what is needed. The goal should be to allow workers to give more time to their families.

That is the goal of the second category of employer response, a category that includes flextime and flexplace, part-time and job-sharing opportunities, as well as various kinds of personal leaves. These are steps in the right direction, but they can have the wrong effect if they are introduced into an organization that continues to use visibility (how many hours an employee is on site) as a signal of its employees' commitment. Since women still feel responsible for various aspects of domestic work, they are more likely to make use of the flexible options listed above.

> And as long as such a differential pattern of use exists, it can only *increase* the disadvantages that women already face in the workplace through the feminization of poverty, the wage gap, the glass ceiling. By itself flexibility superimposed on existing assumptions about the conditions of employment is not likely to change these basic facts. [192]

A number of deeply ingrained practices of American management make women vulnerable to career depreciation if they grasp the two-edged sword of workplace flexibility. For example, they are likely to fail to get on the fast track in which "high-potential employees" are identified in the first seven to ten years of their career—a period when women are most likely to be engaged in family concerns. As one example, a leading university instituted a personal leave provision for child care for its faculty (which would stop the tenure clock). After this had been on the books for fifteen years it was discovered that "no woman who took such a leave has ever subsequently been awarded tenure." [198]

Proposals for Systemic Change

Attempts to fix the system by imposing family policies without more general structural change poses the danger of reinforcing existing gender inequalities. The prevailing assumption is that jobs can be defined independent of the people who will fill them—that employees can be made to fit a single, homogeneous style. The present system, indeed, "is designed to minimize the probability of special treatment for certain groups and is supported by the legal system for just that purpose." [195] However, equality in procedures does not necessarily produce a fair or equal outcome for employees in widely differing family situations.

It is essential for American employers to recognize that the workforce of the present and the future is different from that of the past. Changing demographic patterns create new kinds of diversity for which traditional management approaches are ill-prepared. Research is needed to inform employers of the family circumstances of today's workers. Such research should also illuminate the problems people meet in fitting current organizational requirements. "Identification of the demographic groups that find these requirements most difficult, and the extent to which they are changing, would be a key indicator of where change is needed in order to help employees mesh their concerns with work and family." [198]

A variety of experiments and new approaches are already in place, upon which it may be possible to build the appropriate responses to the new needs. Both employers and employees may benefit from a redefinition of what a career is, facing the fact that it may not be a single long sweep from entry into the work-force until retirement. Instead, "'zero-based budgeting' in careers . . . would involve planning for a particular career segment, perhaps of five to seven years, and then negotiating the level of commitment, the tasks, the compensation and evaluation procedures de novo for the next segment." [195]

An early management specialist, Douglas McGregor, gave the name "Theory X" to the prevailing "scientific management" model of work. It is a hierarchical, distrusting approach that requires visible evidence of commitment (such as the hours that an employee is at his or her station) and that assumes continuity, linearity, and homogeneity in career paths. For today's realities McGregor's alternative "Theory Y" may be more relevant than ever, as a management approach based on "a set of assumptions that people not only enjoy their work but are willing to take responsibility for it." [194] Work–family issues, in particular, must be central to any consideration of systemic change. This is appropriate not only for workers and their families, but also for the organizational flexibility and adaptability required in a rapidly changing environment.

Summary of

The Third Shift

by Arlie Russell Hochschild

[Published in *The Time Bind—When Work Becomes Home and Home Becomes Work* (New York: Metropolitan Books–Henry Holt and Company, 1997), Chapter 14, 197–218.]

The title of Hochschild's 1989 book *The Second Shift* has become feminist shorthand for the double burden on women who both work in paid jobs and do most housework. In this excerpt from her latest book, a case study at a manufacturing plant operated by Amerco (not its real name), a large U.S. company, Hochschild introduces the following idea:

> As the first shift (at the workplace) takes more time, the second shift (at home) becomes more hurried and rationalized. The longer the workday at the office or plant, the more we feel pressed at home to hurry, to delegate, to delay, to forgo, to segment, to hyperorganize the precious remains of family time. Both their time deficit and what seem like solutions to it (hurrying, segmenting, and organizing) force parents . . . to engage in a third shift—noticing, understanding and coping with the emotional consequences of the compressed second shift. [215]

The Relative Emotional Magnetism of Home and Work

Amerco offered a "Work–Life Balance program [which] could have become a model, demonstrating to other corporations that workforce talents can be used effectively without wearing down workers and their families." [197] This model, in which family-friendly options at work (especially flexible or shorter work hours) allow a comfortable balance between work and home, is a reality for an appreciable minority of Americans, but did not take hold in a significant way at Amerco. In attempting to understand this failure, we may contrast the "work–family balance" model with four other modern styles.

- In the "haven model," home is seen as a haven from a heartless world of work.

- In the "traditional model," the man's primary world is at work, the woman's at home.

- The "no-job, weak-family model" is the one described by William Julius Wilson,[1] where people in the inner cities substitute drugs and gangs for worth and security. Its prevalence appears to fluctuate with economic circumstances.

- The last thirty years have seen a rise of the "reversal model" in which the comforts and stimulations that used to be found at home are offered at work, while the home is "taking on what were once considered the most alienating attributes of work." [198]

While the haven and traditional models are generally on the decline in all segments of our society, these shifts are not consistent across all classes. Professional and managerial workers work the longest hours, and the children of higher income families spend the most hours in day care. Some Amerco workers, particularly those with tedious factory jobs, still experienced family life as a "haven," while some men at the top of the corporate ladder maintain a traditional work–family structure with gender-based roles.

Amerco appeared to want to foster a balance of work and family, but instead was most successful at fostering the reversal model. How did this come about? Even while most Amerco workers claimed they needed more time for their families, few took advantage of the company program. Part of the reason may have been lukewarm, or even hostile, attitudes on the part of managers. Other reasons include needing money more than shorter hours, or fear of job loss, or of not being considered "serious players" by peers or supervisors. However, there is a deeper explanation: "Many of them may have been responding to a powerful process that is devaluing what was once the essence of family life. The more women and men do what they do in exchange for money and the more their work in the public realm is valued or honored, the more, almost by definition, private life is devalued and its boundaries shrink." [198]

When Work Becomes Home

"While the mass media so often point to global competition as the major business story of the age, it is easy to miss the fact that corporate America's fiercest struggle has been with its local rival—the family." [204] In this struggle, work has been the winner, expanding both its share of employees' time and its share of their allegiance. Under Total Quality Management, Amerco, like other corporations, invested in the ability of workers to make decisions and began offering moral as well as financial incentives. Amerco takes pains to show appreciation, recognizing achievements in company publications, and holding picnics, holiday parties, and awards ceremonies. People gravitate toward activities that they value and feel valued for performing. Self-perceptions may be influenced by the fact that home life offers few opportunities to make appreciation so explicit and so public. In one study 86 percent of respondents felt their job performance was good or unusually good, but only 59 percent gave their performance at home such high ratings.

Recognition events create a relaxed, social, even playful, atmosphere at work where, according to another study, people, particularly women, are far more likely to find friends than elsewhere. Amerco also provides avenues for employees to achieve personal growth. While seminars on topics like dealing with anger or coping with difficult people are geared toward resolving work-related issues, they help employees with problems at home as well.

Amerco workers were made to feel that the company cared enough to secure their jobs in a challenging marketplace. When Amerco lost market share, it staged a "Large Group Change Event" in the style of a religious revival. The intense atmosphere highlighted the company's commitment to recapturing its competitive position and stimulated workers' commitment to the company's goals. Workers were exposed to confessions of failure and shame and avowals of renewed purpose from company and union representatives, and encouraged to reveal their own frustrations, to offer suggestions, and to "cast out the devil" of petty behavior (like horseplay) that could lower productivity. Workers were tested for personality issues that might obstruct teamwork or performance, and signified commitment by signing banners displayed in the hall.

Events like this generated a moral fervor and a sense of common destiny around the company's agenda. Under the Total Quality rubric, employees were explicitly asked to dedicate themselves to improved quality, but the effect included a new orientation to time. Since responsibility for better quality rested with workers' own decisions and commitment, it required them to become efficiency experts concerning their own jobs and, by extension, their own lives.

When Home Becomes Work

In a broad survey of mainly middle- or upper-class day-care parents, 85 percent said that home often feels like a workplace, while 25 percent said that work often feels like home and another 33 percent that work occasionally feels like home. Only 9 percent believed they balanced work and family "very well," and "only to half of them was home a main source of relaxation or security." For many in this study, "work seemed to function as a backup system to a destabilizing family. For women, in particular, to take a job is often today to take out an emotional insurance policy on the uncertainties of home life." [201]

While work has become permeated with personal satisfaction, emotional content and value-laden activity, home and family life are becoming deskilled, regimented, and pressured. Productive activities like sewing, baking, or caring for elderly relatives have been replaced by commercial substitutes. Recreation often involves watching TV families in scripted relationships.

To spend time with their children, working parents have made "quality time" into a strictly specified obligation rather than an opportunity for spontaneous interaction. So as not to be distracted by unfinished work, one Amerco employee turned reading stories to her sons into a disciplined, focused activity— just like work. Family activities are tightly scheduled, ignoring the leisurely pace that can enhance enjoyment. A cult of efficiency permeates the home, not unlike the scientific management promoted by Frederick Taylor. Food advertisements stress speed of preparation and imply that the food will go down quicker, too—recalling the image of the Billows Feeding Machine from Charlie Chaplin's *Modern Times*, the classic film portrayal of the Taylorized assembly line.

These changes have emotional consequences, especially for children who often resent the increased pressure on their own time, the loss of control over family time, and the unpredictable nature of their parents' attention when work demands may override family members' needs at any moment. Children observed or reported on in this study often acted out frustrations by throwing tantrums, refusing to do what was expected when it was expected, or whining and dawdling when their parents were pressed for time.

Coping with these signs of resistance and maintaining family relationships under stress constitute a third shift. Its central project is paradoxical: management of the emotional fallout from the organization of the second shift around the logic of the first—a project that would not be necessary if home life could unfold according to its own pace and structure. Unfortunately, even parents who are attentive to a child's emotional state cannot always interpret it from the child's own perspective or alter the constraints of their own busy lives. "[E]ven the best of parents in such situations find themselves passing a systemwide speedup along to the most vulnerable workers on the line . . . who signal most clearly the strains in the Taylorized home." [217]

Note

1. William Julius Wilson, *When Work Disappears* (New York: Alfred A. Knopf, 1997). See summary in Part IX.

Summary of

Overwork in the Household

by Juliet B. Schor

[Published in *The Overworked American: The Unexpected Decline of Leisure* (New York: Basic Books, 1992), Chapter 4, 83–105.]

The chronic level of overwork that plagues many American households is not merely a manifestation of our wage-paying jobs. We have typically spent nearly as much time working in the home as we have outside of it. Women bear the brunt of this housework. Although the long hours worked by housewives have a variety of causes, the underlying reason is fundamentally an economic one— the low cost of housewives' labor.

By looking at domestic labor in economic terms, we can better see the economic structures that determine how household work is done. The household has traditionally been outside of the purview of economics, and domestic activity, because it does not generate income, is not included in the economic category of labor. The most convincing argument that the American household is really an economic institution, and that work done there is economic activity, is provided by the finding that, as the paid employment of women grows, more and more household services are purchased in the market.

Constancy of Housewives' Hours of Work and the Upgrading of Standards

Despite the transformations of the twentieth century, one thing remained constant for decades: the amount of work done by the American housewife who does not have another job (outside of the home). The average number of hours worked per week stayed somewhat higher from the beginning of the twentieth century. The odd thing about this constancy of hours is that it coincides with a revolution in household technologies. The amount of capital equipment in the home has risen dramatically, each innovation having the potential to save count-less hours of labor, yet none of them did (except for the microwave oven, a rel-atively recent invention). The use of some appliances, such as freezers and wash-ing machines, actually appears to have increased the amount of time dedicated to housework. An important proximate cause (though it is not the underlying reason) for the constancy of overall household work is that standards rose in step with technological sophistication.

The culture of cleanliness had no place in Colonial America because there were other, far more economically valuable uses for women's labor. However, with growing prosperity many women had more time to devote to housekeep-ing, and higher standards of cleanliness emerged. As housewives achieved easier access to basic necessities, which were increasingly produced outside of the home, they put more effort into expressing values such as nutrition and aes-thetics. All of these trends were supported and encouraged by a new class of homemaking and child-rearing experts and reformers, as well, of course, as by the corporations that had household products to sell.

The trend to "more and better" included all household activities, but the area where the upgrading was the most dramatic was in the care of children. Two or three centuries ago, before the social construction of modern concep-tions of child-rearing and motherhood, parent–child relationships appear to have been much less emotional, partly due to the high probability that children might not survive. Additionally, time for mothering was for many an unafford-able luxury. Attitudes changed during the eighteenth and nineteenth centuries. By the twentieth century ("the century of the child"), increased affection and attention contributed to child survival (and, presumably, welfare), but with it came an immense time burden for mothers.

The Parkinson's Law of housework predicts that "work expands to fill the time available for its completion." Accordingly, "as the market economy pro-duced low-cost versions of what women had made at home, they transferred their labor to other tasks. . . . The most important explanation for the opera-tion of Parkinson's Law in housework was the increasing isolation of the house-wife from the market economy and the resulting devaluation of her time in comparison to what she could be earning in market work" [94] (the opportu-nity cost of her labor). The elimination of alternative uses for a housewife's time artificially deflated the value of her labor.

In addition to family responsibilities at home, outright legal prohibitions such as hiring restrictions, discrimination, job segregation, and social and cultural mores effectively excluded many housewives from the market. Possibil-ities for earning income inside the home were disappearing at the same time as the prosperity of the early twentieth century made it possible for more and more families to afford a housewife. It became a status symbol to have a wife who "didn't work."

Even without the possibility of earning income, household work does have an opportunity cost: the leisure time of housewives. However, this possibility appears to have been neutralized by a combination of factors, including the power of the work ethic, the fact that husbands desire the free services that their wives' labor provide, and the sensitivity of women to the "fairness" requirement that their workload should be comparable to that of their husbands.

The Perpetuation of Domestic Inefficiency

The valuable products of the twentieth-century housewife—well-cared-for homes and children—could have been achieved more efficiently. Many efficient technologies were ignored, discarded, or underdeveloped because the undervaluation of housewife labor created a strong bias against them. Some household services, such as the basic production of foodstuffs, woven materials, and clothing, were taken on by the market. However, the complete socialization, commercialization, and professionalization of other household services, such as laundry, cooking, cleaning, and child care, were never realized despite a turn of the century movement advocating communalization or commercialization.

There are several explanations for the failure of this movement. Businesses preferred the existing system. Men preferred individual attention from their wives. Americans put a high value on privacy and family autonomy. Nevertheless, none of these explanations address the underlying economic issue:

> If the 'price' of each hour of domestic labor had been higher, families would have 'bought' less of it, and standards and services would not have escalated nearly as much. But discrimination and social mores prevented the true opportunity cost of women's labor at home from being taken into account. [96]

Housework Today and Tomorrow

Estimates of working hours indicate that things have started to change, especially for young people. Women are marrying later, unmarrying earlier, having fewer children, and working outside the home more often. "Employed women do about two-thirds as much housework and child care as their unemployed sisters. . . . The processes that raised hours are now operating in reverse: standards are falling, and the range of household services [provided by the housewife] is contracting. The culture of cleanliness is in abeyance."

[103] Women still do about twice as much housework as men, but men's contributions are increasing. This reflects a shift in attitudes and values for both men and women. However, the quality and variety of market substitutes for domestic services still lags, especially in a price range that is affordable for most Americans.

Summary of

The Triangle of the Human Economy—Household, Cultivation, Industrial Production: An Attempt at Making Visible the Human Economy in Toto

by Hilkka Pietila

[Published in *Ecological Economics* 20 (1997), 113–127]

In the processes of modernization and industrialization many functions that had once been performed within the family are transferred to the monetized realm, produced either as public services or as commodities to be purchased on the market. These include the production of food, clothing, and furniture; child and health care; and education and entertainment. Nevertheless, no society has achieved "the extreme form of market utopia" in which work and skills are totally abolished from the private, family realm—in which, "as all labor and skills are absorbed in the market economy, time outside the economic system is reduced to pure unskilled leisure-time." [115]

Instead, there remains a household economy, only part of whose activities have been monetized, but that is, from the human point of view, the primary economy. Here is the locus for the maintenance of human health, mental and physical, as well as for the nurturing and education of future generations. When these essential functions are performed within families they cost time and effort; when they are put into the public sphere they cost money. In traditional economic accounts there is an appearance of economic growth if the same work is shifted from voluntary to paid status. However, it is evident that economic growth is not synonymous with the satisfaction of essential human needs.

Acting as the Background for Theory

This article is based on both studies and activist movements in which the author was involved.

Our point of departure was to find ways of reducing the need for economic growth in a well-off industrialized country like Finland, with a view to de creasing international disparity and extensive exploitation of natural resources. We suggested that revival of the self-reliant, nonmonetary, local as well as household-based production of goods and services makes economic growth unnecessary in small industrialized countries, without unnecessarily jeopardizing the quality of life. [118]

The Nordic women's research group for the "New Everyday Life" focuses on the interplay between private and public spheres. Their vision was of "a society organized in small, well-planned units with a high degree of local self-management." A major problem is that women are working separately "to find individual solutions to collective problems." Thus there is "a need to recreate a functional geographic and organizational level, something that the traditional villages must have been at one time." [121] The main functions to be performed at this intermediary level are local household work, local care of dependents, and local management and production. Much of this work could be organized and carried out by a group of households, rather than on an individual household basis.

Coincidentally, while the women's research group was formulating these visions a village action movement emerged spontaneously in the Finnish countryside. Consisting of 3,000 village committees and affecting the lives of about a half a million people since the 1970s, this movement has revived the structure of country villages, organizing services such as schools, banking, and postal services to replace public services that had been withdrawn. At the core of these successes has been the concept of voluntary teamwork that has proven to be "an effective way of implementing even major projects without money." [122]

Quantitative Measures of Household Work

If the central economic impotence of such activities is to be recognized and integrated into national-level policy, they must cease to be invisible within national accounts. The 1995 Human Development Report of the UNDP estimated that of all the work performed by all the women in the world, one-third is paid and two-thirds is unpaid. By contrast, men receive pay for three-quarters of their working time. In part because it has not been paid for, much of women's work has been invisible in formal economic accounts. This invisible work can be divided into three areas: production, caring, and community management. The most progress has been made in accounting for the first of these. As an example, studies in Finland attempted to evaluate the worth of unpaid work and production in households in the years 1980 and 1990. The total value was found to be between 42 and 49 percent of GDP in both years (depending on the method of estimation). In 1990 women were reported as spending an average of 4 hours a day on such unpaid work, while men spent about 2 hours, 20 minutes. (As compared with a decade earlier, this represented an 18 percent reduction in time for women, and an 18.6 percent increase for men.)

In 1993 the Statistical Division of the U.N. recommended that the difficult issue of accounting for production in households within the System of National Accounts should be resolved by the creation of a two-tier system. The traditional accounting system remains as a "central framework," to be accompanied by "looser satellite accounts which are separate from but consistent with the core national accounts and can measure areas of interest that are difficult to describe within the central framework." [118] It is now recommended by the U.N. that each nation's central framework define production to include goods that are produced in the home, even if they are not paid for. However, services such as cleaning, cooking, and care of children and the elderly remain in the satellite accounts—unless they are purchased through the market (by hiring domestic servants).

While these changes do represent progress, there still has been no formal attention to the third role of women, as community managers. This includes "collective voluntary work for the common good in the neighborhood or in tending the environment, participation in the activities of voluntary organizations, etc." [118]

The Triangle of the Human Economy

A comprehensive framework for the human economy defines it as "all work, production, actions and transactions needed to provide for the livelihood, welfare and survival of all people and families, irrespective of whether they appear in statistics or are counted in monetary terms." [114] The basic components are household, cultivation, and industrial production. The weakness of the traditional approach is that it only perceives the last of these. Nevertheless, industrial production is dependent on the caring, comfort, and health produced through the unpaid work of households, but which it cannot produce itself. Similarly, industrial production cannot make, but is dependent on, the living potential of nature.

Each of these components operates by its own logic. One of these logics has been extensively studied, and the theory resulting from the economic logic of industrial production is too often imposed upon the other two. It is time for a balanced perception of the human economy as a whole, paying equal attention to each of the three components, as well as to their interlinkages.

Summary of

Global Development and Personal Dependency: The High Cost of Doing Well

by Allan R. Meyers

[Published in *World Development* 19, 1 (January 1991), 45–54.]

Changes in demographic patterns in the developed world mean more people are now living with disabilities. Similar changes can be predicted for the developing world. At the same time the process of development is breaking down the family and community support systems that traditionally provided care for the ill and disabled. In the developed world, immigrant women are an important source of dependent care—which, as this article points out, is not a sustainable arrangement. As life expectancy improves for more of the world's population, and more and more people seek caretaking services through market-based resources in a globally integrated economy, competition between the developed and developing world for caregivers is likely to increase.

Disability and Dependency—Industrial Countries

Disability, unlike death or disease, is not a well-defined concept. The operational definition used in this article relies on a person's ability to perform such activities of daily living (ADL) as walking, eating, or grooming, or such instrumental ADL as food preparation or shopping. Although assessment instruments exist for evaluating these activities, data are often unreliable or not comparable across countries.

Even with these problems of measurement, "there is clear evidence of a secular trend toward a greater prevalence of disability in industrial countries." [46] One British geriatrician calls this the "survival of the Unfittest." One of the major reasons is the lengthening of the life span due to improvements in medicine, sanitation, nutrition, and public health campaigns. At the same time, there has been no decrease in the incidence of disability among those who live to be very old. One-third of those over age 85 experience dependency in at least one ADL. Improvements in lifesaving treatments for premature infants and victims of serious injuries (especially young adult males) also mean an increase in the disabled and dependent population.

While there are social benefits to be enjoyed from the prolonged presence of elderly relatives and community members, there are also costs. One estimate of nursing home and home health care costs in the United States for 1986 was

$41 billion, paid mostly by state governments and families. This figure does not include the cost of acute care or related services such as cleaning or assistance with personal hygiene. Neither does this figure include the expenditure (and opportunity cost) of time and effort by relatives and friends of disabled persons in caring for them. One study found that the cost of informal services provided by families and friends to noninstitutionalized older adults (valued at the cost of similar paid services) was greater than the value of formal services received by them. The ratio of informal to formal services is greatest for those who are most impaired.

Projections into the mid-twenty-first century indicate that the proportion of the population that is elderly will rise sharply and the need for services will also rise. A large share of this caregiving will come from family members, especially children, but declining fertility rates, more geographic mobility and greater female participation in the labor force mean that the need for assistance from outside the family will also rise. "At the same time, nursing home aides, home health aides, and personal care attendants are in short and diminishing supply." [48] These workers face poor pay, benefits, and working conditions, and in an expanding service economy are often able to find better jobs.

As a result, the developed countries have come to rely more and more on immigrant women to provide caretaking services, in some cases actively recruiting health and human services personnel offshore. A different pattern, but one with a similar effect (exporting the problem of dependent care) is the movement of older persons from developed to developing countries. In some cases this is a matter of older immigrants repatriating to their country of origin. In others it is a matter of retired persons moving to less expensive or more attractive locations. When this occurs, the same population of women in the developing country are employed to give care. "There is no reason to believe that the women (mainly) of developing countries are any more loving, caring, or compassionate that their North American counterparts (though they may be). Rather, they participate in an implicit economic exchange: North Americans defer or delegate to them care of their disabled and dependent population in exchange for financial resources which they need." [49] North Americans are not the only case. There are Japanese retirement communities in Brazil, to cite one other example.

Transition in the Third World

The populations of developing countries are also aging. By the year 2000 it is projected that there will be as many octogenarians in less developed countries as in more developed countries. By 2025, there will be many more. Although comprehensive formal studies do not exist, it appears that families are the main source of care for the elderly and disabled in less developed nations. "[T]here are few formal paid services in developing countries and little coherent demand (as opposed to need) for such programs." [51] Publicly funded services are also scarce and often limited to special groups such as disabled veterans. Women are the main source of informal care in developing countries, the same women on whom the developed world depends. "If this process—'the compassionate care drain'—continues, developed countries needs will be met, but only at the cost of developing countries' most precious resources and at precisely the time of their own growing need." [52]

Lessons

Developing countries do not need to travel the same path as the industrialized world. While natural growth in disability may not be avoidable, artificial disability and dependency can be reduced if retirement is not mandatory and vocational training is widely accessible. Public policies and taxation can be directed toward preemptive measures to research disease prevention and effective delivery of care. Measures such as famine relief, inoculation, and others that save lives may produce contradictory results if adequate resources are not available to insure the "vitality and viability" of those whose lives are saved.

Countries can support the informal networks that are likely to be the major source of caregiving for the elderly and disabled. Social science researchers can also devote attention to these networks, expanding on anecdotal evidence to develop a more systematic understanding of their role and needs. To the extent that trade in caregivers from less to more developed countries persists, there should be a reciprocal component that ensures that those who emigrate will return with skills appropriate for the growing dependency needs of their home countries.

Finally, a number of inequalities need to be addressed to bring about a more equitable distribution of caregiving services on a global basis: poor pay, benefits, and prestige; the concentration of caregiving work (formal and informal) among women, especially poor and minority women. "We must be sufficiently bold and imaginative to both solve our own problems and prevent them from affecting people in other lands." [53]

Summary of

"Holding Hands at Midnight": The Paradox of Caring Labor

by Nancy Folbre

[Published in *Feminist Economics* 1 (1995), 73–92.]

The title is from a jazz standard that claims that love is a better motive for work than money or fame, defending "personal values against the dictates of the mar-

ketplace." [74] But work based on personal values—caring work—"poses
something of a paradox for economists. If caring is its own reward, it need not
command an economic return. But if caring labor receives no economic return
at all, will it persist?" [74] Since caring labor is generally performed by women,
who generally earn less than men, it poses a dilemma for feminists as well. Do
the rewards of caring labor transcend monetary valuation, or is women's work
undervalued by the marketplace?

The Concept of Caring Labor

This article focuses on motivations, defining caring labor as *"labor undertaken
out of affection or a sense of responsibility for other people, with no expectation of
immediate pecuniary reward."* [75] As well as dependent or family care, it encompasses all labor motivated by a desire to help others. It includes those who
work for wages if they don't work for money alone. A recipient may not welcome an expression of care, or an emotionally attached caregiver might be less
competent than a dispassionate provider. Nevertheless, there is an expected correlation between caring and quality, especially "when part of the task is to make
someone feel cared for, rather than simply to change the bedpan or apply a theory." [75]

Neoclassical economics considers nonpecuniary motives to be exogenously
given preferences. Caring is a form of *altruism,* exogenous and probably bio-
logically determined. However, other social sciences consider several motives
for caring. These motives are related and difficult to distinguish empirically, but
preferences (individual desires), norms (behavior patterns of a particular culture), and values (universal, transcendent principles) can be distinguished analytically. Each category comes to the fore in a different field of knowledge.

Altruism, a psychological concept, involves interdependent preferences
through which one receives pleasure, or utility, from the well-being of others.
Reciprocity is an anthropological concept based on loose implicit contracts that
may, unlike the explicit contracts of market exchange, be fostered by affection
or by a sense of responsibility. Reciprocity might break down if the probability
of eventual payoff declines, but social norms can also influence the supply of
caring. *Responsibility,* the fulfillment of obligations, is a moral category based
on philosophical concepts of right and wrong. "The triad offers three related
escape routes from the individualistic, selfish, and essentially amoral reasoning
of rational economic man." [78]

The Value of Caring Labor

Feminists have suggested that women are penalized for specializing in caring
work, or as one put it, "care is devalued and the people who do caring work are

devalued." [78] Empirical research bears out this undervaluation. One study of compensable factors in occupations found a net negative return to nurturing and a positive return to the exercise of authority. Economists are more interested in how outcomes differ under different institutions than in the ethical dimensions of these outcomes, but feminists face unavoidable personal and intellectual choices.

Neoclassical economics presents a set of assumptions (that utility functions are exogenous and markets are perfect) under which the undervaluation of caring labor disappears. A utility-maximizing individual would forgo possible income to do unpaid (or underpaid) work only if he or she enjoyed greater utility by doing so. "Their actions reveal their preferences." [78] Women earn less than men because of voluntary choices to spend more time doing housework. Women receive more utility from children than men do, and "we are left with the comforting thought that mothers must, after all, be just as happy as the fathers who fail to contribute to their children's support or care, even if they are living in poverty." [79]

Neoclassical theory does admit that markets in the real world are not perfect, and that women's work may well be undervalued. One variation holds that men collude to exclude women from well-paid, high-skill jobs, so women crowd into poorly paid jobs and the oversupply further lowers the wage to a level below equilibrium. The remedy is simple: Eliminate male collusion. But this still does not explain why women crowd into caring work.

Neoclassical economics also accommodates explanations based on externalities. Caring workers may receive "psychic income" from certain kinds of work, creating an oversupply of labor. This oversupply lowers the wage for these jobs, penalizing noncaring workers in them. Externalities can also involve third party effects and information problems. For instance, children are public goods: They grow up to benefit all taxpayers, not just those adults who nurtured them. However, nurturing is difficult to monitor and its specific impact is difficult to define, so day care workers do not recoup their value to society, but experience low pay and high turnover. Nursing is another example. Nurses are hired for certain competencies, but patients receive positive externalities from nurses who are also caring individuals. This affinity for caring work is difficult to find and compensate fairly because both the work and the product are difficult to evaluate.

Institutionalist economics provides an alternative to the neoclassical focus on individualism and contractual exchange. It considers norms, preferences, and values to be partially endogenous and socially constructed, often in opposition to the interests of women. Unlike neoclassicists, institutionalists would claim that the nurturing preference is imposed on women by a sexual caste system with norms and relationships that distort women's decisions. In turn, these decisions internalize and reinforce the sexual division of labor. The nurturing and mediating skills required for women's work encourage identification with the interests of others. Girls who are raised largely by a parent of the same sex, grow up with a less bounded, oppositional sense of self. For institutionalists, caring labor could be a trick to get women to provide low-cost services, or a necessary activity, disproportionately assigned to women.

There is no scientific compass for choosing among preferences, norms, or values, and economists sidestep such choices. For feminists these questions, packaged as the equality versus difference debate, are unavoidable: "Should we recreate ourselves in a more masculine image? Or should we seek, instead, to eliminate the economic penalty imposed on distinctively feminine norms, values, and preferences?" [83] Most feminists favor equality, regarding caring as a quality that handicaps women economically. Women should learn to compete in male-dominated occupations rather than romanticize feminine behavior and differences from men. Changing the rate of return on masculine behavior would involve tampering with a market process and would require collective effort with free rider problems and high transaction costs.

Some feminists are willing to undertake this challenge and to modify or undermine the dynamics of the market. One argument holds that the market economy requires the underlying support of caring work. Some socialist feminists feel that the economy should be organized like housekeeping, giving priority to basic needs, rather than on "masculinist" competitive principles.

Differences among feminists do not hinge on the boundary between neoclassical and institutionalist thought. Either economic framework can be interpreted to support either side of the difference/equality debate. If caring work is correctly valued by the market, those who do it will be those who genuinely prefer it. If the choice of caring work is the result of subordination, a reduction in the supply of caring labor may be desirable. On the other hand, if caring labor provides positive externalities, or if it is necessary but disproportionately assigned to women, a reduction in supply would have adverse social consequences, and policies to address market inadequacies and institutional gaps would be appropriate.

Public Policies and Caring Labor

Policy hinges on values—in this case how much we value caring labor—and also presents paradoxes. A law demanding that everyone do a certain amount of caretaking work would not necessarily increase the supply of real caring labor. On the other hand, providing positive rewards, such as public remuneration, could reinforce the sexual division of labor.

Pro-market and nonmarket arguments also run through debates on family policy and the valuation of household work. Many U.S. feminists support proposals to require studies of the inclusion of household work in national statistics. Some oppose this as romanticizing the sexual division of labor, and favor the "industrialization" of housework and child care. Others feel that quantifying "labors of love" demeans them and privileges market-based work. A similar Catch-22 obstructs agreement on public support for parental labor, such as family allowances or paid leave.

Options should be discussed that fall between the extremes of letting the market establish the value of caring labor and rejecting any monetary valuation at all. Parents "should be entitled to some minimum level of decent support for a form of nonmarket caring labor that benefits society as a whole." [87] Feminism has played an important role in challenging the patriarchal family, helping establish new rights for women and children and demanding a new definition of family commitments that goes beyond traditional, hierarchical, and necessarily heterosexual models. How ironic it would be if progress on this front were neutralized by an individualism so extreme that it renders the best of family values obsolete.

Summary of
Children as Public Goods
by Nancy Folbre

[Published in *The American Economic Review* 84, 2 (May 1994), 86–90.]

"Children tumble out of every category economists try to put them in. They have been described as consumer durables providing a flow of utility to their parents, investment goods providing income, and public goods with both positive and negative externalities. Children are also people with certain rights to life, liberty and the pursuit of happiness." [86] With economic development the cost to parents of raising children rises, but many of the benefits go to society as a whole in the form of Social Security and repayment of public debt. The work of parenting is therefore a public service and nonparents are free-riding on parental efforts. While the nonpecuniary benefits of children may be sufficient for many parents, for economists it is necessary to understand the role of unpaid parental labor in the development of human capital.

Economic Development and the Costs of Children

During earlier periods in the now-developed world, parents were in a position to receive economic benefits from their children. Children often began to work at a young age and, when grown, relied on access to assets like family farms controlled by their parents. Since women had few means of support outside the family, the opportunity cost of raising children was low. Similar conditions exist today in the developing world.

With economic development, the cost of raising children rises. Children stay in school much longer and begin employment later. This improves their future productivity and earning potential, but is more costly for parents. With the growth of labor markets women have more opportunities for economic independence. Geographic mobility also grows, weakening the implicit contracts of family life. Over the long run, fertility tends to fall, but values, norms, and preferences surrounding the family persist. People adjust slowly to these changes, and many families face stressful economic conditions. More and more families are headed by women alone, and poor enforcement of child support from fathers means that women often bear a disproportionate share of the costs of rearing children.

Public policy in the United States and Europe in the late nineteenth and early twentieth centuries began to recognize changes in family structure and developed programs for old age insurance and public assistance for single mothers. These policies have generally provided greater benefits to the elderly than to single mothers and their children, especially in the United States. Social Security has been particularly effective in reducing poverty among elderly men and married couples, but poverty among single mothers and children has grown. Over 40 percent of African-American and Latino children in the United States live in poverty. Even in parts of Europe where benefits are relatively generous, single mothers and children are more likely to be poor than others.

> In short, public policies have reinforced . . . income flows from the young to the old, giving the elderly claims upon the earnings of the younger generation. At the same time, the share of fathers' income transferred to mothers and children has declined, partly as a result of the growth of families maintained by women alone. [87]

Unpaid Parental Labor

Neoclassical economic theory posits a dualistic world in which individuals behave according to self-interest in the marketplace and altruism within the family. The public sector is conceptualized along these lines as well, based either on self-interest or altruism. This formulation ignores the potential for conflicts over resources among groups in society or along generational lines. However, patterns of income transfers, taxation, public debt, investment, and environmental degradation tend to shift a greater financial burden onto the next generation. Expenditures of time, effort, and money by today's parents are important inputs into the ability of the next generation to carry out this responsibility. In addition, the reduction of their children's future disposable income may reduce private transfers of income from children to parents.

The work that parents do in raising children is undercompensated by society and undervalued by economic theory. "Many economists seem to believe that time and energy devoted to children reflect an exogenously given preference that provides a compensating differential for costs incurred." [88] The same line of argument leads to rationalization of the failure of many divorced fathers to pay child support and the greater susceptibility of women to poverty. If women receive greater utility from children either through their own personal preference or through the pleasure of greater contact, then women will take on greater responsibility for them.

Both preferences and commitments are shaped by social norms and values. However, if parents are poorly compensated over the long run, these norms and values may weaken and the supply of parental care may diminish. Recent patterns of divorce and desertion indicate that men are shifting away from family commitments faster than women. Although women and children have no control over this, public policy is far more generous to children of divorced or disabled parents (with no requirement that the other parent work outside the home) than it is to those whose fathers desert them.

New Directions for Family Policy

The benefits that children provide to society impose a collective responsibility that is not being fulfilled. Several policy options have been proposed that reflect very different values. Some would uphold traditional family values (particularly maternal altruism). Others would rely on immigrants to perform household labor. Putting an end to public debt and pay-as-you-go Social Security would prevent nonparents from receiving benefits from parental labor, but would severely limit macroeconomic policy. Social Security could be changed to provide payments only to parents from their own children. However, this ignores the question of equal opportunity and introduces incentives for parents to prefer boys (who will have higher incomes) and to control their adult children's lives in ways that are antithetical to personal liberty and autonomy. Another proposal would pay a "bounty" to anyone who improved children's contribution to society.

The best proposals are those that would distribute the costs of raising children more equally as well as promote equality of opportunity. These include enforcement of child support, publicly supported child care, and compensation for parents through increased tax credits or exemptions and a guaranteed, above poverty level, minimum income. "While there are good reasons to encourage all capable adults to engage in job training or paid employment, it is important to remember that nonmarket work is still work. In fact, it is probably the most important work we do." [89]

PART IX

Human Values in Work

Overview Essay

by Neva Goodwin

The first essay in this book—"The History of Work"—listed some of the differences between work as a topic of theoretical interest to economists versus work as it is experienced by workers, employers, and others in the real world. The simplest view offered by economic theory, in which labor is "just another factor of production," would have much appeal to employers and managers, if could be made operative. For example, in the case of other inputs, a producer can often calculate the relationship between each input's cost and its quality (its productivity) and can then deploy them so as to maximize the value of output with respect to the cost of inputs. It would be ideally convenient for both employers and economic theorists if, similarly, all that had to be taken into account in relation to labor were the productivity of this input, its cost (wages, salaries, and benefits), and the relationship between those two variables. However, both common sense and the extensive empirical evidence reviewed in this volume suggest that this approach is not realistic either in theory or practice.

The essay introducing Part II addressed the uniqueness of labor markets and work processes from the point of view of economic theory. Here we will return to the question of the uniqueness of labor from the point of view of the workers—who know full well that they are not merely another input. From the workers' perspective, the unique character of work can be put under two main headings:

The issue of human dignity. First of all, there are good reasons why productivity—the employers' concern—should *never* be regarded as the only issue of importance. Workers are people, and people are—or should be—served by economic activity, rather than vice versa. To put this in the terms used by philosophers: All human beings should at all times be regarded as ends in themselves, never purely as a means to some other ends.

The issue of motivation. Even if we accept that human well-being is a final goal, and that labor productivity is only a means to that end, we must still pay a good deal of attention to productivity, as one of the significant means to human well-being. When we focus on this subject, the first thing to note is that, unlike other inputs to production, workers have minds of their own. There is an intangible thing, internal to human beings (often referred to as "motivation," sometimes as "morale," "commitment," "responsibility") that affects their performance as workers. Hence, while, in the pursuit of productivity, other inputs merely have to be deployed, workers have to be "managed."

These two issues together set up a tension that has been illustrated in many places throughout this volume. This is the tension between, on the one hand, management's desire to motivate workers simply to enhance productivity. On the other hand, when workers perceive productivity to be the only goal, their motivation is likely to be, at best, shallow, uncommitted, and inclined to erode. Putting these considerations into a broader context, we turn up a question that is often raised by the layperson, but too seldom by economists: Is the economy here to serve the people, or are the people here to serve the economy?

Work as Disutility

As suggested above, the mainstream, neoclassical model that has dominated economics for most of this century has adopted a fairly simple means of dealing with the complexities of labor. Of the two points listed above, the issue of human dignity has received virtually no recognition in standard economic theory, while the issue of motivation has been dealt with by a sleight of hand that chops every working person into two portions. One portion is the consumer, who maximizes his or her utility by allocating available monies to get the greatest possible benefit out of each dollar spent. The other portion is the worker, who perceives work as a *dis*utility to be endured solely to earn the money that will be spent by the consumer-self.

In the ideal neoclassical world, in which jobs are infinitely divisible, there is a single, master calculation on which the worker and consumer-selves collaborate, to determine the point at which the money earned by the last hour of work will yield consumption utility that is exactly equal to the disutility of that marginal work-hour. You are irrational if you work fewer than the optimum number of hours, because then you will forgo a positive amount of utility (the extra utility yielded by the additional income, minus the extra disutility suffered from the additional hours of work). And if you work more than the optimum number of hours, the disutility of that extra time will outweigh the utility of the consumption permitted by the additional income.

Against this neoclassical view the first argument from reality is that jobs are not infinitely divisible. When you take a job, you normally have to accept the hours that the employer regards as standard, and in many cases you risk losing the job if you refuse overtime when it is offered. However, this may be changing for some jobs, so that the neoclassical view becomes, in this respect, less unrealistic. In Part V we saw that "the norm" is getting harder and harder to pin down. The different kinds of work arrangements, with respect to where, when, and for how long each person works, are multiplying rapidly. As a result some workers, particularly those with the most marketable skills, may now be able to choose the job that, at least in terms of work arrangements, more closely matches a marginal calculation of utility and disutility.[1]

On the subject of work as disutility, the Marxian contribution has long been an important part of the discussion. Karl Marx had a lively awareness of the role of work as a part of life's fulfillment, but saw this possibility as most relevant to times other than the era in which he was living. Looking back, it related to craft production (though not to agriculture). Looking ahead, he imagined a utopia in which people could choose to divide their work time between hunting, fishing, and writing. In his own time, however, Marx saw workers as exploited and dehumanized by a system that "alienated" the worker from his work.

An article by Kai Erikson (summarized in Part IX) explores the meaning of Marxian alienation, noting that the psychological effects of work—for good or for ill—are not confined to the workplace, but affect the individual in all aspects of life. Erikson notes that Marx's images of workers of the past (craftsmen) and the present (industrial, assembly line workers) were alike unrepresentative. Nevertheless, the concept of alienation remains relevant, especially where workers either feel that all their work is controlled by others, not themselves; or where they are obliged to focus on only a very narrow part of an activity, without a way to connect with the meaning of the whole.

These alienating job characteristics—often accompanied or created by a management regime of rigid, intrusive rules and close supervision—appear in many writings, in this Part and in the rest of the book, wherever there is discussion of what makes for bad jobs. These themes are so pervasive that it is almost impossible to find a discussion of positive values in work that does not also deal with the negative side. Often, indeed, good work is described largely in terms of the absence of the above-mentioned alienating characteristics.

The View from Management: Frederick Taylor and Theory X

Much of what has been written on work as an important part of an individual's whole life experience has emanated from the field of management studies. While we must remember that the management point of view cannot be identical with the worker's point of view, there is enough overlap that it is worth taking seriously this set of insights into the meaning of work.

A number of exponents of modern management theory were summarized in Parts IV, V, and VI. As one reads through these, it is striking how great the influence of Frederick Taylor continues to be. Almost every modern management theory is described, at some point, in terms of how thoroughly it overturns the tenets of Taylorism. Management approaches of which a given author disapproves may be described as maintaining the old Tayloristic principles. A notable exception to this anti-Taylorism is Peter Drucker, a prominent figure in management studies and also a respected commentator on a wide variety of social issues. He defends Taylor on the grounds that the latter was responsible for what Drucker calls the Productivity Revolution—an increase in output per worker-hour ("labor productivity") that took off in the late nineteenth century in America due to the application of knowledge to the study and the engineering of work. According to Drucker,

> To his death [Taylor] maintained that the major beneficiary of rising productivity had to be the worker, not the owner. His main concern was the creation of a society in which owners and workers, capitalists and proletarians, had a common interest in productivity and could build a relationship of harmony based on the application of knowledge to work.[2]

Taylor emphasized the importance of training, to convey to workers and managers new, more efficient work methods. The discovery and elaboration of these methods was to be performed by "experts," not those closest to the work (workers and managers). The monopolistic limitations on knowledge previously maintained by craft unions were threatened by Taylor's insistence that all manual work—both skilled and unskilled—could be scientifically analyzed, demystified, and made more productive. The unions also were offended by Taylor's dismissal of their own knowledge. Their antagonism explains part of Taylor's bad reputation. Another part was explained, by Drucker, as the hostility that Taylor engendered among capitalists, who did not agree with his goal that the workers should reap the rewards of increased productivity. (This hostility on the part of some capitalists did not prevent others from applying Taylor's methods as a means to greater productivity and profits, as the more familiar portrait of Taylorism suggests.) A third, even more salient reason is detailed below. Before we get there, however, we should pause to ask whether history actually unfolded as Taylor had hoped. Were the workers the beneficiaries of his principles of scientific management? According to Drucker, yes. Workers today receive far higher real incomes for much less work than at the beginning of the twentieth century.

> As late as 1910, workers in developed countries still labored as long as they ever had before, that is, at least 3000 hours per year. Today even the Japanese work only 2000 hours, Americans around 1850 and Germans at most 1600. . . . Other substantial shares of the increased productivity have been taken in the form of health care, which has grown from a negligible percentage of gross national product (GNP) to between 8 and 12 percent in developed countries; and in the form of education, which has grown from around 2 percent of GNP to 10 percent or more.[3]

Even without resolving how much of this century's growth in labor productivity is actually due to Taylorism, it is useful to set Drucker's broad historical view of labor's gain from productivity growth next to the rather gloomier picture we have seen elsewhere in this book, of a relatively recent decline in the portion of growth accruing to less skilled labor.

Taylor appears to have held something very similar to the neoclassical view of work, as purely a means to the final end of consumption (intermediated by income). A century later we find the modern authors of *Your Money or Your Life* urging their readers to reduce their need for income, so as to reduce their need for work. This message is plausible only because we live in the world that Taylor helped to create—a world of such high labor productivity that a much shorter work-week (or a shorter working life, with the ideal of self-financed early retirement) can still, when cleverly managed, support a good life. That is, a life that is considerably less dependent on consumption than what is promoted by the advertisers of the American dream, but that still permits far more comforts and luxuries than were available to our hard-working frontier ancestors.

This is one solution to the disutility of work: Reduce the amount that people do. This solution is unsatisfactory in at least one very important respect. It does not address the psychic needs that appear to be best met in work—for example, the hypothesis stated in the essay by Edward O'Boyle that is summarized here, that "[h]uman beings *need* work itself." [O'Boyle, 118]

Taylor's contribution, directed solely to the ends to which work is a means, ignored the human meaning in the working moiety of the sundered life. This, the deepest reason for his unpopularity, resulted in the dehumanizing management style that was caricatured, as we will see below, as "Theory X." Drucker's defense of Taylor may change our ideas about his motives and give us an appreciation of the productivity gains that have made so much difference in the consumer half of life. But it does not ameliorate the "Theory X"-type effects of Taylorism on the work experience.

The Humanistic Alternative: Douglas McGregor and Theory Y

The critics of Taylorism have been vocal ever since Taylor began his work, at the end of the nineteenth century. Douglas McGregor was one who was especially prominent in the 1950s and 1960s. The "conventional view" of management's task, which McGregor calls "Theory X," is closely associated with the methods that were used to realize Taylor's proposals for increasing worker efficiency. McGregor described Theory X in terms of a set of assumptions about workers—especially, that they are not self-motivated, and that their behavior must be modified and controlled by external forces to overcome an intrinsic dislike of work and an inability to identify with organizational goals.

It is interesting to note that McGregor does also assume a high-productivity world as the basis for his alternative, "Theory Y." In stressing that a "satisfied need is not a motivator of behavior!"[4] he clearly accepted that the multifold increase in output per hour to which Drucker refers both has occurred and has been sufficiently well distributed among workers so that most can meet their survival needs, leaving them poised to focus on "higher" needs. This is the core of Theory Y—the idea that, instead of motivating workers via money and threats (appealing to the needs for survival and security), management should address what is best in the workers. The most relevant needs, in this case, are the social needs for association, for belonging and acceptance, for giving and receiving friendship; the individualistic needs for self-esteem, status, and deserved respect; and the self-fulfillment needs for creativity and continued self-development toward realizing one's own potential.

McGregor pointed out that direction and control are useless for motivating people whose focus has moved on from their primary needs. Hence "[t]he essential task of management is to arrange organizational conditions and methods of operation so that people can achieve their own goals *best* by directing *their own* efforts toward organizational objectives."[5] In 1957, when he first wrote his much reprinted essay, "The Human Side of Enterprise," McGregor did not believe that it was yet possible to create an organization that could fully apply Theory Y; but he shared Taylor's and Drucker's optimistic belief that the social sciences would advance until they could tell us how to answer the basic question of management.

That question may be phrased thus: What changes are required—in corporations, in workers, and/or in society—to create a coincidence of interest between employees and their employers? As early examples of the directions in which he thought managers should look for this answer, McGregor cites a number of ideas that continue to be pursued today: flat organization, assigning as much responsibility as possible to those at the bottom of the organization, sincere (not sham) participation and consultative management, and encouragement of workers to set their own objectives and perform a significant part of their own self-evaluation.

Perhaps the most dramatic way of contrasting the two theories is to imagine them applied to an archetypical form of labor—that which is required to bring forth a baby. An understanding of Theory X in fact gives insight into the way the laboring mother was typically treated in First World hospitals from before World War II until sometime in the 1970s. Specialists would apply their knowledge to inducing the body to do its job, but the woman's part of that job would be minimized, divided up as much as possible among the medical personnel. Ideally, the mother would be unconscious, so that the "experts" had to deal with as restricted a portion of the whole person as possible. By contrast, in a hospital that (knowingly or not) is influenced by Theory Y, the medical personnel stand by as coaches, minimizing their direct assistance except under exceptional circumstances. Their goal is to engage the mother as a whole person, helping her to discover intrinsic resources of mind and spirit as well as of body that she can call on to carry out this labor.

These two approaches—a Theory X version of Taylor's Scientific Management, and a set of possibilities for participation and job enrichment that flow out of Theory Y—have dominated management theories for half a century. Most of today's discussions are still cast in reference to the two poles. As we look around at the world of work, we can easily identify areas where Theory X prevails and principles of scientific management are still used to analyze tasks so that the need for skills is minimized for their efficient performance; and areas where Theory Y is applied to elicit a wider range of immeasurable as well as measurable skills and involvements of a workforce whose diversity is recognized and appreciated. Most workplaces, however, fall between the two extremes, developing their own particular mix of Taylorism (as distinct from Taylor's own ideas), McGregor's ideals, and the modern management theories, most of which appear to be considerably closer to Theory Y than to Theory X. Before we conclude, from the latter fact, that the humanists have triumphed, we should note that the assumptions in the literature are very unevenly represented in the workplace, and the longevity of the current theories is not yet assured. This is an area that goes through fads and fashions of thought with considerable rapidity.

How Social and Psychological Norms Are Shaped by Work

The summary (in Part IX) of a chapter from Robert Lane's book, *The Market Experience*, begins with quotations from four of the great classical economists, each one emphasizing that what is learned during the work experience will shape the rest of a person's life. The psychologists who are also cited by Lane emphasize the ways in that our work shapes our values, contributing to a culture that, among other things, believes in personal efficacy, tends toward the acceptance of diversity, and is inclined to equate income with personal worthiness.

What was required for modern work to have these different effects from earlier forms of work? As noted before, the issue of motivation has a special meaning for the manager or producer who faces the fact (as noted by William Darity and Arthur Goldsmith, summarized here) that you can pay for human capital, but it will only translate into productivity when activated by "psychological capital," or motivation. In the early industrial revolution this reality was revealed in the need for employers to induce workers to want what the employees had to offer. As E.P. Thompson noted, it was "not until the second half of the eighteenth century that 'normal' capitalist wage incentives began to become widely effective."[6] Thompson's famous essay, "Time, Work-Discipline, and Industrial Capitalism," emphasizes the process by which cultures defined by task-orientation (in which work was measured out by what needed to be done) were displaced by time-orientation, until "[m]ature industrial societies of all varieties are marked by time-thrift and by a clear demarcation between 'work' and 'life.'"[7]

This process has not been uniform. Some parts of the world still retain cultures where the slower pace of life and the habits decried as sins by early capitalists (along with their friends in religion, such as the Puritans, Methodists, and Evangelicals) are still accepted as reasonable ways to exist when survival needs do not press. The "sins" that were especially inveighed against were loitering, idling, gazing, and sauntering. In fact these sound rather like modern teenagers "hanging out" at a mall. Clearly, even in the industrialized world not all of culture, or human nature, has changed.

Other exceptions within the modern world are far less benign. Within a society where respectability and legitimate access to society's resources depend on fitting into the culture of employment, those who are totally estranged from that culture are in great peril, and in turn create many dangers for the rest of society. The summary of a chapter from William Julius Wilson's book, *When Work Disappears,* describes the problems of a modern neighborhood when it suffers from persistent joblessness. Role models in such a community are unlikely to possess the characteristics of organization, discipline, or sense of purpose and self-efficacy. These qualities, so necessary to success in our society, are hard to learn in circumstances where there is almost no regular work and few role models for the characteristics that go with modern work attachment.

It may be that one of the constants in human nature is a desire to achieve some notion of success; but the definition of success changes dramatically from one culture to another. In our society, for better or for worse, success is strongly identified with "getting ahead" in terms of having money. The ghetto-related behavior described by Wilson is not caused by a difference from the dominant culture in the definition of success. The difference is that the means of achieving it are virtually beyond reach. The psychological effects on ghetto residents can partly be explained by the "expectancy theory" described in the summarized article by Darity and Goldsmith. Contrary to reasonable expectations, in that context effort does not lead to compensated performance within the economic mainstream.

In the article cited earlier, Lane quotes psychologists George and Caroline Valliant to the effect that a highly significant predictor of mental health is "the willingness and the capacity to work in childhood." [Lane, 247] Rare are the individuals in which such a willingness and capacity can endure if there is no legitimate work to be had.

Beyond the Paycheck

The foregoing discussion has emphasized that, in a society that is defined (as ours is) by a particular, organized approach to work, those who lack access to work suffer great social and psychological disadvantages. This theme is further developed in summaries by Andrew Clark and Andrew Oswald, citing evidence that unemployment is not sought by ordinary people, who are well aware of its demoralizing effects (of many types—not only because of the loss of income); and by Darity and Goldsmith, who stress the lingering ill effects on motivation that result from unemployment.

Going beyond these negative justifications for work, two other summaries comment on the positive values to be found in this part of life. O'Boyle looks at the different kinds of working environment that are needed to satisfy both the individualistic and the social components of human nature. (Here we may see echoes of McGregor's belief in the postscarcity imperative for work to address people's individualistic and social needs.) True to its background in management theory, this article stresses the productivity increases with which managers will be rewarded if they attend to these human needs.

Robert Wuthnow goes further, to examine the evidence that monetary incentives are not all that motivate work. He distinguishes between, on the one hand, the "reward-and-benefit calculations" that the economist and the employer assume, causing them to focus on the wage as prime motivator; and, on the other hand, the moral concerns that rise to the fore when societies have achieved enough affluence so that monetary concerns can (at least in principle) play a smaller role in people's life choices. The moral concern on which Wuthnow focuses is the need for meaning, which causes people to try to shape their lives in ways that can be explained via a consistent and comprehensible "account" or narrative.

The article by Kohn et al., summarized here, is an example of a chorus of voices that point to self-direction in work as a major variable affecting the general well-being of the worker (both on the job and in the rest of life). They correlate the desire for self-direction (both for oneself and for one's children) with a work-based definition of social class: Across several very different cultures, managers and employers are most oriented toward this value, and manual workers least so.

The summary of an article by Randy Hodson pulls together several of the themes we have been developing. Starting with the earliest type of work that seems to fit into the modern conception of a job (work that is done for pay and that is conceptually and temporally distinct from the other, nonwork parts of life), he develops a five-part typology of workplace organization. A number of the characteristics that make work relatively agreeable are depicted by Hodson as highest in early "craft" type of organization, and next highest in the relatively recent experiments with "worker participation," but they took a dip in the historically intermediate stages, of "direct supervision," "assembly line," and "bureaucratic" organization.[8]

Hodson's conclusion echoes Marx's nostalgia for craft production, mentioned earlier. Michael Piore is another writer who also celebrates this form. In the article summarized here, Piore portrays a work system that appears to have achieved at least one of McGregor's goals. Workers and managers in Italian "industrial districts" have adopted as final ends the relational satisfactions gained through a common, productive endeavor. Economic concerns are no longer goals in themselves, but recognized as useful (maybe even necessary) for the end of maintaining an interactive community of equals. Piore adopts Hannah Arendt's differentation between "labor" (necessary for survival), "work" (creating something of lasting value), and "action" (involvement in the community). The work experience as we have discussed it involves all three of these. Piore suggests that the work experience as "action" is key to the success of Italian industrial districts. A tension remains, however, between the motivations offered by income and by the desire to participate in the community. In addition, this analytical scheme seems to slight domestic "labor"—perhaps due to its origins in a Greek civilization where women and slaves, who did the "labor," were lumped together as noncitizens.

The Human Values Achieved through Work

This discussion has led us to consider two sets of human values (not necessarily coincident with economic values) that are especially important with respect to work.

The human values attached to the products of human efforts. How much the workers, or other members of society, need and care about the output of a given work effort is related only very tenuously to the value the market puts on the work. However, for many workers much of the meaning of their lives is derived from the belief that they are producing something of human value. (This was part of Wuthnow's point, as noted above.)

The values that are intrinsic to the experience of work (as distinct from its products). McGregor made a good start in listing these, when he named some human needs that can be filled in work: survival, security, acceptance, association, friendship, self-esteem, status, respect, creativity, and self-development. As he noted, the first two are obviously related to the traditional forms of controlling and motivating labor: wages and the threat of unemployment. Some of the others (such as self-esteem, status, and respect) are also to some degree dependent on an employer in a society where success is defined, in large measure, in relation to jobs and wages.

How do these categories of human values relate to the issues that were raised at the beginning of this essay? In effect, the two issues mentioned earlier—human dignity and motivation—pull in opposite directions on the just-described human values. On the one hand, the issue of human dignity emphasizes the fact that, as human beings, workers are, first and foremost, ends in themselves. According to one common understanding, human well-being is the ultimate purpose of the study of economics and of all of its ancillary branches. The well-being of the worker should be no less a concern, in this respect, than the well-being of the consumer.

However, another understanding of economics that is also commonly found in, for example, introductory textbooks, puts major emphasis on something that most people would regard as a means, rather than an end—namely, economic efficiency. The question is raised (usually no more than once per textbook): "Efficiency to what end?" The answer comes in terms that make it clear that the purpose of efficiency is only the consumer's well-being (and that narrowly defined) for it turns out that the goal of efficiency is to maximize output, and hence consumption.[10]

Raising output depends in important ways on labor productivity; labor productivity depends significantly on motivation. This linkage has been evident as we have reviewed the leading strands in the literature on management theory (in this and earlier Parts of this book). Encouragingly, from Taylor through McGregor, and on into the present, there is a discernible trend toward recognizing that productivity goals cannot be pursued entirely at the expense of quality-of-worklife goals. There remains, however, a gap between the employer's productivity impulse and the essential issue of human dignity.

The Danger of Diverging Opportunities

As we look back over this volume, can we find reason to expect to bridge the gap between employers' and workers' goals? Our conclusion is not very optimistic.

We have surveyed a variety of corporate responses to technological change, globalization, and trade, along with an array of competing management theories. A discouraging impression from this survey is an image of how each of these streams appears to separate and flow into two distinctive channels. One channel is available to people who have education, imagination, initiative, and the social contacts and socializing experiences that will enable them to find "good jobs." The other channel is where the rest of the job seekers must go—those who do not have the necessary personal and/or social attributes, or who, even with most of these attributes, continue to be the victims of discrimination.

"Good jobs" possess some combination of the following characteristics: they offer the worker some choice in how, when, where and how long s/he works; they recognize and support the value of cooperation in the workplace; they permit the worker to identify with and to value the output of the work; they offer opportunities for learning, personal growth, and career development; they provide adequate or good remuneration and benefits.

The existence of good jobs and their relative prevalence in a society has some, by no means simple, relationship with the general level of labor productivity. Exclusive focus on productivity, with maximization of output as the ultimate goal, can sometimes lead to a creative and humane emphasis on what motivates people; however, it will never adequately recognize the issue of human dignity. Still ahead is the job of ensuring that the importance of the latter issue is recognized by all participants in the world of work—from workers to owners of capital. This task can only be undertaken as part of a larger move to reprioritize our goals. Until that more fundamental effort begins, we are unlikely to make much additional progress toward celebrating and building on the human values in work.

Notes

1. An interesting perspective on the work, leisure, and quality of life is provided by the book *Your Money or Your Life* by Joe Dominguez and Vicki Robin. The book asks its readers to examine what they do to earn money; to consider the quailty of life purchased with each additional increment of income; and then to make a realistic cost-benefit analysis along these lines: "Assuming that the purpose of your work is to earn money to support consumption, are you working and spending at the right level?" Some thirty thousand individuals or couples have written to the authors to say that they have carried out the analysis and discovered that their previous package of work and consumption had been elicited by forces in the economy, rather than coming from true needs or wishes within themselves. When they reversed the priority, making the quality of their lives the end and economy the means, they found ways to raise their quality of life, while simultaneously reducing their work effort and their consumption.

These respondents may in some sense appear to be acting as rational neoclassical utility maximizers balancing income and leisure. However, in following Domiguez and Robin's advice to reduce consumption and seek meaningful work, they depart from neoclassical assumptions, which generally imply that individuals maximize consumption and view work as pure disutility.

2. Peter F. Drucker, "The Rise of The Knowledge Society" in *The Wilson Quarterly* (Spring 1993), 61.

3. Ibid., 63–64.

4. Douglas McGregor, "The Human Side of Enterprise," originally published in *The Management Review* 46, 11 (1957); reprinted in *Leadership and Motivation, Essays of Douglas McGregor* (Cambridge, MA.: MIT Press, 1966), 9.

5. Ibid., 15.

6. E.P. Thompson, "Time, Work-Discipline and Industrial Capitalism" in *Past and Present* 38 (December 1967), 81.

7. Ibid., 93

8. For a defense of what bureaucratic organization offers the worker, see Sanford M. Jacoby, *Employing Bureaucracy—Managers, Unions, and the Transformation of Work in American Industry, 1900–1945* (New York: Columbia University Press, 1985).

9. Piore notes that "the distinction [Arendt] wants to make between the two [work and labor] as types of productive activity, is captured by the fact that we speak of the birth process as labor and of an artistic creation as a work of art. The words Arbeit and Werk are used in the same way in German; travail and oeuvre in French." [Piore, 312]

10. The significance of identifying the consumer's well-being—or, more narrowly, the maximization of consumption—as the goal of economics is explored in volumes 2 and 3 in this series [*Frontier Issues in Economic Thought* (Washington, D.C.: Island Press)]. Volume 2 is *The Consumer Society* and volume 3 is *Human Well-Being and Economic Goals*.

Summary of

Learning at Work: Beyond Human Capital

by Robert Lane

[Published in *The Market Experience* (Cambridge: Cambridge University Press, 1992), 237–259.]

[The] understandings of the greater part of men are necessarily formed by their ordinary employments.[1]

It is not sufficiently considered how little there is in most men's ordinary life to give any largeness either to their conceptions or to their sentiments.[2]

The germs of the education of the future are to be found in the factory system. This will be an education which, in the case of every child over a certain age, will combine productive labor with instruction and physical culture, not only as a means of increasing social production, but as the only way of producing fully developed human beings.[3]

The business by which a person earns his livelihood fills his thoughts during by far the greatest part of those hours in which his mind is at its best: during them his character is being formed by the ways in which he uses his faculties at work.[4]

The point of view put forth by the four outstanding classical economists just quoted is no longer in fashion among their heirs, where work is most often viewed as a sacrifice, or disutility, that is undertaken only for wages and consumption gains. Nor is this view fully reflected by the "humanist" critics of modern economic theory, who see the potential for work to provide an enjoy-able exercise of skill, knowledge and effort, but doubt that modern economies can provide such opportunity.

This article employs a definition of work that disengages it from pain or disu-tility: "Work is the effort or activity an individual performs for the purpose of providing goods or services of value to others *or the self* and it is also considered to be work by the individual so involved." [238] To show the important role still played by work in most individuals' development, this article draws on five stud-ies by psychologists who have examined the actual effects of work on workers.

Learning at Work: Effects on Cognition and Personality

Paul Breer and Edwin Locke find that work experiences have a clear and imme-diate impact on basic personal values, such as individualistic versus social orien-tations. An extensive longitudinal study by Melvin Kohn and Carmi Schooler reinforces this conclusion, showing that, for example, "An occupation that re-quires self-direction does not merely recruit intellectually more flexible workers, it develops those cognitive powers of the workers as well." [242] Above all, they emphasize that jobs with *substantive complexity* (usually highly placed, re-sponsible, demanding but rewarding jobs) not only attract workers with match-ing qualities of intellectual alertness and flexibility, self-esteem, and self-direct-edness; they also foster these qualities. By contrast, jobs lacking substantive complexity lead to feelings of alienation.

A similarly constructed study by Jeylan Mortimer and Jon Lorence delves further into the way that early values—specifically those focusing on (1) in-come-maximizing, (2) people-orientation, or (3) intellectual challenge and autonomy—tend to be reinforced, and also subtly altered, by jobs that (in two-thirds of the cases reviewed) are selected by the worker to match their early proclivities. They find that jobs with high incomes tend to decrease an individual's concern for others, while autonomous, challenging jobs seem to increase the worker's people-orientation. (No change in value-orienta-tion was found in the people-centered individuals who took corresponding jobs.)

In developing countries, according to Alex Inkles and David Smith, factory work is the major contributor to the process and direction of change toward modernization—more so than either the traditional culture or formal educa-tion. For example, length of tenure in a factory job is positively correlated with the modern belief in personal efficacy (as opposed to traditional fatalism).

In contrast to what might have been thought to have been a comparable ex-perience by British workers in the late eighteenth and early nineteenth cen-turies, the cost in anxiety and well-being was not high among the modernizing workers. For example, there were no differences between the modernizing group and the traditional village group in the telltale psychosomatic symptoms indicating psychic disturbances. [245]

Finally, psychologists George and Caroline Valliant note that "The willingness and capacity to work in childhood is the most important forerunner—more important than native intelligence, social class, or family situation—of mental health." [247] This observation may be gaining increased salience, as youth employment continues to decline in industrialized countries.[5]

The Process of Learning

A central lesson from these studies is that what is learned during the work experience is very likely to be generalized to all of life. "For example, as in the Kohn and Schooler studies when a worker learns cognitive complexity, a sense of personal control, and self-esteem on the job, these do not evaporate when the worker leaves the job." [248/9] The Valliants pointed out, similarly, that "[p]eople who learned qualities of commitment and preservation at work embodied their qualities in their marital life." [249] And Inkles and Smith found that modern attitudes, such as tolerance for diversity, were also carried home from the factory.

Another lesson is that the most effective learning comes through observation of and interaction with others—more so than learning by precept, or by the purely individualistic work experiences that are sometimes assumed in descriptions of human capital development. Additionally it is interesting to note that pay or other work rewards have a high informational content (regarding the attainment of standards and goals, how one appears in others' eyes, and so on) that may be more important, at least above the subsistence level, than their material values.

Alienated Work

In contrast to the positive effects of work cited so far is the concept of alienation. This has been blamed for static productivity as well as for a variety of reductions of well-being, including intergroup antagonisms, a sense of helplessness in political and social affairs, and a loss of a sense of harmony with nature.

What features of work are most likely to be alienating? Most often cited is lack of participation in the decisions that affect the worker. Additionally, alienation seems to represent a relative absence of the working conditions that were described earlier as contributing to general human development. For example, *self-directed work,* which is substantively complex, loosely supervised, and nonroutine, promotes attitudes of tolerance, respect, and trust. Routine, unchallenging, low-status, heavily supervised work will not play such a developmental role and is likely to reduce self-esteem and create a sense of alienation.

Even here, however, we need to see work in comparison to the rest of the individual's life. A job that to some appears unstimulating, to others might be far better than staying home. While humanists claim that much of modern worklife is meaningless, work-deprivation (as in unemployment) may promote a far worse sense of meaninglessness. An unsentimental view of village life in the Third World contrasts the factory experience as relatively independent and autonomous. Similarly, "a study of women in repetitive, low-complexity, clerical jobs in Chicago found that the social relations at work, not only among themselves but also in 'managing' their managers, were sufficiently engaging to make up for the lack of complexity in the tasks assigned to them." [256]

Conclusion

For many people the worst that can be said about work is not that they have to do it, but that it fails to provide the full benefits of fulfilling experience. Work has the potential to develop cognitive complexity, moral responsibility, self-esteem, and a sense of personal competence; self-directed work can move people to find intellectually challenging uses of their leisure time and to participate in a liberal democracy. This is the standard against which we should judge the success of a society in its provision of work. For a large proportion of the labor force this standard is still out of reach.

Notes

1. Adam Smith, *The Wealth of Nations* (New York: Random House, 1937), 734/5; cited by the author on page 253.
2. John Stuart Mill, "Representative Government," in *Utilitarianism, Liberty, and Representative Government* (London: Dent, 1910), 216.
3. Alfred Marshall, *Principles of Economics,* 8th ed. (London: Macmillan, 1938), 1/2; cited by the author on page 248.
4. Ibid.
5. The five studies referred to are (1) Paul E. Breer and Edwin A. Locke, *Task Experience as a Source of Attitudes* (Homewood, IL: Dorsey Press, 1965); (2) Melvin L. Kohn and Carmi Schooler, *Work and Personality: An Inquiry into the Impact of Social Stratification* (Norwood, NJ: Ablex, 1983); (3) Jeylan T. Mortimer and Jon Lorence, "Work Experience and Occupational value Socialization: A Longitudinal Study," *American Journal of Sociology* 84 (1979), 361–385; (4) Alex Inkeles and David H. Smith, *Becoming Modern* (Cambridge: Harvard University Press, 1974); and (5) George E. Valliant and Caroline O. Valliant, "Natural History of Male Psychological Health: Work as a Predictor of Positive Mental Health," *American Journal of Psychiatry* 138 (1981), 433–440.

Summary of

On Work and Alienation

by Kai Erikson

[Published in *The Nature of Work—Sociological Perspectives,* eds. Kai Erikson and
Steven Peter Vallas (New Haven: American Sociological Association Presidential Series
and Yale University Press, 1990), 19–35.]

The essay on which this summary is based is not a formal inquiry into the relationship between work and alienation, but rather a kind of "aerial reconnaissance," undertaken for the purpose of gathering ideas in preparation for a research project on telecommunications workers. As such, it does not seek to resolve ongoing debates about the meaning of alienation (although it acknowledges them), but rather to draw out some concepts that might be helpful to a sociologist who is thinking about work.

Marx on Alienation

The concept of alienation, developed in the German philosophical tradition, has become most closely associated with the early writings of Karl Marx. Marx related alienation to a specific transition in the history of work—for Marx work is the defining experience of human existence, inseparable from human nature. Not only are humans made for work, humans are made by work. Through the evolutionary process the human brain and body are shaped by labor. In *The Human Condition* Hannah Arendt remarked on "the seemingly blasphemous notion of Marx that labor (and not God) created man or that labor (and not reason) distinguishes man from other animals." [21, Arendt 86]

According to Marx, human beings take up the materials of nature: wood, flint, stone, even a sight or a sound, and make them into objects that, in turn, reveal the true character of humankind. These objects are invested with the energy and skill of the producer who measures himself or herself by the things produced. Industrialization and capitalism disturbed this natural order. The worker no longer owned either the means or the objects of production. A complex division of labor broke work into segments, reducing the role of any individual worker in the production process. Workers no longer produced for their own consumption, but for money—"their experience and ability—their very selves, in fact—are sold at market prices in much the same way as a side of beef or a sack of onions, and in that sense they become commodities themselves." [21]

This separation of workers from the product of their own labor is the source of alienation of human beings from their natural moorings, from each other, even from their own nature as members of the human species. Workers pour themselves into the making of things that are then taken to be sold on someone else's terms. This raid on their personalities is repeated day in and day out, diminishing the human spirit and its moral, perceptual, and intellectual capacities. When labor is but a commodity for sale, laborers are in competition in the marketplace, estranged from each other, too brutalized to experience authentic relationships.

For the modern researcher interested in Marx's views on alienation the question is where in the modern workplace would alienation be most likely to emerge? Four areas are suggested by the Marxist text: (1) where workers are separated from the means of production and from the product; (2) where the worker has no perception of the whole pattern of production or his or her own role in it; (3) where external forces control the labor process; or (4) where work is so divided that only a fraction of the worker's ability is engaged. These reduce to two essential categories: division of labor into narrow specialties and loss of control over the conditions of work.

Where Does Alienation Occur?

The transition Marx described was from the world of the artisan—the craftsman with sure skills and control over his shop, his tools, and his materials—to the world of the industrial worker chained to the machine and the assembly line. These images are symbolic of a certain shift in manufacturing technology, but they are not representative of most workers, then or now. Most workers in the preindustrial era were not artisans in the towns but peasants scattered over vast rural areas. In more recent times, assembly line workers were only a fraction even of manual workers, and that fraction is diminishing in the face of automation.

Agriculture may involve certain craftlike skills, but its labor wore down the peasant in ways that do not correspond to the idyllic view of the artisan. The current situation is different. As workers leave the "satanic mills" for automated workplaces, some observers, notably Daniel Bell and Robert Blauner, have expressed hope that alienation would be reduced and workers would acquire new skills and regain some autonomy in working with production processes reintegrated by automation.

Several other analysts, however, see no reduction in the alienating qualities of work from automation. Work may be less physically strenuous, but the tedium of repetition has been replaced by the tedium of doing nothing but waiting for something to go wrong. Even complex processes require merely attention and reflex rather than mastery or control. Where the artisan inspected the grain of the wood or felt the texture of the weave to accumulate the knowledge of his craft, the worker in an automated workplace has little sensory experience of the production process. Information comes from computer screens or dials, not actual contact with the product.

Computerized equipment can also store the knowledge of the operator, indeed many operators, replacing the experiential record of problems encountered and solved with programmed instructions. The computer "thinks" and makes decisions, leaving unengaged the skill and judgment that make the operator human, programming the worker as well as the machine. The computer can be an instrument of control in another way as well, offering an efficient vehicle for surveillance: timing procedures, counting keystrokes, maintaining a continuous record of performance. Close supervision by itself can feel machinelike, regimenting and hemming in the worker with rules, quotas, and routines. The computer is capable of intensifying this control and rendering it more precise.

How Does Alienation Manifest Itself?

"That is a tougher question than might appear on the surface, because so many different currents of thought have converged on it from so many different ideological directions." [29] Joachim Israel defined one helpful distinction—between "estranging processes" that involve the structure of the workplace and "states of estrangement" that are the psychological effects.

Harry Braverman takes an extreme structuralist position, posing that objectively alienating conditions produce alienated workers no matter what the worker may think or feel. The opposite pole is occupied by Robert Blauner who used surveys of workers' self-reported satisfaction as his primary data. From this perspective, workers are alienated if they feel alienated. For sociologists the dilemma is that alienation is only a useful construct if it is registered in a person's mind and reflected in behavior. But it is naive to think that workers' self-perception always corresponds perfectly to degrading or enhancing aspects of work. (To further confound the question, Marx maintained that one of the characteristics of alienated labor is that it dulls perception, rendering the worker stupefied and lacking self-awareness.)

For the sociologist, the best results will probably be obtained by qualitative field studies "to understand how the ways of work are impressed on the persons exposed to them." [31] If alienation is a state of being, it is not confined to the workplace alone. It influences the rest of the workers' life and, in turn, may be aggravated or compensated for by activities outside the workplace. Work and leisure may be separable in modern life, but the mind is not so easily compartmentalized and the moods of the workplace and the rest of life permeate each other and interact to shape the total pattern of experience.

Even in the confines of the workplace there is room for the play of personality—decorations on a desk, passive resistance on the shop floor, camaraderie. However, alienation can affect personality in insidious ways with classic behavioral manifestations: absenteeism, grievances, quitting, depression, substance abuse. Often the persons who manifest these signs of alienation are not well-equipped to understand their meaning, leaving the trained observer "engaged in a haughty business" of knowing more about people than they know about themselves.

Marx was blunt about the disastrous impact of capitalist production, leaving the worker a debased and crippled idiot. But the researcher should be a little wary of planning "to walk out onto a shop floor somewhere and ask hulking operatives whether the conditions under which they work have stupefied them or made idiots of them." [32] However, finding the right way to ask the right questions may reveal whether alienation in the Marxist sense contributes to certain kinds of callousness characteristic of our times: passionate support for capital punishment, love of guns and other weapons, ultranationalism, xenophobia. "[S]uch questions are important, sympathetic, and in principle answerable." [33]

Summary of

Ghetto-Related Behavior and the Structure of Opportunity

by William Julius Wilson

[Published in *When Work Disappears* (New York: Alfred A. Knopf, 1997), 51–86.]

[T]he residents of . . . jobless black poverty areas face certain social constraints on the choices they can make in their daily lives. These constraints, combined with restricted opportunities in the larger society, lead to ghetto-related behavior and attitudes—that is, behavior and attitudes that are found more frequently in ghetto neighborhoods than in neighborhoods that feature even modest levels of poverty and local employment. Ghetto-related behavior and attitudes often reinforce the economic marginality of the residents of jobless ghettos. [52]

The poorest residents of major cities often live in a socially self-contained world, within which legitimate paid work has largely disappeared. Much has been written about the resulting "culture of poverty," involving behavior and attitudes that make it difficult for the urban poor to get and keep paying jobs. In this article, a leading sociologist argues, on the basis of interviews in inner-city Chicago neighborhoods, that residents of black ghettos often share mainstream beliefs about the value of hard work, honesty, obeying the law, and avoiding welfare—but face a system of constraints and opportunities that prevent them from acting on these beliefs.

The Disappearance of Work

Many of the contemporary problems of the urban poor are the results of persistent joblessness. Such problems have not always plagued the inner city. In the 1950s ghetto neighborhoods were poor and just as segregated as they are now, but they had a high level of employment.

A number of factors have contributed to the decline of the ghetto economy. The decline in mass production and in low-skill, blue-collar jobs, rising educational and training requirements for many occupations, and the growing suburbanization of work have all made employment less accessible to poor inner-city residents. Government policy has also worsened the economic plight of poor neighborhoods. In the decades after World War II, federal programs made mortgages readily available for suburban housing, while constructing massive low-income housing projects in the city, reinforcing residential segregation by race income. Then in the 1980s, as jobs began to disappear from the inner city, changes in federal policy led to drastic cutbacks in basic urban programs just when they were most needed.

The downward spiral of ghetto areas has led to the departure of middle-class and employed working-class blacks, depriving the neighborhoods of resources and role models. In contrast, Mexican-Americans, Chicago's second-largest minority group, are much more likely to live in areas of only moderate poverty, with many small businesses (often owned by Mexicans) and local services.

Models of Success

The lack of jobs in the poorest black neighborhoods translates directly into a lack of male role models who achieve success through legitimate employment. Instead, the men who appear economically successful are engaged in criminal activity, particularly drug dealing. Interviews with young and middle-aged men reveal that they are well aware of this pattern. In some cases, men who had tried to support families on paychecks from legitimate jobs concluded that they could only fulfill their family responsibilities by engaging in at least a little drug dealing.

The drug trade, of course, has caused numerous problems, including the widespread possession and use of guns by drug dealers—many of whom are trigger-happy adolescents. This may decrease social integration, as residents become fearful of leaving the safety of their homes. On the other hand, even the poorest neighborhoods have social networks involving high degrees of interaction. Some parents deliberately pursue social isolation to protect themselves and their children from undesirable behavior patterns that have become local norms. Children raised in impoverished neighborhoods are not only at risk from the dangerous activities around them—they are also unlikely to learn habits and styles of interaction that lead to success in school or work.

The economic segregation of ghetto neighborhoods leads to isolation from mainstream society. Among jobless blacks, women are less likely than men to have friends who are working, married, or have any postsecondary education; blacks, both male and female, are less likely than Mexicans to have a close friend who is employed. Among those who are employed, blacks are less likely than Mexicans to report that a friend or relative helped them find their current job.

The Culture of Poverty

> [T]he total culture of the inner-city ghetto includes ghetto-related elements, but it also includes a predominance of mainstream elements. Many media discussions of the 'underclass' often overlook or ignore these mainstream elements. [67]

Survey research shows that nearly all inner-city blacks believe that plain hard work is important in getting ahead. Nonetheless, they live in circumstances that do not always allow them to act on this belief. Those who work in low-skill, low-paying jobs, often with long commutes on public transportation, typically have little or no prospects for advancement on their current jobs, and no opportunities for education or training for better jobs. Meanwhile, the temptations of unemployment and illegitimate sources of income are ever-present. In stable neighborhoods, economically marginal individuals face greater social pressure to engage in legitimate, mainstream activities. In ghetto neighborhoods, on the other hand, means of adapting and surviving economically gain a local legitimacy, regardless of how the larger society views these actions.

Some ghetto-related behaviors, such as street corner panhandling, may be situationally adaptive. Other practices, including idleness and public drinking, may be verbally condemned by many residents, but still culturally transmitted by example or role modeling. Regardless of the community's beliefs, it lacks the basis to create and enforce alternative models. Accidental cultural transmission occurs when behaviors are functional in a dysfunctional environment: Adolescent males, denied other forms of accomplishment, learn that they gain respect when they carry and are willing to use assault weapons.

Joblessness and Efficacy

Regular employment provides organization, discipline, and a sense of purpose in life. Prolonged unemployment can create the opposite traits. Lack of a formal job need not imply idleness, but even difficult informal endeavors are unlikely to involve regularity and consistency in hours of work. The problems created by this lack of structure are more severe when they are shared and reinforced by others in the neighborhood. One of these shared problems is a perceived lack of "self-efficacy," that is, the absence of the belief in one's own ability to act and accomplish one's goals. People may acquire a feeling of futility either because they doubt their own abilities or because they believe they face an unresponsive or hostile environment. Both varieties of futility are strengthened by unemployment, particularly when it is long-lasting and widespread in the community. The ghetto community develops a low collective efficacy, which is spread via the process of accidental cultural transmission. This is both a consequence of, and a cause of, the weak labor-force attachment of many residents.

As confirmed by the Chicago interviews, people get tired of trying to save money, find work, or find better housing when their repeated attempts have ended in failure. Survey respondents blamed their failure to find work on competition from foreigners, the scarcity of jobs, the government's failure to provide jobs, lack of access to decent jobs in the suburbs, and the need to care for their children. Only a few saw racial prejudice as the major obstacle they faced.

As this list suggests, many are making rational decisions based on the limited choices available to them. Although welfare recipients received meager cash payments, they were (at the time this was written) eligible for food stamps and Medicaid. Most of the jobs they could get were at or close to the minimum wage and did not include health benefits. Leaving welfare to take such a job, and then paying for health care, would be an economic step down, not up. Likewise, leaving a minimum wage job that provides no benefits is not always an enormous loss. Many welfare recipients want to leave welfare and find work, but their environment gives them no viable opportunities to do so—and all too many opportunities to absorb behaviors and attitudes that arise from, and reinforce, the absence of work.

Summary of

Unhappiness and Unemployment

by Andrew Clark and Andrew J. Oswald

[Published in *Economic Journal* 104 (May 1994).]

Unemployment in most of the Western industrialized economies is worryingly high. How serious a problem this is depends in part on whether people are voluntarily or involuntarily unemployed. Yet economists have done little empirical work to investigate this question. This article, using psychological methods, relies on British survey data to test whether the unemployed are more or less happy than those who have jobs, the implication being that people would not voluntarily choose unemployment if it makes them unhappier.

As in much statistical research, this study cannot prove causation. Relative unhappiness among the unemployed might not be a function of their job status, but of their preexisting personality or other factors. However, the study does show that the unemployed are more unhappy—and the authors suspect that there is a causal relationship.

Unemployment and Unhappiness

The British Household Panel Study, surveying a random sample of about six thousand Britons active in the labor market in 1991, asked a series of twelve questions relevant to well-being, such as: "Have you recently: (1) felt constantly under strain? (2) been able to enjoy your normal day-to-day activities? (3) been feeling unhappy and depressed?"

A simple scale can be constructed by counting the number of questions on which an individual reported being fairly or highly stressed. The highest possible level of distress is 12, the lowest is zero. For the 522 unemployed persons in the survey, the average level was 2.98, about twice the figures for those who were employed (1.45) and self-employed (1.54). The significance of the average for those without jobs is made stronger by looking at the distribution of answers. More than half of all respondents reported a mental distress score of zero, with 76 percent reporting 2 or lower.

Mental distress is also found disproportionately among women, people in their thirties and forties, and to a small degree among those with higher levels of education. Within each of these groups, distress is higher for those who are unemployed. Comparing across regions of the country, it appears that it is less harmful psychologically to be unemployed in regions where average unemployment is higher—where there are many other people in similar situations.

Regression results, using four different equation specifications, all yield results in which unemployment is a statistically significant predictor of high mental distress. Other factors that predict relative unhappiness are being separated or divorced, and having children, especially one child; but joblessness is the strongest predictor. Factors that were not significant include race and income. The regression results suggest that, in terms of the 12-point "distress scale" described above, losing your job is equivalent to moving from 0 to 2, or from 1 to 4.

The authors conclude that their results justify a rejection of the idea that unemployment is voluntary. They therefore suggest that "British policy measures aimed at cutting out supposedly high levels of voluntary joblessness would be misguided." Instead, since unemployment appears to be involuntary, "The State may have to look elsewhere for ways to tackle unemployment, and perhaps consider methods of directly raising the number of jobs rather than reducing the number of benefit claimants." [648]

Summary of

Social Psychology, Unemployment, and Macroeconomics

by William A. Darity, Jr., and Arthur Goldsmith

[Published in *Journal of Economic Perspectives* 10, 1 (Winter 1996), 121–140.]

The traditional macroeconomic approach to unemployment depicts a one-way chain of causation in which wages, employment, and productivity are affected by "given" psychological factors such as tastes, motivations, and endowments of human capital. This article draws on the work of numerous social psychologists to describe the relations among these variables as a feedback loop, wherein psychological factors are reciprocally affected by the economic variables. The interesting results of such interdisciplinary cross-fertilization include a proposal for reshaping human capital theory, and reasons to question the existence of a natural rate of unemployment.

Motivation and Human Capital

It is useful to understand human capital as divided into two conceptually distinct parts. Conventional human capital, based in skills as well as physical health, defines an individual's ability to initiate and complete tasks. Ability, however, does not predict action. If we want to know what will come of the potential described in skill-based human capital we have to add in the factor of motivation. This is what explains "effective human capital"—the portion of an individual's innate and learned capacities that will be actually realized.

Standard measures of conventional human capital include education, experience, tenure, and aptitude. Economic studies of the correlation of these factors with real wages suffer from omitted variable problems that are likely to lead to unreliable estimates of the various factors that determine wages and/or productivity. What is omitted may be broadly termed motivation. It is the psychological capital that determines the extent to which the more commonly measured aspects of human capital will be turned into effective human capital. Since psychological capital is likely to be correlated to some extent with the standard measures of human capital, and since some aspects of motivation may be jointly determined with personal productivity, the results will be skewed if randomness is assumed for this omitted variable. Nor can it be treated as a time-invariant variable whose impact is not contingent on any observable regressor, since motivation is determined in important ways by the individual's employment history.

Unemployment and Motivation

It is evident that unemployment can affect an individual's psychological well-being. The responses that have been observed include depression, anxiety, low self-esteem, and strained personal relations. Going beyond common-sense observation, there is an extensive literature[1] that explores the two-way causal links between unemployment and psychological health, or ill-health. The mechanisms that complete the linkage from unemployment to psychological health to motivation are explicated in "expectancy theory," currently the most widely accepted and empirically verified theory of motivation.

> This theory posits that a person's motivation is directly related to beliefs that: (1) effort will lead to performance . . . (2) performance will be rewarded by compensation, opportunities to use skills, security and opportunity to develop professional relations; and (3) the rewards contribute to the realization of individual goals like autonomy, achievement, self-respect, status, recognition, friendship and security. [125]

Job loss, often experienced as a negation of some or all of these beliefs, can be a traumatic blow to self-esteem and can create feelings of helplessness or lack of control over one's life. Such feelings are a common precursor to depression and are also known to "reduce motivation and result in detrimental cognitive effects that hamper learning." [124]

> To the extent that unemployment leaves a psychological imprint that persists following reemployment, individuals suffer lower self-esteem, learned helplessness, and a loss of the latent byproducts of working (like practice in time management), and their personal productivity is likely to suffer. Personal productivity of 'survivors' is also expected to decline, as they witness the trauma of their coworkers. . . . Therefore, a deterioration in psychological well-being brought about by a recession triggers a subsequent decline in productivity across the labor force. [132]

Quantifying the Connection between Unemployment and Emotional Well-Being

The propositions put forth here are that unemployment damages psychological well-being and that psychological well-being has an effect on productivity (via job attachment, as well as through both cognitive and emotional effects). These propositions are not reflected in standard economic analyses because economists have generally accepted the impossibility of making interpersonal comparisons or of measuring psychological variables. However, this is an area in which there has been notable progress in recent decades. Tests of convergent validity (comparison of different measurement instruments, as well as self-reporting, to see if they achieve like results), of stability (does the same test generally produce similar results if repeated, say, two weeks later?), and of internal consistency have shown reason to place considerable confidence in several psychological survey tools that have now achieved a long history.

Goldsmith, Veum, and Darity (1995), estimating separately the impact on wages of both skill-based human capital and psychological capital, have found that, while both are important determinants of productivity, "a 'one-unit' improvement in psychological capital has a much larger effect on productivity than an equivalent increase in skill-based human capital. For females, in particular, the impact of human capital is heavily contingent upon motivation." [129]

A Behavioral Macroeconomic Model

What would a macroeconomic model look like, if it represented the influence of psychological well-being on productivity and labor-force participation? As an example, we may consider how the ramifications of an employment shock work their way through an economy over time.

In a conventional economic model a sharp drop in employment is followed by equilibrating forces that will affect the price of labor until "the economy returns to its original real levels of employment, output and wages, but with nominal wage and output price deflation. In such a model, the short-term experience of joblessness has no long-term effect on workers, nor on supply and demand for labor." [132]

In contrast, a model that explicitly included the interconnections between a society's economic vitality and its psychological health, and that recognized the long-lasting cognitive and emotional damage of unemployment, would show some different possible consequences to a rise in joblessness. On the supply side the effect can be either increased or reduced labor supply, because, while emotional distress may create discouragement, leading to less attachment to work, it can also create a "trauma escape" effect, in which workers are willing to accept lower real wages in order to obtain a job. In either case, however, the debilitating effects of unemployment are expect to reduce the efficiency of labor, and will therefore reduce aggregate labor demand. This may cause unemployment to rise further, and may be the explanation for the persistence of episodes of lowered employment.

Given this psychological link we may find a new, less desirable equilibrium, even if unemployment is eventually reduced—not only because of wage or price rigidities, but also as a result of unfavorable labor force histories. "Ultimately, with a labor force showing lower participation, employment and productivity, the output of the economy will be lower than the original potential. . . . Thus, the story of the intermediate run must include not only flexible nominal wages, but the productivity and labor market attachment consequences of joblessness. . . ." [132]

Note

1. Reviewed by Norman T. Feather in *The Psychological Impact of Unemployment* (New York: Springer-Verlag, 1990).

Summary of

The Need for Work as Such: Self-Expression and Belonging

by Edward J. O'Boyle

[Published in *The Social Economics of Human Material Need,* eds. John B. Davis and Edward J. O'Boyle (Carbondale: Southern Illinois University Press, 1994), 116–142.]

This is a chapter from a book that sets forth some of the principles of "social economics"—an alternative to the conventional economic paradigm. A major difference between the two views of production theory is that conventional economists focus on instrumentality, and either set aside the problem of human dignity or presume that human material need is satisfied entirely through money. Social economists, in contrast, insist that instrumentality is subordinate to dignity and that because of the duality of human material need human beings are not satisfied by money alone. Human beings *need* work itself. [118]

The chapter summarized here briefly notes that the term "work" can be broadly interpreted to include, for example, parenting; however, the writer then turns to exclusive consideration of the experience that employees have in working for an employer.

Human nature is dualistic, containing both individual and social components. The individualistic part of human nature seeks self-expression. The social part requires a sense of belonging. In the workplace these aspects express themselves through individual effort, on the one hand, and teamwork on the other. Effective workplace management fosters and supports both sides of the workers' dual nature.

Self-Expression: Meeting the Need of the Individual for Work as Such through Individual Contribution

On the individualistic side, each human being needs work as an opportunity to contribute something that represents his or her unique endowment of skills and talents. Such work simultaneously makes a contribution of something that is special and lasting, and also has the practical result of contributing to the individual's survival. Employers also benefit from the uniqueness of individual abilities, which offer a wide variety from which to draw when carrying out a production process.

At the same time, human beings are unique among factors of production in that they alone may, and often do, make the choice to withhold some of their productive energies. Conventional economic theory and practice has tended to respond to this fact by encouraging close monitoring of worker effort. The social economics alternative is "to restructure the work itself to make it more attractive and to reward the employees for the additional work effort on grounds that a more attractive workplace makes for a *permanent* increase in work effort and revenues. . . ." [120] The positive motivation that can be set up in this way encourages workers to propose the myriad small innovations that can result in continuous product improvement. This is the mechanism that accounts for the success, for example, of total quality management.

When people are deprived of the opportunity to work, or to do work that exercises individual skills and talents, these idle capacities are in danger of deteriorating through nonuse. On the positive side, unlike other factors of production, human capacities grow and develop—rather than being depleted—through use.

Balancing Individualistic Needs with the Social Needs for Belonging and Teamwork

> Teamwork is organized by enlarging human motivation from individual goals pursued competitively to include common goals pursued cooperatively. To be successful, teamwork requires a blending of self-interest and a genuine concern for others. This blending is achieved (if at all) with some difficulty. [127]

A person who is working alone on a project for which she has responsibility is likely to combine, automatically, thinking and doing. Group work unfortunately has the side effect of making it possible to separate the thinking and the doing tasks, giving the former to individuals identified as management and the latter to those identified with labor. This creates a hierarchical structure and makes true teamwork much more difficult.

Group behavior includes another potential downside. In the process of creating boundaries that establish who is *in* the group, there is also an assumption that others are *out* of it. When such exclusion is defined on the basis of gender, nationality, race, age, or religion, it becomes discriminatory as well as exclusive. On the positive side, the interaction between the social satisfactions of teamwork and the gratifications of individual contribution includes some reinforcements for cooperation. For example, important aspects of learning occur through cooperative work (in teams, in mentoring situations, and so on), thus enhancing the individual satisfaction of effective self-expression.

Ideally, workplace teams are formed not only for the goals of production but to enhance the development of such essential personal qualities as responsibility, cooperation, solidarity (in which "a human being finds fulfillment by adding to the fulfillment of others," [134]) and caring.

> Teamwork depends on management's valuing workers sufficiently as human beings to actively involve them in the decisions as to how the work is to be done. Belonging is the fruit of such valuing. This involvement, which affirms the workers as more than mere instruments of work, provides them with additional means for effectively caring for one another on a regular basis. [131]

The Role of Management in Creating a Healthy Workplace

Effective managers, recognizing the dualism in workers' needs and motivations, will establish a dual system of rewards to reinforce both types of contribution. They will recognize the firm's self-interest in the fact that "[w]orkers whose need for self-expression is unmet are dissatisfied workers and that dissatisfaction, in turn, encourages them to withhold some of their productive energies, to become less efficient, and to be less concerned about quality." [126] The other side of human nature that must be expressed by work is even less recognized in the typical employment situation today. Our society's emphasis on competition has resulted in an unbalanced system of rewards that does not sufficiently emphasize the importance of cooperative behavior. Possibilities for rectifying this imbalance might include, for example, systems of gain-sharing; cash bonuses tied to the achievement of collective goals; in-kind bonuses; and intangible symbols of the company's recognition of especially effective group efforts.

The firm's interest is clearly related to the promotion of a partnership between the firm and the workers, wherein the firm gains in quality and productivity because the workers are responsible and committed, while the workers achieve an experience that is essential to their fulfillment as human beings. Firms that wish to reap these benefits cannot do so by faking a commitment to their workers. When work is organized so that it is possible to treat the workers like interchangeable parts the workers become, in effect, "more object than person." [123] A healthy workplace requires that workers are truly seen as ends in themselves, not merely as means to the firm's ends.

Summary of

Shifting Perspectives: The Decoupling of Work and Money

by Robert J. Wuthnow

[Published in *Poor Richard's Principle: Reconciling the American Dream Through the Moral Dimension of Work, Business, and Money* (Princeton, NJ: Princeton University Press, 1996), 85–104.]

By the beginning of the twentieth century mainstream social scientists had shifted from a paradigm that placed economic behavior in the context of broader values to one that viewed work and money in isolation. As new immigrants poured into the United States, the American Dream became framed in terms of work and money. Today, when individuals are asked why they work, the overwhelming answer is "to make money." It seems to follow that "economic decisions compose a self-contained system, operating in terms of reward-and-benefit calculations, while moral commitments and values constitute a separate realm." "Money is in this view regarded as a universal exchange medium that translates labor into a commodity capable of being expended on any valued pursuit. We need to rethink the relationship between work and money, therefore, if we are to make a valid place for moral discourse to be considered." [87]

Working for Money

Several surveys have tested the adequacy of the assumption that people work solely to make money. This assumption would be supported by findings that people rank monetary awards high among job values, that people would not work if they were not paid, that people would work more if they were compensated more, that career changes occur because of opportunities for more money, and that job satisfaction is closely associated with pay. On each count, however, the surveys suggest otherwise.

For example, in a study on American values in the 1980s, 91 percent of those surveyed argued that it is better to work at a job with lower pay than a higher paying job with low job satisfaction. In another analysis of 2778 employees leaving the federal government, only 10 percent responded that a desire to earn more money was their reason for resigning. More significant were issues of job satisfaction, stress, and conflicts with personal interests and lifestyles. Finally, in a study where people were asked if they would not work if they had all the money they needed, 78 percent reported that they would continue to work.

Surveys such as these may suffer from intrinsic biases; for example, it could be that people are more comfortable *talking* about job satisfaction and working hard than they are about *talking* about wanting a lot of money. People may in fact work because they want lots of money. Even if this is true, there is something in our culture that makes it hard for individuals to capture all of their values of work in solely monetary terms.

The Post-Scarcity Thesis

Some observers of the workforce suggest that a decoupling of work and money occurs when societies reach a certain level of affluence. In much of the developed world individuals achieve a standard of living that could, in theory, greatly reduce the monetary concerns of the average wage earner. When such a standard of living is reached, the values associated with work are said to shift toward emotional and intellectual gratification. Some evidence supports this thesis. A survey conducted in Japan proposed: "Since I have achieved some material wealth, I would like to improve the spiritual aspects of my life." [91] Fifty percent of those surveyed agreed, while only 34 percent said they wanted to continue to improve their material standard of living. At the same time, studies conducted in Canada, the United States, and France document a series of conflicting trends. The importance of money may wax and wane over short periods of time, but it remains a subject of high concern for most people at all levels of income.

Working to Give a Legitimate Account

"How people understand their work, their money, and the relation between the two is a complex cultural matter. Instead of arguing simply that people work to make money, we need to pay closer attention to these cultural matters." [92] This article proposes that a primary function of work is that it offers people a way to give a legitimate account of themselves. Accounts are a key element of the process by which we ascribe meaning to our behavior and express ourselves in public. They "connect the particular act under question to values and ways of talking about values that are acceptable in a given social context." [93] The main consequence of emphasizing legitimate accounts is that human action must then be understood in terms of the social and cultural context within which it occurs, rather than being seen only as a function of the exchange of goods, services, and other resources. While money is not absent from these accounts, they go well beyond an understanding of the individual as an isolated decision maker who rationally calculates, for economic reasons alone, what work to do and how much to do.

In this context, work is a human enterprise, not simply as a function of "economic man." [93] If people do not work simply to earn incomes, but to provide themselves and each other with legitimate accounts, then work and money cannot be considered part of a utilitarian discourse in the manner portrayed by economists. A theory of legitimate account suggests that people will consider the value of their work and self in relation to a wider set of cultural values, personal obligations, and perceptions of who they are. Not only do they seek meaning in the accounts they construct around their work—work can be an important element in people's efforts, more broadly, to give meaningful accounts of themselves.

Emphasizing the framework of accounts is distinct from emphasizing the subjective meaning that people give to their working lives. Subjective meanings that people attach to their work can largely be hidden from view, and may even be unknown to the individual. An account, by definition, occurs in public. In most cases people will give an account that is close or identical to their own feelings and beliefs. They can then honor their own accounts sufficiently to stay committed to a particular activity, to regard that activity as being meaningful, and to feel good about themselves when engaged in that activity.

Putting It All Together

Drawing from original research on the changing meanings of white-collar work (drawn from a later chapter in the book), it can be seen that

> [o]n the whole, the accounts people give of their work reveal that it is, in most cases, meaningful to them. The reason they feel committed to their work and expend so much energy on it is that they feel right about it, and it in turn makes them feel right about themselves. Everybody has moments of doubt when they wonder if they are pursuing the right career, and they know their current job is by no means perfect. Being able to tell stories to themselves and to their acquaintances, however, sustains them from day to day. We fail to understand the significance of these accounts if we assume, as much of the published literature does, that people somehow start out their adult lives with a certain set of values, search the labor markets until they find some line of work consistent with these values, and then live happily ever after. [133]

Summary of

Position in the Class Structure and Psychological Functioning in the United States, Japan, and Poland

by Melvin L. Kohn et al.

[Published in *American Journal of Sociology* 95 (January 1990), 964–1008.]

This article explores the ways in which workers' positions in the process of production affect psychological functioning, in a Western capitalist country (the United States), a non-Western capitalist country (Japan), and a socialist country (Poland). Specifically, it examines the psychological effects of social class, defined in terms of ownership and control of the means of production, and control over the labor power of others. It finds social class to be consistently related to valuing self-direction for one's children, being intellectually flexible, and being self-directed in one's orientations to self and society. However, the relationship between social class and a sense of distress (versus subjective well-being) is weaker and less consistent.

The article asks four questions. First, is it possible to conceptualize and index social class consistently in three such diverse societies? Second, is social class distinguishable from social stratification? Third, does social class have similar psychological consequences in all three countries? And finally, what explains the psychological effects of social class?

Conceptualizing Social Class and Stratification

The study is based on three very similar, detailed surveys of random samples of employed men, conducted in the United States in 1964 with a follow-up in 1974, in Poland in 1978, and in Japan in 1979. In each case the respondents' descriptions of their work situations was used to define their social-class positions, with appropriate national differences in the indices employed.

For the United States and Japan, it was appropriate to distinguish employers, the self-employed, managers (employees who have substantial numbers or multiple levels of subordinates), first-line supervisors (who have moderate numbers, or only one level, of subordinates), nonmanual workers, and manual workers. Manual and nonmanual workers are distinguished because the latter generally have much greater control over their own conditions of work. In socialist Poland, in the Communist era, there was no category of employers, but the other distinctions all applied; an additional distinction was made between factory workers and nonproduction manual workers. Factory workers were viewed as central to the centralized organization of the economy and had greater power and privileges than other manual workers.

Social stratification was measured, in all three societies, by a combination of occupational status, job income, and educational attainment. The correlation of stratification with class is strong, but far from perfect. In each country, all three components of stratification, as well as the combined index, are substantially correlated with class. Much but far from all of the correlation results from the sharp differences in stratification positions of manual and nonmanual workers. If these two groups are combined into a single category, the correlations between stratification and class are weaker, but still substantial.

The first two questions were answered in the affirmative. Broadly comparable indices of social class were developed for all three countries. These indices are highly correlated with, yet distinct from, social stratification.

Class and Psychological Functioning

The surveys contain extensive psychological data, which have been analyzed by the authors in several other publications. In this article, they focus on four key aspects of psychological functioning: parental valuation of children's self-direction versus conformity to external authority; intellectual flexibility; self-direction versus conformity in one's own orientation to self and society; and a sense of distress versus well-being. The hypothesis that these factors are related to social class is largely confirmed by the data.

The first three factors are strongly correlated with class, in a manner that is largely consistent for the three countries. In the United States, managers and employers have the highest scores on parental valuation of children's self-direction and on intellectual flexibility. Nonmanual workers are next, followed by first-line supervisors, then the self-employed, and finally manual workers. The ranking is virtually the same for self-directedness of orientation. Rankings in Poland are quite similar to those in the United States. The correlation coefficients are even similar in size. Factory and nonfactory manual workers have very similar scores. The correlations of psychological factors with social class are somewhat lower, but still significant, in Japan. The rankings generally parallel those for the United States.

The correlation of social class with distress is lower; it is inconsistent across countries. For the United States, the pattern parallels the other three factors, with employers, managers, and supervisors the least distressed, and manual workers the most distressed. For Japan, an intermediate pattern, with managers and employers among the least distressed, but nonmanual workers by far the most distressed social class. For Poland, the pattern is nearly the opposite. Managers are among the most distressed social class; manual workers are among the least distressed.

Explaining the Relationships

Social class is strongly correlated with social stratification. Therefore, it is necessary to test whether class and stratification have independent psychological effects. The relationship between stratification and the psychological factors remains highly significant even when statistically controlling class. Controlling stratification markedly lowers the effects of class, but of the nine correlations with class (three psychological factors in three countries), seven remain significant.[1] Thus class and stratification have independent effects on psychological functioning.

The authors' preferred hypothesis is that occupational self-direction explains most of the relationship between class and psychological functioning. Their measure of occupational self-direction combines the substantive complexity of work (the extent to which work requires thought and independent judgment), closeness of supervision, and routinization (repetitiveness and predictability of the job). The occupational self-direction index, and all three of its components, are substantially correlated with class in each country. The relationship is especially strong between class and substantive complexity of work.

Statistically controlling for occupational self-direction eliminates most of the correlation between class and the first three psychological factors, in all three countries. This is consistent with the hypothesis that class matters psychologically in large part because people of more advantaged class position have greater opportunity to be self-directed in their work. Once the relationships are controlled for occupational self-direction, there is little if any gain in explanatory power when controls are added for the social and demographic backgrounds of workers, or for social stratification.

Social Class and Distress

The anomaly is the relationship of social class to distress, which is not cross-nationally consistent. Part of the explanation is that occupational self-direction did not have cross-nationally consistent effects on distress. Another part of the explanation is that other job conditions, such as job risks, uncertainties, and protections, had effects countervailing to those of occupational self-direction. These job conditions were differently related to social class in capitalist and socialist societies.

Note

1. The correlations for Japan of class with parental valuation of self-direction, and with self-directedness of orientation, are no longer significant when controlled for social stratification.

Summary of

Dignity in the Workplace Under Participative Management: Alienation and Freedom Revisited

by Randy D. Hodson

[Published in *American Sociological Review* 61 (October 1996), 719–738.]

Studies of work tend to focus either on technological, organizational, and environmental factors or on the struggle between workers and managers for control of the labor process. Drawing on the work of Robert Blauner and Richard Edwards, this article combines elements of both perspectives (along with recent developments in labor–management relations) into a new schematic, then reviews several dozen studies for evidence of meaning and autonomy in relation to workplace organization.

Alienation and Freedom

Blauner described four models of work organization that emerged historically in concert with the progression of production technologies and persist in the modern economy. Using survey data and case studies of typical industries, he analyzed the quality of work under each regime. He found that measures of job satisfaction traced a U-shaped pattern across these four types of work, indicating that skill and autonomy fell from high levels and then rose again.

Craft work, exemplified by the printing industry, is the earliest model. Workers enjoyed stable employment, control over the labor process, a strong organizational culture, interesting work, and opportunities to learn and use skills. Work was an end in itself and an important part of personal identity. As *machine-powered* production developed, such as in the textile industry, craft workers were replaced and oppressive supervision was put in place to monitor large numbers of unskilled workers and female laborers. Workers looked outside the workplace—to family, religion, and community—to reduce alienation. When *assembly-line* work emerged, typical of automobile production, the work process became highly rationalized. The handling and transportation of materials throughout the factory could be done by unskilled operators who remained disenfranchised and alienated. *Continuous process* production in the chemical industry, however, moved products through various processing stages without human handling. Workers monitored equipment, stepping in only to solve problems. This work required knowledge, good judgment, and alert crisis response skills, and marked an upward turn in quality-of-work indicators.

Richard Edwards, in his 1979 book, *Contested Terrain*, associated trends in workplace organization with systems used to control the workforce. Edwards' historical model of workplace control has five components: direct personal control, foreman's control, technical control, scientific management, and bureaucracy. As with Blauner's chronological sequence, each form coexists with others as it emerges. The model developed here synthesizes these two frameworks into a five-part typology while also accommodating recent trends in technology and industrial relations:

WORKPLACE ORGANIZATION	CHARACTERISTICS
Craft	High training and worker control over daily decisions
Direct supervision	Day-to-day decisions made by supervisor
Assembly line	Flow of work controlled by conveyors
Bureaucratic	Decision making based on rules
Worker participation	Regular solicitation of worker input

This schematic forms the basis for analyzing several aspects of job quality. Evidence for the analysis was developed from an exhaustive search of workplace ethnographies, selection of facilities that captured relevant concepts, and careful coding to produce comparable data. Eighty-six ethnographies reporting on 108 separate cases met the criteria for inclusion in this analysis.

Working with Dignity

Workers develop strategies to maintain dignity, protect themselves from abuse, and establish individual identity. These strategies, which can range from sabotage to withdrawal of cooperation, "are autonomous behavioral agendas that arise in response to the demands of the workplace. . . . Thus, worker strategies are attempts to defend or regain dignity in the face of work organizations that violate workers' interests, limit their prerogatives, or otherwise undermine their autonomy." [722]

Two realms of work experience and activity were analyzed in relation to the five types of work organization described above: task-related and coworker-related work. Four task-related aspects have been identified as important in literature on the workplace: (1) *job satisfaction* and (2) *pride* indicate attitudes toward work; (3) *insider knowledge* comes from on-the-job learning and can be a source of bargaining power; and (4) the *effort bargain* reflects workers' enjoyment, their perception of the fairness of rewards, and their power relative to management. Three coworker-related experiences are also important in the literature: (1) *solidarity*, or the willingness of workers to defend each other from management, other workers, or customers; (2) *peer training* as an indicator of knowledge not possessed by management; and (3) "the prevalence of *social friendships* [which] is one of the most significant indicators of a positive work experience." [724]

Data Analysis

The task-related and coworker-related variables found in the selected ethnographies were noted as present or absent, or scaled according to intensity or prevalence. The values were entered into ordinary least squares regressions as dependent variables, with the five types of work organization as independent variables. The results are similar to Blauner's U-shaped pattern, with indicators of job quality falling from high levels in craft-like jobs to lower levels in more controlled work settings, then rising again in situations that encourage worker participation in decision-making processes. However, there are variations in the pattern for different outcome variables. Although they rise from the lowest points, most do not achieve the high levels initially established under craft-based work. The resulting pattern is more like a backwards "J."

Job satisfaction, pride, and effort are lowest under direct supervision, then reach new highs under worker-participation regimes, with effort slightly higher under participation than under craft organization. Insider knowledge is lowest in assembly-line work, where job content is rigidly prescribed. It reaches its second peak under bureaucracy, where it can be useful to skirt or manipulate the rules, and then drops slightly again.

The coworker-related variables also drop sharply once craft-based work is replaced by more regimented forms. Each of these three variables reaches its lowest point under a different organizational regime. Solidarity is lowest under bureaucracy, where workers are stratified and competitive. Peer training is lowest under direct supervision. Social friendship is lowest under assembly-line work that tends to enforce isolation. Skill and autonomy, introduced as mediating variables, have positive effects on both task and coworker variables, but they can only reduce, not eliminate, the effects of the work organization variables.

Discussion and Conclusion

Continuous process technology never became as prominent a part of workplace organization as Blauner expected, though the work experience recovered some of its meaning and autonomy as participatory forms of production became more prominent. For most of the indicators studied, craft-based organization retained the highest values. References to worker or observer statements in the ethnographic material indicate ambivalence about the consequences for workers of participatory regimes. Some observers or analysts see positive effects from team-based management, while others see it as a form of "self-subordination" or "estranged participation" that puts workers' insights at the service of work intensification. One worker described it as the best and worst kind of situation.

Participatory forms of work organization are still in early stages of development. As with management objectives, the evolution of future structures of labor–management relationships will reflect the efforts of workers to defend their dignity and increase their well-being. To analyze and understand these new patterns, students of industrial relations "will need to incorporate not only the existing concepts of management exploitation and worker resistance, but will also need to include a renewed role for concepts like worker pride, insider knowledge, friendship, and peer support." [735]

Summary of

Work, Labor, and Action: Work Experience in a System of Flexible Production

by Michael J. Piore

[Published in *Transforming Organizations*, eds. Thomas Kochan and Michael Useem (Oxford: Oxford University Press, 1992), 307–318.]

In recent years, a number of studies have confirmed the notion that since the 1970s there has been a trend toward smaller business units in the industrial economies. This is a marked difference from the tendency of the earlier postwar decades. The neoclassical competitive market model may have been useful in explaining the operations of larger units, but falls short of being able to describe these new trends. Drawing from case studies of Italian flexible specialization and the philosophical categories developed by Hannah Arendt in *The Human Condition* (1958), an alternative analytical perspective is offered that captures the salient features of work experience in these newly emergent forms of industrial organization.

The Characteristics of Industrial Districts

A growing number of case studies can be summarized as observing the following characteristics of industrial districts: (1) Technological dynamism that continuously changes product types and production techniques. (2) A close relationship with the culture and community of the geographic region in which they are lodged; described by some as a "thickening of industrial and social interdependencies in a certain place." [309] (3) Commercial networks, with the ability to cooperate among firms. Producers even visit each other's production facilities as if there were few trade secrets to be lost. (4) A combination of seemingly contradictory traits of competition and cooperation. (5) "The spontaneous and unpredictable character of success and failure." [309] (6) A "bottoms-up" approach to innovation where changes in product and technique occur with shop-level input.

A few general observations may be made about the kinds of public policies that are supportive to such industrial districts. Firms within these districts have common needs such as research and development, training and education, and coordination of production on production-related activities when there are economies of scale. These may include, for example, financial services, common eating facilities, or medical care. Their success also depends on observation of a common set of standards and norms, with some means of enforcement. Of special importance are the norms or laws that limit competition. While there is little agreement about the historical or other processes that give rise to institutions that can supply these public goods in the particular fashion required to enable dynamic cooperative action within a network of small firms, one aspect of leadership does stand out: a willingness to spend a major part of the leaders' time in mediating disputes.

Hannah Arendt and the Human Condition

In *The Human Condition,* Hannah Arendt distinguishes three modes of productivity: *work, labor, and action.* Originally conceived of in the structure and philosophic tradition of the Greek city-state and the later analytical structure of Marx, these categories can be particularly useful in understanding work experience in industrial districts.

For Arendt, work and labor involve relationships between humans and their physical environment. With work, the product is characterized as permanent, and it achieves an independent existence. Thus, through work humans are able to exert a kind of immortality. Labor, on the other hand, is associated with the services and consumption that ensure basic needs for human survival. Most important is her concept of action, which is "the activity through which individuals reveal themselves to other individuals, and through which they achieve meaning as persons." [312] Likewise, action is dependent on human plurality, "the twofold character of equality and distinction."[1] Similar to the civic life of the Greek citizen in the city-state, action is an end in and of itself because it is how people define themselves as men and women, but action is also a means to an end because the sequence of actions over one's life (work) constitute a story that is told in the community.

Arendt argues that action has disappeared from human activity. In the world of mass production, work has been reduced to labor by the removal of contemplation and discourse from production. Individuals have therefore cut themselves off from other people, withdrawn into themselves, and have lost their ability to act. The flexible specialization of small firms in industrial districts might thus best be understood in terms of a return to action.

Industrial Districts as Action

If production is conceived of as an arena of action, apparently contradictory characteristics of industrial districts are explained, and it can be seen why they maintain their strength. By thinking of production as "an arena of discourse and a stage for action," [314] one can understand the workings of the bottom-up network of producers, employees, and politicians that characterizes the open production process of small firms and their ability to be innovative. The work-place can then be seen as a realm where those involved reveal themselves to each other as individuals. The act of producing goods and services in collaboration with others eases the transition back and forth between production, on the one hand, and the politics of the organization of production, on the other.

The paradox of competition and cooperation also dissolves under such a framework. Industrial districts have been described as paradoxical because they were viewed from a model in which work is a means toward an end of individual income. It was therefore hard to understand how the notion of individual profit maximization could be consistent with the need for collaboration. What results is that

> [w]e have mistaken competition for the individual's attempt through action to differentiate himself or herself. What appear to be collaborators or cooperators in the market model are interlocutors in the discourse through which the differentiation of the individual occurs and the audience for the story of a life which actions create. [315]

The essential concept in Arendt's view of action, as extended to contemporary industrial districts, is therefore the notion of a community of equals wherein the individual can differentiate his or her self. Arendt also believed that communities should be small (as are industrial districts), but that size and the creation of a community of equals are not enough since the culture of the community must also value action enough to enter this realm of productive relationships.

Public Policy

What does this discussion of action contribute to the public policy problem of creating and maintaining industrial districts of this kind? The problem can be split into two components. The first is how to foster a sense of a need for action in a community. Very little can be gleaned on this subject from the case studies or from economic theory. It remains an issue for further study. The second regards the problem of labor.

Flexible specialization in small industrial districts reconciles the means and ends of production. In mass manufacturing, the production process is a means of securing income. In flexible specialization, the production process is a means to get income *and* an active source of meaning in one's life. Balancing these two purposes is the central public policy problem to be resolved. The question thus remains

> [h]ow is it possible to ensure that production serves as an effective means for the community's survival without having the members of the community become so preoccupied with income that action, which makes the community dynamic in the first place, loses its centrality in the community's value system? [316]

Note

1. Hannah Arendt, *The Human Condition* (Chicago: University of Chicago Press, 1958); cited by the author, 313.

Subject Index

Absenteeism, 3
Absorptive capacity of the natural environment, xxxvi
Accounts, emphasizing the framework of, 380–81
Acquisitions, 206
Action disappearing from human activity, 389–90
Active learning techniques, 127
Activities of daily living (ADL), 339
Advertising industry, xxxi–xxxii, 236
Affirmative action, 9, 261
AFL-CIO, 218
Africa, 98
African Americans:
  apparel industry, 96
  biculturalism, 263
  college graduation, 262, 285
  contingent work, 183
  ghetto-related behavior and the structure of opportunity, 368–71
  middle class, 261
  motivational and relational skills, 12
  poverty, 346
  segmentation, labor market, 40
  soft skills, 262
  wages, 9
  see also Diversity and difference in the workplace
Agency theory, 227–28
Aggressive behavior, deemphasizing, 309
Agriculture:
  Agricultural Labor Relations Board, 237
  exports, 268, 295
  history of work, 2
  labor–management relations, 234–38
  peasants, 366
  sharecroppers, semi-feudal, 6
  women, 98–99
Algorithmic organization, 153–57
Alienation:
  computers, 144
  culture of, 263
  and freedom, 385–86
  how long does it manifest itself, 367–68

Marxian economics, 351, 365–66, 368
  self-directed work, 363
  social relations at work, 364
  where does it occur, 366–67
Altruism, 342, 346
Amerco, 330, 331
American Dream, 173, 261, 379
American Farm Bureau Federation, 235
American Federation of Labor (AFL), 260
Andon lights, 139
Antidiscrimination legislation, 188, 190
Anxiety about the nature of work, xxx
  contingent work, 173–76, 181–85
  developed countries, employment and productivity in, 177–81
  flexibility, sustainable, 208–13
  home-based work, 205–8
  informal economy, 199–204
  internal labor markets, 171–73, 192–95
  market-mediated work, 185–88
  rethinking employment, 189–92
  segmentation, toward a new labor market, 195–98
Apparel industry, 66, 94–97, 204
Argentina, 104
Artisans, 2–6, 366
Asia, 98, 292–95, 303
Assembly-line work, 366, 385, 387
Attitude, 262–63, 288
Australia, 225, 231, 232
Austria, 225
Automation:
  alienating qualities of, 366
  assembly line workers, decline of, 366
  cooperation and worker responsibility, increasing, 158
  informated workplace, 143, 146, 147
  insurance industry and production organization, 153–57
  programmable, 238–40
  sociology of deskilling and, 167–68
  Total Automation Index, 131
Automobile industry, 116, 129–35

Baby, delivering a, 354–55

Banking, consumer, 196
Bargaining, wages determined through, 91, 231
  see also Collective bargaining
Bauman Foundation, xxviii
Behavioral macroeconomic model, 375–76
Belonging and self-expression, 376–79
Benefits, human investment, 211
Best practices, 122, 123, 125
Biculturalism, 263
Bill collecting, 273–74
Biological explanations of differences between people, 259
Blacks, see African Americans; Diversity and difference in the workplace
Boycotts, 236–37
Bracero Program, 235, 237
Brand-name producers, 236
Brazil, 104
Bretton Woods agreement, 116
Buffers, 130, 131
Bureaucratization of employment, 172
Bureau of Labor Statistics, U.S., 173, 175, 181, 186
Bureau of National Affairs (BNA), 186
Bureau of the Census (BOC), 186

California, 96–97, 204
Canada:
  caring labor for the young/old/sick, 319
  cooperative system of industrial relations, 34
  money and work, decoupling, 380
  rights of workers, 35
  training, 231
  unions, 232
  wage curve, 26
Capacity, preventing excess, 127
Capital-intensive processes, more/less, 5–6, 163
Capitalism, 6, 9, 326
  see also individual subject headings
Caring labor for the young/old/sick:
  children as public goods, 345–47
  diversity and difference in the workplace, responding to, 326–29
  economic instruction, viewing the household as an, 333–36
  emotional consequences of compacted home life, 329–33

feminist theory, 344
gender and family issues in the workplace, 312–15
globalization and labor, 339–41
goals regarding women's market/nonmarket work, conflicting, 299–300
historical changes in household division of labor, 316–19
household services, socialization/commercialization/professionalization of, 335
Human Development Report of the United Nations, 300–301
human economy in toto, making visible the, 336–38
male work profile impacting women, 301–2
market equality vs. domestic responsibility, 306–7
  paradox of, 341–45
prescriptions and policies, 307–10
progress over last twenty years in reporting of women's work, 319–23
Soviet Union and Central-Eastern Europe, former, 323–26
sustainable society, 13
unfair burdens, 304–6
women's labor force participation, 302–4
Catholicism, 291
Census of Service Industries, 186
Centralization, index of, 226
Centralized industrywide systems of bargaining/negotiations, 231
Change, resistance to, 124–25
Children:
  baby, delivering a, 354–55
  cost of raising, 306
  economic efficiency, 315
  impoverished neighborhoods, raised in, 369
  learning society, 212
  mobility and family responsibilities, occupational, 278–79
  parent–child relationships, 334
  as public goods, 345–47
  textile industry, 5
  time debate, household, 316–19
  wages, mother's, 313
  work in childhood, willingness and capacity to, 356, 363

see also Caring labor for the young/old/sick
China and women workers, South, 292–95
Choices, career, xxiii
Civil rights, 9, 96, 261
Class background and service sector jobs, 279
Class structure and psychological functioning, 382–84
Cleanliness, culture of, 334, 335
Clothing industry, 66, 94–97, 204
Coal mining, 5
Coca-Cola, 236
Code-switching, 263, 288
Co-determination rights, 247–48
Coevolutionary model of technoorganizational change, 121–25
Cognition and personality, learning at work influencing, 361–62
Cognitive dissonance and caring labor for the young/old/sick, 300
Cohesiveness, group, 229
Collaborative relationships, 146
Collective bargaining, 224, 225, 239–40, 243
Collective responsibility, 146
College, 162, 262, 285, 313
Commission on the Future of Worker-Management Relations, 217
Communication function of works councils, 246
Communism, collapse of European, xxxv
Compartmentalization, 263
Compensation and output per worker, 73–74
see also Globalization and labor; Wages
Competence, high minimum level of, xxv
Competition, xxxi, 196, 201, 378
Complexity, substantive, 362
Computers:
    alienating qualities of, 144, 366
    automation and production organization, 153–57
    conduct of work within the workplace, changing, 117
    ergonomics, 159
    immigration and offshore production, incorporation of Third World

women into wage labor through, 297
    inequality, computing, 161–67
    labor demand, changing, 196
    monitoring, 145
    production represented and controlled by, 151
    skill?, the end of, 146–49
    skills mismatch, 81, 82
    see also Technology
Conflict and contention, processes of, 33–34, 59
Congress of Industrial Organizations (CIO), 260
Consensus management, 139
Consultation and co-determination, 247–48
Consultative participation, 217, 228
Consumer Price Index (CPI), 74
Consumer prices, 74
Consumers and workers, relationship between interests of, xxxvii
Consumption, xxxii, xxxviii, 6
Contention and conflict, processes of, 59
Contested Terrain (Edwards), 385–86
Contextual knowledge, 154
Contingent work:
    anxiety about the nature of work, 173–76, 181–85
    changing labor supply, 196–97
    Europe, 231
    goals regarding relationship between women's market/nonmarket work, conflicting, 299–300
    skilled, 197–98
    United States, 233
    see also Flexibility
Continuous process production, 385
Contracting out, 174, 185
Contracts, work, 57–59
Control, labor:
    Contested Terrain, 385–86
    discrimination, 31
    fundamental mechanisms for, three, 37–38
    homogenization, 6
    labor power, extraction of labor from, 29–30
    neo-Hobbesian model, 32
    performance concerns, 195
    technology, 31

Control, labor (*continued*)
  unemployment, 30–31
  see also Power
Convergent validity, 375
Cooperatives, producer, 12, 221–22,
  228–29, 248–56
Cooperative system of industrial
  relations:
  automation, 158
  education within a, 212
  model, cooperative, 34
  participation, worker, 20
  partnership between the firm and
    workers, 378–79
  productivity, labor, 35
Core employees, 197, 207
Core labor force, 209
Corporate culture, male-dominated, 313
Corporations, transnational, 83
Cost-based strategies, 233–34
Cost-benefit calculations and mother-
  hood, 307
Cost of job model, 33
Cotton, 6
Councils, work, 12, 219–21, 234,
  245–48
Counterproductive growth, xxxvi–xxxvii
Coworker-related work, 386–87
Craft work, 152, 385, 387
Crime and erosion of earnings/
  employment of black men in
  the 1980s, 285–86
Cuba, 204
Cultural expectations and caring labor,
  309
Current Population Survey (CPS), 173,
  181
Curve:
  labor demand, 216
  labor supply, 3–4
  Phillips, 28
  U-shaped curve and women
    participating in work force, 290,
    291, 303, 385
  wage, 18–19, 25–28
Cycles, business, 39, 187, 229–30, 251

Data, egalitarian access to, 146
Data entry jobs, 154–56
Day labor, 174
Decentralization, 201, 231
Declaration of the World Summit on
  Social Development, 108

Declining Significance of Race (Wilson),
  260
Defeminization, 291
Defensive innovation, 62, 70
Democratic party, 243
Democratic principles in firms, barriers
  to, 255–58
Denmark, 248, 251, 319
Department store industry, 196
Dependability, 262–63
Dependency and disability, 339–40
Depression, the Great, 7, 123
Deprivation theory, relative, 47, 48–49
Deregulation, 196
Deskilling of workers:
  homogenization, 8
  Labor and Monopoly, 36
  Marxian economics, 115
  sociology of automation and, 167–68
  technology, 11
Despotism, 292–95
Devaluation of women's work, 305–6,
  342–43
  see also Caring labor for the
    young/old/sick
Developed countries, 62
  agriculture, 2
  caring labor for the young/old/sick,
    299, 308
  decay and uncertainty, images of,
    117
  disability and dependency, 339–40
  employment and productivity in,
    177–81
  immigration and offshore production,
    incorporation of Third World
    women into wage labor through,
    295–98
  informal economy, 202–4
  learning-centered social institutions,
    212
  mistrust between developing and, 106
  policy options, 109–12
  small, 65
  transition to the information society,
    210–13
  wage inequality, male, 224–27
  see also Globalization and labor;
    individual subject headings
Developing countries:
  caring labor for the young/old/sick,
    340–41
  cheaper labor, 117

export platforms, international
investment in, 267–68, 295–98
factory work, 362, 364
gender issues, 98
immigration and offshore production,
incorporation of Third World
women into wage labor through,
295–98
informal economy, 201
labor standards and protectionism,
106
mistrust between developed and, 106
working conditions, 66, 98–101
see also Globalization and labor
Development, important role of work in
individuals', 361–64
Dignity, human, 349, 359, 385–88
Disabilities, care for individuals with,
306–7, 339–40
Discrimination, 19, 31, 45–46
Disposable labor force, 209
Distress, 372, 384
Distributive justice, 192
Disutility of work, 350–51, 353
Diversified quality production, 127–29
Diversity and difference in the workplace
apparel industry, 96–97
black men in 1980s, erosion of
earnings/employment in, 283–86
China, women workers in South,
292–95
emotion work, 273–76
feminization of labor force, 290–91
gender roles in the workplace, 263–64
identity, personal, 259
immigration and offshore production,
incorporation of Third World
women into wage labor through,
295–98
mobility, racialized jobs and upward,
261–63, 280–83
queues, labor market, 264–66, 269–73
racial interactions, 260–61
responding to increasing, 326–29
service sector jobs, 276–80
soft skills and black mens' employment
problems, 286–89
women in the global workforce,
266–68
Divorce, 303
Domestic labor, 299, 321
see also Caring labor for the
young/old/sick

Domestic responsibility vs. market
equality, 306–7
Dominican Republic, 100
Downgrading of labor, 200
Downsizing, 190, 191, 206
Drugs, illegal/addictive, xxxi, 285, 369
Dual employment relationships, 20–21,
104, 184, 196

Economic nationalism, xxv–xxvi
Economic Policy Institute (EPI), 173
Economic rationality, 301–2
Economic theory, see Labor economics;
Neoclassical economics; Theory,
economic
Education:
black men in 1980s, erosion of
earnings/employment in, 285
college, 162, 262, 285, 313
councils, work, 246
industrial districts, 389
information-based society, 212
service sector jobs, 279
skill requirements, 82
Soviet Union and Central-Eastern
Europe, former, 324
standards, national, xxv
trade as solution to problems caused
by, 110, 111
varied labor supply and rising levels of,
197
women's participation in the labor
market, 303
Efficiency:
computer rationalization, 155
cooperatives, producer, 253
defining, 31
domestic inefficiency, the perpetuation
of, 335
efficiency wage model, 33
home becomes work, when, 332
internal labor markets, 189
intervention, motives for, 109
leave policy, family, 315
neoclassical economics, 59
purpose of, 359
scientific management, 116
sociotechnical systems, Swedish, 126
technology, 36–37
wages, 43–44
wage theories, 19, 41
X-efficiency theory, 118
Effort bargain, 386, 387

Effort into final output, transformation
    of, 33–34
Elasticities, 64, 71
Elderly care, 308, 339–40
Electric power, 122–23
Emergencies and andon lights, 139
Emigration, transforming internal
    migration into, 295–98
    see also Immigration
Emotional well-being and
    unemployment, quantifying
    connection between, 374–75
Emotion work:
    African Americans, 262
    diversity and difference in the
        workplace, 273–76
    growing importance of, 287
    home becomes work, when, 332–33
    Managed Heart, The, 265–66
    Second Shift, The, 329
    see also Caring labor for the
        young/old/sick
Employing Bureaucracy, 189
Employment:
    artisans, 2–6, 366
    black men in 1980s, erosion of
        earnings/employment in, 283–86
    bureaucratization of, 172
    core labor force, 209
    coworker-related work, 386–87
    decline in industrial, 9–10
    elasticity of labor demand, 64
    exit-voice model, 50–53
    fairness in distribution of work of all
        types, 299, 300
    Fordist work process, post-, 149–53
    Japanese management techniques,
        138–39
    labor from labor power, extraction of,
        29–30
    learning at work, 361–64
    leave, parental, 313–14
    methodology for analyzing levels of,
        101–2
    motherhood and, conflict between,
        326
    politics and economics of global,
        101–5
    primary sector jobs, 38–43, 46
    quantitative measures of household
        work, 337–38
    satisfaction, job, 385

secondary sector jobs, 39, 41–43
security, job, 138, 183, 229, 232–33
segments, restructured into three
    principles, 197–98
standards, labor, 67–68, 105–8
stratification of, 12
supply curve, labor, 3–4
technology and quality of, 157–61
temporary, 174, 185, 188, 191, 197,
    231
tenure, job, 51, 52, 190
trade and U.S. labor markets,
    international, 76–80
uniform conditions of, pressing
    industry/government for, 242
wage curve, labor contract model for,
    27
white-collar, 381
see also Anxiety about the nature of
    work; Caring labor for the
    young/old/sick; Contingent work;
    Globalization and labor; Industrial
    relations; Workers; Working
    conditions
*Employment Relations in a Changing
    World Economy* (Locke, Kochan &
    Piore), 231
Energy, cheap, 5
Enforcement and informal economy,
    203
Engineers, 115, 151, 152–53, 177–78
England, *see* United Kingdom
Enlightenment and dualism between
    rational activity of the mind and
    irrational activity of the body,
    263–64
Equal Employment Opportunity
    Commission, 261
Equilibrium, integrated and
    partially/fully segregated, 49–50
Equity, focusing on the availability of,
    257
Equity rule/theory, 44–45, 47
Ergonomics, 159
Estranging processes, 367, 388
Europe:
    caring labor for the young/old/sick,
        308, 323–26
    centralized industrywide systems of
        bargaining/negotiations, 231
    collective bargaining, 224
    contingent work, 231

councils, work, 220
employment, decline in industrial, 10
feminization of labor force, 290–91
internal labor market theory, 195
Keynesian welfare state, 211
leave, parental, 314
low-skill workers, 227
policies for wages and employment, 111
poverty, 346
recovering economy, 116
unemployment, 210
unions, 161, 225
wage inequality, male, 225
women's labor force participation, 302, 303
Exchange rates, 188
Exclusionary approach to labor organization, 260
Exit-voice model, 50–53, 216
Expectancy theory, 356
Exploitation, labour, 106
Exports, 267–68, 295–98
see also Globalization and labor
External environment models, 194
External labor market, 197

Facing Up to the American Dream (Hochschild), 261
Factor price equalization, 78
Factory work, 122, 292–95, 362, 364
Fair wage–effort hypothesis and unemployment, 22, 47–50
Families:
devaluing the essence of family life, 330–33
factory regime and familial hegemony, 293–94
learning-centered social institutions, 212
leave policy, family, 313–15
models, work, 330
nuclear, 13
policy responses, 347
service sector jobs, 278–79
single mothers, 346
unpaid parental labor, 346–47
values, return to family, 325–26
women's participation in the labor market, 303
see also Caring labor for the young/old/sick

Far East, 303
Farm worker organizing, 235–36
see also Agriculture
Fat and Mean: The Corporate Squeeze of Working Americans and the Myth of Managerial "Downsizing" (Gordon), 64, 80
Feedback on technological design/ implementation, 161
Feminist Politics and Human Nature (Jaggar), 263
Feminist theory:
caring labor for the young/old/sick, 306, 344
household dynamics, 322
Marxian economics, 264
production politics, 292
radical, 264
socialists, 264
Feminization of labor force, 98–99, 271–72, 290–91
Financial markets and the political structure of the enterprise, 255–58
Finland, 337–38
Firing employees, 188
Firm, theory of the, 36
Flexibility:
best-practice systems, 123
contingent work, 181–85
decentralization accompanied by, 231
manufacturing, American, 149–53
national contexts, differing, 232
staffing, 186–87
transformation of work and employment, 208–13
wage, 187
white and black women, 279
see also Contingent work
Flexible specialization:
automation, programmable, 240
capacity, preventing excess, 127
contradictory tendencies on issue of skills, 148–49
focus of, 127
newly emerging forms of industrial organization, 388–91
turbulent market conditions, 128
Flight attendants, 273–74
Ford Foundation, xxviii
Fordism, 123, 133, 149–53
Formal labor markets, 102–3

Fragmentation of jobs and new
    technologies, 158
France:
    cooperatives, producer, 12, 248
    cooperative system of industrial
        relations, 34
    councils, work, 220
    money and work, decoupling, 380
    rights of workers, 35
    training, 231
    work-sharing model, 211
Freedom and alienation, 385–86
Free riding firms, 55
Friendships, social, 386–87
Fund for the Future, xxviii

Gain sharing, 229
Garment industry, 66, 94–97, 204
Gated communities, xxv
*Gender and Family Issues in the
    Workplace* (Blau & Ehrenberg), 312
Gender issues/differences:
    feminization of labor force, 98–99,
        271–72, 290–91
    gender-neutrality, 327
    global economy, 98–101
    household responsibilities, men taking
        on more, 315
    male work profile impacting women,
        301–2
    occupational segmentation, 312–13
    production politics, 292–93
    rational activity of the mind and irra-
        tional activity of the body, 263–64
    wage inequality, male, 224–27
    see also Caring labor for the
        young/old/sick; Diversity and
        difference in the workplace;
        Women
Germany:
    collective bargaining, 225
    computing inequality, 164–67
    contingent work, 231
    cooperative model, 34
    councils, work, 220
    diversified quality production, 127–29
    flexibility, 232
    rights of workers, 35
Ghetto-related behavior and the
    structure of opportunity, 368–71
Global Development And Environment
    Institute (G-DAE), xxvii

Globalization and labor:
    apparel industry, 94–97
    caring labor for the young/old/sick,
        339–41
    changing structure of markets, 196
    gender issues/differences, 98–101
    grappling with, 65–67
    inequality and falling real wages,
        82–87
    Japan, 91–94
    labor markets, international trade and
        U.S., 76–80
    Latin America, 101–5
    participation, employee, 227
    policy responses, 67–68, 109–12
    skills mismatch between labor supply
        and demand, 80–84
    technology/trade and measurement,
        61–65
    trade and demands for skilled and
        unskilled workers, 88–91
    transformation of work and
        employment, 208–13
    unskilled workers, how trade hurt,
        69–72
    wages in the 1980s, international trade
        and American, 73–76
    women in the workplace, 66, 98–101,
        266–68, 290–98
Global substitute, 322
Goals, bridging gap between employers'
    and workers', 359–60
Good jobs, 10, 359–60
Gourmet food stores, 297
Government:
    black men in 1980s, erosion of
        earnings/employment in, 286
    China, women workers in South,
        294–95
    cooperatives, producer, 253
    ghetto-related behavior and the
        structure of opportunity, 369
    human-centered systems, 136
    informal economy, 200, 202–3
    learning-centered social institutions,
        212
    protectionism, 103–4
    skill level of employees, 227
    see also Policy responses; Politics
Grape production, 236–37
Greek civilization, 358, 389
Gross domestic product (GDP), 338

Gross national product (GNP), xxxi, 291, 323
Group identity/behavior, 259, 264, 378

Harmonization, 106–7
Harrod's Law, 179
Haven model, 330
Health insurance, xxv, 183, 184
Healthy workplace, creating a, 378–79
Heckscher–Ohlin trade theory, 71, 77, 88
Hierarchical systems, 115, 143–45, 152, 256
High school/college wage differential, 162
High-value added strategies, 233
Hiring employees, 188, 190, 287–88
Hispanic Americans:
  apparel industry, 97
  contingent work, 183
  informal economy, 203–4
  poverty, 346
  see also Diversity and difference in the workplace
History of work:
  beginning, in the, 2
  discipline and technology, 4–6
  factories and families, 6–7
  labor economics, 16–17
  preindustrial work, 2–4
  twentieth century, rise and fall of the late, 8–10
Holistic/dignified approach to production, 136
Holland, 319
Home and work, interchangeability of, 331–33
Home-based work, 176, 205–8
Homogenization, 4, 6–8
Hong Kong, 292–95
Household division of labor, historical changes in the, 316–19
  see also Caring labor for the young/old/sick
Housewives, 6–7, 333–35
  see also Caring labor for the young/old/sick
HRM Policies Index, 131
Human capital and motivation, 373–74
  see also Neoclassical economics
Human-centered systems, 13
  alienation, 365–68

class structure and psychological functioning, 382–84
development, important role of work in individuals', 361–64
dignity, human, 385–88
disutility of work, 350–51
flexible production, 388–91
ghetto-related behavior and the structure of opportunity, 368–71
goals, bridging gap between employers' and worker's, 359–60
lean production, 130
money and work, decoupling, 379–81
paycheck, beyond the, 357–58
personnel management, 172–73
productivity, labor, 140–43
scientific management, relationship of modern management theories to, 351–53
self-expression and belonging, 376–79
social and psychological norms shaped by work, 355–56
technology and human resources, integrating, 129–35
Theory Y, 353–55
unemployment/social psychology and macroeconomics, 373–76
values achieved through work, 358–59
workers' perspective on unique characteristics of work, 349–50
Human Condition, The (Arendt), 365, 388, 389–90
Human Development Report of the United Nations, 300–301
Human economy in toto, making visible the, 336–38
"Human Side of Enterprise, The" (McGregor), 354
Human survival and wages, xxxvi
Human Well-Being and Economic Goals, 120
Humor reinforcing labor and gender relationships, 267
Hungary, 324
Hunter–gatherer communities, 2

Identity, personal, xxiii, 259, 264
Immigration:
  apparel industry, 97, 204
  caring labor for the young/old/sick, 340

Immigration (*continued*)
  disabilities, care for individuals with,
    307
  farm worker organizing, 235–36
  offshore production and,
    incorporation of Third World
    women into wage labor through,
    295–98
  twentieth century, early, 6
  wages influenced by, 83, 86
  work ethic, 288
Imports, 70, 82–83, 95
  see also Globalization and labor
Improvement, continuous, 138–39
Incentives:
  agency theory, 227–28
  contracts, work, 59
  cooperatives, producer, 249–50
  councils, work, 246
  scientific management, 116
  supervision and high wages as
    competing, 43–46
  transactions, motivation to complete,
    23–24
  wage, normal capitalist, 355–56
  see also Motivation
Inclusive approach to labor organization,
  260
Independent contracting, 174, 205,
  206–7
Individual effort and productivity, 20,
  33, 57
Individual enterprise level, industrial relations moving toward the, 231
Individualism of the efficiency wage
  model, 19
Individualistic part of human nature,
  376–78
Industrialization:
  female migration, 295–98
  industrial districts, 388–91
  industrial divide, 123
  Industrial Revolution, 4–7, 326, 355
  labor process, 115–16
  postindustrial society, 178–79
  preindustrial work, 2–4
  see also Developed countries;
    Globalization and labor;
    Manufacturing
Industrialization and Industrial Man
  (Kerr, Dunlop, Harbison &
  Myers), 113

Industrial relations:
  agriculture, 234–38
  automation, programmable, 238–40
  common patterns of, four common,
    231–32
  cooperatives, producer, 221–22,
    248–55
  councils, work, 245–48
  financial markets and the political
    structure of the enterprise,
    255–58
  human economy in toto, making
    visible the, 336–38
  inequality of labor market
    opportunities, 12, 82–87,
    161–67, 191
  management, changes in, 216–18
  participation and productivity,
    relationship between, 227–30
  productivity growth, 32–35
  training, 191
  transformation of, 231–34
  wage inequality, male, 224–27
  see also Alienation; Cooperative system
    of industrial relations; Unions
Inequality of labor market opportunities,
  12, 82–87, 161–67, 191
  see also Segmentation, labor market;
    Wages
Informal economy, 11, 102–3, 199–204,
  320–21
  see also Contingent work
Information technology, 123, 124,
  143–46, 208–13
Innovation, 232, 256
Input valuation, 322
Insider knowledge, 386, 387
*Instability and Change in the Global
  Economy* (MacEwan & Tabb), 98
Institutional change, 35
Institutionalist economics, 8, 17, 22–24,
  343–44
Insurance industry and computer
  rationalization, 153–57
Integrated equilibrium, 49
Interaction skills, 288–89
Internal labor markets:
  factors causing firms to move to, 55
  market-mediated work, 185
  pressures against, 189–90
  support for, 189
  theory and change, 192–95

World War II, period immediately
following, 171–73
*Internal Labor Markets and Manpower
Analysis*, 173, 189
Internal revenue service (IRS), 203,
206, 208
International Conference of Labor Force
Statisticians in 1954, 320
International Labor Organization (ILO),
105, 108
International Monetary Fund, 290, 291
International Motor Vehicle Program
(IMVP), 129
Interpersonal jobs, xxiii, xxiv
Intervention, motives for, 109
Investment/finance and producer cooperatives, 250–51, 254–55
Islam, 291
Italy:
collective bargaining, 225
contingent work, 231
cooperatives, producer, 12, 248, 249,
251, 252–55
cooperative system of industrial
relations, 34
councils, work, 220
flexible specialization, 127, 128
rights of workers, 35
unions, 232

Japan:
class structure and psychological
functioning, 382–84
contingent work, 231
cooperative system of industrial
relations, 34
flexibility, 232
globalization and labor, 65–66,
91–94, 116
internal labor market theory, 195
lean production, 118–19, 123,
126–28
management techniques, 136–40, 193
Mexico, work organization in, 136–40
money and work, decoupling, 380
participation, employee, 230
rights of workers, 35
stagnation, economic, 10
transition to the information society,
210
unions, 232
working conditions, 135–36

Joblessness, persistent, 369
see also Unemployment
*Job Queues, Gender Queues—Explaining
Women's Inroads into Male
Occupations* (Reskin & Roos), 269
Job satisfaction, 385–87
Job security, 138, 183, 229, 232–33
see also Anxiety about the nature of
work
Job Study, 209
Job tenure, 190
John D. and Catherine T. MacArthur
Foundation, xxviii
Jurisprudence, industrial, 23
Just-in-time inventory policies, 130, 139

Kennedy administration, 235
Keynesian economics, 17, 211
Korea, South, 26

Labor and Monopoly Capital
(Braverman), 36, 115
Labor economics:
alternative theories, 1, 17–18, 53–56
analytical frame, 56–59
conclusions, 24
efficiency/unemployment and work
incentives, 18–20
exit-voice model, 50–53
fair wage–effort hypothesis and
unemployment, 47–50
history of, 16–17
industrial relations and productivity
growth, 32–35
institutions, persistence of, 22–24
market model and the new dissent,
16–18
production process in competitive
economies, 29–32
radical political economy, 35–39
segmentation, labor market, 20–22,
40–43
supervision and high wages as
competing incentives, 43–46
theory and empirical evidence,
connection between, 15
uniqueness of, 15–16
wage curve, 25–28
see also Theory, economic
Labor markets, formal and informal,
102–3
see also Employment

Labor process under industrialization,
    115–16
Latin America, 66–67, 99, 101–5, 303
Latinos, *see* Hispanic Americans
Layoffs initiated by the employer, 52,
    53, 229–30
Leadership, 124, 389
Lean production:
    Japan first to use, 123
    organizational logic of, 129–31
    parallel structures, participation
        occurring via, 128
    post-, toward, 133–36
    quality control circles, 126–27
    research/questions/methods and
        evidence, 131–32
    support and criticism for, 118–19
Learning at work, 361–64
Learning-centered social institutions,
    211–13
Leave policy, family, 313–15
Legislation:
    antidiscrimination, 188, 190
    Civil Rights Act of 1964, 261
    Equal Pay Act, 184
    Family and Medical Leave Act of
        1993, 184–85, 313
    informal economy, 203
    National Labor Relations Act of 1935,
        235
Legitimate account, working to give a,
    380–81
Leisure time, 309
Lettuce, 237
Lithuania, 324
Living design influencing caring labor,
    309
Localistic despotism, 293–94
Local self-management, society
    organized around, 337
London (England), 3
Long-cycle production, 135
Long-term employment relations, 229
Low-skilled workers, 69–72, 198,
    226–27

Machine-powered production, 385
Macroeconomic models, 28, 188, 373
Mainstream jobs, 281
"Making of the Black Middle Class,
    The" (Collins), 261
Malfeasance, controlling worker, 29–32

Managed Heart, The (Hochschild),
    265–66, 273
Management:
    agriculture and labor–management
        relations, 234–38
    healthy workplace, creating a, 378–79
    Japan, 136–40, 193
    managers, the role of, 216–18
    owners and managers point of view on
        work, xxx
    personnel, 172–73
    team-based, 151, 377–78, 387–88
    technology, 160
    theories, xxx, 46
    workers' know-how transferred into
        management functions, 144
    see also Scientific management
Manufacturing:
    African Americans, 262
    export, 296
    flexibility in American, 149–53
    import competition, 82–83
    Japan, 92
    productivity growth, 74
    technological change, 76
    unions, 172
    wages and trade patterns, 77–78
    worker participation programs, 161
    see also Globalization and labor
Manufacturing Consent, 292
Maquiladoras, 138, 201
Marginalist revolution of the 1870s, 16
Market equality *vs.* domestic
    responsibility, 306–7
Marketing Experience, The (Lane), 355,
    361
Market-mediated work, 174–75, 185–88
Market model and the new dissent,
    16–18
Married women in the labor force,
    303–4, 313
Marxian economics, xxxiv, 19
    alienation, 351, 365–66, 368
    deskilling of workers, 115
    disutility of work, 351
    feminist theory, 264
    homogenization, 7–8
    household dynamics, 322
    power, 59
    production process in competitive
        economies, 29–32
Mass production, xxiii, xxiv

action disappearing from human activity, 389–90
core institution of Industrial Age, 116
household durables, 178
lean production contrasted with, 130–31
standardization of products/processes/labor/cost and accounting methods, 123
Maternity leave, 315
Maximization, principle of, 18, 24
Meaning and autonomy in relation to workplace organization, 385–88
Means/end distinction, xxxii–xxxiii, xxxvi–xxxviii
see also Segmentation, labor market
Measurement and reporting of women's work, 319–23, 337–38
Mediating disputes, 389
Meetings, short daily, 139
Men:
  contingent work, 184
  corporate culture, male-dominated, 313
  household responsibilities, taking on more, 315
  male work profile impacting women, 301–2
  wage inequality, 224 27
  see also Diversity and difference in the workplace; Gender issues/differences
Mental distress and unemployment, 372
Mergers, 206
Mexican Americans, 369, 370
Mexico, 136–40, 204
Miami, 204
Microeconomic theory, 16–17
Microfoundations model, 18
Micropolitical effects of restructuring, 152
Microprocessor-based technologies, 129
Middle class, 6, 261, 274, 369
Middle East, 98, 303
Migration, relationship between labor market niches and female, 295–98
see also Immigration
Minimum wage, 87
Minorities, 9–10, 96–97
  see also African Americans; Diversity and difference in the workplace; Hispanic Americans

Mississippi, 96
Mobility, occupational:
  racialized jobs and upward, 261–63, 280–83
  segmentation, labor market, 40
  service sector jobs, 276–80
  training, 191
Modern Times (movie), 332
Money, decoupling work and, 379–81
  see also Wages
Monitoring, 159
Monopoly union model, 215–16
Morale, xxx, 191
Motherhood, 307, 326
  see also Caring labor for the young/old/sick
Motivation, xxx
  African Americans, 12, 288
  agency theory, 227–28
  and human capital, 373–74
  productivity, 355
  workers with a mind of their own, 349–50
  see also Incentives

Nationalism, economic, xxv–xxvi
National Longitudinal Survey of Young Women (NLS), 277
Nature of Work—Sociological Perspectives, The (Erikson & Vallas), 365
Neoclassical economics, xxx, 17
  black mobility in white corporations, 280, 282–83
  caring labor for the young/old/sick, 342, 343
  communism, collapse of European, xxxv
  disutility of work, 350
  dualistic world of self-interest and altruism, 346
  efficiency, static, 59
  household dynamics, 322
  inequality of labor market opportunities, 21
  larger vs. smaller units, 388
  Marxian economics, xxxiv
  past, stuck in the, 7–8
  poverty, xxxviii
  skill differences, 41
  union model, monopoly, 215–16
  wage curve, 26–27
Neo-Hobbesian model, 32

Netherlands, 220, 308
Networks, 57–58, 127, 209
New Deal, 241
New York, 95–96
New Zealand, 321
Niche production areas, 152
1970s, transformation of work since the, 9–13
No-job/weak family model, 330
Noncompetitive labor market explanations of wage curve, 27–28
Nonstandard work, *see* Contingent work
North, policy options for the, 109–12
  see also Developed countries
North America, 302–3
  see also Canada; United States
North Carolina, 96
North–South Trade, Employment and Inequality (Wood), 180
Norway, 225, 231, 232, 301, 319
Nuclear family, 13
Nursing homes, 339–40

Obsolescence, rapid, 190
Occupational labor markets (OLMs), 53–56
Office technology, 119, 153–57
Offshore production and immigration, incorporation of Third World women into wage labor through, 295–98
Oil prices, 116
Older workers, 213
Oligopolies, xxiv, 196
On-call workers, 174
Opportunistic rule, 44–45
Opportunity cost, 322
Opportunity structures, expanding, 153
Organizational Choice (Trist), 135–36
Organizational forms, adoption of new, 124–25
Organizational structure, 239–40
Output per worker and compensation, 73–74
  see also Globalization and labor; Productivity, labor; Wages
Output valuation, 322
Outsourcing, 78
Overworked American, The: The Unexpected Decline of Leisure, 333
Owners and managers point of view on work, xxx

Paradigm shifts and diffusion, 123–24
Parental labor, unpaid, 346–47
  see also Families
Parental leave, 313–14
Parkinson's Law of housework, 334
Participation, employee, 20, 217, 227–30
  see also Cooperatives, producer
Partnerships, *see* Cooperative system of industrial relations
Part-time workers, regular, 174, 197, 231
Patriarchal authority, 100
Paycheck, beyond the, 357–58
  see also Wages
Paying for Productivity (Blinder), 227
Peasants, 366
Peer training, 386
Pension plans, 184, 191
Performance-based models, 194–95
Performance/skill-related pay systems, 232
Permanent employment, 92–93
Permissive technologies, 117
Personality and cognition, learning at work influencing, 361–62
Personnel management, 172–73
Personnel supply services employment, 186, 187
Petrochemical industry, 234
Phillips curve, 28
Piece-work type incentive plans, 46
Plywood industry, 222, 248–49
Poland, 324, 325
Policy responses:
  bottom, racing back from the, 67–68
  caring labor for the young/old/sick, 308–9, 344–45
  developed countries, 109–12
  diversity and difference in the workplace, 327–28
  families, 347
  gender and family issues in the workplace, 315
  industrial districts, 389, 390–91
  labor standards, 105–8
  single mothers, 346
Politics:
  agriculture and unionization, 235
  feminist theory and production, 292
  global employment, economics of, 101–5

radical political economy, 35–39
unions, 243
see also Government
*Poor Richard's Principle: Reconciling the
    American Dream Through the
    Moral Dimension of Work, Business,
    and Money*, 379
Population Reference Bureau, 304
Ports of entry, 172
Poverty:
    culture of, 370
    ghetto-related behavior and the
        structure of opportunity, 368–71
    middle class falling into, 261
    neoclassical economics, xxxviii
    prostitution, 100
    Social Security, 346
    welfare system, 9, 211, 327, 371
    working conditions, 303
Poverty and Discrimination (Thurow),
    270
Power:
    corporate, wage squeeze and, 84
    councils, work, 245–46
    extraction of labor from labor, 29–30
    Marxian economics, xxxiv, 59
    substitutability of labor, 90–91
    technology and the dynamics of,
        169–70
    unions and political, 243
    see also Control, labor
Preindustrial work, 2–4
Prices:
    consumer and producer, 74
    Consumer Price Index, 74
    elasticities, 71
    factor price equalization, 78
    Harrod's Law, 179
    oil, 116
    productivity, labor, 173, 178
    skill intensity, 71–72
    Stolper-Samuelson theorem, 74–75
    trade influencing, 85–86
Pride, 386, 387
Primary sector jobs, 38–43, 46
Printing industry, 385
Privatizing the benefits of caring labor,
    309
Producer cooperatives (PCs), 221–22,
    228–29, 248–55
Producer prices, 74
Product-development cycles, 190

Production Organization Index, 131
Production Politics, 292
Production process:
    alternative models, 125–29
    capitalist control over the, 6
    China and women workers, South,
        292–95
    class structure and psychological
        functioning, 382–84
    computers, 144, 151
    coordination of production on
        production-related activities, 389
    craft-based, 152
    feminist theory and production
        process, 292
    holistic/dignified approach, 136
    informal economy, 201–2
    insurance industry and computer
        rationalization, 153–57
    job satisfaction, 385
    long-cycle production, 135
    newly emerging forms of industrial
        organization, 388–91
    shifts, five major, 122
    subcontracting, 185
    subsistence production, 320
    unions, 242–43
    Walrasian/Neo-Hobbesian and
        Marxian models, 29–32
    see also Lean production; Mass
        production
Productivity, labor:
    absence of gains in, 82
    compensation and output per worker,
        73–74
    cooperatives, producer, 249–50, 255
    cooperative system of industrial
        relations, 20, 34, 35
    developed countries, employment and,
        177–81
    employment growth dynamics, 173,
        179–80
    gap between wage growth and, 63
    human-centered systems, 140–43
    Human Condition, The, 389
    individual effort, 20
    industrial relations and growth of,
        32–35
    informal economy, 201
    information technology, 124
    means/end distinction, xxxii–xxxiii,
        xxxvi–xxxviii

Productivity, labor (*continued*)
    owners and managers point of view on
        work, xxx
    participation, employee, 227–30
    prices, 178
    Productivity Revolution, 352
    psychological capital, 355
    scientific management, 352–53
    services *vs.* manufacturing, 74
    society's point of view on work,
        xxxi–xxxiii
    technology, 75
    Theory Y, 354
    voice, expression of, 216
    Volvo plants, 134–35
    wages, 38–39
    workers with a mind of their own,
        349–50
Profits, xxxviii
    cooperatives, producer, 249, 250, 253
    falling U.S., 116
    participation, employee, 229
    size, firm, 39
    voice, expression of, 216
Programmable automation (PA),
    238–40
Proletarianization, 4, 7–8
Prostitution, 99–100
Protectionism, 103–4, 106, 109–10
Psychic income, 343
Psychological functioning and class
    structure, 382–84
Psychological norms shaped by work,
    355–56
Public funding for training, 55
Public goods, 54, 345–47, 389
Puerto Rico, 100
Purex, 236

Quality control circles, 126–27, 138
Quality time, 332
Queues, labor market, 264–66, 269–73
Quitting jobs, 51–53

Racial issues/minorities, 12, 260–61
    see also African Americans; Diversity
        and difference in the workplace;
        Hispanic Americans
Radical political economy (RPE), 20,
    35–39
Railroads, 5
Ranking systems, 264–66, 269–73

Rational activity of the mind and
    irrational activity of the body,
    263–64
Rational expectations model, 18
Rat-race equilibrium, 314
Reagan administration, 95
Reciprocity, 342
Redistribution of income, 109, 110–11
Reform movement, 172–73
Regression analysis, 284
Regulation, institutional, 55
Regulatory barriers, removal of, 196
Relational skills, 262, 273–76, 286–89
Religion, 356
Representative participation, 217, 228
Research agenda, topics for a,
    xxxv–xxxviii, 131–32, 163,
    389
Responsibility, 342
Reversal model, 330
Rhythms of nature and preindustrial
    work, 3
Rights of workers, 34–35, 229
Risk behavior, modeling, 257, 258
Robotics Index, 131
Robust types of work organization, 154,
    156
Role models, 356, 369
Routinized jobs, xxiii
Runaway shops, 78
Rural areas and export manufacturing,
    268
Rural household industry, 2–3

Saint Monday's celebrations, 3
Scandinavian countries, 305, 308, 327
Scarcity thesis, post-, 380
Schenley, 236
Schools, *see* Education
Schumpeterian school, 124
Science-based technology, 114
    see also Technology
    Scientific management:
    automation, programmable, 240
    incentive-based system of
        compensation, 116
    Marxian economics, 115
    modern management theories to,
        relationship of, 351–53
    Theory X, 329
    twentieth-century manufacturing
        organized around, 133

workers' know-how transferred into management functions, 144
Search theory, 7
Seasonal fluctuations, 187
Secondary sector jobs, 39, 41–43
Second Shift, The (Hochschild), 329
Segmentation, labor market:
  empirical evidence, 41
  equilibrium, segregated, 49–50
  explaining, 45–46
  gender and family issues in the workplace, 312–15
  ghetto-related behavior and the structure of opportunity, 368–71
  labor economics, 20–22, 37–38, 40–43
  new, toward a, 195–98
  supervision and high wages as competing incentives, 43–46
  testing the theories, 42–43
  unionism, industrial, 4
  women and minorities, 38
Segregated equilibrium, 49–50
Selection criteria for this book, xxxiii–xxxiv
Self-directed work, 363
Self-efficacy, 370–71
Self-employment, 174, 205, 207–8
Self-expression and belonging, 376–79
Self-interest, 346
Self-subordination, 387
Seniority system in Japan, 93
Service sector jobs:
  expansion of, 271, 303
  mobility, race/class and occupational, 260, 266, 276–80
Set-asides, minority, 261
Sex-related tourism, 99–100
Sharecroppers, semi-feudal, 6
Shared control, 239, 240
Sin, perception of, 356
Single mothers, 346
Size, organizational, 39, 239
Skills:
  artisans, 2–6
  computers and upgrading, 162–64
  contingent work, 197–98
  cyclical shortages, 55
  employment relations, recent trends in, 191
  flexible specialization, 148–49
  good jobs, 359–60

government workers, 227
human capital theory, 41
learning-centered social institutions, 211–13
low-skilled workers, 69–72, 198, 226–27
mismatch between labor supply and demand, 80–84
occupational labor markets, 53–56
prices, 71–72
relational, 262, 273–76, 286–89
soft skills, 262, 286–89
technical change, skill-biased, 86
technology and the end of, 146–49
wages and role of, 17
women, 148
see also Globalization and labor
Slave labor, 6
Slow pace of life, 356
Social change in the work process, 23
Social corrosion, 111
Social crisis around transition to information society, 210
Social economics, 376
Social Economics of Human Material Need (Davis & Boyle), 376
Social effects caused by disintegration of collective
  processes surrounding work, 201
Social exchange theory, 47
Socialism, 264, 291, 323–26
Socializing the costs of caring labor, 308
Social norms shaped by work, 355–56
Social part of human nature, 376–78
Social process models, 194
Social relations at work, 29, 368
Social Security, 346
Social welfare system, 8–9, 211, 327, 371
Society's point of view on work, xxx–xxxiii
Sociology of deskilling and automation, 167–68
Sociotechnical organizational change, 121–25
Sociotechnical systems, Swedish, 126, 128
Soft skills, 262, 286–89
Solidarity, 386
South, globalization and jobs moving, 61

see also Developing countries;
  Globalization and labor
Soviet Union, former, 323–26
Spain:
  cooperatives, producer, 12, 248
  councils, work, 220
  temporary employment, 231
  training, 232
Specialized services, 187, 188
Specialized substitute, 322
Specialty goods, 297
Staffing flexibility, 186–87
Standard Classification of Occupations,
  322
Standardization, xxiii, 123
Standards:
  educational, national, xxv
  labor, 67–68, 105–8
  producers, judging performance of,
    58–59
Statistical Process Control (SPC),
  151–52
Status attainment theory, 280
Steam engine, 122
Steel industry, 5, 140–43
Stolper–Samuelson theorem, 74–77,
  88
Stone Age affluence, 2
Structure of the firm, 36
Subcontracting, production, 185, 233
Subjective experience of workers, 16
Subsidized wages, xxv
Subsistence production, 320
Substantive complexity, 362
Substantive participation, 217, 228
Substitutability of labor, 90–91
Supervision, 43–46, 145
Supply-and-demand analysis of wage
  curve, 26–27
Surveillance, 30, 31, 145, 146
Survival techniques, 302
Sweatshop conditions, 94
Sweden:
  cooperatives, producer, 248, 251
  participation, employee, 230
  sociotechnical systems, 126, 128
  training, 232
  Volvo, 133–36
  wage determination, centralized, 225
  welfare model, Scandinavian, 327
System of National Accounts (SNAs),
  301

Task-orientation, 3, 356, 386–87
Taylorist approach, *see* Scientific
  management
Team-based management, 151, 377–78,
  387–88
Technology:
  auto industry, 129–35
  coevolutionary model of
    technoorganizational change,
    121–25
  control over employees, 31
  defensive innovation, 62, 70
  deskilling of workers, 11, 36
  differential patterns of technological
    change, 76
  flexibility in American manufacturing,
    149–53
  goals, clear idea of final, 120
  heterogeneity of, 45
  hierarchy, the limits of, 143–45
  housewives' hours of work, 334
  human-centered systems, 129–35,
    140–43
  Industrial Revolution, 5
  inefficiency, 36–37
  information technology, 123, 124,
    143–46, 208–13
  Japanese work organization in Mexico,
    136–40
  labor process under industrialization,
    115–16
  lean production, toward post-, 133–36
  new directions and new, 116–20
  occupational labor markets, 54–55
  power, the dynamics of, 169–70
  production, alternative models of,
    125–29
  productivity, labor, 75, 140–43
  quality of employment, 157–61
  skill?, the end of, 146–49
  skill-based technical change, 86
  as a social object of organization,
    168–69
  sociology of automation and deskilling
    theory, 167–68
  technical jobs, xxiii, xxiv
  transformations, visions of sweeping,
    113–14
  wages and, reduced, 72, 81, 89
  see also Computers
Telecommuting, 159, 205–6
Temporary help, 185

buffering regular employees from fluctuations in demand, 188
defining, 174
growth of, 197, 231
point of entry, 61
Tenneco, 236
Tenure, job, 51, 52, 190
Textile mills, 4–5
Theory, economic:
agency theory, 227–28
backdrop for understanding contemporary contributions to subject of work, xxxiv–xxxviii
compensation growing at same rate as output, 73
computer use, wage differential for, 164–65
conventional and alternative, 1–2
cooperatives, producer, 252–53
feminist theory, 264, 292
firm, standard economic theory of the, 227
gaps in contemporary research, xxxv–xxxviii
institutionalist economics, 8, 17, 343–44
internal labor market theory, 192–95
Keynesian economics, 17
macroeconomic models, 28, 188, 373–76
management theory, xxx, 46
microeconomic theory, 16–17
past, three theories stuck in the, 7–8
social economics, 376
socialism, 324
sociology of automation and deskilling theory, 167–68
status attainment theory, 280
Theory X, 329, 353–55
Theory Y, 353–55
unskilled workers and globalization, 69–70
see also Labor economics; Neoclassical economics
Third World, see Developing countries; Globalization and labor
"Time, Work-Discipline, and Industrial Capitalism" (Thompson), 356
Time Bind—When Work Becomes Home and Home Becomes Work, 329
Time debate, the household, 316–19
Time-orientation, 356

Tisch Library, xxvii
Tobacco products, xxxi
Tomatoes, 237
Total Automation Index, 131
Total quality management (TQM), 331
Toyota, 134
Tracking performance, 145
Trade, xxv, 10–11, 291
see also Globalization and labor
Traditional model, 330
Training:
industrial districts, 389
industrial relations, recent trends in, 191, 231
peer, 386
polarization between jobs based on new practices and those that aren't, 234
public funding for, 55
scientific management, 352
trade, as solution to problems caused by, 110, 111
Transactions, 57–58
Transformation of Work, The (Wood), 238
Transforming Organizations (Kochan & Useem), 326
Transnational corporations, 83
see also Globalization and labor
Transparency, computer age version of universal, 145
Triangle of human economy, 338
Trust hypothesis, 46
Tufts University, xxvii
Turbulence in the American Workplace, 173
Twentieth century, rise and fall of the late, 8–10
Two-tiered society/workplace, xxiv–xxvi, 206, 211

Understanding the Gender Gap (Goldin), 303
Unemployment:
agriculture, 235
control, labor, 30–31
Europe, 210
fair wage–effort hypothesis, 22, 47–50
ghetto-related behavior and the structure of opportunity, 369
incentives, 46
insurance system, xxv

Unemployment (*continued*)
  Keynesian economics, 17
  low-skilled workers, 198
  persistence of, 15–16
  politics of, 102
  self-efficacy, 370–71
  social psychology/macroeconomics
    and, 373–76
  Soviet Union and Central-Eastern
    Europe, former, 324–25
  Sweden, 133
  traditional approach to labor
    discipline, 230
  transition to the information society,
    210
  unhappiness and, 371–72
  wage curve, 25–28
Unhappiness and unemployment,
    371–72
Unions:
  African Americans, 284
  agriculture, 235–37
  apolitical, 8
  changing environment, response to,
    218–19
  councils, work, 220
  craft-based, 6
  decline in, 86–87, 190, 218, 232,
    234
  Europe, 161, 225
  home-based work, 176, 207–8
  informal economy, 201
  internal labor markets, 189
  Japan, 93
  Latin America, 67
  lean production, 136
  median wage, 216
  Mexico, Japanese work organization
    in, 140
  political economy of agriculture and,
    235
  reorganizing work, efforts at, 232
  reviving labor, strategy for, 241–44
  rules of the workplace, negotiating
    the, 172
  scientific management, 239, 352
  segmentation, 4
  tenure/quits and separations, 50–53
  trade, international, 75–76
  traditional unionism, 242
  wages, 27, 41, 91, 224
  what do unions do, 215–16

  women workers in South China,
    294–95
United Farm Workers (UFW), 234–37
United Kingdom:
  caring labor for the young/old/sick,
    301, 307, 317–19
  cooperative model, 34
  cooperatives, producer, 248
  councils, work, 220
  flexibility, 231
  preindustrial work, 2, 3
  rights of workers, 35
  unemployment and rise in earnings, 85
  unhappiness and unemployment,
    371–72
  unions, 87, 232
  vocational training, 231–32
  wage curve, 26
United Nations, 300–301
United States:
  caring labor for the young/old/sick,
    307, 317–19
  class structure and psychological
    functioning, 382–84
  contingent work, 181–85, 233
  cooperative model, 34
  cooperatives, producer, 248–49, 251
  councils, work, 220–21
  flexibility in American manufacturing,
    149–53
  married women, 303–4
  money and work, decoupling, 380
  reorganizing work, efforts at, 232
  rights of workers, 35
  unions, 224
  wage inequality, male, 224–27
  worker participation programs, 161
  World War II, economy unscathed
    after, 116
  see also individual subject headings
University of California, 237
Unskilled labor, 62, 69–72, 88–91,
    109–12
Urban informal sector, 102
Use of Buffers Index, 131
U-shaped pattern of women
    participating in work force,
    290, 291, 303, 385

Validity, convergent, 375
Valuation of labor time spent in
    household production, 322

Valueless jobs, xxxvii
Value of work to the worker, xxxvii–xxxviii
Values, family, 325–26
Values achieved through work, 358–59, 362
Vertical disintegration, 196
Village action movement, 337
Virtuous circle, 173
Visibility and shared information, adapting to, 146
Vocational training, 231–32
Voice within the firm, worker, 51, 52, 216, 218
Volatility in earnings and hours worked, 90
Volunteer work, 321
Volvo trajectory, the, 133–35

Wages, 15
    average, 73–74
    black men in 1980s, erosion of earnings/employment in, 283–86
    computing inequality, 161–67
    contingent work, 183
    cooperatives, producer, 252, 254
    curve, wage, 18–19, 25–28
    decoupling money and work, 379–81
    discrimination, 31
    fair wage–effort hypothesis and unemployment, 22, 47–50
    flexibility, 187
    gender issues/differences, 299
    hourly, xxiv
    human survival, xxxvi
    immigration, 83, 86
    incentives, normal capitalist, 355–56
    inequality of income, 82–87, 224–27, 233
    institutions, wage-setting, xxiv
    Japan, 93
    Keynesian economics, 17
    market-mediated work, 187
    median income and unions, 216
    minimum, 87
    national income accounting, 320–21
    parental labor, unpaid, 346–47
    paycheck, beyond the, 357–58
    performance/skill-related pay systems, 232
    policy responses, 110–12
    productivity, labor, 38–39, 63
    psychic income, 343
    redistribution of income, 109, 110–11
    relative wage performance, 74–75
    scientific management, 352
    sectoral differences, 188
    service sector jobs, 278
    skills, role of, 17
    subsidized, xxv
    supervision and high wages as competing incentives, 43–46
    technical jobs, xxiv
    theories, wage, 19, 41
    twentieth century, rise and fall of the late, 9–10
    uniform conditions of, pressing industry/government for, 242
    women, 99, 291, 303, 313
    workers' point of view, xxx
    see also Globalization and labor; Segmentation, labor market
Wealth in a two-tiered society, xxiv–xxvi
Web of rules, 114, 115
Welfare, 8–9, 211, 327, 371
When Work Disappears (Wilson), 259, 356, 368
White-collar work, 381
White people, 9, 276–80
    see also Diversity and difference in the workplace
Wisconsin, 208
Women:
    complexity jobs, low-, 364
    contingent work, 184
    devaluation of work, 305–6, 342–43
    education, 303
    globalization and labor, 66, 98–101, 266–68, 290–98
    Hispanic Americans and informal economy, 203–4
    industrialization, 5
    irrational onto, unfair projection of the, 264
    married women in the workforce, 303–4, 313
    maternity leave, 315
    motherhood, 307, 326, 346
    primary sector jobs, 38
    service sector jobs, 266
    skilled trades, 148
    technology and quality of work, 160
    tenure, job, 190
    textile industry, 5

see also Caring labor for the
  young/old/sick; Diversity and
  difference in the workplace
Women's Research and Education
  Institute (WREI), 174
Work, three points of view on, xxx–xxxii
Workers:
  assembly-line, 366, 385, 387
  consumers and, relationship between
    interests of, xxxvii
  core employees, 197, 207
  government, 227
  know-how transferred into
    management functions, 144
  low-skilled, 69–72, 198, 226–27
  participation programs, 161
  partnership between firm and,
    378–79
  perspective on work, xxx, 349–50
  rights of, 34–35, 229
  technology and the role of, 160–61
  unskilled, 62, 69–72, 88–91,
    109–12
  value of work to, xxxvii–xxxviii,
    349–50
  see also Deskilling of workers;
    Employment; individual subject
    headings

Workers, Managers, and Technological
  Change (Cornfield), 234
Work ethic, 288
Work–family balance model, 330
Working conditions:
  contingent work, 184–85
  developing countries, 66, 98–101
  ergonomics, 159
  Japan, 135–36
  monitoring, 159
  self-directed work, 363
  telecommuting, 159
  unions, 95
  Volvo plants, 134–35
  women's participation in the labor
    market, 303
Works councils, 219–21, 234, 245–48
Works Councils: Consultations,
  Representations, and Cooperation
  in Industrial Relations, 245
Work-sharing model, 211
Work Transformed (Shaiken), 117
World Bank, 290, 291
World War II, 7

X-efficiency theory, 118

Your Money or Your Life, 353

Name Index

Abraham, Katharine, 174, 185
Ackerman, Frank, 1, 15, 61, 121
Addison, John, 223
Adler, Paul, 148, 150
Akerlof, George, 22, 47
Albin, Peter, 153
Amott, Teresa, 269
Amsden, Alice, 67, 69
Appelbaum, Eileen, 118, 125, 153, 172, 173, 177, 181
Arendt, Hannah, 365, 388, 389, 391
Aronowitz, Stanley, 146
Autor, David, 86, 119, 161

Bailyn, Lotte, 305, 309, 326
Barbash, Jack, 24
Barley, Stephen, 119, 167
Bartlett, William, 221, 252
Batt, Rosemary, 118, 125
Beck, John, 119, 149
Becker, Gary, 17
Bell, Daniel, 366
Bell, Ella, 263, 269
Belman, Dale, 63, 76
Benería, Lourdes, 66, 98, 302, 310, 319
Bentham, Jeremy, 145
Benton, Lauren, 199, 202
Berggren, Christian, 118, 133
Bernstein, Aaron, 177
Bhagwati, Jagdish, 68
Bianchi, Suzanne, 311
Black, Sandra, 223
Blanchflower, David G., 18, 25, 84
Blau, Francine, 216, 224, 306, 309, 312
Blauner, Robert, 150, 366, 367, 385
Bleaney, Michael, 25
Blinder, Alan, 227
Bluestone, Barry, 121
Blumenberg, Evelyn, 66, 94
Bonin, John, 221, 248
Boserup, Esther, 266, 269, 290
Bound, John, 262, 283
Bowles, Samuel, 19, 29
Boyle, Edward, 376
Braverman, Harry, 8, 36, 115, 121, 147, 150, 367

Breer, Paul, 362, 364
Browne, Harry, 118, 136
Buchele, Robert, 19, 20, 25, 32
Burawoy, Michael, 292
Burggraf, Shirley, 310, 312

Cable, John, 252
Çagatay, Nilüfer, 266, 290, 311
Campbell, Duncan, 69
Cappelli, Peter, 118, 175, 189
Carnoy, Martin, 176, 177, 208
Carswell, Bruce, 217–18
Cassirer, Naomi, 181
Castells, Manuel, 113, 120, 176, 177, 199, 202, 208
Chandler, Alfred, 4, 14
Chavez, Cesar, 236
Christensen, Kathleen, 176, 205
Christiansen, Jens, 19, 20, 32
Clark, Andrew, 357, 371
Clinton, Bill, 217
Cobble, Dorothy, 205
Collins, Sharon, 261, 269, 280
Commons, John, 17
Cooke, William, 223
Cornfield, Daniel, 234
Craig, Ben, 223

Darity, William, 355–57, 373, 375
Davis, John, 376
DeFazio, William, 146
Dickens, William, 21, 40
DiNardo, John, 86, 119, 164
Doeringer, Peter, 21, 171, 177, 189
Dominguez, Joe, 360
Dougherty, Laurie, 113, 171, 259
Drago, Robert, 43
Drucker, Peter, 352, 360
Du Bois, W. E. B., 260, 268
Dunlop, John, 17, 113, 120

Edwards, Richard, 4, 37, 385
Ehrenberg, Ronald, 306, 309, 312
Elgar, Edward, 69
Ely, Richard, 17
Erikson, Kai, 351, 365
Estrin, Saul, 252

Farber, Henry, 223
Fernández-Kelly, M. Patricia, 176, 202
Folbre, Nancy, 305, 310, 341, 345
Ford, Henry, 116, 133
Foucault, Michael, 145
Freeman, C., 122, 125
Freeman, Richard, 22, 50, 68, 91, 216, 221, 245, 262, 283

Galbraith, John K., 8
Gallagher, Kevin, 121, 215
Garcia, Anna, 202
Gershuny, Jonathan, 307, 316
Gintis, Herbert, 222, 255
Glyn, Andrew, 14
Goldin, Claudia, 14, 303, 310
Goldsmith, Arthur, 355–57, 373, 375
Gómez-Buendía, Hernando, 66, 101
Goodwin, Neva, xxix, 299, 349
Gordon, David, 4, 7, 64, 80
Greenaway, David, 25

Harbison, Frederick, 113, 120
Harris, Jonathan, xxvii, 121
Harrison, Bennett, 121, 175, 177
Hartmann, Heidi, 119, 157
Hicks, John, 16
Hirschman, Albert, 23, 50, 216
Hochschild, Arlie R., 262, 265, 273, 305, 329
Hochschild, Jenifer, 261, 269
Hodson, Randy, 357, 358, 385
Hudson, Ken, 181
Hughes, Alan, 14
Hyman, Richard, 223

Ichniowski, Casey, 140
Inkles, Alex, 362–64
Israel, Joachim, 367

Jacoby, Sanford, 172, 177, 189, 361
Jaggar, Alison, 263, 269
Jones, Derek, 221, 248, 252
Jong-Il, You, 69

Kahn, Lawrence, 216
Kalleberg, Arne, 181
Katz, Lawrence, 119, 161
Kaufman, Bruce, 24, 223
Kelly, Maryellen, 238
Kerr, Clark, 17, 24, 113, 120, 192
Keynes, John M., 16
Kiron, David, 13, 121

Kleiner, Morris, 223
Kochan, Thomas, 129, 216, 217, 223, 231, 326, 388
Kohn, Melvin, 362–64, 382
Kosters, Marvin, 68
Krafcik, John, 118, 129
Kraft, Kornelius, 223
Kraut, Robert, 157
Krueger, Alan, 86, 119, 161, 223
Krugman, Paul, 68
Kuhn, Thomas, 123

Lane, Robert, 355, 361
Lang, Kevin, 21, 40
Lawrence, Robert, 62, 71, 73, 79
Lazear, Edward, 221, 245
Lazonick, William, 68
Lee, Ching K., 266, 292
Lee, Eddy, 67, 105
Lee, Thea, 63, 76
Leibenstein, Harvey, 118
Levine, David, 217, 227
Liebenstein, Harvey, 19
Lincoln, James, 65
Lipietz, Alain, 14
Lobodzinska, Barbara, 302, 310, 323
Locke, Edwin, 362, 364
Locke, Richard, 216, 231
Lorence, Jon, 362, 364
Lynch, Lisa, 223

Mabbett, Deborah, 68
MacDuffie, John, 118, 129
MacEwan, Arthur, 98
Marsden, David, 23, 53
Marshall, Alfred, 16, 364
Marx, Karl, 8, 16, 351, 367, 368
Mathews, John, 118, 119
Matthaei, Julie, 269
McGregor, Douglas, 329, 353–55, 360
McKersie, Robert, 185
Meyers, Allan, 269, 306, 339
Mill, John S., 364
Mortimer, Jeylan, 362, 364
Moss, Philip, 262, 263, 286
Murphy, Kevin, 84
Myers, Charles, 113, 120

Nakata, Yoshifumi, 65
Noble, David, 115, 121
Noyelle, Thierry, 175, 195

O'Boyle, Edward, 353

Omi, Michael, 260, 268
Ong, Paul, 66, 94
Osterman, Paul, 175, 192
Oswald, Andrew, 18, 25, 357, 371
Özler, Sule, 266, 290, 311

Pencavel, John, 223
Perez, C., 122, 125
Perlman, Richard, 43
Perot, Ross, 73
Pietila, Hilkka, 336
Piore, Michael, 21, 123, 148, 171, 177, 189, 231, 358
Pischke, John-Steffen, 86, 119, 164
Pollock, Michael, 177
Portes, Alejandro, 176, 199, 202
Power, Marilyn, 266, 276
Prennushi, Giovanna, 140
Putterman, Louis, 221, 248

Rasell, Edith, 181
Rebitzer, James, 20, 35
Reich, Michael, 4
Reich, Robert B., xxiii, xxvi
Reskin, Barbara, 181, 265, 269
Robin, Vicki, 360
Robinson, John, 307, 316
Rodrik, Dani, 64, 88
Roediger, David, 260, 269
Rogers, Joel, 219, 223, 241
Roos, Patricia, 265, 269
Roosevelt, Franklin D., 261
Rosenberg, Sam, 266, 276

Sabel, Charles, 123, 148, 238
Sachs, Jeffrey, 70–72
Sahlins, Marshall, 13
Salter, W. E. G., 172, 173, 177, 178
Samuelson, Paul, 16, 30
Sapsford, David, 25
Sassen-Koob, Saskia, 267, 268, 295
Schettkat, Ronald, 177
Schooler, Carmi, 362–64
Schor, Juliet, 305, 333
Sengenbrenner, Werner, 69
Shaiken, Harley, 117, 118, 121, 136
Shatz, Howard, 70–72
Shaw, Kathryn, 140
Singh, Ajit, 14
Sivard, Ruth, 302, 310
Slaughter, Matthew, 62, 71, 73, 79, 84

Smelser, Neil, 60
Smith, Adam, xxxiv–xxxv, 16, 364
Smith, David, 362–64
Smith, Stephen, 252
Solow, Robert, 15
Sorge, Arndt, 223
Spalter-Roth, Roberta, 181
Stewart, Ian, 25
Stigler, George, 17
Stone, Philip, 311
Strasser, Susan, 14
Strauss, George, 223
Streeck, Wolfgang, 223
Swedberg, Richard, 60
Szalai, Alexander, 311
Székely, Gabriel, 136

Tabb, William, 98
Taylor, Frederick, 115, 133, 138, 332, 351
Thomas, Robert, 234
Thompson, E. P., 3, 4, 355, 360
Thurow, Lester, 264, 269, 270
Tilly, Charles, 5, 14, 23, 56
Tilly, Chris, 5, 14, 23, 56, 262, 263, 286
Tilly, Louise, 157
Trappe, Heike, 312
Trist, E., 135
Tyson, Laura D., 217, 227

Useem, Michael, 129, 326, 388

Vallas, Steven, 119, 149, 365
Valliant, Caroline, 356, 363, 364
Valliant, George, 356, 363, 364
Veblen, Thorstein, 6
Vobejda, Barbara, 311

Waldfogel, Jane, 311
Webster, David, 181
Welch, Finis, 84
Wever, Kirsten, 223
Wilson, William, 14, 259, 268, 269, 288, 330, 356, 368
Winant, Howard, 260, 268
Wood, Adrian, 62, 69, 109, 180
Wood, Stephen, 153, 238
Wuthnow, Robert, 357, 379

Yellen, Janet, 22, 25, 47

Zuboff, Shoshana, 119, 143